SHOULD WOMEN BE PASTORS AND LEADERS IN CHURCH?

My Journey to Discover What the Bible Says About Gender Roles

DR. BILL RUDD

WESTBOW
PRESS®
A DIVISION OF THOMAS NELSON
& ZONDERVAN

This book is a work of non-fiction. Unless otherwise noted, the author and the publisher make no explicit guarantees as to the accuracy of the information contained in this book and in some cases, names of people and places have been altered to protect their privacy.

WestBow Press books may be ordered through booksellers or by contacting:

WestBow Press
A Division of Thomas Nelson & Zondervan
1663 Liberty Drive
Bloomington, IN 47403
www.westbowpress.com
1 (866) 928-1240

Because of the dynamic nature of the Internet, any web addresses or links contained in this book may have changed since publication and may no longer be valid. The views expressed in this work are solely those of the author and do not necessarily reflect the views of the publisher, and the publisher hereby disclaims any responsibility for them.

Any people depicted in stock imagery provided by Getty Images are models, and such images are being used for illustrative purposes only.
Certain stock imagery © Getty Images.

ISBN: 978-1-9736-3058-6 (sc)
ISBN: 978-1-9736-3057-9 (hc)
ISBN: 978-1-9736-3059-3 (e)

Library of Congress Control Number: 2018906998

Print information available on the last page.

WestBow Press rev. date: 07/10/2018

Dedicated to scores of godly women who have affected my life, but most of all to:

Linda Aurora Koskela Rudd (my mother)

Gloria Jean Lampiris Rudd (my wife)

Angela Joy Corbin (my daughter)

Contents

Introduction

This book is about a journey—a very personal journey. It's about my journey to discover what the Bible teaches about gender roles—primarily in the church, but incidentally, though no less important, in marriage. Why I went on that journey, how it unfolded, and where it led me—those subjects fill the pages of this book. The journey has been terrible and wonderful. It has been gut-wrenching and fun. It has been challenging and rewarding. It has brought me grief and given me hope.

I hope you'll join me on this journey. Perhaps you'll be shocked, as I was, about some things I discovered in the Bible. Perhaps you will be challenged to think biblically in ways you did not anticipate. After all, a closed mind is a dangerous thing. If you love God and the Scriptures, whether or not you agree with me at every point, I believe that you will appreciate how seriously and reverently I have attempted to unpack what the Bible teaches on this crucial topic.

For all who feel passionately about this subject in either direction, I plead with you to read this book *all the way to the end*. Don't make up your mind part way through and set this aside. Something might really surprise you (and hopefully *bless* you) just around the corner.

A Little about Me

I am undeservedly blessed and intensely grateful that the Bible has been a central part of my life since I was a preteen. I have often said that one of the three most important decisions of my life was my life-changing preteen commitment to read from the Bible every day.

Because of some amazing mentors,[1] I was given numerous opportunities to preach in churches and youth rallies beginning when I was twelve years old.[2] I've been a vocational pastor for more than fifty years and estimate I have preached or taught well over 12,000 sermons and lessons based on my understanding of the Bible. In college, my major was Bible and my minor was biblical Greek. Seminary opened the world of biblical Hebrew to me and provided great tools for exegeting the Scriptures with integrity. My master's and doctoral programs focused on the biblical languages, exegetical studies, theology, and on pastoral ministry. It's been a great privilege to teach as an adjunct faculty member in two seminaries and to preach in many Christian colleges and universities.

I say all this only to emphasize that I have been incredibly blessed to have been able to spend nearly all of my life immersed in the study and teaching of the Scriptures and hope that I'm able to continue that until I die or Jesus returns.

I Was Wrong

Therefore, it is no small thing for me to have to admit that for the vast majority of those years I WAS WRONG in my understanding of a key Bible teaching. I say that with great regret and shame and include in this book what I have verbalized to many whom I have taught and led, "I am so very, very sorry. Please forgive me." I am painfully aware of the warning of James 3:1: "Not many of you should presume to be teachers, my brothers, because you know that we who teach will be judged more strictly."

This book results from a long journey—a journey that dragged me from a sincere but erroneous understanding and teaching of the Bible regarding

---

[1] Pastor Bob Russell, Pastor Paul VanGorkom, and Pastor Glenn Williams were some of the first. Before them, when I was twelve years old, Helen Wamhoff, pastor's wife and my first Youth Ministry leader, gently *coerced* me to preach my first sermon (a brief and very unimpressive presentation on Matt. 7:7, 8). That Sunday night I was "bitten" by the teach-the-Bible bug.

[2] Please don't be impressed—I've reviewed some of those original sermon notes and they were REALLY BAD! I am thankful for welcoming churches across the Upper Peninsula of Michigan such as Calvary Baptist (Sault Ste. Marie), Hulbert Baptist, Newberry Free Methodist, Cedarville First Union Church, the Soo Salvation Army, etc.

gender roles in the church to what I am now convinced is a more accurate understanding of what the Bible actually teaches regarding this crucially important topic.

If over the first near half-century of Bible study, teaching, and preaching someone had asked me which of my beliefs I might someday have to reconsider, gender roles would not have appeared anywhere on the list. It wasn't even a blip on my radar screen. I felt totally convinced that the position I had been taught and accepted was solidly grounded in a correct understanding of the very obvious teachings of Scripture. In retrospect, I realize that I had simply accepted what I had been taught and never seriously investigated the Scriptures on my own—they seemed so clear. So, what happened that I have now moved from a complementarian to an egalitarian[3] understanding of the biblical data? That is the journey this book describes: how I came to consider the possibility I was wrong about what the Bible said and what convinced me I had no choice but to change my position and share that change with others.

It is inevitable that someone will accuse me of making this change based on a desire to be politically correct or to win the approval of some individual or group. I vigorously reject any such suggestion! To the degree I am self-aware, this study and my change are based on a desire to please God by accurately exposing what the Scriptures actually teach no matter where the chips fall. No one should change their beliefs and values based on a head count of who will agree or disagree. Frankly, in this change, among my friends and acquaintances, more will disagree than agree with my change. Those who know me well know my temperament pushes me toward pleasing people with whom I have a relationship (to a fault when I am not vigilant). In this change of belief, it should be clear that I'm not holding a wet finger to the wind to see which way I should go. If I wanted to please the majority of those who have been my friends through the years, I would not change my position.

No one with a high view of the Scriptures lightly changes their interpretation unless convinced by overwhelming evidence from the Bible

---

[3] A simplistic definition is that complementarians believe that God created men and women equal, but that men are, by the Creator's design, intended to lead while women are to follow. Applied to church ministry, women are prohibited from teaching or holding positions of authority over men. In contrast, egalitarians believe that while the Creator's design included male and female completing each other, it neither intended nor required any gender-based restrictions on women regarding teaching or leading.

itself. It is my passionate prayer that every reader of this book will do their very best to approach this study with an open mind, setting aside preconceived ideas and commitments and asking God's Spirit to "guide them into all truth" (John 16:13)[4] and asking *the Anointing* who is the Holy Spirit, to *teach them about all things* (1 John 2:27).

I Dare You

I pray that my readers will dare to allow the Scriptures to speak for themselves rather than allowing ecclesiastical tradition, historical precedent, denominational creed, respected leaders' dogmatism, embarrassment over admitting error, fear of rejection and criticism, or barely conscious personal bias to influence their understanding.

We often make heroes of those past trailblazers and martyrs who bucked tradition and sometimes had to stand against the nearly unanimous teachings of the church and its leaders, often at great personal risk. Think of Martin Luther, Athanasius of Alexandria, John Wycliffe, John Huss, William Tyndale, John Knox, John Bunyan, Copernicus, Galileo, Dietrich Bonhoeffer, Dr. Martin Luther King Jr., and others. We must, like them, be willing to consider that the crowd can be wrong—even the so-called "biblical" crowd.[5] "To the law and to the testimony: If they speak not according to this word, it is because there is no light in them" (Is. 8:20 KJV).

Take the risk! Join me on a journey to discover what the *Bible* says about gender roles in church ministry and leadership—*Sola Scriptura*[6] and *sola Deo gloria!*[7]

---

[4] Unless otherwise noted, all quotations from the Bible will be from the New International Version, 1984 edition.

[5] See chap. 2: "When the church was horribly wrong."

[6] Latin expression meaning that the Scriptures alone are the basis of Christians' faith and practice.

[7] Latin: *for the glory of God alone.*

The Beginning of the Study

An early, much shorter version of this study was initially prepared for the elder and ministry teams[8] at Calvary Church in Muskegon, MI. I am immensely grateful to those dearly loved colleagues for their courage and graciousness through months of study and interaction. They modeled passion to discern what the Scriptures teach, courage to consider alternative understandings to what they had assumed, and unity despite differences. Our process of study was designed for a group in which few, other than myself, had formal, academic biblical training, and none (other than myself) had a background in biblical languages. Despite that, our study included attention to careful exegesis including serious consideration of how the biblical languages informed the interpretation of relevant passages.

While revising and greatly expanding those early drafts, I hoped that eventually my audience might include not only pastors and laypeople but also seminarians and their professors. I say this with no small measure of fear and trembling as I am very much aware that my strengths are more in the realm of a ministry practitioner than as an academic scholar. In the course of my study and many months of seemingly endless revisions and edits, the emergence of a rapidly expanding body of advancing scholarship regarding gender roles in the Bible continually challenged me to include additional material including that which was technical and scholarly. Knowing that some of the "tribes" I have associated with are at times insulated from new streams of biblical scholarship outside their trusted sources, particularly those with an egalitarian bent, I have attempted to balance "popular" with "scholarly." Hopefully, the tone of this study is pastoral while including material which is academic.

My dear friend Dr. Bill Brown, an accomplished author, told me, "There is never a time one is finished with their writing. There is just a time to stop." That time has come. I hope that some of those who honor me by reading this book will offer their observations, suggestions, criticisms, and corrections, which may lead to future revisions that could produce an improved study.

---

[8] A big "thanks" is due to the Ministry and Elder Teams of Calvary Church in Muskegon, MI, who were part of that study: Carrie Albright, James Bean, John Grasley, Greg Munson, Aaron Rosema, Joy Rosema, Pastor Jeremy Sandison, Pastor Keith Sandison, and Jill Young.

Please send your input to drbrudd@msn.com. If this study encourages you to think biblically, would you be so kind as to recommend it to others?

A Few "Nuts and Bolts"

A few notations regarding details of audience, style, format, etc., may be helpful as my readers navigate the pages to follow.

Too Deep, Too Shallow, or, Just Right?

I am a pastor, not a scholar. It has been my privilege to serve as an adjunct professor in two seminaries, but my work was primarily in areas of ministry praxis rather than scholarship (homiletics, pastoral competencies, etc.). I am very much aware of my limitations. In some parts of this book I have pushed the boundaries by attempting to include material probably "above my pay grade." I have worked hard to be accurate in what I have written and to reference scholarly resources that I have learned from. I sincerely hope that this will make the book worthy of consideration for some who, unlike me, qualify as scholars.

As a ministry practitioner, it has been my goal for this book, at least the greatest part of it, to be accessible to every pastor as well as to the average Christian. My seminary Homiletics Professor, Dr. Paul Fink, challenged my classmates and me with memorable sayings such as, "Put the cookies on the lower shelf," and "Remember, you're not feeding giraffes." While I have attempted to do that, perhaps parts of this presentation will stretch some of my readers, even as some of my sources have challenged me. I hope if some readers struggle with sections I have failed to make sufficiently interesting or understandable, they will skim through those places and re-engage on the other side. Eat the fish; leave the bones.

I really hesitate to say this, but if someone is tempted to not even try, or becomes discouraged and thinks about quitting, they can skip to the short chapter-by-chapter summary at the beginning of chapter 12 to get a brief overview of the book. That might also help some to select the chapters most relevant to where they are in their own gender roles journey. Knowing that some may skip around rather than reading from beginning to end, I have included more repetition than might otherwise be warranted. But please remember that the unfolding chapters build on what has gone before and are incomplete without persevering from the beginning all the way to the end. The ideal is to read this book from the beginning all the way to the end.

Discussion Aids for Small Groups

"For Discussion" material is at the end of each chapter. If small groups chose this book as a twelve-week or longer study, these could guide their discussion after each has read the chapter beforehand. I recognize that the length of some chapters could be challenging for a twelve-week small group curriculum. Therefore, some groups may choose to take a longer time.

Greek and Hebrew Words

Normally, the first discussion of a particular Greek or Hebrew word will include both the Greek or Hebrew form and the English transliteration, for example: ἡσυχία (*haysuxia*). There are a few times when the Greek word is repeated, but normally, after the first use, only the English transliteration will be used.

Words of Deep Gratitude

Gloria, my Junior High sweetheart and faithful wife, partner, friend, lover, and ministry associate for more than fifty years deserves many crowns in heaven for all the ways she has enhanced my life, passionately partnered in ministry, filled our church and home with beautiful music, sat by herself in church, poured herself out for our children and grandchildren, invested herself in hundreds if not thousands of women, and tolerated my lifetime of too much closeting to prepare many thousands of sermons and now this book. Our four children are the joy and pride of our lives. Unique, bright, creative, inquisitive, opinionated, insightful, winsome, delightful, and successful in each of their own life pursuits, Andrew, David, Daniel, and Angela, and their spouses, have all challenged and shaped my thinking in so many ways. We jokingly (kind of) say, "We taught them to be independent thinkers, but not quite THAT independent!" Whether or not they fully agree with all I have written, the fingerprints of each of their influence are all over the best parts of this book, but not on any of its errors and flaws.

My parents, Dr. Edward and Linda Rudd, profoundly influenced my life by their relentless and unconditional love, instruction, support, godly example, constant prayers, wisdom, generosity, and encouragement. They have been in heaven for over fifteen years and I miss them so much. No matter how bad it might be, they would be thrilled to see this book and without doubt would have shamelessly promoted it and purchased scores of copies to pass out. Similarly, Gloria's parents, Andrew and Marge Lampiris, were the epitome of outstanding in-laws and exemplary followers of Jesus in so many ways. They always supported my ministry pursuits even though they took their daughter and grandchildren many miles away from them.

I followed my older brother Terry to the same college and seminary and then into pastoral ministry. His legacy of a life of ministry faithfulness, wisdom, and effectiveness is greatly valued. He modeled godly pastoral ministry, exceptional preaching, and a lifetime of growth.

Growing up, pastors and youth leaders taught me, mentored me, loved me, were patient with me, believed in me, gave me opportunities to serve and minister, and constantly encouraged me. Thank you to all of you! I am so thankful for each of you.

It is unrealistic to name all the ministry colleagues (staff and lay) with whom it has been my privilege to serve at Calvary Baptist Church (Sault Ste. Marie, MI), Grace Bible Church (Elkhart, IN), Perry Baptist Church (Perry, MI), Grace Gospel Church (Huntington, WV), and Calvary Church[9] (Muskegon, MI). Each of you helped me to grow. It was an honor and privilege to serve with you whether as an intern, youth pastor, or senior pastor. Each congregation had exponentially more people who were loving, authentic, and encouraging than those who (painfully) were not. Your faces are often in my mind, memories, and prayers. Thank you for putting up with me, helping me to grow, and giving me the privilege of serving Jesus with you. Valued ministry friends, too many to name, include pastors of churches other than where I have served, as well as teachers and professors. They have left their imprints on my life and ministry. I am so grateful to each one!

---

[9] A.k.a. Calvary Baptist Church.

I need to acknowledge the editorial assistance that came from my dear wife, Gloria (my best helper and loving critic), as well as from several amazingly generous friends who volunteered to invest in searching out portions of my manuscript to identify errors and needed improvements or to give helpful advice: Janet Stapleton (church member), Dr. Lynette Simm (author and university professor), Dr. Gailord Weeks (psychologist), and Kristen Stagg Gardner (author). Although their contributions differed in size, I am deeply grateful for their friendship and wise input at important points in the project. Despite my limited budget, Amy Nemecek greatly improved segments of my writing by her professional editing skill and the suggestions it spawned. Also, without the staff of Westbow Press, I'm not sure when this project might have become reality.

Any remaining spelling and grammatical errors, impossibly long and clumsy sentences, stylistic disasters, boring paragraphs, and theological missteps are entirely my responsibility.

My Invitation

And now I invite you to come with me on a journey of extreme importance to discern the mind, heart, and purposes of God regarding gender roles in the church.[10] I hope and pray you will do so with an open heart and mind, willing to allow the teaching of the Scriptures to challenge and change your thinking and values as you constantly call on God the Holy Spirit to "guide you into all truth (John 16:13) and to "teach you about all things" (1 John 2:17).

---

[10] While beyond the scope of this work, some passages relevant to the focus on gender roles in the church engendered important and probably controversial observations and conclusions regarding gender roles in marriage and society. While these are not the focus of this study, I hope that my readers will give careful consideration to the observations I have included.

1

My Too-Slow, Personal Journey

A little like the Three Bears' porridge, some journeys are *too fast*. Others are *too slow*. Only a few are *just right*. My biblical journey regarding gender roles in the church has been slow—*way too slow*! In retrospect, it included move than a half-century of traveling in the *wrong direction*! Maybe my way-too-slow-journey can help some others to get it *just right*.

When you've been walking in one direction for more than fifty years, turning around is a big deal—especially if the previous direction took you farther and farther away from the truth, however sincerely that path was followed. I invite my readers to join me in the journey. Allow the compass of the Holy Scriptures to judge whether I'm now on the right path.

Does It Really Matter?

So how big a deal is it what someone believes about gender roles in the church? Does it matter if women can serve in other ways, but not as leaders, pastors, elders, or Bible teachers over men? How much difference does it make whether or not the Bible actually commands women to be silent in church, especially when it comes to teaching or leading men?[11]

When I was a seminary student and a part-time youth pastor in Indiana, a wonderful couple in the church, Frank and Reva Welker, "adopted" Gloria and me. Their love, hospitality, generosity, encouragement, help, and godly

---

[11] "I do not permit a woman to teach or to have authority over a man; she must be silent" (1 Tim. 2:12).

example had a wonderful influence on our lives. Because our parents were hundreds of miles away, Reva determined that she would spoil us with her mothering. I learned many great lessons from Frank, the volunteer Sunday School superintendent at church, who operated his own business building truck campers as part of the area's booming RV industry. But Frank had a disadvantage compared to his competitors. He had lost a hand in a corn husking machine when he was young. It was amazing to watch him work. Most of the things he did "required" two hands, but he had learned to adapt and did them with one and an arm that ended at the wrist. He was remarkable! Most people with two hands would never have done what he did, let alone with only one. There's a reason God designed us with two hands.

What if men and women are like two hands God designed to build Jesus' church? What if the complementarian belief[12] has cut off one hand so that, at least in key leadership and teaching roles, the church is working one-handed? How might it affect the effectiveness of the church if it functioned with both hands? What if that really was God's plan from the beginning? What difference might it make?

A Female Pastor—Can You Do That?

Visiting Maple Grove Community Church during their honeymoon, Brendan and Tanya glanced at each other with raised eyebrows when they realized that the pastor was a woman. Both came from churches where there had been unchallenged agreement that the Bible limits the pastoral office to men. They grew up being reminded that the Bible commands that women "should remain silent" in the church (1 Cor. 14:34) and that they are not permitted "to teach or to have authority over a man" (1 Tim.2:23).

Just a few weeks earlier Brendan's pastor, Rev. Cal Samson, had preached that the reason many churches were compromising on that conviction was a desire to be *politically correct* and to be accepted in a culture that rejects God and His truth. When a ripple of "amens" signaled the congregation's approval, Tanya whispered impishly in her fiancé's ear, "That sounded like a lot of masculine voices."

After church that day, anticipation of their fast-approaching wedding

---

[12] Complementarians believe that God created men to lead and women to follow.

quickly overshadowed any questions they might otherwise have discussed about gender roles in the church. Besides, it was easier to just go along with the program than to risk questioning such a strongly held conviction of their church, especially when the Scriptures seemed undeniably clear.

But on that honeymoon Sunday, over lunch in a fancy Italian restaurant, the newlyweds talked about the sermon. They agreed that the sermon was both biblically sound and personally relevant. But actually, they talked less about the sermon than about the gender of the person who delivered it. "I had a hard time getting past the fact that the pastor was a woman," Tanya reflected. "But once I did, I thought the sermon was really great. I've heard a lot of sermons on that passage, but she brought out some insights I don't remember ever hearing."

"Maybe that's because women don't think like men," Brendan said half teasingly as he reached out to gently wipe spaghetti sauce off Tanya's chin with his thumb.

"No kidding," Tanya responded, the corners of her eyes crinkling in a way that Brendan thought was really cute. "Maybe if there were more women pastors we'd all be able to think more biblically."

Brendan rolled his eyes.

"Seriously," she continued, "I did an online Bible study on gender roles last year and it left me more confused than ever. It seemed that in different passages the Bible contradicts itself by advocating for both sides of the question. I'd never admit it at our church, but some of the things Paul wrote in his New Testament letters seem downright misogynistic. It's like he had a grudge against women. Seriously, some of my friends think the Bible was written by men and for men, portraying an exclusively male God."

"I know what you're saying," Brendan responded, "but we've always been taught that the Bible is trustworthy and doesn't contradict itself. I guess I've just gone along with what my pastors have taught and never seriously looked into the question for myself. On the other hand, if the Bible is so clear about this, why is there so much debate about it? Haven't some denominations even split over this? Do you think it's all about compromise, or is it possible that the church has gotten it wrong for hundreds of years? Is that even conceivable?"

Brendan rubbed the hockey scar on his chin the way he did sometimes when he was concentrating hard on something.

"What are you thinking about?" Tanya pressed.

"Well, I was just remembering when Tommy Sanders stayed over and went to church with me one Sunday."

"Is he the one you played hockey with in high school?" Tanya asked. "The one you hoped would become a Christian?"

"Yeah, that's Tommy. Anyway, after church he asked me whether our church ever had a woman pastor. I told him no and showed him the verse about women being silent in church. I remember the stunned look on his face. He said, 'Women can't talk in church? You can't be serious!' He would never come back to church with me after that."

"While we're on the subject," Tanya said with a conspiratorial wink, "what about the whole thing about wives submitting to their husbands? Maybe we should take another look at that too . . . or is that a little too threatening for your macho ego?"

"Ouch!" Brendan held his hands over his gut as if he'd been stabbed. "Now you're really going too far. Give a woman an inch and she'll always—" He was interrupted by a good-natured slap on his arm. "Okay, okay. I know when it's time to stand down. I guess we ought to take another look at what the Bible says about that too. But where do we start?"

"We can figure that out . . . but not today." Tanya leaned in close to Brendan's ear as she seductively whispered, "I've got something else in mind when we get back to the hotel. Maybe we can investigate some gender roles of our own."

You Can't Overstate the Importance of This Issue!

Brendan and Tanya's honeymoon might take priority over their doing an in-depth study of the gender roles issue, but to keep putting it off isn't a realistic option for Christians and churches, given the far-reaching implications that surround the controversy. Where a church stands regarding gender roles either includes or excludes at least half of its members from leadership and teaching roles and also has profound effect on the day-to-day dynamics of every marriage. Depending on one's perspective, the unbending requirements of the traditional majority view are either *really good* or *really horrible* for churches and marriages. Furthermore, no matter which position it affirms, a church potentially pleases or offends many people *inside* the church and potentially either raises or devastates its *desirability quotient* for a far greater number of people *outside* the church—people the church desperately wants to bring to Christ.

Excluding women from church leadership and maintaining the traditional position of the church that calls on women to submit to their husbands may be accepted by many conservative church insiders, but to many outsiders these viewpoints appear ludicrous and old fashioned at best and unthinkably oppressive at worst. There are exceptions to this aversion. For example, many Muslims have no problem with strict religious and marital requirements for women's silence and submission. However, Christians and non-Christians alike almost universally condemn Islam as abusive to women, especially as practiced in nations where it is the majority religion. Is this condemnation of Islam hypocritical for complementarian Christians? Though some of the external expressions and the extent of their application may differ, the *underlying view of gender roles* may be uncomfortably similar.

Many Christians are embarrassed by the gender restrictions in their churches. They may have experienced ridicule or rejection from their non-Christian friends and they may have winced under accusations that Christianity perpetuates the abusive oppression of women. For many followers of Jesus, it has become increasingly difficult to defend a position that is not only culturally reprehensible, but more importantly that seems out of character with the God they encounter in the scriptures. If they were honest, many would say that the gender-based restrictions and mandated submission just don't *feel right* to them in spite of their inability to reframe a handful of relevant Bible passages that seem to lend strong support for gender-based leadership restrictions in the church as well as for male authority in marriage. Those Scriptures are: 1 Corinthians 14:33–38 (women must be silent in church), 1 Timothy 2:11–15 (women must be quiet in church and cannot teach men or be a leader), Ephesians 5:22–24, and Colossians 3:18 (wives must submit to their husbands in the same way they do to the Lord).

Understood traditionally, many Christians and churches feel duty bound to affirm and practice those biblical directives no matter how others may think or react. Many affirm that we must obey God even if we don't understand or agree right now. He is good, and whatever He commands is good. God's thoughts and ways are higher than ours (Is. 55:8) so we must trust and obey believing that someday we will understand.

There Are Alligators in This Pond

Whether a church excludes or includes women in pastoral and preaching roles, strong emotional responses are elicited that can be highly divisive in denominations, churches, and families. It's not unusual for opposing sides to characterize themselves or their antagonists with labels such as *faithful to the Scriptures* and *orthodox,* as *compromisers* and *Liberals,* as *old fashioned* and *irrelevant,* or perhaps even as *raving Fundamentalists* or *radical feminists.* Craig Blomberg, distinguished professor of New Testament at Denver Seminary, recalls one of his seminary professors asserting that "Christians who found no timeless restrictions on women's roles in home or church were 'either exegetically incompetent or biblically disobedient.'"[13] So much for open-minded and respectful debate!

When a long-time ministry friend learned that I was writing a book about gender roles in the church, he wrote the following concerns: "Brother Bill, I don't know where you are headed in your book. I believe there are very clear areas of ministry for women as they are gifted by our Sovereign Lord. I also believe there are definite areas of ministry designated by our Sovereign Lord not suitable for the woman. Just briefly expressing my concern that we as unashamed Baptists hold to what the clear teaching of the Bible is on this subject."

I get it! The passages mentioned above appear on the surface to be crystal clear about gender-based restrictions in the church and home. I appreciate my friend's willingness to share his concern that I not abandon what he believes is a clear and important Bible teaching. I share his commitment to pleasing God and following the Scriptures. At the same time his words reveal how strongly he is convinced that this is a settled and non-debatable issue for anyone who is submitted to the sovereignty of God and the authority of the Bible. Clearly it is his conviction there is no wiggle room on this topic and no need to even consider the possibility of being mistaken in one's interpretation. None at all! Hopefully that is because he has done a careful, exegetical study of the relevant Bible texts with a teachable spirit. But, with only two highly disputed passages in the entire Bible that *specifically* address church gender roles, it is

---

[13] Craig Blomberg, foreword in Michelle Lee-Barnewall, *Neither Complementarian nor Egalitarian: A Kingdom Corrective to the Evangelical Gender Debate* (Grand Rapids: Baker Academic, 2016), Kindle Loc 66.

more than a little troubling when the topic is treated as if it were a "virgin birth" level doctrine, especially when one is confronted, as I was, with some shocking discoveries about the two key passages.

Regretfully, I was reminded of how often I have been guilty of a closed-minded dogmatism that reflected little humility, teachability, or awareness of my personal fallibility or of my vulnerability to deception—either by self[14] or by others. Too often, confident in my convictions, I did not exemplify a genuinely teachable spirit. I repent that too often I have acted as if my personal interpretations of the Bible were inspired and inerrant and therefore beyond questioning, rather than affirming that the orthodox doctrine of inspiration and inerrancy applies ONLY to the biblical autographa,[15] *not* to every or any *translation* or human *interpretation* throughout the centuries. When I believe that my interpretations of the Bible are authoritative and unassailable, I act as if they are inspired by the Holy Spirit in the same way as the writings of the prophets, apostles, and even the red-letter words of Jesus. The Bible, *correctly understood*, is trustworthy. My *interpretations* of the Bible are vulnerable to error. If this is not true, how can one explain all the firmly held denominational differences? Why do Christians who share a high view of Scripture disagree on topics like the mode and subjects of baptism, details of eschatology, forms of church government, spiritual gifts such as speaking in tongues, etc.?

However entrenched or open someone may be regarding their understanding of the relevant Scriptures that discuss gender roles, neither ignoring the controversy nor insisting that one's view is so certain that there is no reason for debate continue to be realistic options for churches. The issue will not go away because a church ignores it either out of closed-minded confidence or fear of disagreement. Burying one's head in the sand is seldom an effective strategy. Hiding behind clichés like "because the Bible says so" or "that's so out-of-date" won't bring resolution or peace.

While contemplating whether we want to wade into this theological pond full of alligators, we must recognize that especially for many millennials and upcoming generations who are already wrestling with difficult challenges to

---

[14] "The heart is deceitful above all things and beyond cure. Who can understand it?" (Jer. 17:9).

[15] The autographa are the original copies of the authors' writings of each book of the Bible in Hebrew, Aramaic, or Greek.

their beliefs, the apparent misogyny of the church alleged to be supported by these Scriptures can be the final nail in the coffin of the faith they grew up with. This is a common mantra among the growing number of *de-churched believers* whose creed is "yes" to Jesus but "no" to the church. All of that highlights the importance of the question: *"What did Jesus say about gender roles in marriage and the church?"*

What Did Jesus Say?

What Jesus did and said about any issue becomes normative for all who claim to be His followers. In the gender roles debate, His example and teachings should seize our attention. Throughout His ministry Jesus was shockingly countercultural in His inclusion and elevation of women and was tellingly silent regarding hierarchical gender roles—both in church leadership and in marriage. The value of an argument based on silence may be disputed, but *the absolute silence of Jesus* on a topic of such importance screams for further consideration.

On the other hand, Jesus did speak about the creation of the first male and female, quoting the Genesis passages that emphasized not hierarchy but identity, unity, and equality: "'Haven't you read,' He replied, 'that at the beginning the Creator 'made them male and female,' and said, 'For this reason a man will leave his father and mother and be united to his wife, and the two will become one flesh'? So they are no longer two, but one. Therefore, what God has joined together, let man not separate'" (Matt. 19:4–6).

The significance of Jesus' teaching, silence and practice regarding gender roles will be considered in much more extensively in chapter 3.

A No-Win Situation

On the traditional side of the issue, there are many sincere and committed Christians who, even if some of them might have angst about it, feel biblically obligated to maintain gender-based leadership restrictions in the church and the home. They feel conscience-bound to obey what appear to be very clear biblical requirements overtly stated in passages such as 1 Corinthians 14:33ff, 1 Timothy 2:11ff, and Ephesians 5:22ff, and alleged to be implied elsewhere in the Scriptures. Even if their position is unpopular, politically incorrect, and offensive to some church insiders and to most outsiders, they believe that they must not compromise obedience to what the Bible teaches.

At the same time, gender role issues increasingly affect the reputation and witness of the church with unbelievers. The secular culture in the West is increasingly passionate about gender equality and women's rights and therefore frequently condemns the church not only as anachronistic and hopelessly irrelevant, but worse, as stubbornly misogynistic in its blindness to and ugly perpetuation of the oppression of women. This has been highlighted even more by the exploding "#MeToo" movement that calls attention to the correlation between men with power and the sexual assault of women.

On the other hand, if a church with long-held convictions on either side of the gender roles controversy embarks on a new, open-minded investigation of the relevant Scriptures, it risks an immediate backlash of misunderstanding, conflict, division, and condemnation. This knee-jerk reaction often comes merely because the question has been raised—not because the biblical evidence for or against gender-based hierarchy has been reverently reexamined. It is the classic dilemma of being caught "between a rock and a hard place." All too often this results in a church losing dissatisfied members from both sides. Whatever position is reaffirmed or adopted, the church's unity, stability, testimony, and influence are imperiled with adherents, non-adherents, or both.

One would think there would be broad agreement among all believers that pursuing and practicing biblical truth is always appropriate and must take precedence over tenuous or pseudo peace and unity. When the Bible addresses a controversial issue, we must not run away from carefully examining what it says. At the same time, in this and every difference over doctrine or practice, it should be assumed that Jesus' followers, in the spirit of Romans 14:1–4, would model mutual acceptance while not judging, looking down on, or condemning those with whom they disagree. Such love and respect are not inconsistent with each being "fully convinced in his own mind" (Rom. 14:5).

But, passions run high regarding gender roles. Illustrating the strong opinions on the topic, John Dickson writes: "The question of women delivering sermons in church is a touchy one for many evangelical Christians. For some it is even a test case of whether someone *is* an evangelical. I remember the dismay of one of my pastor friends when he was told by his ecclesiastical supervisor, 'It is sinful for a woman to preach, and sinful for a man to let her.' Such language powerfully raises the stakes. We want to get this issue right."[16]

I understand that some of my longstanding friends may be surprised, disappointed, or even shocked that I would embark on this journey rather than simply reaffirm the traditional complementarian position which I have held most of my life. I plead with them to not dismiss this book without first reading it in its entirety. Please resist the temptation to read in order to either refute or affirm what I have written. Please read with an open. Remember Solomon's wise counsel: "He who answers before listening—that is his folly and his shame" (Proverbs 18:13). If you do not find in the chapters that follow a careful, reverent, unbiased, in-depth, and credible exegesis of the relevant Scriptures, then you should reject my conclusions. But please, don't allow tradition, stubbornness, over-confidence, fear, laziness, or any other motive to cause you to reject my findings out of hand without even exploring their validity.

The Two Primary Positions on Gender Roles in the Church

Historically, there are two primary positions regarding gender roles in church ministry. While there is a spectrum of beliefs about gender roles, most lie on a continuum between complementarianism and egalitarianism.

Broadly speaking, **complementarians** believe that the genders are equal but have different roles including hierarchical distinctiveness at least in marriage and the church. Some extend the hierarchical requirements beyond marriage to business, government, and all social relationships and interactions. These believe that it violates God's created order for a woman to exercise authority over a man in any realm. Some therefore suggest that it is an expression of God's judgment on sin whenever in biblical history He permitted a woman to rule, as in the story of Deborah[17] in Judges 4-5 or in a passage such as Isaiah 3:11–12.[18] Regarding church ministry, in the complementarian view, women are prohibited from leadership over (at minimum in a *pastoral* or *elder* capacity) or from teaching adult males in

---

[16] John Dickson, *Hearing Her Voice* (Grand Rapids: Zondervan, 2014), 11.

[17] How Deborah fits in the gender roles debate will be discussed in detail in chap. 11.

[18] "Woe to the wicked . . . women rule over them."

church. Most complementarians apply hierarchical roles to marriage—the husband is to lead and the wife is to submit. A lesser number apply their position to all male/female relationships.

On the other hand, **egalitarians** believe that the genders are equal and that God intended no hierarchical gender distinctions in marriage, the church, or in any other area of life. In this view, there should be no gender-based restrictions on women for leadership or ministry in the church, nor any gender-based authority in the home or any other realm.

Variations of both views are held by many biblical scholars, respected Christian leaders, and ordinary Christians. Nuanced applications play out differently from church to church and home to home. Some believers are egalitarian regarding church ministry but complementarian about marriage or vice versa. In reality, some Christians give lip service to a complementarian view of marriage but practice egalitarianism in most of their day-to-day marital interactions.

Both predominant positions *claim* considerable exegetical support insisting that interpreting the Bible provides evidence that supports them. Each reference the same proof texts but obviously interpret them in different ways. *Both* positions struggle to address other texts, occasionally even within the same paragraph. This poses serious exegetical challenges and/or apparent contradictions for their positions. It is the goal of this study to present serious and credible exegesis for every relevant passage, including the most challenging ones, to arrive at a consistent position regarding gender roles in the church and beyond. This study proposes to present a careful interpretation of the relevant texts to provide a consistent and comprehensive advocacy and defense of an egalitarian position leaving no exceptional passage that contradicts this conclusion.

It should be acknowledged that the terms "complementarian" and "egalitarian" sometimes carry negative baggage, do not always communicate clearly,[19] and have sometimes been used in ways that are imprecise, derogatory, and stereotypical. But they can be helpful as *shorthand* representations of the two positions and will hopefully be used both accurately and respectfully in this study.

---

[19] For example, egalitarians believe that the genders are *complementary*, but reject any suggestion of hierarchy.

Where We're Going

So why should there be another book on gender roles in the church? I write hoping my story and what I have learned may resonate with others who love and are committed to the Scriptures and who will take a fresh look to be sure they got it right regarding this very important theological and practical issue. Perhaps my journey and **shocking** discoveries in key biblical texts will provide new insights about what the Bible says about gender-based restrictions in the church. Looking back, I'm embarrassed and regretful that my journey was so slow and pray this study will contribute to a reformation of biblical understanding and implementation in gender roles. The outcome for churches, marriages, and for men and women of all ages is potentially transformational.

The primary focus of this study is on gender roles in the church. The similarly challenging and crucially important issue of gender roles in marriage will primarily be addressed as part of the consideration of the concession passages (chap. 5) and the headship passages (chap. 6). A more extensive examination of Ephesians 5:21–33, Colossians 3:18, Titus 2:5, and 1 Peter 3:1–6 is very important but beyond the scope of this study. Gender roles in marriage will be considered primarily as that topic intersects with gender roles in the church. However, assessing God's creation intent for the genders has implications for all relationships inside and outside the church.

As part of these considerations, an interpretive insight will be presented that has radical implications—that the practice of gender roles in a Christian marriage should embody and preview New Creation values. Those values were inaugurated by Jesus' death, resurrection, and ascension, and constitute the reinstatement of original creation values.

My Personal Journey

Through more than fifty years of pastoral ministry, I accepted and taught a version of complementarianism contending that women are free to minister in any way in the church except in the office of pastor or deacon. Believing that 1 Corinthians 11:3–16 provides obvious permissions related to the later restrictions in 1 Corinthians 14:33–40 and 1 Timothy 2:11–15, I taught that women could teach men in church if they were under the authority of a male pastor. However, I had no reasonable answer to the question, "In what way does a teaching woman demonstrate that she is under a male's authority?" Based on 1 Corinthians 11:3–16,[20] I half-heartedly argued that the sign of being under male authority was a head covering—either some scarf or hat or, more likely, that her "long hair is given to her as [in place of] a covering" (1 Cor. 11:15). However, neither I nor anyone I knew proposed any clear definition of what such a hat or scarf should look like—what size, color, material, or style was necessary, or how much of the woman's head actually had to be "covered." Should it be a lovely bonnet, a tiny doily, a stylish hat, a bridal-type veil, or a dark-colored burka with eye slits so she could see? Nor was I aware of any widely accepted standard for how many inches of hair were required or how it should be styled to qualify as "long." Somehow, I overlooked these significant inconsistencies in my position. In reality, I didn't have to think about it because women seldom if ever preached.

I also believed and taught that wives are responsible to submit to their husbands as they would to Christ. I defended these gender-based assignments from my traditional understanding of the Scriptures whose interpretation I assumed to be clear and unquestionable as in Ephesians 5:22–24. I accepted what I had always been taught and never pursued my own in-depth study of the biblical material with open-minded intent to be sure that I had been taught correctly. I completely missed what should have been obvious indications in the text that the traditional understanding had serious problems. I tried to salve the harshness of the wife's duty to submit by emphasizing the husband's requirement to love his wife in a totally unselfish, sacrificial manner—being Jesus to his wife. Nevertheless, I taught that a wife was obligated to submit to her husband in *everything* unless in so doing she would disobey a clear command from God, her higher Authority (a principle illustrated in Acts 4:19).

In the last venue of my full-time pastoral ministry I served for 32 years at Calvary Church in Muskegon, Michigan. I retired on September 11, 2016.[21] The church held a moderate complementarian tradition throughout its 111 years of history, maintaining that all aspects of ministry are open without

---

[20] "The woman ought to have a sign of authority on her head" (1 Cor. 11:10).

[21] I am now "Pastor Emeritus" at Calvary Church, a kindly bestowed title with virtually no expectations.

gender restriction except the offices of pastor/elder and deacon. While women participated and led in *many* aspects of the church ministries including worship leading and a handful of times in team-teaching a sermon, they did not engage in a "pastoral" teaching role—though what constituted a "pastoral" teaching role had never been specifically defined. No staff women were given the title of "pastor" even though precisely the same position was sometimes filled by a male "pastor."[22] Lay or staff elders were always required to be male. Practically speaking, though a woman could have chaired a major church decision-making entity such as the Building or Finance Committees, it didn't happen. In retrospect, that was not because no qualified woman was ever available, but because of a latent or semi-conscious but real gender bias.

Over the years at multi-denominational pastors' fellowships I occasionally encountered women pastors. Based on my understanding of the Scriptures, I could not have supported them as pastors in our church, but, respecting the autonomy of those churches, I never felt I had to make that an issue. Clearly, they interpreted the Scriptures differently than I did. I never engaged in a conversation with them on how their role could be supported by Scripture.

During my fifty plus years of pastoral ministry, on a few occasions I briefly thought about gender roles only to defend my predetermined interpretations that someone had questioned. I don't recall ever seriously considering any biblically-based arguments to the contrary. I didn't think there were any that were credible. Sometimes I saw an intriguing book title or article on the topic, but, upon inspection, I was unimpressed by the "evidence" presented from the egalitarian side. The arguments seemed based more on political correctness than on careful exegesis of the Scriptures. For this reason, I was able to easily dismiss those few challenges that came even from people I respected and cared about because I felt conscience-bound to stand for what I believed to be a biblical mandate. During those decades, I felt no need or pressure to reexamine or to change my position despite some discomfort about it that nagged at the edges of my psyche.

---

[22] For example, women served as the "Director" of Children's Ministries. Somehow, the hypocrisy of these title differentiations escaped me, or at least, didn't bother me enough to move me to either reexamine my interpretation of the Scriptures or the integrity of my verbal gymnastics. I am so sorry Sarah, Jana, Jill, and Carrie. During my tenure, you all served as highly effective colleagues and valued friends with remarkable attitudes despite our biased policies.

At the time, I was unaware of a growing body of literature based on solid exegesis that undermined the traditional view and supported egalitarianism. Tribalism thrives when the culture, beliefs, and values of other tribes are not sought out, or are largely ignored or summarily dismissed. The "bubble" I lived in was such that evidence that might refute my views normally did not even appear on my radar screen. My theological radio stayed on one station—the one that supported the convictions I had adopted. Everyone lives in a bubble—some much larger or smaller than others. It requires curiosity, humility, and serious intentionality to explore outside familiar and comfortable boundaries. I felt safe within my complementarian silo.

A Crack in My Complementarian Foundation

Knowing my displeasure with the sources I had casually explored, my daughter Angela sweetly encouraged me to look at a book she thought I might want to investigate because, she suggested, the author affirmed a different position than mine supported by serious biblical exposition. She was right! In Stanley Grenz's book, *Women in the Church: A Biblical Theology of Women in Ministry*,[23] I was confronted with serious biblical arguments against gender restrictions in church leadership. He suggested alternative and credible ways of interpreting key passages that I had thought could only be read as prohibitive mandates regarding women assuming the pastoral office and functions.

This was significant! Now to maintain a sense of integrity, I had to reexamine my understanding of those and related texts throughout the Scriptures. I began to discover a large and rapidly expanding[24] world of scholarly studies of the Bible that advocated egalitarianism. I had been unaware

---

[23] Stanley Grenz, *Women in the Church: A Biblical Theology of Women in Ministry* (Downers Grove, IL: Intervarsity Press, 1995).

[24] James R. Beck, ed., *Two Views on Women in Ministry* (Grand Rapids: Zondervan, 2009), Kindle version, loc. 195–200) refers to the "remarkable volume" of "new literature that has emerged since 2001" regarding biblical teaching on gender roles and affirms that "advancing scholarship can sometimes set forth an entirely new line of reasoning that can help on side or the other better explain its case." He concludes that "we must all stay abreast of cutting-edge scholarship if we are going to participate in this debate effectively."

of these—but then, I had not been looking for them. Even while writing this study, new scholarly and popular biblical literature has continually emerged and/or come to my attention often affirming and expanding my emerging understanding of the relevant Scriptures. Much like so many other areas of knowledge, science, and technology, there has been an avalanche of relevant new information and scholarship[25] that has enhanced our ability to interpret and apply the Scriptures.

This accelerating growth in knowledge should be no surprise to Bible students. God told the prophet Daniel this would characterize the end times: "But you, Daniel, shut up the words and seal the book, until the time of the end. Many shall run to and fro, and knowledge shall increase" (Dan. 12:4 ESV). While the prediction alerts us that the understanding of prophecies relating to the eschaton will advance as the time of their fulfillment draws near, it seems to also apply to the astonishing growth in all areas of knowledge. The more time humans have to "subdue" the earth (Gen. 1:22), the more the multifaceted and seemingly unlimited macro and micro treasures God placed within His creation will be unearthed, whether mind-boggling technological capabilities, new cures for disease, beneficial uses for organic and inorganic substances, previously unknown species, or new comprehensions of biblical truth.

Throughout my study, I also explored numerous pro-complementarian resources to maintain objectivity and to test the arguments of one against the other. I was forced to examine my own biases and the assumptions I had accepted uncritically so I could attempt to apply careful exegetical analysis to the Scriptures. But the most important discoveries were from my own examination of the Biblical text itself.

Oops, I Had a Big Problem

At one point in my journey, I was preaching through the three relationships of Ephesians 5:21 to 6:9 in a sermon series entitled "Body Building: Back

---

[25] For example, better understanding of biblical languages (grammar, syntax, vocabulary, cognates, etc.), historical and cultural backgrounds, archeological discoveries, etc. The explosion of recent scholarly literature about the Scriptures is a wonderful if not also a bit intimidating help for Bible study, not only producing wonderful new insights but also sometimes challenging traditional understandings.

Down." The sermons focused on wives and husbands, children and fathers, and slaves and masters. I had already given one sermon about marriage in which I presented the same moderate complementarian view I had always taught from Ephesians 5:21–33, that is, that wives must submit to their husbands in everything unless it forces them to disobey a clear command of Scripture.[26] I emphasized how this submission was ameliorated by the requirement for husbands to cherish their wives with self-sacrificing and nourishing love. Husbands must never abuse their authority through selfish demands or behavior.

Then, as I was working ahead on Ephesians 6:5–9 (slaves and masters) I suddenly realized that over the years when teaching those verses, I always treated them as if they were about modern employee and employer relations (labor and management) rather than about actual slaves and masters which is the obvious *literal* focus of the passage. I had to acknowledge that I had made that substitution for two reasons: (1) the employee/employer relationship was much more accessible, relevant, and practical for my twentieth- and twenty-first century American audiences, and (2) I assumed, without any exegetical support in the text, that the passage *could not* be endorsing the institution of slavery so it had to be handled in some different way. But now I was forced to acknowledge that I had always bypassed *interpretation* of the text to substitute more a culturally acceptable *application* of the passage. Recognizing that Paul was addressing three *parallel* relationships, I had to face several questions: "What does slavery have to do with marriage?" "If God affirms male authority in marriage and parental authority in families, doesn't it follow that God also affirms the authority of masters over slaves?" "Does the Bible approve of slavery?"

Later I realized that this was only one of four very significant *tip-offs* in the passage (these will be examined in detail in chapter 5) that suggested that the traditional approach to the passage might be both overly simplistic and also patently incorrect in dealing with the central theme that ties the three relationships together in a coherent and cohesive whole. This theme has radical implications for how the passage should be interpreted.

That day I was forced to look again at the whole passage—to reexamine

---

[26] A principle regarding the precedence of God's law over man's which the apostles illustrated in Acts 4:19, "Judge for yourselves whether it is right in God's sight to obey you rather than God."

the three relationships to discern an interpretive key that would enable me to understand and apply them consistently without violating the obvious *parallelism* and other frequently overlooked elements of the passage. I had to be faithful both to the context and to all parts of the text regarding these three interrelated relationships, each of which, I now recognized, portrayed the *oppressed* party in relationship with their *oppressor*. The conclusions I arrived at transformed not only how I interpreted the three parallel relationships in the Ephesian passage, but also how I now apply them in today's culture, especially regarding gender roles in marriage

When the "light came on" about the underlying intent of Ephesians 5 and 6—the need to *make temporary relational concessions* in an oppressive culture for the sake of peace and the Gospel—I realized that an important pillar supporting the case for patriarchal hierarchy was seriously flawed. The principle that **temporary concessions must sometimes be made in an oppressive culture in order to promote peace and the advance of the Gospel**, could also apply to a number of other Scripture passages regarding gender roles. This transformative understanding of Ephesians 5:21–6:9, coupled with the conclusions I was reaching in my gender roles studies in other texts, especially in 1 Corinthians 14 and 1 Timothy 2, ultimately congealed in my journey toward egalitarianism. My conclusions about the three relationships and how this relates to the gender roles discussion will be seriously and thoroughly examined in chapter 5, "Submission—a Personal Tipping Point."

Standing at "Ground Zero"

As important as the concession principle was in my journey, the most significant outcome of my reexamination of key passages was a shocking discovery regarding the only two passages in the entire Bible that speak directly to the issue of gender-restricted roles in the church: 1 Corinthians 14:33–35 and 1 Timothy 2:11–15.[27] Those two prohibition passages are **ground zero** in the gender roles debate. Arguably, how one understands these two

---

[27] The focus of 1 Corinthians 11:1–16 is more on "head coverings" than on gender roles. However, because Paul assumes that a woman can pray or prophesy in church if her head is covered, the passage does speak to the gender roles issue. However, rather than restricting women's participation in church, Paul unquestionably assumes it.

central passages most probably, though perhaps subconsciously, influences how they interpret every other possibly relevant Scripture before and after them. As a result, those related passages are often interpreted predictably along party lines often without having received the same careful, exegetical analysis as would normally be applied.

My stunning discovery was that four key Greek words in 1 Corinthians 14 and 1 Timothy 2 were, in virtually all English versions, translated in ways that are at best inconsistent, inadequate, unclear, or misleading, and at worst, deceptive. These paradigm-shifting conclusions will be carefully developed in chapters 7–9. When I first began to see the stunning implications of these translation issues, my confidence in my newly entertained egalitarian position was a bit tentative because I felt rather alone in my understanding. What kind of arrogance would be required for me to think I had discovered something of such significance? If I were correct, why were other interpreters not seeing these same things that now seemed incontrovertible? Why did the most popular and influential Bible versions perpetuate these inadequate, unclear, or misleading translations? How could my rather simple investigation unearth such shocking and transformative conclusions? Who do I think I am to raise these issues?

I now realize that my ignorance of prior and supportive biblical scholarship was due to my lack of awareness of a growing body of interpreters making these same points. It is extremely difficult to fulfil the demands of pastoral ministry, prioritize one's family, and at the same time remain connected to the ever-growing stream of biblical scholarship that especially flows from academic centers such as seminaries and graduate schools. Most people (including me) primarily know those resources promoted and affirmed in their own denominational or self-reinforcing tribal communities. Significant time, investigation, and open-minded effort are required to search out resources outside of those that are familiar and only buttress one's existing positions. I realized that the seeds planted by these observations had perhaps been sown in my mind by others but it was probably not sufficiently open for me to latch onto them. I came to realize that the "new" path I thought I had discovered on my own was not so new and was now being reinforced again and again. For example, imagine my delight when I discovered four animated videos[28] that paralleled many of my own discoveries in a brief, entertaining, and convincing way!

These crucial translation issues will be thoroughly addressed in later chapters. Also noted there will be the little-known but astounding and credible evidence from some of the most ancient New Testament manuscripts that 1 Corinthians 14:33–35 may be a later scribal addition to Paul's letter, neither written by him nor inspired by the Holy Spirit. While experts in textual criticism[29] do not all agree on this, the possibility is monumental for the gender roles debate.

It is the assessment of this study that these inadequate and misleading, if not deceptive, translations in most English versions have profoundly influenced the gender roles debate in support of complementarianism and have been used to buttress the imposition of silence and leadership restrictions on women in the church. The consequent erroneous understanding of the prohibition passages has had significant and unwarranted influence on how other passages throughout the Scriptures from Genesis 1 on have been translated and understood.

The paradigm-shifting result of these translation issues in 1 Corinthians 14 and 1 Timothy 2 is so important for the gender roles discussion that I seriously considered addressing them near the beginning of the book—fearing some readers might not persevere to chapters 7–10. However, I determined that by initiating the gender roles study at the beginning of God's written revelation in Genesis 1–3, we can first lay an essential foundation about God's intent for the genders (chap. 3) and the origin of hierarchical distinctions (chap. 4). That way we can consider gender roles in the unfolding of the BIG STORY of the Bible. This will provide a much better context in which to consider the concession passages (chap. 5), the headship passages (chap. 6), and the prohibition passages (chaps. 7–10). After that, this study will include an overview of how women actually ministered to and led God's

---

[28] "Should Women Teach in Church," Sharp Videos, *https://www.youtube.com/playlist?list=PLOMFMVk5oX41sBBX-U9kcfaB_trmKj3Ox*

[29] Textual criticism is the science of reconstructing the original writings of the Bible. There are, for example, 25,000 copies or partial copies of the New Testament books and letters with no two exactly the same. No original copies exist. Textual critics attempt to use all of these copies to reproduce the original writings. Because of the vast number of copies, it is possible to produce an extremely accurate reproduction of the originals.

people in both Testaments and in early church history (chap. 11). Finally, the study will conclude with a practical consideration of "Where do we go from here?" (chap. 12).

Studying in Community

My investigation of the gender roles study moved to another level when the elders and staff of Calvary Church accepted my encouragement to begin an intensive group study of the topic. One result of Western modernity on the church has been the over-emphasis on an <u>individualistic</u> approach to the Christian life including Bible study and interpretation. This may have been influenced by a misapplication, over-emphasis, or over-reaction in Reformation theology promoting the priesthood of *individual* believers. Sadly, this often eliminates or reduces the balance, accountability, and breadth of understanding that comes from differing perspective, gifts, and experience inherent to studying, interpreting, and applying the Bible in company with others.

Our church leadership project took place as part of the "unfinished business" I hoped to complete in the final eighteen months before I retired after thirty-two years of pastoral ministry at Calvary Church. The elders and ministry team (staff) responded very positively to my recommendation that during the transition time we would engage in a diligent study of gender roles in Scripture in order to either reaffirm, reform, or replace the church's complementarian tradition prior to my retirement. After considering an overview of the Scriptures and topics as taught by both positions, it was determined that various ones from the two groups would prepare and present studies followed by group discussion regarding gender roles looking through four biblical "lenses:"

1. Creation, fall, and new creation,
2. Male headship passages,
3. Prohibition passages, and
4. Examples of female leadership and ministry in the Bible.

As the elders and staff prepared and gave presentations on these four topics, all agreed that it was crucial from the outset for each one to do their best to understand both major views before settling on a personal or corporate position. It was our goal that before affirming or arguing one's own view or preference, there should be a full and accurate comprehension of the opposing view(s). All this was to be done in the spirit of Proverbs 18:2, 13: "A fool finds no pleasure in understanding but delights in airing his own opinions ... He who answers before listening— that is his folly and his shame." This was essential so that in all the discussions that followed the presentations, there would be a serious effort to listen and understand before disagreeing with and advocating for alternative understandings.

This book was born out of the journey I have described, enhanced by the presentations and interactions with colleagues, and shaped by the many discoveries from my own personal translation and study of the Scriptures, including exegetical insights from scores of books, articles, blogs, etc. While all four "lenses" were important in my journey, the most stunning and transformative discoveries came about, as described above, while analyzing and exegeting the two "ground zero" prohibition passages, 1 Corinthians 14:33–38 and 1 Timothy 2:11–15. The discovery that four key Greek words in the two passages had clearly been translated in an *inadequate, misleading, or possibly even blatantly deceptive* manner in nearly all English translations with roots at least back to the Latin Vulgate caused me to wonder if there could have been a centuries-long gender-based patriarchal prejudice reflected in their translation and interpretation. Whether or not it was part of an intentional patriarchal conspiracy, the result of unconscious gender-bias, or a sincere but unquestioning and dangerous acceptance of hierarchical tradition, only God knows.

The possibility of a pervasive bias should not be surprising, since the struggle for control between the genders and the imposition of male rule, are a universal, ongoing reality resulting from Adam and Eve's sin (Gen. 3:16[30]). Translation bias as a motive in the English translation of the *ground zero* texts cannot be proven beyond question, however, my new understanding of those two passages was the tipping point in my journey from a complementarian to a more egalitarian understanding of the biblical data.

---

[30] God said to the woman: "your desire shall be contrary to your husband, but he shall rule over you" (Gen. 3:16b, ESV); "you will desire to control your husband, but he will rule over you" (Gen. 3:16b, NLT).

What's at Stake?

What are the implications of moving from a traditional complementarian to an egalitarian understanding of the Scriptures? First, from a biblical standpoint, my journey has resulted in an ability to confidently interpret the gender roles passages in a manner consistent with each other and with the larger themes and teachings that pervade the Scriptures. It has given me the ability to harmonize those passages that had previously appeared to be blatantly contradictory. These important exegetical insights have also eliminated the nagging sense of discomfort from interpretations that seemed inconsistent with the character of God as beautifully revealed in Scripture, with the teachings, silence, and example of Jesus, and with the inherent attractiveness of the Gospel in a broken world where selfishness, injustice, oppression, prejudice, and abuse are far too prevalent evidences of human sinfulness.

From a practical standpoint,[31] these corrected understandings of the Scriptures open the door to at least 50% of church attendees to employ their gifts, abilities, and experience in ministry positions and opportunities previously denied to them. Many would assert that in reality, women make up as much as **two-thirds** of church-going believers. The potential of significantly enhancing the leadership, ministries, teaching, and outreach of the church by this inclusion is enormous. Imagine the result of doubling the number of potential leaders and teachers in the church with one simple change! The practical outcome of my journey is the removal of a huge barrier that turns many people away from the church and from Jesus and His Gospel. Both insiders and outsiders have been disgusted and appalled by what they deem to be the perpetuation of an institutionalized denigration and oppression of women based solely on their gender. A great deal is at stake!

A striking illustration of what's at stake comes from the realm of Bible translation—not, however, the seemingly endless task of producing and marketing yet another English version of the Scriptures (there are already approximately 900 partial or complete English versions of the Bible). I'm

---

[31] It is crucial to understand that in studying gender roles, a follower of Christ must be motivated by and committed to pleasing God and being guided by the Scriptures rather than by a desire to please people and be guided by cultural norms or political correctness.

talking about the epic task of translating the Bible into all the languages of the world so everyone can hear and read God's message in their own tongue. "Although in the 1930s and 1940s there was hesitancy to send female missionaries globally, Wycliffe Bible Translators went against the norm. In particular, Wycliffe had been a place where unmarried women had been able to bring their Bible translation skills to the table . . . If it hadn't been for single women over the 70-year history of Wycliffe, half of the translations wouldn't have been completed . . . Today women make up 85 percent of the translation force with Wycliffe."[32] Wow! In the face of that astonishing revelation, ask the questions, "What's at stake if women are excluded from ministry because of their gender?" "Is it possible that by translating the Bible into many hundreds of languages, women have wrongly assumed the role of teaching men?" "Should all these translations be redone by men?"

Coming Up Next

In the next chapter, we will be reminded that through the ages, the church at large has sometimes been tragically mistaken in significant Bible interpretations. Some of these errors have had momentous negative influence on world-view, theology, morality, and life. They stand as a stark reminder we should not assume that because a particular interpretation has enjoyed long and widespread acceptance, that is no guarantee of its accuracy. Christians believe that the Scriptures are trustworthy, but not necessarily our fallible interpretations of them.

FOR DISCUSSION

1. Growing up, how were gender roles in marriage perceived and practiced by your parents, grandparents, or other close relatives? Where do you think these values came from? Were they always assumed to be correct or were they debated? Were those gender roles ever altered? Why or why not?

---

[32] Tara Beth Leach, *Emboldened: A Vision for Empowering Women in Ministry* (Downers Grove, IL: Intervarsity Press, 2017), Kindle, 106–7.

2. In the churches you have attended, what ministries and roles were open to or denied for women? What were the most common ministries carried out by women in those churches? How difficult would it be if the church had to fill all those roles with men?

3. Have you ever attended a church where a woman served as a pastor? What were her responsibilities? How was her work the same as or different from male pastors? What was your impression on the effectiveness of her ministry?

4. Describe sermons or lessons you have heard about gender roles in the church. How have you been exposed to serious presentations of both views?

5. If you've ever talked about it, what do your unchurched friends think about the typical complementarian position regarding women's position in marriage and in church leadership? If you haven't discussed it with them, what would you guess their views might be?

6. If your daughter or granddaughter said that she believed God was calling her to be a pastor, what would you tell her?

7. Read Proverbs 2:1–6. What do these verses suggest about how we should study the Bible? Why do you think it is difficult for people to study a controversial topic such as gender roles in the Bible with an open mind? As you study this topic, how can you be sure that your subconscious prejudices or church traditions don't unduly influence how you interpret the Bible? Why do you believe that you are willing to study with an open mind even if the Bible might teach something different than what you now believe about gender roles?

8. What do you think is God's view of women? Regardless of one's view on gender roles in marriage and the church, how can the church portray God's values regarding women?

2

When the Church Was Horribly Wrong

I was lost! Panic squeezed my heart as if it were in the grip of an icy hand. I knew we couldn't be lost for long—the woods weren't big enough. I knew that if we walked a straight line in any direction it was less than a half-mile to a road or path I would recognize. But it was embarrassing . . . and the "straight line" would be through thick woods, rough terrain, and skin-tearing thickets. I was a teenager guiding my youth group on a hike and this was my turf—the hundred plus acres of woods surrounding our family cabin where I had spent "kazillion" days since I was four or five years old.

But here I was, trying to act calm, cool, and in control so nobody would figure out that we were lost. I was leading my peers including the cute redhead I wanted most to impress. I didn't want anyone to realize my fear before I could recognize a trail, big rock, unusual tree, or other landmark in the woods around us that would tell me our location and the right direction to go. It was now obvious that we had been going in the wrong direction for quite a while.

When I finally figured out where we were, with a great sense of relief I guided my hiker friends in a different direction—this time the right one— the one that would lead us to our desired destination, out of the woods.

The sense of fear followed by relief is fresh in my memory even now about sixty-five years later. I had thought I was going the right way, but instead was going farther and farther away from our destination. It was painful to recognize that I had been mistaken, but it surely felt good to start moving in the right direction. Hopefully my teenaged friends never guessed that they had just experienced a brief illustration of Jesus' parabolic teaching about the "blind leading the blind" (Luke 6:39, 40).

My gender roles journey has parallels to my teenage experience. I was confident about my gender roles position, believing it to be firmly based on the Scriptures. I was tragically ignorant that my faulty interpretations had been carrying me farther and farther from what the Bible actually taught about gender roles in the church and the home. It was very troubling when I realized that the biblical "markers" that had assured me I was on track had been misperceived. Sadly, longstanding traditional teachings on gender roles, like direction-giving highway signs switched around by mischievous pranksters, have misguided generations of Christians who were as sincere in following those directions as most of those who gave them.

As I opened my mind to the possibility that I had been wrong, the biblical foundations on which my position was built began to show fissures. I was forced to consider the possibility that, no matter how sincere I may have been, my position regarding gender roles had been mistaken. Could I have been moving in the wrong direction throughout my fifty plus years of pastoral ministry, Bible study, theological training, and Bible teaching? As disconcerting as it was to face my long journey in the wrong direction, after correcting my course there has been a wonderful sense of relief and fulfillment as well as a compelling sense of responsibility to share what I have learned with others.

Often the church has been right. Sometimes the church, or parts at least, has been wrong—big time! A few tragic historical illustrations will be considered below. Whenever the church is wrong many people are damaged—people inside the church, people outside the church, and people wrestling with questions about where they should be. Whether the church was right or wrong, it also mattered a great deal how the members responded to each other in their disagreement. Too many times even when the church was right, it has displayed an arrogant, overbearing, and judgmental spirit that offends and repels rather than engages or attracts those who disagree or those who do not believe. Therefore, it is essential for the church not only to get things right, but also to harmonize conviction with kindness, humility, and a teachable spirit.

Disagreement and Divisiveness

An essential safeguard against misguided or premature confidence is a sincere effort to pursue open-minded listening and study while consciously rejecting the tendency to quickly disagree and to argue before understanding an opposing perspective or position. Solomon gave an essential warning: "A fool finds no pleasure in understanding but delights in airing his own opinions . . . He who answers before listening—that is his folly and his shame" (Prov. 18:2, 13). In the gender roles debate, the ideal is that both sides would be able to articulate the opposing position before arguing confidently for their own.

Especially in the last century, the issue of church gender roles has increasingly become the focus of passionate debate and painful division in Jesus' church. Both positions are practiced by various denominations and churches, though the complementarian has been embraced by the majority. Pastors and church members line up on both sides of the debate. Because both positions are highly offensive to many people, there is no "safe" or non-divisive position.

Sixty-five years ago, when *Father Knows Best* was one of the most popular television shows, Robert Young and Jane Wyatt portrayed a somewhat idealistic complementarian marriage that reflected the prevailing values of the secular culture in America as well as in the church. In recent decades, however, the complementarian position has become repulsive to many people who do not attend church and to a good number of those who do. While that change of values is not exclusive to any generation, it is especially common today among younger generations. Complementarianism is often seen as an expression of the institutional perpetuation of male domination and the abusive oppression of women.

While the egalitarian view is looked on more favorably by a growing number of believers, it is common for more conservative and fundamentalist complementarians to perceive and characterize that change as a *compromise* for cultural acceptability and political correctness and/or as an accommodation to the influence of "radical feminism." I hope this study will model respectful disagreement over the interpretation and application of biblical truth without impugning the motives of individuals whose differing strong convictions may be a sincere expression of their understanding of the Scriptures.

On both sides, unconscious bias frequently lurks just below the surface and may exert varying degrees of unwarranted influence on their thinking. In any case, when experiencing disagreement, Jesus' church, more than any other institution, should model respectful dialogue as an example to an American culture that seems to have lost that ability—an essential for healthy community life whether church, family or society. While debating this topic, it would be good to remember the oft quoted statement, "In essentials, unity; in non-essentials, liberty; in all things, charity."

In Romans 14 Paul encouraged believers in the church in Rome to accept, not pass judgment on, not look down on, and not condemn those who disagreed with them on "disputable matters." It should be possible then, for believers to disagree in the gender roles dispute without demonizing, disrespecting, or separating from each other. Paul's admonition is not an excuse for either ignoring or minimizing the importance of the topic, because he declares regarding disputable matters that "each one should be fully convinced in his own mind" (Rom. 14:5). Obedience to Paul's instructions should help to preserve peace and unity in the church. But it is not a panacea, because unlike the primarily individual and potentially private decision on what to eat (Rom. 14:2ff), the gender roles decision affects the entire church in a very public way as it encourages or rejects the participation of approximately 50% of the adult congregation regarding leadership and teaching every week.

Nearly every gathering of the church is a very public exhibition either of the exclusion or the inclusion of women, who constitute at least half of the adult congregation. Members of churches with a long complementarian tradition may be so used to this exclusion that it doesn't feel either strange or shocking, but those without that tradition as well as many from a younger generation may experience embarrassment, shock, or even revulsion at what feels to them to be antiquated, illogical, bigoted, unjust, and oppressive. Many of these will push back against the tradition or will *vote with their feet* as they exit either to seek what they perceive to be a more relevant expression of their faith and values or far worse, to walk away from their faith altogether.

It is important to affirm that Christians believe there are times when God's ways surpass human comprehension (Is. 55:9; Rom. 11:33, 34) and inclination (Eph. 4:18; Rom. 8:7) and may therefore be misunderstood or rejected by many people, especially unbelievers (Ex. 23:2) and immature believers. Christians believe that faithfulness to the Scriptures is a value higher than approval by the culture. For example, Christians cannot avoid the "offence of the cross" (Gal. 5:11) and remain true to the Gospel. The message of the cross is at the center of their faith. The cross is offensive because it exposes human selfishness and sinfulness as well as inability to remedy personal guilt and condemnation. Only through Jesus' substitutionary death on the cross and victorious resurrection is forgiveness possible. Likewise, Christians must not interpret the Scriptures regarding gender roles motivated by a desire to please anyone but God. They should not be motivated to please either those who are not predisposed to submission to biblical values, nor to those who affirm either a complementarian or egalitarian understanding of the Scriptures. At the same time, whatever their position regarding gender roles, they must not allow stubbornness, arrogance, over confidence, or ignorance to keep them from doing their best to be sure that they are correctly handling the Word of truth (2 Tim. 2:15).

When the Church Was Really Wrong

Christians must acknowledge that large segments of the church have vehemently held to interpretations of specific Scriptures later proven to be incorrect. Historically, numerous examples may be found of widely held interpretations of Scripture that many in the secular culture rejected and that later had to be acknowledged by the church as erroneous. Sometimes, large numbers of Christians accepted a particular position or even a whole scheme of doctrine as orthodox until some brave individual[33] or many in concert paid a great price to challenge that view so compellingly that ultimately the church was forced to take a new look at applicable Scriptures. Many would point to the Protestant Reformation as a dramatic illustration of this dynamic.

---

[33] For example, Athanasius of Alexandra who in the fourth century was the chief (and sometimes seemed like the only) defender of Trinitarianism against the Arian heresy. For his stand for truth, he suffered seventeen years in exile and came to be characterized as "Athanasius Contra Mundum" (Athanasius against the world).

What Do You Mean, "The Earth Isn't the Center of the Universe"?

Historically, the church has sometimes adamantly opposed new scientific theories as contrary to Scripture, only later having to acknowledge that it was their *interpretation* of the Scriptures rather than the scientific theory that was incorrect. Copernicus (1473–1543), who had been in good standing with the church, brought its wrath upon himself when he wrote that the earth orbits the sun rather than vice versa. The great reformer "Martin Luther called Copernicus 'a fool who went against Holy Writ' and an 'upstart.'"[34] Regarding Copernicus, Luther said, "There was mention of a certain new astrologer who wanted to prove that the earth moves and not the sky, the sun, and the moon. This would be as if somebody were riding on a cart or in a ship and imagined that he was standing still while the earth and the trees were moving."[35] Luther was absolutely confident that his position was grounded in reason and in Scriptures such as the story told in Joshua 10: "Even in these things that are thrown into disorder I believe the Holy Scriptures, for Joshua commanded the sun to stand still, and not the earth."[36] Today we understand that the Bible authors sometimes used the *language of appearance*, even as today's scientifically savvy television weather persons talk about the sun rising and setting when it is actually the earth turning.[37]

Galileo (1600s), the "father of modern science," embraced Copernicanism and challenged the long-accepted belief that Scripture taught a geocentric universe. "The matter was investigated by the Roman Inquisition in 1615, which concluded that heliocentrism was 'foolish and absurd in philosophy, and formally heretical since it explicitly contradicts in many places the sense of Holy Scripture' . . . He was tried by the Inquisition, found 'vehemently

---

[34] Paul Poulton, *Genesis for Ordinary People* (Eugene, OR: Wipf and Stock, 2014), Kindle, 2.

[35] Keith Mathison, "Luther, Calvin, and Copernicus—A Reformed Approach to Science and Scripture," June 1, 2012, Ligonier Ministries blog, https://www.ligonier.org/blog/luther-calvin-and-copernicus-reformed-approach-science-and-scripture/

[36] Ibid.

[37] This is an excellent reminder that an overly literalistic interpretation of the Scriptures can lead us astray and can naively disrespect what the Bible is and how God intended that it should be read and understood.

suspect of heresy', and forced to recant. He spent the rest of his life under house arrest."[38]

Today everyone agrees that most scientists and church leaders in Galileo's day were wrong and that our solar system is heliocentric. Today all Christians acknowledge that a correct understanding of the Scriptures is consistent with this universally accepted scientific fact.

God Approves of Slavery . . . Not!

Tragically, there was a more recent time when large numbers of Christians were horribly wrong. Many Christians and Christian leaders in the United States believed in and fought vigorously to perpetuate the horrific institution of slavery. Many defended slavery by using (today we would say "misusing") Scripture. "In the years preceding the Civil War in America, Christian ministers wrote nearly half of all the defenses of slavery. Methodist pastor J. W. Ticker told a Confederate audience in 1862, 'Your cause is the cause of God, the cause of Christ, the cause of humanity. It is a conflict of truth with error—of the Bible with Northern infidelity—of pure Christianity with Northern fanaticism.' Divisions over the morality of slavery split Baptist and Methodist denominations in America in two."[39]

The phenomenon of a youthful London preacher, Charles Spurgeon, exposed the depth of pro-slavery sentiment in the American South. Spurgeon is perhaps the most famous and most respected nineteenth century pastor, often known as "the prince of preachers." He is recognized not only for his eloquence, but also for his theological brilliance and courageous proclamation of the truth even when it was unpopular. Many thousands flocked to hear him preach at multiple services every week at the massive Metropolitan Tabernacle in London. It was a mega church long before the onslaught of contemporary mega churches. His weekly sermons were printed and distributed around the world—like nineteenth century sermon podcasts. What is not widely known is the vitriolic hatred he engendered in the American South because of his anti-slavery position. All over the South church members and pastors

---

[38] "Galileo Galilei," Wikipedia article.

[39] Rachel Held Evans, *Searching for Sunday* (Nashville: Thomas Nelson, 2015), Kindle, pp. 75, 76.

publicly burned his books. Anticipating a possible American preaching tour, the twenty-four year old was widely vilified and his life was threatened.

After a massive burning of his books in Montgomery, Alabama, in February 1860, a local newspaper article stated: "We trust that the works of the greasy cockney vociferator may receive the same treatment throughout the South. And if the pharisaical author should ever show himself in these parts, we trust that a stout cord may speedily find its way around his eloquent throat."[40] Many pastors and whole denominations railed against him and banned his books.

Christian George, curator of the C. H. Spurgeon Library, described the fury against the young abolitionist:

> By 1860, slave-owning pastors were 'foaming with rage because they [could not] lay hands on the youthful Spurgeon.' His life was threatened, his books burned, his sermons censured, and below the Mason-Dixon Line, the media catalyzed character assassinations. In Florida, Spurgeon was a 'beef-eating, puffed-up, vain, over-righteous pharisaical, English blab-mouth.' In Virginia, he was a 'fat, overgrown boy'; in Louisiana, a 'hell-deserving Englishman'; and in South Carolina, a 'vulgar young man' with '(soiled) sleek hair, prominent teeth, and a self-satisfied air.' Georgians were encouraged to 'pay no attention to him.' North Carolinians 'would like a good opportunity at this hypocritical preacher' and resented his 'endish sentiments, against our Constitution and citizens.' The Weekly Raleigh Register reported that anyone selling Spurgeon's sermons should be arrested and charged with 'circulating incendiary publications.'[41]

---

[40] Christian George, "Why the American South Would Have Killed Charles Spurgeon," The Gospel Coalition blog, March 1, 2017, https://www.thegospelcoalition.org /article/why-american-south-would-have-killed-charles-spurgeon?utm_source =feedburner&utm_medium=email&utm_campaign=tgcblog#When:2017-03-01T06:00:00+00:00

[41] Ibid.

Two years after President Lincoln's Emancipation Proclamation, the Klu Klux Klan (KKK) was founded with a purpose to establish white Protestant Christianity by whatever means were necessary and claimed that Jesus was the first Klansman. Prayers and hymns went up around the Christian symbol of the cross which was set on fire. The KKK was relaunched under the leadership of Methodist preacher William Joseph Simmons in 1915. He and his white partners climbed Stone Mountain where they set up an altar and a burning cross beneath which they laid a Bible, a sword, and an American flag. Simmons declared that angels were surrounding the mountain and singing hosannas because the KKK was being revived.[42] Professing Christians and pastors permeated the KKK membership and proudly proclaimed the support of the Bible in what we now recognize was a horrendously evil perversion of Scripture misused to defend their diabolic bigotry. To whatever degree it supported or failed to condemn this horrific evil, the church was wrong—very, very wrong.

Slavery in the United States was not merely a way-over-the-edge theological, academic, or social debate. In addition to the wicked, horrific, and unimaginable suffering inflicted on millions of slaves,[43] the nation was ripped apart. Families, churches, and communities were divided. Ultimately, it led to the death of well over a half million soldiers in the Civil War. The ghastly consequences and legacy of slavery continue to affect generations today more than most white people are willing to acknowledge. Slavery is an ugly and indelible blot on the history of the United States and of the church of Jesus Christ in parts of the United States.

Thankfully, even prior to President Lincoln's Emancipation Proclamation, many voices decried the evil of slavery. The abolition movement grew as more people opened their minds to its anti-slavery message and as more consciences

---

[42] DeNeen L. Brown, "The preacher who used Christianity to revive the Klu Klux Klan," The Washington Post, April 6, 2018, https://www.msn.com/en-us/news/us/the-preacher-who-used-christianity-to-revive-the-ku-klux-klan/ar-AAvHTXw?li=BBnb7Kz

[43] While not wishing in any way to diminish the incalculable awfulness of Hitler's anti-Semitism, it can be noted that there were nearly twice as many slaves in America as Jews who died in the holocaust. Both were unimaginably evil. Sadly, Americans are quick to condemn the Nazis but cling to the myth of American exceptionalism, a "Christian nation," a city on a hill whose history is terribly tarnished by its oppression and murder and robbery of Native Americans and slaves. The church can be wrong!

were awakened. But it was a long, slow battle. Much more recently, Dr. Martin Luther King Jr. experienced apathy and opposition from many white pastors who should have been his strongest backers. In an interview he stated, "The most pervasive mistake I have made was in believing that because our cause was just, we could be sure that the white ministers of the South, once their Christian consciences were challenged, would rise to our aid. I felt that white ministers would take our cause to the white power structure. I ended up, of course, chastened and disillusioned."[44]

I wish I could say I have always appropriately opposed racial bigotry and hatred. As a student in a Christian university in the South at the zenith of the Civil Rights Movement, I heard its president in chapel messages assert that the Negro race was inferior along with numerous other racist and hateful remarks, shrouded in misused "biblical" justification. I disagreed but am deeply sorry and ashamed that I didn't stand up and yell "No! That's wrong!" and then walk out in protest shaking the dust off my feet. If I had done that, I would have been "shipped" immediately and escorted off campus. Think of it! That was a well-known, widely respected, so-called Christian university whose evil, bigoted views and segregationist policies were affirmed by a huge constituency of churches and pastors for decades during my lifetime. The church can be wrong!

Thankfully today, while pockets of racism remain, the majority in the Western world (believers and unbelievers) agrees that slavery and racial bigotry are reprehensible and inexcusable evils.[45] Today Western Christians unanimously use the Scriptures to oppose them.

Could the Church Also Be Wrong about Gender Roles?

Is it possible that a similar awakening is gaining support today regarding gender roles in the church? It is striking that in the past, pro-slavery Christians argued that Ephesians 6:5–9 implied God's approval of slavery, while in the

---

[44] Andy Gill, "The American Church and Our Ties to White Nationalism," *Patheos*, June 22, 2017, http://www.patheos.com/blogs/andygill/american-church-ties-white-nationalism/?utm_medium=email&utm_source=Newsletter&utm_campaign=Progressive+Christian&utm_content=43.

[45] Tragically, ethnic bigotry and systemic racism continue in alarming numbers—mostly in the shadows, but too often openly.

present, pro-complementarian Christians argue that in the same paragraph, Ephesians 5:22–33 illustrates God's approval of patriarchy. Wait a minute! Stop and reread that last sentence and allow it to sink in. If complementarians now reject slavery but embrace patriarchy, are those positions hermeneutically and logically contradictory?

These are textually connected, related, and parallel relationships in which the oppressed and their oppressors are instructed. The inconsistency of making one relationship a perpetually binding hierarchy while rejecting a similar understanding of the other is blatant and without a trace of textual support. Chapter 5 will propose an interpretive principle that resolves this tension, harmonizes the three relationships, and eliminates the inherent hypocrisy of rejecting slavery as evil while embracing and enforcing patriarchy as divinely intended.

Although Christians must sometimes be willing to be out-of-step with the culture when core beliefs or values conflict, nevertheless in the face of widespread disagreement by reasonable people, Christians should not be unwilling to reexamine their *interpretations* of the Bible with an open mind. The choice is not necessarily between the Bible and godless secularism as some more conservative evangelicals or fundamentalists might propose, but sometimes is between the Bible as popularly or traditionally understood and the Bible as correctly interpreted.

As made-in-the-image-of-God, Holy Spirit-indwelt-and-taught followers of Jesus (Gen. 1:26, 27; 1 Cor. 3:16; 6:19; 1 John 2:29), we should know that a believer may appropriately feel uncomfortable with an interpretation of Scripture even though unable at the time to rationally explain why. This may be God's Spirit testifying in concert with the believer's spirit about gender roles apart from intellectual comprehension—much like the Holy Spirit's ministry of assurance within the spirit of a true believer ("The Spirit himself testifies with our spirit that we are God's children," Rom. 8:16).[46] Sometimes the intellectual and rational awareness lags behind the spiritual witness within.

If believers feel uncomfortable with a particular teaching of Scripture and, as nearly as possible for fallen people, are rejecting personal bias or

---

[46] The subjectivity of this dynamic coupled with the deceptiveness of the human heart (Jer. 17:9) and the pervasive vulnerability to subconscious bias all together suggest that this principle must be applied carefully with due respect for the margin of error.

perspective, such a "pause" in their Spirit should be taken seriously and lead them to additional, open-minded study of the Scriptures. Sometimes a believer's spirit resonates with a particular cultural awakening or movement such as the abhorrence of slavery. This resonance with a value held by many in the secular culture is sometimes not the result of a willingness to compromise nor a desire for cultural approval, but rather is because unbelievers are capable, as a result of God's image in them and His providential working, of arriving at what is true and beautiful. While not all "truth" claims are true, all genuine truth is God's truth wherever it appears. Even atheists or demons[47] may sometimes adopt and proclaim pieces of truth.

Recognition of Gender Bias

The prevalence of disagreement regarding gender roles among committed Christians should engender humility and a teachable spirit. If the Scriptures do not teach contradictory positions, it is obvious that many Christians affirm a position that is unbiblical. Unless everyone is willing, like Jesus' disciples, to sincerely ask, "Is it I, Lord?" (Matt. 26:22), the polarization will be perpetuated and no one will move beyond their entrenched dogmatism. Humility demands we sincerely ask, "Could I be wrong about gender roles?" Stubborn personal certainty and a teachable spirit are incompatible. Whenever there is widespread disagreement among Christians who share a high view of the Scriptures, the appropriate response is a willingness to reexamine the issue with an open mind and heart.

With regard to the gender roles debate, it is essential to recognize and identify one's personal, complex, and often subliminal *biases* and how they potentially influence their opinions and interfere with their objectivity when examining this issue. Biases arise out of one's upbringing, relationships, enculturation, and life experiences. Everyone has biases and most are unaware of what theirs are.

I was reminded recently about the power of bias after watching President Donald Trump's State of the Union address and the follow-up analyses by pundits, politicians, and people in general. If someone's bias or presupposition

---

[47] The maniac's demons correctly announced Jesus' identity: "Jesus, Son of the Most High God" (Mark 5:7).

was that the president was doing a good job for the country, they concluded that the speech was stellar, unifying, and full of truth and hope. On the other hand, if a listener's presupposition was that the president was a terrible person who didn't tell the truth and was causing irreparable harm to the nation, the speech was hollow, full of falsehood, divisiveness and empty boasting. It was like they all listened to two totally different speeches. Both viewpoints cannot be correct, but presuppositions have powerful influence over what we look for, what we perceive, how we respond, and what we think we know.

The power of presuppositional bias is such that if listeners were divided by their feelings about the president prior to listening to the speech, their post-evaluations would be totally predictable. This is true to such an extent that one wonders if the ability to analyze and think critically is completely negated by bias.

Similarly, if someone presupposes from 1 Corinthians 14 and 1 Timothy 2 that women are to be silent in church and are not permitted to hold positions of teaching or authority over men, then that bias will have powerful influence over how they understand and interpret *every other Scripture passage* that might be related to the gender roles issue. If, on the other hand, a person's presupposition is that what the Bible teaches about God's character and creation, and about Jesus' teachings and example support the absolute equality of men and women and allow for no gender-based hierarchical distinctions, then that bias will influence how they interpret *every relevant passage* including 1 Corinthians 14 and 1 Timothy 2 and lead to conclusions that support their pre-understandings.

Is it possible that presuppostional gender bias is so strong that interpreters are unable to analyze and think critically about how to understand Bible texts and are therefore incapable of changing their position regardless of what the Scriptures actually say? This is a possibility that should terrify every Christian who looks to the Scriptures as their rule of faith and practice. The danger that presuppositional biases will stifle the guidance of the Holy Spirit in the study of the Scriptures is very real.

Biases may subconsciously lead to efforts to please others. This can contribute to undue favor and a lack of objectivity regarding a view held by people whose opinions or approval one values. It can also lead to the practice of eisegesis (reading one's bias into the text) rather than exegesis (allowing the text to speak for itself).

With regard to interpreting the Scriptures that address gender roles, it would be difficult to overstate the subtle and pervasive gender bias that has permeated all human culture since Adam and Eve's sin and the consequent battle of the sexes—a tragic struggle that men most often win (Gen. 3:16[48]). To varying degrees, everyone is subconsciously affected by this ubiquitous patriarchal gender bias either by buying into or strongly reacting against it. It would be naïve to assume these biases have not affected the church's understanding of this subject. It would be naïve for me to assume that such biases have not affected me.

The best safeguard against biases is the awareness that one has them and to have a truth-telling friend, associate, or even critic who will help to expose those biases. The more aware a person is of their own biases, the less likely it is that they will subconsciously affect their perspective and values. Unfortunately, personal bias is like a blind spot. By definition, it is a *blind* spot, that is, one is *blind* to it. For sinful people, self-awareness is not natural. Self-awareness must be diligently, relentlessly, and sometimes ruthlessly cultivated. Openness to discovering one's own subconscious biases coupled with an intentional pursuit of a teachable spirit and a humble dependence on the Holy Spirit's guidance[49] will help to root out and put away long-standing subliminal prejudices and presuppositions.

As far as humanly possible, one must not embark on a reexamination of the biblical data regarding gender roles inclined to prove either a complementarian or egalitarian conclusion. Sometimes, for many reasons, we all have a preferred outcome, but when studying the Scriptures, we must continually resist any tendency to affirm our will rather than God's.[50] We must do our best to have an open mind as we consider the arguments and evidence from many perspectives and viewpoints.

---

[48] "Your desire shall be contrary to your husband, but he shall rule over you" (ESV).

[49] "But the anointing that you received from him abides in you, and you have no need that anyone should teach you. But as his anointing teaches you about everything, and is true, and is no lie—just as it has taught you, abide in him" (1 John 2:27).

[50] "Your will be done on earth as it is in heaven" (Matt. 6:10); "Going a little farther, he fell with his face to the ground and prayed, "My Father, if it is possible, may this cup be taken from me. Yet not as I will, but as you will" (Matt. 26:39).

The Pervasiveness of Sinful Male Domination

It is important to acknowledge that male domination has almost universally prevailed since Adam and Eve's sin brought ruin into God's till then perfect creation and set in motion the gender wars predicted in Genesis 3:16 ("you will desire to control your husband, but he will rule over you" [51]). The patriarchal outcome of those conflicts ("he will rule over you") is as certain as the other tragic consequences of sin's curse announced in the text: snakes will crawl on their bellies, women will experience pain in childbirth, food production will require painful and sweaty toil, thistles and thorns will attack our gardens, and death will return us to dust (Gen. 3:14–19). These are all *consequences*, not *commands*! Clearly, patriarchy results from sin, not from the *intent* of the Creator. This will be discussed in much more detail later in this book. As will be further demonstrated, whenever the church asserts that it is God's *intent* for men to rule over women, the church is wrong . . . as wrong as it was in declaring slavery to be God's intent. The next chapters will demonstrate that patriarchy was no more God's creation intent than were death and the body's return to dust.

It may be impossible to fully gauge the widespread, detrimental influence gender presuppositional bias has had and continues to have on all cultural institutions including business, government, the family, religion, and the church. The stained-glass ceiling in the church is as real in many churches as the infamous glass ceiling is in the corporate and political worlds.

In contrast to lofty assertions regarding the absolute equality of all people, the pervasiveness of male dominance over women in the United States of America is illustrated by women not even being allowed to vote throughout the nation until less than 100 years ago (August 18, 1920). That came only after a long, ugly battle. For many centuries in most parts of the world women could not be educated, own property, control their own income, testify in court, hold public office, obtain a divorce, obtain equal pay for equal work, etc. This is still true in many parts of the world, especially in many Muslim-majority nations.

Even in the United States it was only a few decades ago (1981) that the US Supreme Court ruled unconstitutional that the husband held sole control

---

[51] New Living Translation.

of marital property. Less than thirty years ago (1988) it was determined that educational institutions receiving federal assistance would have to provide equal athletic opportunities for women. Still today the gender pay gap[52] and the glass ceiling limiting access to CEO and upper management positions in the workplace continue to reflect significant gender bias—all this despite and in contradiction to our oft-repeated pledge of allegiance: *"with liberty and justice for all."* After more than 240 years, the United States has yet to elect its first female president or vice president.

Apart from the question of gender roles in church, it seems self-evident that Jesus' followers should view these illustrations of the denigration and subjugation of women in society with repugnance even as most people now feel abhorrence about the devaluation and subjugation of fellow human beings as slaves.[53] They should consistently oppose the persistent remnants of every expression of prejudice, racism, sexism, ageism, and injustice in our culture and its institutions, including, or especially, in Jesus' church.

Egalitarians argue that in ancient Israel and the early church, despite primarily patriarchal and oppressive surrounding cultures, there were numerous illustrations of women in key leadership and ministry roles. This will be demonstrated extensively in chapter 11. In spite of those biblical examples, complementarianism has been the majority view in Christendom throughout most of church history. Significant opposition to complementarian understandings of Scripture are relatively recent. "While the whole of Christian history contains sporadic examples of unusually prominent women in the church, most Christians did not begin to seriously

---

[52] "It takes women on average 15 months to earn what men do in a year. The average gender pay gap across the nation: Full-time working women earn 82 cents for every dollar earned by men ... Women's pay lags men's by 26 cents, data says," Muskegon Chronicle article, 4/9/2017. A white man's lifetime wages are projected at $2.7 million while a white woman's is $1.5 million (55%). The gap is about the same for Hispanics but not quite as pronounced for Blacks. Muskegon Chronicle article, 10/15/2017.

[53] This is not at all to suggest moral equivalence between slavery and gender bias. While both of those may be practiced with varying degrees of prejudice, injustice, and cruelty, the evils often associated with slavery far exceed the problem of college women having less opportunity then men to participate in inter-collegiate sports or to secure a high-paying CEO position. Further, this distinction should not suggest any justification of gender bias however severe or mild—only to be sure to not minimize the all-too-common horrific abuses associated with slavery in its various forms.

consider the question of equality or the ordination of women until the Society of Friends (Quakers) in the early 1800s. Arguably every decade since the 1860s has seen a new denomination accept the ordination of women as pastors and elders."[54]

"Until very recently (ca. 1980s), traditional readings have assumed the ontological inferiority of women through the entire history of interpretation, and it is implausible to think that an interpreter can effectively shed the foundational assumptions of the traditional view and still coherently maintain the remainder of interpretations and applications virtually intact."[55] As long as interpreters harbor traditional assumptions about gender roles, it is virtually impossible for them to look at the biblical texts without prejudice that frames and limits the interpretive options and conclusions they will consider. This greatly increases the vulnerability of the church to once again being tragically wrong. Regarding gender roles, could it be that much of the church is wrong again? Is egalitarianism the next Copernican, abolitionist, and suffrage revolution?

A New Breeze Is Blowing and It's an Egalitarian Gale

Patriarchal-supporting interpretation has been assumed correct and has permeated the teaching in the vast majority of Christian colleges and universities, seminaries, publications, parachurch ministries, and church pulpits for centuries in the Western world. If there has been a monopoly-like patriarchal domination at the *spring* of biblical teaching, should anyone be surprised that the *river* flooding the Christian culture has largely reflected male domination? It is only recently that a new and growing *stream* of serious biblical interpretation supporting an egalitarian understanding of Scriptures has been entering the *sea* of Christian thinking. The rise of egalitarianism and of both scholarly and popular literature supporting it have been growing exponentially throughout the last decade.

In a recent check, Google's search engine instantly provided well over 890,000 sites one could explore on the subject of "gender roles egalitarianism."

---

[54] "Egalitarianism," online article, http://www.theopedia.com/egalitarianism
[55] Cynthia Long Westfall, *Paul and Gender: Reclaiming the Apostle's Vision for Men and Women in Christ* (Grand Rapids: Baker Academic, 2016), 4.

At the same time, bing.com served up over 12,6000,000 results for those words. The more specific moniker, "egalitarianism in the church," offered, in one second, 13,600,000 sources to explore. Whatever one's position on the topic, Pandora's Box has been opened regarding gender roles in the church, and the discharge cannot be put back.

But when an interpretation of Scripture has had such long and widespread domination, its ascendancy is self-perpetuating and difficult to dethrone. Such dominance should not be viewed either as an argument for or against its continuation but suggests that consideration of an alternative should be undertaken with a spirit of seriousness and caution. The core doctrines of orthodoxy, as expressed for example in the Apostles' Creed, have dominated biblical interpretation through the ages, and should therefore never be challenged lightly. But hopefully no one would list gender role beliefs as a core doctrine of orthodoxy on a par with those in the Apostles' Creed. It is not included in *any* of the ancient creeds. Nevertheless, if any long- and widely held theological understanding is challenged by serious, exegetically-driven alternative views, integrity demands that it be given serious consideration and not be treated as off-limits for respectful and careful examination.

Remember, This Is <u>Really</u> Important!

Given the current ecclesiastical landscape, it would be difficult to overemphasize the importance of the gender roles issue in the church for at least these reasons:

1. Both complementarians and egalitarians sincerely believe that *faithfulness to the Scriptures is at stake*. While it is possible that within both camps there are those whose motivations are not based on biblical evidence, it is hoped that the majority's sincere desire is to practice with integrity what they believe the Bible teaches. Christians believe that obedience to Scripture, even when unpopular or difficult, will ultimately be seen to reflect the loving will and plan of God. But <u>both gender roles views cannot be correct</u>. One is true to the teachings of Scripture and one is not. It is incumbent on every serious Christian to discern which is right.

2. Gender roles in the church is a crucial issue because of the *potential* to either more than double or to reduce by more than half the pool of potential leaders and teachers in the church. Based on whether there are biblical gender restrictions for ministry, the outcome will include harnessing or bypassing half or more of all the gifts, passion, energy, experience, knowledge, and perspective in the church, at least at a leadership level. Egalitarians might argue pragmatically that the outcome of this debate could *revitalize* or partially *paralyze* the church.[56] Egalitarians assert that eliminating gender restrictions could be a catalyst for generating renewal in the church. **Imagine using two arms instead of one!** Complementarians, however, would understandably object to negatively characterizing their position based on potential numerical loss of ministry personnel, citing obedience to biblical conviction as the higher value. "If this is God's plan," they would argue, "whether we understand now or not, it is best for everyone in the church, including women!" Ultimately the question does not boil down to pragmatics but Scripture. The stakes are too high to not engage in careful examination of the relevant Scriptures.

3. This issue is pivotal because many people *inside the church* are making up their minds whether to stay or move on depending on how this issue is resolved. For many, on both sides, the gender roles position reveals the heart and values of an institution. Sadly, there is no longer a "safe" position. Some people will probably eventually leave over this issue regardless of where the church stands.

4. The outcome of this debate is momentous because many *outsiders* see the church as just another institution that oppresses women and they use this perception to justify rejecting Christ and His church. The effectiveness of the church's witness about the character of God, the relevance and ethic of the Bible, and the equality of the genders is and will be affected. Nevertheless, the Scriptures, not pragmatics, must

---

[56] "Roughly 1 in 3 of all Master of Divinity students is female, according to The Association of Theological Schools. This trend spans back several years. And yet, as Barna reported, less than 10 percent of all lead pastors are women." Ashley Emmert, "The State of Female Pastors," Christianity Today, October 15, 2015. https://www.christianitytoday.com/women-leaders/2015/october/state-of-female-pastors.html

ultimately prevail but pragmatic implications may validly invigorate renewed investigation of the biblical data.

What If?

What if, as chapters 7–9 will propose, the unclear or misleading translations in the most popular and influential English versions have inappropriately and profoundly influenced debate to support patriarchy and have been used to support the imposition of silence and leadership restriction on women in the church?

What if the *misinterpretation, misapplication, and neglect of numerous relevant passages throughout the Scriptures* have robbed women of opportunities to employ their God-given gifts in Jesus' church and have robbed churches of the benefits of the full-orbed leadership and instruction achieved by including women who represent more than half of their members?

What if these errors have for centuries hindered the witness, example, and influence of the church regarding gender role equality as a testimony against the often-predominant cultural norm for limiting, subjugating, oppressing, silencing, and even abusing women?

What if the church's failure to liberate women from a key residual part of sin's curse has robbed the world of an important "sign" of the now-and-future kingdom of God on earth and the values of the New Creation?

What if well-meaning and sincere followers of Jesus have too often joined ranks with less "innocent" domineering males to perpetuate this perversion of God's creation intent and of Jesus' redemptive restoration of those original values?

If these "what ifs" are even remotely possible then no follower of Jesus should resist an open-minded and sincere reexamination of the biblical data to be sure that the church has not been wrong again on gender role restrictions as it was on a geocentric universe, Reformation-exposed theological errors, and the institution of slavery.

What if you are wrong in your current position on gender roles? Would you want to know? Do you dare to investigate?

The church must not be wrong about gender roles. Too much is at stake!

FOR DISCUSSION

1. Read Romans 14:1–23. What were the disputable matters the Christians in the church at Rome were struggling with?
2. Make a list of what Paul told the Roman believers to do and not do regarding those with whom they disagreed?
3. How can you tell the difference between a "disputable matter" and an issue over which there is *no room for disputation* because of the clarity of Scripture?
4. What are some significant "disputable matters" facing the church today?
5. Do you think the gender roles issue is a "disputable" matter? Why or why not?
6. Whether or not you believe that the gender roles issue is biblically debatable, what specific directions from Paul in Romans 14 could validly be applied to this controversy among Christians in your church?
7. What biases do many people have about gender roles? Where do they come from? What are some biases you might have that could affect how you view this topic? How aware do you think you are about your own biases and what gives you that confidence?
8. As you pray, ask God to work in your church to bring about unity regardless of the level of agreement on the gender roles dispute. Pray that you and others in your group/church would be sensitive to the Holy Spirit's guidance as you study the Scriptures highlighted in this study.

3

What God Intended from the Beginning

If you had been a woman leading the children's ministries at Riverview Community Church[57] you would not have had the same title as a male who held the same position even though the job descriptions were identical. A man was called "Pastor" of Children's Ministries, while a woman was designated "Director" of Children's Ministries. The title "pastor" not only carried more authority than "director" but also qualified for higher compensation on the church pay scale. A male pastor also could serve as an elder while the female director could not. But the only difference between the two individuals was *gender*. When the children's ministry position was vacant, no title or salary were assigned to the job description until it was known whether the candidate who would receive the call was male or female.

Female "directors" also didn't preach in the worship services at Riverview. Women participated freely in many church ministries, including some in the worship services such as the music ministry, making announcements, leading in prayer, or reading Scripture, but they didn't preach. There wasn't any written policy or constitutional "rule" prohibiting women from preaching, but it was an unspoken tradition.

Over the years, though Riverview dealt with some controversies and occasionally some mild disagreements, the gender roles issue was simply not on the radar screen. As in many churches with a complementarian tradition, there was no debate. Anyone who disagreed probably realized there was no sense of need for any discussion so either stuffed their disagreement or quietly slipped away to look for another church. The long-standing complementarian

---

[57] Not its real name.

position was just assumed by everyone—at least so it seemed. In reality, only God knows what was in people's hearts, how many people left the church or didn't join it because of this view, or how many disagreed but were afraid to voice their objections, didn't want to rock the boat, or lacked the ability to present an alternative position from the Scriptures.

In all of this, Riverview Community Church mirrors many thousands of churches throughout the United States and the world who affirm and practice the gender-based restrictions that represent the complementarian position. These include thirty-five-member congregations and megachurches, evangelical churches and mainline denominations, diverse churches and homogeneous churches, Pentecostal churches and liturgical churches, 100-year-old churches and recent church plants, the Roman Catholic Church and the Eastern Orthodox Church, Baptist churches and Presbyterian churches. The gender-based ministry restrictions aren't limited to a few sophisticated or off-the-wall mostly-similar congregations.

What is undeniable at Riverview is that at least 50% of the members were prohibited from serving in the top positions of leadership such as pastor and elder. Half of the members see zero examples of people like themselves serving and investing their abilities in key leadership roles. Half of the members exist in an environment where their voice and perspective are not heard or valued on important issues affecting 100% of the congregation. Church leadership regularly makes important decisions affecting everyone but that lack the perspective, creativity, diversity, and experience of 50% of those affected. Some may argue that the male leaders receive input and counsel from women, especially their wives. However, that input differs vastly from what would be received by having women actually sitting at the table engaging fully in the free exchange and discussion of ideas and then participating in making the final decisions.

Why is the gender-restrictive model at Riverview pervasive throughout Christendom? Was this the way God intended from the beginning? Did God create men to lead and women to submit? Are men born with a leadership gene? Are women born with a submission gene? Those questions are really at the heart of the gender roles debate.

Many Christians are polarized over whether or not God, from the beginning, planned for men to be leaders and women to be followers. Some assert that the respective leader/submitter roles were inherent to God's creation design for the genders. Others strongly disagree and contend that the creation accounts emphasize the identity, equality, and oneness of the genders and that any gender role hierarchy violated God's creation intent and was a tragic *result* of sin's entrance into the world. These views seem so far apart there is little room for compromise. How can people committed to and reading the same Bible come to such diametrically opposed views? Obviously, a careful examination of God's original plan for the relationship and roles of men and women is vital if God's intent for the genders is to be realized.

Back to the Future

Beginning at the beginning is a good thing. Therefore, turning to the opening chapters of Genesis to search out God's intention for His creation is an essential starting point.

Some Bible scholars suggest that the first appearance of a topic in Genesis, the Book of beginnings, is a key to understanding later appearances of the same topic throughout the Scriptures. For example, while the illustration may be more striking than prophetic, it is nevertheless interesting to note that the first use of the word "love" (אָהַב,'ā·hăḇ) in Genesis is a reference to a father who loved his only son and gave him as an offering (Gen. 22:1, 2). He did this on a mountain in the region of Moriah (Gen. 22:1). Centuries later, Solomon built the Temple on Mount Moriah, the place God designated for Israel's offerings (2 Chron. 3:1) which pointed to the offering of Jesus on the Cross.

The significance of the themes introduced in the opening chapters of the Bible (Gen. 1, 2) is elevated by the realization that many of them will reach their fruition in the *new creation* as beautifully portrayed in the concluding chapters of the Bible (Rev. 21, 22). These Genesis/Revelation themes are like beautiful bookends for God's unfolding story that develops between. These chapters introduce the key themes of God's epic story and the conclusion and fruition of those themes.

The answers to three questions are foundational to construct a biblical view of gender roles in the home, church, and society today:

- What was God's original intention for gender roles as revealed in the Genesis 1 and 2 accounts of Creation?

- Regarding gender roles, what was the result of the Fall described in Genesis 3?
- How are gender roles portrayed in their future actualization in the New Creation?

Creation

It is my assertion that the Genesis 1 and 2 account of the original creation identifies *no hierarchical distinctions based on gender.* Those chapters give no indication of hierarchical roles for leadership or authority related to maleness or femaleness. "Conspicuously absent in Genesis 1–2 is any reference to the divine prescription for man to exercise authority over woman . . . The total absence of such a commission indicates that it was not part of God's intent . . . Any teaching that inserts an authority structure between Adam and Eve in God's creation design is to be firmly rejected since it is not founded on the biblical text."[58]

The Persistent Problem of Bias

It must be acknowledged that not all Bible students and scholars agree with this confident assertion. It is my belief that an unbiased and straightforward reading of these chapters in isolation from the rest of the Bible would never lead to the conclusion that God's original intent was for Adam to have authority over Eve. Unfortunately, my assertion about an *unbiased* reading is naïve because everyone brings their biases, often subconscious, to their understanding of the text. None of us can read those chapters apart from the subtle influence of (1) our personal background and experiences, (2) the sermons and studies to which we have been exposed, (3) our awareness of New Testament passages that appear to call on women to be silent and to not have authority over men in the church, and (4) our desire to please and not disappoint people we respect who share or have influenced our current position on gender roles.

Additionally, the pervasive domination of patriarchy throughout society

---

[58] Michelle Lee-Barnewall, *Neither Complementarian nor Egalitarian,* 121.

and the church has powerfully, though perhaps subtly, prejudiced our understanding of these passages. Many of us, by our backgrounds, have been predisposed to look at the creation and fall stories through complementarian lens. The challenge of performing exegesis (drawing out what the text actually says) rather than eisegesis (reading one's own biases into the text) is real. For many people, the subconscious bias and predisposition toward a complementarian understanding of the Scriptures are so powerful and pervasive that to even question it is tantamount to questioning biblical orthodoxy.[59] Aversion to an open-minded consideration of what was perceived to be on the edge of heresy is a powerful motivator to *not rock the theological boat.* This may help to explain the paucity of egalitarian literature until the relatively recent avalanche of scholarly books, papers, blogs, etc., written from an egalitarian standpoint.

A recent study revealed that people are much more influenced by their political party connections than by the actual content of its policies. The study involved an experiment to determine the power of bias to influence people's feelings about a policy. In a survey of over 1000 voters in the United Kingdom, they discovered that responses were strongly influenced by a policy's perceived connection to a political party much more than by its actual content. For example, when Labour supporters thought the policy came from Labour there was strong support. However, support plummeted when it was described as a Conservative policy. Similarly, if Tories thought the policy came from their party, they were four times more likely to approve of it. "The results show that voters interpret policies through a lens of their feelings for the party. If they dislike a party, they'll interpret any policy through a negative filter . . . policy is far less influential than existing party affiliation."[60]

What does this mean for the gender roles issue? It suggests that many people may subconsciously support complementarianism or egalitarianism based on who they believe holds to the views, more than by their actual

---

[59] In the church I had pastored for thirty-two years, when I first presented a possible egalitarian understanding of the Scriptures regarding gender roles, a few people quickly left the church. It was as if I had changed my position on the deity of Christ.

[60] Richard Shotton, *"Marketing triage: why brands need to categorize consumers into three groups"* (12/13/2017), https://www.linkedin.com/pulse/marketing-triage-why-brands-need-categorise-consumers-richard-shotton/?trk=eml-email_feed_ecosystem_digest_01-recommended_articles-12-Unknown&midToken=AQFXXojqsMrwPQ&fromEmail=fromEmail&ut=2tg7X-wTzoXo01.

understanding of the relevant biblical data. In reality then, which position on gender roles is held by an individual's theological tribe will have subtle but strong influence over how they process what the Scriptures actually say. If I and my tribe are complementarian, it will be hard for me to have an open mind when considering research supporting an egalitarian position. The same is true for someone who lives in an egalitarian tribe.

The bias issue is compounded further by the prospect that most of our English translations appear to have been significantly influenced by gender bias in key passages including 1 Timothy 2:11–15. This frightening and crucially important issue will be illustrated and discussed at length in chapters 7 through 10.

It is *essential* to be aware of one's own biases and their influence on how they interpret the Bible. One must be ruthlessly committed to preventing those biases from closing one's mind to biblical understandings that might challenge the party line regarding gender roles.

From the Beginning: Gender Equality

What seems indisputable in the creation accounts is that both male and female were created in God's image[61] as equal partners to exercise dominion over the creation. Genesis 1:27–28 states: "So God created man in his own image, in the image of God he created him; male and female he created them. God blessed them and said to them, 'Be fruitful and increase in number; fill the earth and subdue it. Rule over the fish of the sea and the birds of the air and over every living creature that moves on the ground.'" There was no distinction, gender-based or otherwise, in the assignment to the two image-bearers to steward God's creation.

Genesis 5:1–2 also teaches that both Adam and Eve were created in God's image: "This is the list of the descendants of Adam. When God created humankind, he made them in the likeness of God. Male and female he created them, and he blessed them and named them 'Humankind' when they

---

[61] A comparison of Colossians 3:10–11 and Galatians 3:26–28 reveals Paul's understanding that both male and female bear the image of God as restored in Jesus' inauguration of the new creation.

were created."[62] Adam's declaration about Eve in Genesis 2:23 is pertinent: "because she was bone of his bones, flesh of his flesh." The text then affirmed them as "one flesh" in Genesis 2:24 which description is reiterated in Paul's description of marriage in Ephesians 5:31. Eve is threefold in the image of God because she was formed directly by God in his image; she, in contrast to Adam's from-dirt-formation, was formed from Adam; and she became one flesh with Adam, God's image bearer, in their sexual union.[63]

In spite of the clear affirmations that both male and female were made in God's image not only in the Genesis creation account but also assumed in Paul's description of the new creation (Col. 3:9, 10[64]), some complementarians argue that men are made in God's image but women are not. Some claim that 1 Corinthians 11:7 supports this view because it affirms that a man is made in God's image but does not specifically state the same for a woman: "A man ought not to cover his head, since he is the image and glory of God; but the woman is the glory of man."

The context of this statement in 1 Corinthians 11:2–16 is a very challenging passage as virtually all commentators acknowledge. The passage includes some rather obscure and challenging statements and prompts numerous difficult questions including: Who bears the divine image? What does "head" mean? Which references to "head" are physical, hierarchical, or relating to origin? How do men or women *dishonor* their heads by covering or not covering them? Why is it a shame for a woman to "cut" or "shave" her hair? Is a woman supposed to never cut her hair or merely to not cut it so it is "short"? How short is "short"? What does it mean to be the "glory" of another? What does it mean to be created "for" someone? What do angels have to do with humans having a sign of authority on their head? How are men and women independent of each other? How does nature teach us it is "disgraceful" for a man to have "long" hair? How long is "long"? Which of these issues were culturally-specific to the first century, or more specifically to first century Corinth, and which are timeless and universal?

Wow! Frankly, the passage is an interpreter's nightmare. The widely

---

[62] NRSV.

[63] Cynthia Long Westfall, *Paul and Gender*, 65.

[64] "Do not lie to each other, since you have taken off your old self with its practices and have put on the new self, which is being renewed in knowledge in the image of its Creator."

disparate explanations are like a theological quagmire that has engendered far more confusion and disagreement than consensus even among those who agree on the gender roles issue. Perhaps this is one of Paul's writings Peter described as "hard to understand" (2 Pt 3:15, 16). It is not the ideal kind of passage on which to anchor a confident position regarding an issue as important as gender roles in the church. Dogmatic positions should not be based on very challenging passages about which there is a great deal of disagreement among Bible students and scholars. While not Gospel truth, there is merit in the colloquial saying: "The main things are the plain things and the plain things are the main things."

The topics mentioned above from 1 Corinthians 11 are like pieces of a very complicated puzzle that in order to see the picture correctly must all fit together in precisely the right way. The lack of broad consensus in interpreting this chapter suggests:

- either no one has yet correctly put all the pieces together so that broad interpretive consensus is engendered, or else
- gender bias has stood in the way of reaching any such harmonious agreement.

However, some comprehensive interpretive approaches to 1 Corinthians 11 are emerging in the writings of contemporary theologians and Bible students. In recent decades, the same staggering advances and progress in the explosion of knowledge in the sciences and technology also exist in biblical studies. They have enjoyed a deluge of new linguistic, historical, and cultural understandings regarding the biblical languages and times. These are increasingly shedding new light on challenging Bible passages and will hopefully continue to bring about increased interpretive clarity and consensus among Bible scholars with regard to difficult passages such as 1 Corinthians 11.[65]

The Genesis 1 and 1 Corinthians 11 portrayals of Eve being made in the image of God and being the glory of Adam are not incompatible but complementary. She was both because God made her in His image, not from

---

[65] Cynthia Long Westfall's recent (2016) volume, *Paul and Gender: Reclaiming the Apostles' Vision for Men and Women in Christ*, includes excellent illustrations of recently emerging biblical scholarship relevant to the gender roles debate.

the ground like Adam, but from Adam himself—from a rib taken from his side. First Corinthians 11:7 states that "A man . . . is the image and glory of God; but the woman is the glory of man." As such women are the *glory of the glory*[66] *and of the divine image.* This is not a diminishment of her identity but an enhancement of it. After the creation of Adam, God's pronouncement was "not good" (Gen. 2:18), whereas after the creation of Eve, Adam's completion, God pronounced everything He had made as "very good" (Gen. 2:18; 1:31).

At the conclusion of a complex but extremely helpful discussion Westfall offers a summary that helps to bring together (a) the various elements of this passage in light of Paul's other New Testament writings, (b) his overarching theme in 1 Corinthians 11, (c) the cultural background of the ancient world, (d) relevant data from related extra-biblical sources,[67] and (e) other related biblical texts. She writes:

> In conclusion, though woman is man's glory (in contrast with man being only the image and glory of God), it does not follow that Paul is indicating that woman does not bear the image of God, or that she has a lesser glory than the

---

[66] Ibid, Westfall, 65.

[67] The Scriptures include references to or quotations from at least thirty non-canonical that include pagan writings and authors (see Wikipedia article, "Non-canonical books referenced in the Bible," https://en.wikipedia.org/wiki/Non-canonical books referenced in the Bible) such as the "Book of Jasher" (Joshua 10:13), "the book of the annals of Solomon" (1 Kings 11:41), and the "Book of Enoch" (Jude 14). With few exceptions, Christians unanimously agree that these books do not bear the stamp of divine inspiration but do contain some true statements and accurate information that biblical authors quote or reference. Westfall argues cogently that 1 Corinthians 11 may "have strong textual ties with 1 Esdras 4:14-17" in which "there are too many associations . . . for them to be coincidental." The 1 Esdras text has remarkable parallels both to 1 Corinthians 11 and to Genesis 2:24, that provide very helpful interpretive clues for understanding Paul's discourse about men and women. Ibid, pages 66-68. 1 Esdras is primarily a repetition of the book of Ezra with shorter sections from 2 Chronicles and Nehemiah. A few chapters of the book contain material not found elsewhere in the Bible. 1 Esdras was included in the Septuagint (Greek translation of the Old Testament from which Jesus sometimes quoted). It was quoted by early church leaders such as Origen. The Eastern Church included 1 Esdras in the canon, but the Western Church did not. It is included in most Roman Catholic translations of the Bible, but not in most Protestant versions.

man. The Pauline corpus maintains that all believers, male and female, are on exactly the same footing in terms of the ontological image and glory of God. Female believers are renewed in the image of God in the same way as men. However, when it comes to external appearance, there is a difference between the glory of men and the glory of women. In common with the culture, Paul believed that God created women to be more attractive or more glorious, so that she is the glory of man. This becomes a pragmatic problem at the very point when women attempt to manifest the Spirit in prophesying (1 Cor. 11:5; 12:7, 10), or when they lead in prayer in order to worship God. However, the mandate to veil should be understood neither as a polemic against women nor a subordination of women to men, because veiling was their protection and a sign of whatever status and honor a woman could possess in the Greco-Roman culture. Therefore, in cultures that veil, women have often tried to resist the command by husbands or authorities to unveil. It was a privilege and a protection that Paul extended to all women in the congregation in reformation of the cultural practice.[68]

Regardless of how one understands the more obscure parts of the passage, what is clear and indisputable in 1 Corinthians 11:2–16 is that:

- The Scriptures, when correctly interpreted, do not contradict each other.[69]
- Obscure passages should not be interpreted in ways that contradict clear primary texts.
- Paul assumed that women would participate in worship gatherings by praying and prophesying. In those activities, it seems undeniable that women were expected to lead other worshipers, including men through prayer and preaching (prophesying), otherwise the other

---

[68] Westfall, *Paul and Gender*, 69, 70.

[69] Most, not all, Christians would affirm this view of Scripture. It is the perspective from which this book is written.

parts of the passage, however difficult they may be to interpret, make no sense at all. The text assumes the presence of both men and women in the services in which women prayed and prophesied.

While 1 Corinthians 11:2–16 remains a challenging text to interpret in a way that is comprehensive and produces consensus concerning all of its elements, it is crystal clear that Paul condoned women's participation in key roles which shaped and directed mixed gender worship gatherings. The question was never *whether* women would lead the church in prophesying (preaching) and prayer, only *how they should be groomed or attired* while doing so.

Back to the Beginning—What about Authority?

Considering my assertion that there are no gender-based hierarchical distinctions in God's creation design, it is helpful to remember that in that perfect, pre-sin world there was no selfishness, competition, conflict, pride, ambition, jealousy, manipulation, or desire for domination. There was no need for a list of laws because unconditional love was their natural predisposition and constant practice. There was therefore no need or inclination for either gender to have authority over the other.

In contrast, in the fallen creation, governing authority is necessary to curb the selfish desires and ambitions of sinful people and to minimize and resolve the conflicts and violence born out of their selfishness. In the beginning, the only authority was God and the authority He assigned to both Adam and Eve to exercise in partnership over His creation (Gen. 1:28).

Since humanity's fall into sin, multiple layers of authority including governmental (Rom. 13:1ff) are now essential so as to maintain an imperfect and fragile peace in sin-tainted societies. The alternative is division, exploitation, violence, and chaos as was illustrated in the time of the Judges when "Israel had no king; everyone did as he saw fit" (Judg. 21:25). Authority structures were necessary to attempt to keep a peaceful and just society. Even regulations regarding divorce and remarriage, according to Jesus, were given "because your hearts were hard. But it was not this way from the beginning" (Matt. 19:8). God's original design for His perfect world included no hard hearts and no hierarchical distinction between the genders.

It is not that authority is inherently evil. God's absolute authority functions in perfect harmony with His essential being and His character of holiness, love, grace, mercy, righteousness, justice, and kindness. His authority is consistent with and flows out of His infinite perfections and out of His sovereignty and superiority over everyone and everything. He is the authoritative Creator. Everything else is His subservient creation.

As divine image-bearers Adam and Eve exercised God's authority over His creation as equal partners with no stated or implied difference of rank or any suggestion of hierarchy in their essential beings or relationship to each other. "God blessed them and said to them, 'Be fruitful and increase in number; fill the earth and subdue it. Rule over the fish of the sea and the birds of the air and over every living creature that moves on the ground'" (Gen. 1:28). Genesis 1 and 2 emphasize Adam and Eve's unity and equality, not their dissimilarity or disparity of rank. Clearly that was God's original intent. However, in the now fallen world, all subsequent human authority, whether sanctioned by God (Rom. 13) or illicitly commandeered, is flawed due to depravity and naturally tends toward exploitation and oppression.

In contrast, there were no authority issues prior to the entrance of sin. Notably, the creation story in Genesis 2 describes God dividing the first human being by removing his rib in order to form a second human being so that they could enjoy a side-by-side co-regency and face-to-face intimacy made possible by their inherent identity, similarity, and equality. They were literally *made of the same stuff.* Adam responded with a powerful acknowledgement of that unity and oneness, "This is now bone of my bone and flesh of my flesh" (Gen. 2:23). In marriage, the two were re-joined to become one (Gen. 2:24). Stackhouse observes, "I cannot imagine a stronger set of images of coequality, partnership, and the like."[70]

The Image of God Is Unrelated to Gender or Marital Status

N.T. Wright argues that both male and female were created in God's image (Gen. 1:26, 27) and that gender was not an aspect of being God's image-bearers:

---

[70] Stackhouse, *Partners In Christ: a Conservative Case for Egalitarianism,* 47.

Many people have said, and I have often enough said it myself, that the creation of man and woman in their two genders is a vital part of what it means that humans are created in God's image. I now regard that as a mistake. Not only the animal kingdom, as noted in Genesis itself, but also the plant kingdom, as noted by the reference to seed, have their male and female. The two-gender factor is not at all specific to humans, but runs right through a fair amount of the rest of creation. This doesn't mean it's unimportant it means if anything it's important; being male and being female, and working out what that means, is something most of creation is called to do and be, and unless we are to collapse into a Gnosticism, where the way things are in creation is regarded as secondary and shabby over against what we are now to do with it, we have to recognize, respect and respond to this call of God to live in the world he has made and as the people he has made us. It's just that we can't use the argument that being male-plus-female is somehow what being God's image bearers actually means.[71]

Being made in God's image is not an equation such as *Adam + Eve = God's image*. Rather, *Adam = God's image* and *Eve = God's image*. Wright's argument undermines any claim that created gender differences inherently require that one gender has authority and the other is responsible to submit. Both the man and the woman, *individually and separately,* are complete divine image-bearers. Recognizing that gender existed in the prior creation of animals and plants reveals that gender is not a factor in humans being made in God's image. Nor is the union of male and female required to fully reflect God's image. Both male and female are image-bearers by God's creation, not by their marriage or by physically becoming *one* through sexual union. Genesis does not teach that the image of God is incomplete in the male or female apart from union with the other. An unmarried person of either gender is made in the image of God just as is a married person. A single

---

[71] N. T. Wright, *"Women's Service in the Church: The Biblical Basis,"* a conference paper for the Symposium, 'Men, Women and the Church,' St John's College (Durham, 9/4/2004): http://ntwrightpage.com/Wright_Women_Service_Church.htm

woman or man is not an incomplete image-bearer. If someone becomes a widow or widower they do not cease to be God's image bearer until or unless they remarry. Recognizing that both male and female are individually and equally made in God's image undermines any suggestion that one, by virtue of their gender, inherently has authority over the other.

Complementarians Offer a Very Different View of Creation

In jarring contrast to these conclusions, complementarians argue that from the beginning God intended for Adam to have a position of authority over Eve. Because they can cite no statement which asserts either gender possessing authority over the other, they must appeal for evidence in supposed *implications* they project onto the texts. For example, they assert that:

(1) patriarchal hierarchy was *implied* when God gave exclusively to Adam (not Eve) both the creation mandate and the prohibition regarding the tree of the knowledge of good and evil;

(2) the *order* of creation—Adam first, then Eve—*implied* his predominance;

(3) Adam's *naming* of Eve (even as he had named the animals) *implied* his authority over her;

(4) Eve's creation to be Adam's "helper" (Gen. 2:18) *implied* a supporting role under the leadership of Adam; and,

(5) the designation of the wife as the "weaker partner" in 1 Peter 3 *implied* a creation- and gender-based need for her husband's leadership over her.

It would be impossible to prove and perhaps for anyone to self-perceive, but it is my strong suspicion that if a person studied the Genesis creation account without first having been enculturated in a male-dominated society or exposed to a complementarian understanding of the New Testament prohibition passages, they would never arrive at the five conclusions stated in the previous paragraph. Interpreters must always be alert to their vulnerability to read into texts supposed *evidence* supporting their positions. Looking at the creation account isolated from gender role predilections would overwhelm one with a sense of Adam and Eve's equality, partnership, and oneness—not with any sense that that Adam possessed authority over Eve. That simply is not in the Genesis text.

However, once a person has become convinced of a complementarian understanding of 1 Corinthians 14:33–35 and 1 Timothy 2:12–15, the temptation to artificially impose those apparent hierarchical concepts back onto the creation account is both subtle and powerful. Interpreters, whether complementarian or egalitarian, fall into party lines in their interpretation of *both*—the creation account (Gen. 1, 2) and the prohibition passages (1 Cor. 14 and 1 Tim. 2). Despite the order and wide separation of their appearance in the Scriptures, it would be difficult to win a chicken-and-egg argument about which passage has influenced understanding of the other, or whether both were considered purely on their own merits with no influence from the other. However, it could reasonably be argued that the primacy of the creation account should influence the understanding of the later and arguably more obscure passages rather than vice versa.

That said, let's consider those five complementarian assertions which they allege are based on the Genesis creation account and on the New Testament reference in 1 Peter 3, all of which they assert portray creation-based gender-distinctions.

(1) The Creation Mandate and Prohibition Concerning the Tree of Knowledge

First, the argument that God's creation mandate was given exclusively to Adam overlooks or suppresses contradictory information within the text. Genesis 1 clearly indicates that God's assignment to subdue and to rule over the creation was given "to them," that is to *both* Adam and Eve who, in the immediately previous verse, were *both* said to be created in God's image. It seems irrefutable that God's creation mandate to rule over and care for the creation was given to *both* Adam and Eve together with no hierarchical elevation of one as the leader in fulfilling this assignment.

Genesis 1:26–31 states (emphasis added):

"Then God said, 'Let us make man in our image, in our likeness, and let them rule over the fish of the sea and the birds of the air, over the livestock, over all the earth, and over all the creatures that move along the ground.' So God created man in his own image, in the image of God he created him; male and female he created them. God blessed them and said to them, 'Be fruitful and increase in number; fill the earth and subdue it. Rule over the fish of the sea and the birds of the air and over every living creature that moves on the ground.' Then God said, 'I give you every seed-bearing plant on the face of the whole earth and every tree that has fruit with seed in it. They will be yours for food. And to all the beasts of the earth and all the birds of the air and all the creatures that move on the ground—everything that has the breath of life in it—I give every green plant for food.' And it was so. God saw all that he had made, and it was very good. And there was evening, and there was morning—the sixth day."

Some assert that Genesis 2 adds the clarifying detail that God's assignment to subdue and rule creation was first made to Adam alone, prior to Eve's creation, thus suggesting a hierarchical role. However, God's command to Adam in Genesis 2:15–17 says nothing about the creation mandate which Genesis 1:28 states was given to "them."

As for the argument that male authority is demonstrated by God's giving exclusively to Adam the prohibition against eating from the tree of the knowledge of good and evil, two things should be noted:

(1) Although the text states that the prohibition was given to "the man" (Gen. 2:16, 17) and this appears to precede the creation of Eve (Gen. 2:18), to build an argument for hierarchy on this goes far beyond what the text actually states. Nothing in the text connects the communication of the prohibition to a leadership role. Further, to assume that the prohibition was given only to Adam is an argument from silence as we have no way of knowing if God also reiterated it in her presence.

(2) More important, even if the command was given to Adam prior to Eve's creation, it does not logically follow that he and all men after him

therefore hold a position of authority over women. This conclusion is an arbitrary hypothesis lacking any textual support. As presented above, the references to God's communication about the trees in the garden comes in the context of clear and repetitive assertions of Adam and Eve's essential unity and identity.

It is possible that the description and prohibition concerning the two trees was positioned thematically in the chapter rather than chronologically as part of the larger description of the garden home God prepared for the crown of His creation (Gen 2:8–17). This description included the instructions to "till and keep" the garden (2:15–17) with the clarification that while tending the garden the fruit could be freely enjoyed from any tree except one.

On the other hand, if one assumes a chronological sequencing in Genesis 2, it could reasonably be argued that this command had to be given prior to Eve's creation because otherwise Adam might have innocently munched on the easily accessible deadly fruit while he was naming the animals, much like a modern descendent of Adam gulps down ballpark franks while watching a baseball game. If one assumes a literal/historical, 24-hour understanding of Genesis 2, in six hours, taking five seconds to analyze and to invent a descriptive label for each animal, only 4,320 species would be completed. Whether this staggering task is an argument against such a literalistic interpretation, as a tribute to Adam's stellar intellect, or as an indication that Adam needed only to start the project rather than to complete it to recognize his aloneness, my point is that most men would want a snack during such a challenging and demanding task. Whatever one's hermeneutical approach, the unfolding story necessitates that Adam receive a *heads up* about the malignant tree to protect him until his soul mate arrived.

The text gives no indication on how long Adam was alone. It appears to have been within the sixth day of the creation week, but that raises the interpretive question of how long the creation days were. Although many fundamentalist and evangelical scholars adamantly insist on seven back-to-back, sequential 24-hour days (and a young earth), it should be remembered that such a literalistic interpretation may be a minority view both among contemporary global Christians as well as throughout much of church history. Revered church father, "Augustine, writing in the early fifth century, noted, 'What kind of days these were it is extremely difficult or perhaps impossible to determine' (City of God 11.7)."[72] From ancient rabbis to esteemed orthodox stalwarts such as B. B. Warfield, interpretations other than the literal day/ young earth views have been embraced or seen as compatible with Scripture.[73] This is pointed out not to be sidetracked from the gender roles topic or to take sides in the hotly debated science/Scripture issues but to indicate that, if one assumes that they were the two original humans and that Genesis 1 records actual history, the time between Adam and Eve's creations could have been as little as a few hours to as much as a number of days, weeks, or months. How long did it take Adam to name some or all of the animals and come to grips with his aloneness? Whether hours or weeks, if Adam was like many of his always-hungry descendants, grabbing something to nibble on from the wrong tree was probably too great a risk to delay announcing the prohibition till after Eve's arrival. Thus, it is reasonable to assume that if God gave Adam the prohibition about the tree prior to Eve's creation, it was simply to prevent an inadvertent eating due to ignorance while he was still alone in the world. There is no text-based reason to assume that the sequence of events in Genesis 2 provides evidence for male dominance based on Adam, not Eve, having first received Eden's single prohibition.

In contrast to complementarian assertions, Genesis 1 and 2 present Adam and Eve as equal image bearers and co-regents over God's creation. Further, Adam's announcement, "bone of my bones and flesh of my flesh" (Gen. 2:23), along with God's "one flesh" pronouncement (Gen. 2:24) preclude any hierarchical elevation of one gender over the other. Any such suggestion of hierarchy seems not only absent from but also abrasively out of sync with what the account actually and unequivocally states.

---

[72] "Biblical Reasons to doubt the creation days were 24 hour periods," The Gospel Coalition (1/28/2015): https://blogs.thegospelcoalition.org/justintaylor/2015/01/28/biblical-reasons-to-doubt-the-creation-days-were-24-hour-periods/

[73] This includes well-known scholars with a high view of Scripture such as J. Gresham Machen, Edward J. Young, Carl Henry, and Gleason Archer. https://blogs.thegospelcoalition.org/justintaylor/2015/01/28/biblical-reasons-to-doubt-the-creation-days-were-24-hour-periods/

(2) The Order of Creation

Second, complementarians frequently argue that gender-based hierarchy is implied by the order of creation, that is, by the fact that God created Adam *before* Eve. It is my opinion that if someone's unbiased study were restricted to the Genesis creation account, it would be highly unlikely that they would conclude that hierarchical significance is conveyed by the order of creation. Nothing in the text gives any hint leading to that conclusion. On the contrary, the repetitive emphasis of the account is on the essential identity, unity, and equality of male and female.

I believe that no one would come up with this argument from Genesis 1 and 2 unless they read back into it a complementarian predisposition and/or a complementarian understanding of 1 Timothy 2:13 ("For Adam was formed first, then Eve") and/or of 1 Corinthians 11:8–10 ("For man did not come from woman, but woman from man; neither was man created for woman, but woman for man. For this reason, and because of the angels, the woman ought to have a sign of authority on her head").[74] In other words, the conclusions they assume from (or read into) the creation account, which does *not* assert hierarchy based on the order of creation, may be artificially imposed because of biases or considerations other than a careful exegesis of Genesis 2.

This interpretive dynamic appears to be backwards when the clear teaching of Genesis 1 and 2 is adjusted to conform to an unclear and much disputed interpretation of 1 Timothy 2 and 1 Corinthians 11. While later passages may add details and give additional insights, the prior and primary creation text, Genesis 2, should inform the interpretation of the much later, more debated, and somewhat obscure passages; not vice versa. Creation is the primary theme of Genesis 2, whereas it is a minor, secondary topic in the two passages focused on proper order in the church (1 Tim. 2 and 1 Cor. 11). Additionally, if, as will be asserted in chapters 6 through 10, the complementarian understanding of those New Testament passages is incorrect, then it follows that their order-of-creation conclusions from Genesis 2 are strongly suspect or totally invalid and should be rejected.

In all of these passages, the issue is not whether Adam was created first but rather is what the significance of that prior creation was or was not.

---

[74] These texts will be considered in detail in a later chapter.

Regarding 1 Timothy 2:11–13, complementarians assert that Paul used the order of creation to support his prohibition of women from teaching or assuming authority over men: "A woman should learn in quietness and full submission. I do not permit a woman to teach or to have authority over a man; she must be silent. For Adam was formed first, then Eve." It's easy to understand how a surface reading of the typical English translation could lead to that conclusion. However, I will argue that those complementarian conclusions from 1 Timothy 2 are incorrect. It will be demonstrated that Paul did not prohibit women from teaching or from being a pastor nor does the order of creation support such a limitation. Rather, as will be seen, he instructed women regarding the peace-promoting spirit they were to exemplify while learning, teaching, and leading in the gatherings of the church.

Paul's statement about the order of creation in 1 Timothy 2 should be understood in the context of the specific issues Paul addressed in Ephesus where Timothy had been assigned as his apostolic representative. This included (1) the prevalence of false teaching in Ephesus, (2) the powerful influence of the female-dominated Artemis cult[75] coupled with popular proto-Gnostic[76] myths regarding Eve, (3) the false teaching that Eve preceded Adam in creation, and (4) the problem in Ephesus of women teaching and commandeering authority in an argumentative, abusive, and domineering manner.[77] When these factors are considered and the correct interpretation exposed, the order of creation argument supporting patriarchy vanishes.

Contrary to complementarian assertions, there is no hint whatsoever in the text of Genesis 1, 2, suggesting hierarchal roles based on Adam's creation before Eve's. Both God's stated intent for and Adam's immediate response to Eve's creation (Gen. 2:18–24) are about her oneness with him and her suitability to alleviate his aloneness because she, unlike the animals, is his equal, made of the same stuff.

---

[75] "The city clerk quieted the crowd and said: 'Men of Ephesus, doesn't all the world know that the city of Ephesus is the guardian of the temple of the great Artemis and of her image, which fell from heaven?'" Acts 19:35.

[76] Proto-gnosticism involved false teachings that later evolved into the full blown heresy referred to as Gnosticism.

[77] See the discussion in chapter 10 regarding the meaning of ἡσυχία (*haysuxia*) and αὐθεντεῖν (*authentein*).

The argument asserting male authority based on priority of creation in Genesis 1, 2 is further undermined by the recognition that the animals, birds, and fish were all created *before* humans. The entire creation story **builds up to a zenith** in the creation of Adam and Eve who will rule over everything created before them. Therefore, based on that recognition, perhaps Eve, not Adam, is at the apex of the ascending order of creation. She, not Adam, would be creation's top dog. Some jokingly suggest that with Eve, God "finally got it right." However, no credible biblical scholar makes these assertions because the text asserts no hierarchy based on the order of creation.

Significantly, when Jesus, the Creator (John 1:3), quoted from the creation account, He never mentioned Adam's prior creation. Rather, He spoke as if Adam and Eve were created at the same time: "'Haven't you read . . . that at the beginning the Creator 'made them male and female'?" (Matt. 19:4). Obviously, Jesus did not choose this opportunity to assign or assume any hierarchical significance to the order of creation. Perhaps then, neither should we.

Some complementarians suggest that the hierarchical implications of prior creation are related to the ancient tradition of the firstborn holding a position of ascendancy over those born later. This argument from *primogeniture* suggests that it was God's plan to give the firstborn ascendancy—thus Adam, the first of God's children, had the place of predominance. However, the firstborn argument seems to be an unsubstantiated logical leap to impose either on Genesis 1, 2 or on 1 Timothy 2:13. Further, "In Hebrew tradition the firstborn did carry the most significant status in the family (e.g. Gen 38:27–30). But already in the Old Testament, God shows that he does not necessarily follow this human ordinance, for he chose Jacob, not Esau (Gen 25:21–26). In Romans Paul cites this passage as a precedent for God's gracious reversal in his dealings with humankind (Rom 9:10–13)."[78] Additional illustrations of the firstborn being displaced by a younger sibling in God's evaluation or program include: Cain and Abel, Esau and Jacob, Ishmael and Isaac, Reuben and Judah, Reuben and Joseph, Manasseh and Ephraim, Aaron and Moses, Eliab and David, Amnon (or Chileab after Amnon's death) and Solomon, and the first Adam and Jesus, the "last Adam" (1 Cor. 15:45).

The point is that God's sovereign grace, not primogeniture, often prevailed over birth order in biblical scenarios. "In fact, rather than appealing to Adam's firstborn status as the basis for a permanent male-dominated

---

[78] Grenz, *Women in the Church,* Loc.1596.

hierarchy, Paul declares that in Christ the creation order of woman coming *from* man is balanced by women giving birth *to* men (1 Cor 11:11–12)."[79] Further, Jesus announced that in His Kingdom, "the last will be first, and the first will be last" (Matt. 20:16). Thus, it is evident that the text of Genesis 1, 2 does not indicate that because of Adam's prior creation God intended for him and all his male descendants to have authority over Eve and all their female descendants.

(3) The Naming of Eve

Some argue that evidence for Adam's position of authority over Eve in the original creation is found in that he named her (Gen. 2:23; 3:20). The assertion is that the act of naming signifies superiority and/or authority over those being named, as illustrated in Adam's naming of the animals.

The fact that this idea is accepted by many as self-evident without any supporting evidence either from the Genesis 2 text or from any other Scriptures suggests that it also might be rooted in gender bias. In the first applicable Scripture (Gen. 2:23), when Adam exuberantly declared, "she shall be called 'woman' for she was taken out of man," it was not so much an act of naming as it was an understandable celebratory reaction[80] to seeing the woman for the first time and recognizing that God had provided him with a corresponding partner. It was a recognition "that Eve's femaleness (*issah*) complemented his maleness (*is*)."[81]

The actual naming of Eve didn't occur until <u>after</u> the fall (Gen. 3:20, "Adam named his wife 'Eve' because she would become the mother of all the living"). Any conclusion about it being an indication of original creation hierarchy between the genders is inaccurate. Rather, the immediate and precedent context of Eve's naming is God's pronouncement of the consequences of sin, including the wife's "desire" to control and the now-to-be-prevailing domination by the husband: "And you will desire to control your husband, but he will rule over you" (Gen. 3:16b, New Living Translation). This was

---

[79] Ibid.

[80] A tongue-in-cheek preacher suggested that when Adam awakened to the sight of Eve, he yelled, "Woo man!" ("woman") as an expression of his ecstatic delight.

[81] Grenz, *Women in the Church*, 1591.

the tragic new reality in the fallen world inhabited by self-seeking sinners. Men and women will fight to manipulate and control the other and men will ordinarily prevail in that struggle. Male domination was never God's plan based on His creation design. It is the tragic consequence of sin's ruinous entrance into God's creation and it predominates in all places and times in this broken world.

It seems evident that Adam's naming of Eve was not a demonstration of creation-based headship. Rather it was a prediction of her role in the new fallen world as "the mother of all the living."[82] Adam's stated reason for Eve's name, "because she would become the mother of all the living," sounds much more like an *elevating pronouncement of honor*, rather than one which *put her in her place* under his authority. Perhaps that is because her name would serve as a reminder of God's redemptive promise that her Offspring would be the One to free the creation from Satan's bondage and all the terrible consequences of sin[83]—hardly a designation of a perpetual role of submission. It is significant that in one of the *prohibition passages*, Paul recalls the promise of Genesis 3:15 which was fulfilled through "the [τῆς] childbearing" by Eve's descendant, that is, as a result of the birth of Eve's promised Progeny, Jesus.[84] He was to launch the new creation, including women's salvation from the bondage of sinful patriarchy, exploitation, and oppression.

Further, it is devastating to the naming argument to note in Genesis 16:13 that Hagar named God: "She gave this name to the Lord who spoke to her: 'You are the God who sees me,' for she said, 'I have now seen the One who sees me.'" Identically the same Hebrew word (קָרָא, *qara*) is used for Adam's naming of the animals (Gen. 2:19) and Eve (Gen. 3:20) as is used for Hagar naming God. Obviously, absolutely no one would suggest Hagar had authority over God because she *named* Him. The same argument could be made from numerous other examples of humans *naming* God, such as Exodus 17:15; Judges 6:23; et al.

It is important to note regarding the naming of the animals in Genesis 2:

---

[82] "Adam named his wife Eve, because she would become the mother of all the living" (Gen. 3:20).

[83] "And I will put enmity between you and the woman, and between your offspring and hers; he will crush your head, and you will strike his heel" (Gen. 3:15).

[84] "But women will be saved through [the/ τῆς] childbearing—if they continue in faith, love and holiness with propriety" (1 Tim. 2:15).

First, the Genesis 2 story is not about sovereignty, rule, or authority. In Genesis 1 man and woman *together* in the image and likeness of God are given a God-like dominion over all living creatures. But there is no basis whatsoever for carrying this argument over into the narrative of Genesis 2 in order to construct a hierarchy in which God gives authority to the man to exercise dominion over the woman.

Something different is going on in Genesis 2. The naming of the animals is not an expression of the man's authority over them, as though it corresponds to God's giving of dominion to the man and woman in Genesis 1:26, 28. It is a way of *identifying* what the animals are in relation to the man. It forms part of the search for a suitable helper. God resolves to make a "helper fit for him". He creates the beasts from the ground and brings them to Adam to "see what he would call them". Adam gives them their names but he fails to *identify*, a suitable co-worker or companion. So God creates the woman not from the ground but from Adam's side, which means that Adam can identify her as ʾisha because she was taken from ʾish (Gen. 2:23).

Secondly, naming in scripture is a way of determining the essential character or identity or purpose of something or someone . . . One person names another not because he or she has authority over the named person but because he or she is *the right person to identify or determine the essential significance of the named person.* This is where the 'privilege' comes into it. Adam names the woman because he is in the best position to understand the significance of the fact that she was created not from the earth as a different species but from his own bone and flesh.[85]

---

[85] Andrew Perriman, *"When Adam names the woman he does not exert authority over her:"* http://www.postost.net/2015/11/when-adam-names-woman-he-does-not-exert-authority-over-her. Note that this article gives numerous examples of "naming" in Scripture to support its assertion that naming does not demonstrate authority over.

Rather than signifying his authority over her, Adam's naming of Eve is instead a beautiful announcement of their equality of origin and nature, both created and made by God out of the same material and thus totally "suitable" (Gen. 2:18) for absolute partnership in carrying out the creation mandate together.

(4) The Woman as "Helper"

An important complementarian argument is the assertion that Eve's design for a role of submission to Adam's authority was demonstrated in Genesis 2:18 by her creation to be his "helper" (עֵזֶר, 'ē·zĕr).[86] Genesis 2 makes no statement about Adam being Eve's "head"[87] or "leader." But, according to complementarians, the idea is inherent in the woman's designation as "helper," which, they assert, indicates the woman's supportive role regarding the man's priorities, agenda, direction, leadership, and authority.

Does the idea that "helper" implies "under the authority of" suggest *inferiority*? Most complementarians say "no," and insist that the "helper" argument does not imply inferiority of nature, identity, or worth for women. Nevertheless, many egalitarians believe this is a semantical dodge. At its core, the complementarian understanding of "helper" as well as its practical outworking, to most anyone except perhaps to complementarians, feels like the assignment of a lesser role—a role suggesting not merely gender-based subordination but also inferiority. Regardless of equality or inferiority implications, Egalitarians strenuously object to any suggestion that "helper" implies that woman is to be the man's subordinate assistant.

Although not all believed that males are superior to females, it was common among the Reformers to narrowly define and limit the role of women to that of wife and mother. Many Christians today are ignorant of the strongly patriarchal heritage which the Reformation passed on. Martin Luther shockingly said, "The word and works of God are quite clear, that women were made either to be wives or prostitutes. Men have broad and large chests, and small narrow hips, and more understanding than women, who

---

[86] "The Lord God said, "It is not good for the man to be alone. I will make a helper suitable for him" (Gen. 2:18).

[87] The concept of "head" and "headship" will be addressed later in chapter 6.

have but small and narrow breasts, and broad hips, to the end they should remain at home, sit still, keep house, and bear and bring up children."[88]

Such views of women and their role did not originate with Luther or the Reformation. Revered early church father, Augustine (Bishop of Hippo, 354–430), had difficulty understanding how Eve could be Adam's "suitable helper" other than by procreation. He couldn't conceive of any way she could help him other than by bearing children. He believed that she certainly would not help him tilling the ground. In his mind, two same sex friends living together was more pleasurable than the cohabitation of husband and wife.[89]

Regarding the idea that God created woman primarily to procreate, Mowczko observes: "I cannot see that the respective punishments for Adam and for Eve signify that Adam tilled the earth on his own without any help from Eve, either before or after the first sin, or that Eve went through childbirth on her own without Adam's help and support. Furthermore, Genesis 5 tells us that Adam was 130 years old when he seemingly had his third son, Seth. What has Eve been doing all these years? It is difficult to accept [the] proposition that for decades on end she is inside having children while Adam is out there sweating and struggling with the soil."[90]

In sharp contrast to Augustine and Luther, Mowcyzko quotes Kenneth Bailey who asserts concerning the Genesis 2 account of Eve's creation: "It was not *Eve* who was lonely, unable to manage and needed help. Instead, it was *Adam* who could not manage alone. Eve was then created as an *'ezera* [feminine of *ezer*] . . . a powerful figure who comes to the help/save someone who is in trouble. The Hebrew word *'ezer* is often used for God . . . The word 'ezer does not refer to a lowly assistant but to a powerful figure who comes to help/save someone who is in trouble . . . Women, as descendants of

---

[88] Libby Anne, "What Women Lost in the Protestant Reformation," (11/30/2017), Patheos: http://www.patheos.com/blogs/lovejoyfeminism/2017/11/what-women-lost-in-the-protestant-reformation.html?utm_medium=email&utm_source=Newsletter&utm_campaign=Best+of+Patheos&utm_content=57

[89] Perhaps his own relational history is reflected in his negative attitude toward being married to a woman. Augustine had a son by his fifteen-year lover, broke up with her to be engaged to a ten year-old heiress, then decided instead to become a celibate priest for the rest of his life.

[90] Ibid.

Eve, are placed by God in the human scene as the strong who come to help/ save the needy (the men)."[91]

"All of the other occurrences of *ezer* in the OT have to do with the assistance that one of strength offers to one in need (i.e., help from God), the king, an ally, or an army. There is no exception."[92] This revelation undermines any suggestion that Eve's creation to be Adam's "helper" suggests any hierarchy of man over woman.

How did Eve *"help"* Adam? The text (Gen. 2) gives no answer to that question other than the implication that her help was to overcome his aloneness.

> Nothing is said in the text about procreation as being the "help" Adam needed. Rather, God put a spotlight on Adam's aloneness by the assignment to name the animals. This assignment heightened Adam's awareness that nowhere in creation was there a *kenegdo*, an equal who corresponded to him (Gen. 2:18-20). The moment God brought Eve to Adam, the problem of aloneness was solved by the gift of his equal, a perfectly compatible companion.
>
> Despite what some may suggest, there is no mention of permanent or fixed gender roles in Genesis 2. And nothing in Genesis 2 or 3 implies that the woman continues to be primarily identified or defined as Adam's helper. Likewise, the man does not continue to be primarily identified or defined by his task of naming the animals.
>
> The scriptures give us no reason to think that Eve's station in life was marked by a one-sided help or service to her husband, or that Adam's station in life was to receive his wife's help without also helping her. Furthermore, the idea that women are to help men, but men are not to help women flies in the face of both common sense and the repeated New

---

[91] Ibid.

[92] Stanley Gundry and James R. Beck, eds. *Two Views on Women in Ministry*, (Grand Rapids: Zondervan, 2005).

Testament teaching that we are to love one another. Surely, an obvious expression of loving someone is helping them. Helping someone is not a gender role.[93]

But, given the patriarchal foundation laid by revered church leaders such as Augustine and Luther, it should not be surprising that to this day large segments of the church believe that restrictive and, in the minds of many, subservient ("helper") gender roles were God's plan for women. Though they might object to some of the offensive statements by Augustine and Luther, theirs is the spring from which the stream of the "Biblical Manhood and Womanhood" movement has flowed. This "Neo-Reformed" movement for which John Piper is a prominent spokesperson holds to complementarianism as the third of the "Twelve Features of New Calvinism."[94] They firmly embrace the argument that "helper" portrays the role of the woman as a follower of the man despite the many textual and linguistic evidences to the contrary.

It would be impossible to prove a link between patriarchy and the recent #MeToo movement and the explosion of accusations by women regarding sexual assault and misconduct by men in places of power, but one cannot help wonder if the subtle message of patriarchy, long proclaimed by large portions of the church, overtly or subtly affirms male domination of women and the perception that women exist for the benefit of men. After all, God created them to be men's "helpers." For fallen men, it is an evil but somewhat understandable step to the assumption that women exist for the pleasure of men. Some of patriarchy's fruit may indeed be more rotten than would like to be considered.

Many complementarians object to the assertion that their view of "helper" suggests male *superiority*. They argue that authority does not imply superiority. They point out that God sometimes delegates His authority to human representatives (for example those in government, Romans 13:1-7) without ascribing superiority of worth or identity above those whom they rule. However, unlike the complementarian's woman, the authority bestowed on a governmental official is not based on gender. It is a temporary, tentative,

---

[93] Mowczko, Three Scholars with Two Views.

[94] Jared Oliphint, "John Piper's Twelve Features of the New Calvinism," *Reformed Forum* (blog), March 17, 2014, https://reformedforum.org/john-pipers-twelve-features-new -calvinism/

sometimes precarious and provisional authority based on their current position or office.[95] It is unrelated to their gender identity. The person who holds governmental *authority* ordained by God (Rom. 13:1) is often a woman. The submission God requires to be rendered to human rulers has nothing to do with a permanent, creation-based or gender-based role. If at any time a governing party no longer holds their position, their authority instantly evaporates. It is neither permanent nor inherent to their person, identity, essence, or gender.

What about Jesus' submission to the Father?

Another complementarian argument suggesting that submission does not indicate inferiority is based on Jesus' submission to the Father. Jesus is equal and one with the Father, not inferior to Him, yet during His incarnation, He practiced submission. Virtually all Trinitarians would agree with this teaching regarding the relationship of the Incarnate Son with His Father. However, Jesus' voluntary and temporary submission was an aspect of His humble self-emptying related to His incarnation as described in Philippians 2:6–8 (emphasis added): "Who, being in very nature God, did not consider equality with God something to be grasped, but made himself nothing, taking the very nature of a servant, being made in human likeness. And being found in appearance as a man, he humbled himself and became obedient to death— even death on a cross!"

There is a world of difference between Jesus' submission and that of the complementarian's woman. Jesus' "temporary functional subordination to the Father"[96] was completely voluntary and in no way related to His divine essence, whereas the submission of women envisioned by complementarians was permanently imposed by God and is inseparably related to their female essence. In contrast, Jesus' submission was not based on anything inherent to His divine nature or essence. Jesus' submission to the Father was unrelated to who He was and is in His identity and essence. In His nature and essence,

---

[95] Whether inherited through a "royal blood line," selected by vote, or commandeered by power and/or violence.

[96] Millard J. Erickson, *Introducing Christian Doctrine* (Grand Rapids: Baker Book House, 2001), 221.

Jesus was and is God, equal and one with the Father. Jesus' submission was voluntary and temporary, related to His Incarnation not to His nature. He submitted to God the Father as the God-man, not as the pre-incarnate divine Son of God. This is in stark contrast with the woman's submission required by complementarians which is related to who she is in her identity and essence—to her gender. It is a permanent and essential aspect of who she is. That is NOT what Genesis 1 and 2 teach!

Jesus' voluntary submission was self-imposed. The complementarian woman's submission is involuntary—supposedly imposed by God from the beginning of her creation. In contrast to Jesus' temporary submission, the complementarian woman's submission, because it is based on her created essence, is forever. Therefore, to defend the complementarian's permanent, gender-based submission by comparing it to Jesus' temporary, voluntary submission to the Father is inappropriate. What could be a valid comparison would be between Jesus' temporary and voluntary submission for redemptive purposes and a Christian woman's temporary, voluntary, self-sacrificing submission to her husband in an oppressive culture as a concession and accommodation for the sake of peace and the promotion of the Gospel. She may choose to incarnates Jesus' redemptive submission in her marriage to bring about her husband's salvation and sanctification.

How far does the submissive helper role apply?

Male authority implied by the woman's designation as *helper* is, according to complementarians, God's assignment to males in *marriage*. But most complementarians also extend the authority/submission relationship to roles in the church, and some, to the roles of males and females in general, thereby prohibiting female board members, business owner/operators, employers, managers, supervisors, principals, CEOs, mayors, judges, senators, presidents, etc. (unless all whom they lead are women).[97] In all of these instances, complementarians would insist that male authority does not imply female

---

[97] The pervasive patriarchy practiced for centuries both in society and in the church, is evidenced in the *glass ceiling* that has hindered and limited women from gaining access to positions of authority or power in all levels of church, business, and government as well as in the unjust wage disparity all of which continues to be prevalent in the USA today.

inferiority. Without intending at all to minimize the more egregious horrors of the institution of slavery, telling women that their required submission to men is not an indication of inferiority would be a little like telling slaves that their required submission to their masters was not based on perceived inferiority. That would be a hard sell!

Think about this—if complementarians do not apply male authority in all of the above mentioned societal applications of gender-based restrictions, it is problematic for their position. Those who call for gender role hierarchy only in marriage, or even in marriage and the church but not in society, must then explain why, if the submissive role is *gender*-based, it does not apply to all women (married or single) in all relationships with men.

Unless they assert male dominance over females in every circumstance, complementarians must answer the questions: "What is it about the *feminine gender* which, by God's design, predisposes married women to submit to their husbands, but does not also do so in all other female-male relationships?" "Is the supposed *helper gene* only activated by a wedding or by walking into a church building?" "Is the *helper gene* turned off if the woman is single or widowed?" Otherwise, "Why are married women not required to submit to all men rather than only or first to their husbands?" "If submission is *gender*-based, why is a twenty-nine-year old single female not obligated to submit to all males in her life regardless of their age or marital status? Or is she?" "Should all complementarians adopt the view that the female gender, by design, assigns women to be *'helpers'* to all males?" "If submission is by God's design *gender*-based rather than *role*-based (wife), doesn't it have to apply across the board?"

Perhaps for many complementarians, these implications go way too far. Most would be uncomfortable applying their view of God's creation intent for Adam and Eve universally to all male/female relationships. But if submission to men is God's plan for women from the beginning *based on their gender*, does it not follow that all women must submit to all men? It would seem that the only exceptions would be that the authority of men over women cannot supersede the authority of God, her husband, or perhaps her father. Those relationships would be primary, but if submission is *gender*-based, they would not be exclusive. That view may be palatable for fundamentalist Islamists, many cults, or even for some fundamentalist Christians, but would be extremely difficult to swallow for most evangelical and mainline Christians and perhaps almost vomitus for the majority of people in contemporary western cultures. Even more importantly, that view does not seem compatible with the spirit of Jesus demonstrated in His actions and words regarding women or with the Old and New Testaments' positive portrayals of women leading men.[98] If complementarians are hesitant to adopt this broad and consistent application of *gender-based* submission of all women to all men, perhaps they need to rethink the supposedly creation/gender-based assumptions on which their view depends.

However, the issue regarding Genesis 2:18 is not whether God sometimes delegates His authority to humans to represent Him without indicating they are as superior as He to those whom they rule. Rather, the question in Genesis 2:18 is whether "helper" in that verse suggests any gender-based hierarchy or any such assignment of authority and submission. The complementarian understanding of "helper" misrepresents the meaning of the Hebrew word (עֵזֶר, *ezer,* "help"). The meaning of "helper" does not suggest being under authority. "Help" is most often used in the Old Testament to describe what God does for His people (16 of 21 occurrences).

Actually, based on the predominance of the "help" references referring to God, if the issue were authority, a person could more reasonably argue from Genesis 2:18 that females are to exercise authority and superiority over males. "Poor, lonely Adam," it could be argued, "couldn't even make it through his first 24 hours without help." But in reality, the concept of "helper" is not about who has authority over whom, but about one *providing assistance and strength* to another—like the help God provides for His people.

To overcome this difficulty, some complementarians argue that God subordinates Himself to the agendas of humans to help them. This suggestion is seriously problematic for at least two reasons. First, God does not help humans by abandoning His own agenda to adopt theirs. That would not be helpful, it would be disastrous! Second, it overlooks that when God chooses to "*help*" us, He is still infinitely superior to us and retains His authority over us. In the most common Old Testament use of the term, the One who is incalculably superior to them stoops down to "*help*" His needy people. Similarly, Jesus' incarnation to help us with our greatest need did not diminish His absolute deity, sovereignty, superiority, and Lordship over us.

A simple survey of a few Old Testament references to God *helping* His

---

[98] See chapter 11.

people exposes the error of suggesting that Eve's role of helping Adam was like God *subordinating* Himself to us and to our needs. See, for example:

- "My father's God was my **helper**; he saved me from the sword of Pharaoh" (Ex. 18:4);
- "There is no one like the God of Jeshurun, who rides on the heavens to **help** you and on the clouds in his majesty" (Deut. 33:29); and
- "Yet I am poor and needy; come quickly to me, O God. You are my **help** and my deliverer; O LORD, do not delay" (Ps. 70:5).

God helps His people with their needs because of His awesome superiority and power motivated by His love.

The point of Genesis 2:18 is that God created Adam for relationship with another who was *suitable* as his equal so as to relieve his aloneness, and there was no other created being capable of fulfilling that need. "The Hebrew word translated 'helper' does not imply the idea of subordination but designates the female as the one who rescues the man from his loneliness."[99] Adam needed his *from-a-rib-made-woman*, not to rule over her, but to relate and partner with this one who was "bone of his bones and flesh of his flesh" (Gen. 2:23).[100]

This is important! Eve was not made simply to be Adam's "helper." She was made to be a "helper suitable" (נֶגֶד, *neged*) for him. She was *suitable* because she was his equal, not inferior to or below him as the animals were. It is the fact that Eve was not *below* him, but *in front of/opposite/nearby* him (the meaning of *"suitable"*) that enabled her to resolve Adam's aloneness (Gen. 2:18). The emphasis is on equality not on inferiority and not on a supportive role based on male authority and female submission.

(5) The Weaker Gender

One other argument some might make to suggest that God's initial design of man and woman included a created, gender-based difference requiring

---

[99] Grenz, *Women in the Church,* 1591.

[100] It is difficult to discover the source, but the following quote is often attributed to Matthew Henry: "Eve was not taken out of Adam's head to top him, neither out of his feet to be trampled on by him, but out of his side to be equal with him, under his arm to be protected by him, and near his heart to be loved by him."

male leadership is found not in the Genesis creation account but in 1 Peter 3:1–7. This is a classic passage used to assert the requirement for wives to submit to their husbands: "Wives, in the same way be submissive to your husbands" (1 Peter 3:1). In verse 7, the conclusion of the paragraph, Peter wrote, "Husbands, in the same way be considerate as you live with your wives, and treat them with respect as the weaker partner." The suggestion is that the women are *weaker* by nature—by the way God designed them from the beginning. For some this becomes an argument favoring the need for men, the *stronger* gender, to lead.

However, because the Scriptures do not explain or define in what way women are *weaker,* this becomes a matter for pure conjecture. Is she weaker physically, emotionally, intellectually, socially, spiritually, or some combination of these, and in what sense does that justify her need to submit rather than lead, if it does? Every reasonable person today would acknowledge knowing some women whose superior strength over men is evident in some or all the areas listed above.

Some complementarians attempt to define "weaker partner" as a gender-based vulnerability to being deceived as Eve was in the first temptation. They may attempt to garner support from 2 Corinthians 11:3 and 1 Timothy 2:14. However, 1 Peter 3 makes no such connection between being "weaker" and being more easily deceived. If that were the issue, submitting to a husband who does not "believe the word" (a non-believer) would hardly seem to be the cure. The reference to Eve's deception in the original sin in 1 Timothy 2:14 will be discussed further in chapter 10.

Others would argue that "weaker" may simply refer to the fact that on average, women are physically smaller in stature than men and have less muscle mass. Men's stature and muscle mass advantage often enables sinful husbands to physically dominate or abuse their wives and, in contrast, provides loving husbands opportunities to honor their wives through deferential or gallant assistance in circumstances where the husband's size or strength are an advantage. But a difference in stature or muscle mass has nothing to do with the capacity to lead or to exercise authority. Alexander the Great (5'8"), Napoleon (5'6"), Joan of Arc (5'2"), Hitler (5'10"), Winston Churchill (5'7"), Gandhi (5'4"), Martin Luther King Jr. (5'7"), and Mother Teresa (5'4") did not wield influential leadership or strong authority because of their superior size or muscle mass. A generous assessment of my dear wife Gloria's height is barely five feet tall, but everyone who knows her would acknowledge that her excellent leadership ability has no correlation to her stature.

History is replete with illustrations of great leaders who were *weaker* than others as typically designated. Think, for example, of U.S. President Franklin D. Roosevelt who was physically weaker than most others in that he was dependent on a wheelchair or leg braces. FDR was anything but a *"weaker"* president! History remembers him as an effective and powerful leader despite his physical weakness. Being stronger physically or intellectually is not a predictor or qualifier for effective leadership. Being 6'9" and 400 pounds does not guarantee leadership acumen. Despite average size and muscle mass differences, modern scientific study disproves any broad characterization of one gender as *weaker.*

It is nonsense to suggest that all women as a class are weaker than all men. However, "What is not nonsensical, sadly, is that in a patriarchal society, Peter is telling the simple truth—economically, politically, legally, educationally— when it comes to most dimensions of social power, women *are* weaker than men."[101] The woman's weakness in those ways is imposed on her by oppressive and exploitive men. This seems most likely to be Peter's meaning of women being the "weaker partner." It was not a statement of some innate, gender-based difference, but of the tragic reality of women's experience in a male-dominated and oppressive culture. It is the brutal reality predicted due to sin in Genesis 3:16: "Your desire shall be for your husband, and he will rule over you." Rather than men taking advantage of the hierarchical weakness imposed by sinful society, Peter instructs husbands to respond to their wives with consideration, honor, and respect, recognizing them as fellow-heirs of God's grace.

First Peter 3:1–7 fits the pattern of Ephesians 5–6 and Colossians 3–4 by advocating temporary accommodations to patriarchy—here applied specifically to a marriage involving an *unbelieving* husband who obviously had not adopted radical new creation values of equality and mutual submission as required by Ephesians 5:21 ("Submit to one another out of reverence for Christ"). The wife's submission (as in several of the other concession passages such as Titus 2:4, 5) is stated to be for the sake of keeping peace and of advancing the gospel with the goal that the unsaved husband would be won over. As in the other passages dealing with temporary concessions,

---

[101] Stackhouse, *Partners in Christ,* 77.

the weaker (powerless) party must sometimes voluntarily submit to the party with hierarchical strength, and the party with power must treat the powerless party with honor, respect, and kindness. How to correctly interpret the *concession passages* will be presented in chapter 5.

Incidentally, if complementarians believe this passage is prescriptive for today, shouldn't they be teaching all wives to call their husbands "master" (1 Pt. 3:6)? I am not aware of any complementarian who would advocate for that or perhaps who would *dare* to do that! Complementarians might argue against advocating for the "master" title today by proposing that some aspects of this passage are prescriptive (such as "submissive") and others are descriptive (such as "master"). This appears to be a forced and artificial distinction in that Sarah's responses to Abraham are the example on which Peter bases his requirement for submission. And no textual evidence is advanced instructing how to discern which parts of the paragraph are prescriptive and which are descriptive. Apparently, interpreters are left to arbitrarily decide that for themselves based on which parts of the text, in their mind, pass the culturally or personally acceptable test.

Incidentally, for those who like to cite Sarah's designation of Abraham as "Lord" (κύριον, *kurion*) as evidence supporting patriarchy, it would be important for them to note that a literal translation of 2 John 1 reveals that the Apostle John addressed his letter to the "chosen lord" of the church (ἐκλεκτῇ κυρίᾳ, *eklektay kuria*) who was a <u>woman</u>! Although, there is dispute on whether the recipient was the female leader/pastor of the church,[102] a prominent lady in the church (perhaps it met in her house), or a metaphor for the church, in any case, in the verse the apostle unquestionably uses the feminine form of "lord." How stunning it would be if a prominent English version dared to legitimately and literally translate it, "her chosen lordship."

Whatever Peter intended by designating wives as the "weaker partner," his call for husbands to "honor" them is not at all the same as instructing them to *lead, exercise authority over,* or "lord" *it over* their wives who must submit because of their weakness. That is not Peter's point. The text includes no such suggestion. Honor can flow up or down between the powerful and the powerless despite authority or subservience, position or anonymity, strength or weakness. Honor flows up in that all humans should honor God and children

---

[102] Chapter 11 argues that an unbiased interpretation of the text and context supports the view that the "chosen lady" is the female leader/pastor of the church.

are to honor their father and mother (Eph. 6:2). Believers are commanded to "honor the king" (1 Pt. 2:17). Power flows down as when autocratic King Xerxes delighted to honor his loyal subject Mordecai (Esther 6:6). Xerxes did not in any sense submissively place himself under Mordecai's authority. The powerful monarch greatly honored his much weaker subordinate by recognizing and rewarding his courageous and beneficial actions. Obviously, to honor someone can be unrelated to his or her comparative status.

This is a good place to ask the question, "What did Jesus say about creation design and intent for the genders?" After all, He was the Creator God Who, in Genesis 1, 2, brought all things into existence (John 1:3, 10; Col. 1:16; Heb. 1:2).

Jesus' Commentary on Gender Roles in Creation

Jesus quoted from Genesis 1:27 and 2:24 in Matthew 19 and Mark 10 when His opponents questioned Him about the lawfulness of divorce. His response regarding divorce focused on God's *original intent* for marriage: "It was not this way from the beginning" (Matt. 19:8). His creation-account quotation was, "But at the beginning of creation God 'made them male and female.' 'For this reason a man will leave his father and mother and be united to his wife, and the two will become one flesh.' So they are no longer two, but one. Therefore, what God has joined together, let man not separate" (Mark 10:6–9). Jesus' argument assumed that male/female diversity in creation was consistent with their essential identity and equality whereby God joined them into "one flesh." Jesus' entire case was built on the oneness which marriage accomplishes in the union of male and female—a oneness which must not be severed by divorce.

In Jesus' quotation from Genesis 2 the emphasis on becoming one speaks to Adam and Eve's inherent identity. Adam found no complement to resolve his aloneness in any of the animals (Gen. 2:18–20). The revelation of this dissimilarity seems to be the purpose of God's assignment for Adam to name the animals. Because Eve, unlike the animals, was created from him to be like him and equal to him, she became one with him. This essential oneness is antithetical to any effort to separate Adam and Eve by hierarchy, rank, position, or authority as an expression of some supposedly fundamental gender difference.

Neither Genesis 1 and 2 nor Jesus' quotation of those texts in Matthew 19 and Mark 10 give even the slightest hint of hierarchy in gender roles. If it were important for Jesus to affirm male authority in marriage, this was the time to do it—when He was rehearsing the nature of marriage as God intended from the beginning. Instead, Jesus' commentary emphasized the fundamental identity, unity, and oneness of male and female.

Remember that Jesus is the Creator—the God of Genesis 1, 2 who created everything. Jesus created Adam and Eve. John 1:3 declares, "Through him all things were made; without him nothing was made that has been made." Therefore, everything Jesus, during His incarnation, said and did regarding male and female relationships, *reflects His creation intent* initially. He is "the image of God," (Col 1:15) "the radiance of God's glory and the exact representation of His being (Hebrews 1:3). Therefore, whatever Jesus said or did regarding gender roles is a perfect revelation of God's creation intent.

What Else Did Jesus Say about Gender Roles?

Because Jesus' teachings and actions regarding gender roles will not be discussed elsewhere in this study, a few observations will be included here. What Jesus said and did, or did not say and do, are of paramount importance because Jesus is the perfect revelation of God.

Think about it: if there exists a God who determined to reveal Himself by becoming a human, what would He probably do? Most probably He would reveal His identity by doing things no mere human could do such as performing supernatural acts as *signs* of Who He was. This Jesus continually did! Further, would not the actions and words of this God-man reveal what God was like? If that God were capricious, frightening, unloving, cruel, unkind, and distant, wouldn't those characteristics show up in how the incarnate God lived and related to people? Instead, throughout His life, teaching, and interactions, Jesus revealed God to be relentlessly welcoming, loving, gracious, merciful, compassionate, unbiased, kind, patient, righteous, and just.

If we read parts of the Bible (for example in the Old Testament) and from them deduce negative things about God, then perhaps we have misread or misinterpreted those passages, because Jesus is the ultimate and perfect revelation of God (John 1:18; 14:9; 2 Cor. 4:4; Col. 1:15; Heb. 1:3). If painful life experiences have made us vulnerable to assuming negative things about God, perhaps our perspective is too limited and/or short-sighted. Do you want to know what God is like? Look at Jesus!

Looking at Jesus is therefore a important thing to do if we want to know God's heart and will regarding women and their role in His creation and His church. It seems highly significant that in all of Jesus' extensive teachings recorded in the Gospels there is *not one word* suggesting hierarchy between the genders. Jesus' silence speaks volumes.[103] At the same time, Jesus' consistent inclusion and elevation of and response to women was radically counter-cultural in the very patriarchal, exploitive, and oppressive culture of the first century. Arguably the answer to the question, *"What did Jesus say about gender role hierarchy?"* is **NOTHING!**

But while Jesus said nothing to support gender-based hierarchy, His actions and words constantly contradicted gender bias, restriction, and oppression in the culture. Jesus praised Mary for leaving the expected female role of preparing and serving the meal for the men so she could join the circle of His male disciples (Luke 10:38ff). Clearly Jesus welcomed her into this relationship normally reserved exclusively for males. The Kingdom of God that Jesus brought near upended the values and biases of depraved earthly kingdoms.

Jesus honored the deferential request and startling challenge from a Canaanite woman who, it could be argued, respectfully *taught* Him why it would be appropriate for Him to heal a Gentile woman's daughter. This was during the season of His public ministry when His focus was on "the lost sheep of Israel" (Matt. 15:21ff). Jesus, of course, did not need her instruction.

---

[103] The" silence of Jesus" during His earthly ministry would be a worthwhile study to identify the topics and doctrines which either He chose not to discuss or which the Gospel writers, guided by the Holy Spirit, omitted. Those who believe that "all Scripture is God-breathed" (2 Tim. 3:16) typically do not give extra weight to the "red letter" sections (red ink being the way Jesus' spoken words are designated in some editions of the Bible). Nevertheless, it would be worth considering why Jesus chose to ignore some seemingly vital topics (such as gender roles) while emphasizing others. At minimum it would seem to be an indicator of relative importance of the themes which He emphasized or ignored.

He was neither ignorant of the things she would say nor reluctant to do what she requested. Rather, He facilitated an opportunity for her to confess her faith and to highlight important truths in a shocking and memorable manner. That the Gospel writer included this story about a Gentile woman speaks volumes regarding the Gospel in relationship to both ethnicity and gender.

Although Jesus' portrayal of the family did not specifically address gender roles, His teachings potentially envisioned significant realignments of familial priorities. The Old Testament descriptions of the family are typically patriarchal. In contrast, Jesus, in His teaching about His now-and-future kingdom, challenged basic family structures in a patriarchal culture by placing loyalty to God and Himself above loyalty to family (Matt. 10:37; 19:29; 23:9; Mark 10:29; Luke 14:26).

In Jesus' kingdom, there is no elevation of males over females. Further, His hard-to-fully-interpret prophecies about radical changes regarding marriage in the resurrection (Matt. 22:30; Luke 20:35) imply a total end in the new age to any marital patriarchy with its legacy, priority, ascendancy, or advantages. Note the context of His teaching in verses 22-28—it was all about assuring that a man would have an heir to carry on his name and estate. In the fallen world the wife of these seven brothers is part of his property. Her role is simply to bear a child to give an heir to and to perpetuate the name of her husband. If a wife died, there was no requirement for her sisters to marry her husband in order to carry on her name and produce an heir for her estate. She gave up her name when she married and she had no inheritance to pass on. It all belonged to her husband. But in the new age, one-sided patriarchy is banished forever—a tragic vestige of sin's curse. No longer is a wife her husband's property whose role is to serve him!

Jesus referred to a female pagan ruler, the Queen of Sheba, as a positive example of passionate pursuit of God's truth.[104] Not everyone would agree that that this was a tacit approval of a woman holding a high position of authority over men, but it seems unlikely that Jesus would select such an illustration if a woman ruling over men was a rebellious violation of God's creation design.[105]

---

[104] Matt. 12:42 and Luke 11:31 refer to the story recorded in 1 Kings 10:1ff and 2 Chron. 9:1ff.

[105] A national female ruler was not a total anomaly in the Bible in spite of the pervasive gender bias in most of society. Queen Athaliah had ruled the Southern Kingdom of Judah (2 Kings 11:3) prior to good King Joash. The Scriptures reveal that she was heartless in

Rather, Jesus seemed often to relish opportunities to challenge cultural bias by selecting those from the devalued segments of society to be the heroes of His teaching and stories (e.g. the poor, sinners, women, children, and Gentiles such as the Good Samaritan).

Women played a prominent role in bearing testimony to Jesus from His mother's womb to His empty tomb. His birth, identity, death, and resurrection were defined by the witness of women. Theirs were the first human voices testifying about His incarnation and His resurrection. It was to a *Gentile woman* that Jesus first unequivocally identified Himself as the Messiah (called Christ): "I who speak to you am He" (John 4:25, 26). The Greek text of that stunning announcement is even more revelatory. Jesus called Himself "**I am**" (Ἐγώ εἰμι, *ego eimi*), identifying Himself with the God of the Exodus—the God who spoke to Moses from the burning bush and revealed Himself as "I AM" (Ex. 3:14).

That this revelation was given to a woman is shocking to anyone with patriarchal bias. Her testimony turned a city to Jesus (John 4:28–30, 39–42). Some call the Samaritan woman *"the first Gospel evangelist."* Given the prevalent cultural devaluation of women, these are stunning revelations of God's radically different perspective about them.

Elizabeth declared Jesus' Deity while He was still in Mary's womb (Luke 1:41–45). Likewise, Jesus' glorious, theology-ridden prenatal announcement was delivered by His mother Mary in her now famous "Magnificat" memorialized in the Scriptures in Luke 1:46–55. When newborn Jesus was brought to the Jerusalem Temple, a female prophetess, Anna, delivered the first Jesus-centered sermon in the Temple courtyard (Luke 2:36–38).

During His earthly ministry, Jesus shattered cultural standards by welcoming women alongside men to receive His teaching (Matt. 14:21; 15:38), by interacting with them one-on-one (John 4:1–26; 8:1–11, 11:1–45; 12:1–8), and by including them as regular traveling partners and ministry assistants

---

the elimination of potential rivals, even her own family, but there is no biblical indication that she was unfit to rule because of her gender. It is not commonly known that a few decades before the birth of Jesus, a woman, Salome Alexandra, known as Alexandra of Jerusalem, ruled the Jewish province of Judea from 76 to 67 B.C.E. Though rare, having women in the highest possible positions of authority was not unknown among God's people during biblical history including prophetesses and Deborah's leadership and judgeship prior to the monarchy.

along with His apostles and others (Mark 15:21; Luke 8:2, 3). To some extent, Jesus' ministry was only possible because it was bankrolled by several apparently wealthy women who were part of the traveling entourage that accompanied Him on His itinerant ministry: "These women were helping to support them out of their own means" (Luke 8:1–3). Jesus touched women (Matt. 8:14, 15; Luke 8:54) and allowed them to touch Him (Mark 5:27, 28; Luke 7:36–39; John 12:1–8).

At a time when Jesus' male disciples were tone deaf to His frequent predictions about His approaching death, only Mary (the sister of Lazarus and Martha) seemed to hear and believe His announcements. Her extravagant act of anointing His feet prefigured His death but also triggered the hypocritical criticism by the spiritually dense and self-righteous male disciples (John 12:1–12). Jesus praised Mary's unforgettable visual sermon and promised it would be rehearsed wherever the Gospel would be preached in the world (Matt. 26:6–13; Mark 14:3–9; John 12:1–8). The Gospel writers included reports of the importance of "*many*" women in relationship to Jesus at His crucifixion (Matt. 27:55; Luke 23:27; John 19:25) when nearly all of His male apostles had fled in fear. Jesus would have been alone in that horrific time if He had not discipled women who would turn out to be His most loyal, fearless, and exemplary followers.

Then Jesus chose women to be the first witnesses and preachers of His resurrection (Matt. 28:5–10; Luke 24:9, 10, 22–25; John 20:1–18)—a stunning selection, given the cultural norm prohibiting women from being witnesses in court because they were considered unreliable.[106]

Some would raise the question, "If Jesus believed in no gender-based ministry restrictions, why did He choose twelve men to be His apostles?" In addition to the parallelism of twelve male apostles to lead the new people of God even as twelve male patriarchs led the old people of God, this may well have been a necessary accommodation[107] to the male-dominated first century culture before Jesus' inauguration of the new creation. This question

---

[106] Zhava Glaser, "Jesus and the Role of Women," Jews for Jesus on line newsletter: "Women were not allowed to testify in court. In effect, this categorized them with Gentiles, minors, deaf-mutes and 'undesirables' such as gamblers, the insane, usurers, and pigeon-racers, who were also denied that privilege."

[107] The need for temporary concessions in male-dominated, hierarchical cultures will be discussed in chapter 5.

will be addressed further in chapter 11 where evidence will be presented demonstrating the existence of female apostles in the early church along with additional explanations as to why Jesus' initial apostles were all males.

In summary, it seems evident that the Gospels include zero examples of Jesus teaching in favor of hierarchical gender roles. Further, egalitarians find support for their inclusive position based on (1) Jesus' emphasis on the oneness and equality of men and women in the Old Testament creation account, (2) His consistent elevation and inclusion of women including welcoming their presence and participation in His ministry and in the most intimate inner circles of His disciples, (3) His selection of women as the primary witnesses and proclaimers of His mission from His mother's womb to His empty tomb, and (4) Jesus' striking *silence* regarding male leadership and female submission in any relationship including marriage and ministry.

There is <u>nothing</u> in the teachings and practices of Jesus' public ministry to challenge the assertion that His original creation design included no gender-based hierarchical distinctions. This is especially important when we are reminded that the Jesus of the Gospels is the God of Creation in Genesis 1, 2. Therefore, what He said and did in His incarnation reveal His intent for the genders from the beginning of creation.

Conclusion Concerning Creation Design

Therefore, it is evident that God's original created design was for absolute equality of the genders. Although there obviously is some diversity in roles as in those based on created anatomical differences (only the woman can house in her womb, give birth to, and breastfeed a child) as well as on some less obvious neurological and psychological differences, there is no indication in Genesis 1, 2 of any kind of gender-based hierarchical roles involving authority or superiority. There is no hint of Adam being the leader and Eve the submitter, only multiple indications of their unity, equality, co-regency, and partnership. Before the ruination brought by sin, there was no reference at all regarding any hierarchy. It was unnecessary because there was no interpersonal conflict, competition, ambition, or sense of need for one gender to dominate the other.

How gender roles were affected by the ruinous results of sin's entrance into the world will be considered in the next chapter, as well as what those roles look like in the already–not yet New Creation Jesus inaugurated by His death and resurrection.

FOR DISCUSSION

1. Some people believe that God created men to lead and women to follow their leadership. What would most unchurched people think about that? Why are many women be offended by those ideas?

2. What scientific evidence are you aware of that might confirm or refute that men are naturally inclined to lead and women to follow? Are men by nature better suited to lead then women? Why or why not? Are women by nature more suited to follow than to lead? Why or why not?

3. What are some leadership traits that seem more natural to men? What are some leadership traits that seem more natural to women?

4. Give examples from history and contemporary society of women who have been or are outstanding leaders. Give examples from the Bible of women who exhibited effective leadership ability. In some marriages, the wife is a more natural leader than the husband. How does that fit with the idea that men are designed to lead and women to follow?

5. Read Genesis 1:26–28. The word "them" obviously refers to both Adam and Eve. List the specific things the text says that included both Adam and Eve. What does this passage suggest about the roles of men and women?

6. Read Genesis 2:18–25. What indications do you find that the passage is more about the differences between Adam and Eve or their similarities? What, if any specific things does the passage say about whether the man or the woman is to have authority over the other?

7. In the Gospels, Jesus said nothing about men being responsible to lead and women to submit. Why do you think He said nothing about this important issue and what is the significance of His silence? Jesus quoted from the creation account in Genesis 1, 2 in Matthew 19:4–6. What was Jesus' emphasis about the genders in this passage?

8. Why do you think many Christians and churches are so divided and polarized about gender roles in the church and in marriage? What are some things you could do to promote unity in the church even when there is disagreement about a topic like this?

4

How the Gender Wars Started and When They Will End

Have you ever been in a disagreement with your spouse or a friend and suddenly realized that you had no idea how the fight started? It's hard to resolve conflict if you can't remember what prompted it.

Regarding the huge chasm in Jesus' church over the role of women, a proper understanding when and how the gender wars began could be an important key to resolution—at least to the debates over gender roles in marriage and the church. Further, what the Bible teaches about when the battle of the sexes will end conveys crucial understanding germane to the whole discussion. A correct understanding of ONE BIBLE VERSE in its context has earthshaking implications regarding the *origin* of the battle of the sexes and on *how to accurately interpret* the rest of the relevant Scripture passages.

The Epic Story of Everything

That single verse, Genesis 3:16,[108] has a momentous place in God's epic story told in the Holy Scriptures. After all, **the Bible is a story**. The Bible includes many stories but all together they make up one story—one big story

---

[108] "To the woman he said, 'I will greatly increase your pains in childbearing; with pain you will give birth to children. Your desire will be for your husband, and he will rule over you.'"

sometimes called the "meta-narrative" that simply refers to one overarching, universal story that encompasses and unifies all other stories into one.

The Bible is the story of the world; the story of the human race; the story of everything. It is my story, your story, everyone's story, but supremely, it is God's story. It is the story which explains everything; the story reflected in all great stories; the story of which all other stories are a part. It is the story that answers the big questions asked by philosophers and thinkers through the ages: Who am I? Where did I come from? Why am I here? Where am I going? In other words, the story reveals my identity, my origin, my purpose, and my destiny. The story that is the Bible is the story that helps me understand what's going on in the world; why the world is so great and so awful; why people act like they do; why I act like I do; and what's going to happen in the future.

The Bible is the story so far in the true novel God is still writing. The Bible is a love story. It is the story of the cosmic battle of good and evil. It is the story of a great rescue operation. It is the story about how God, through Jesus, is rescuing and restoring His ruined creation back to its original perfection. **The Bible is the story of JESUS!**

To correctly understand any individual part of the Bible such as the gender roles issue, it is essential to see it in relationship to the big story of the Bible. Where and how does it fit within the *four movements* of this epic story? One way to characterize those movements is:

Creation → Rebellion and Ruin → Redemption → Restoration.

Previously, we focused on the first part of God's big story, Creation—the creation of all things, specifically what the Genesis 1 and 2 accounts reveal about the creation of Adam and Eve, the first male and female. Those chapters assert the absolute equality and unity of the genders and portray absolutely no gender-based hierarchy in Adam and Eve's roles and relationship. Their perfect relationship was part of the perfect world—beautiful in every way—judged by God as "very good" (Gen. 1:31).

Tragically, the second movement of the Bible's Big Story, Rebellion and Ruin, recounts Adam and Eve's sin and how terribly it changed everything! They, all their descendants, and the whole creation, were horrifically affected by sin's curse. Retaining the afterglow of the original creation while also displaying the tragic outworking of sin left Adam and Eve and all their descendants *beautiful and broken* like everything else in God's creation. We are all beautiful/broken people living in a beautiful/broken world.

One especially terrible consequence of the original sin was **patriarchy,** the rule of men over women and consequently, the unending war of the genders—the ubiquitous battle for control.

We must now examine the origin of patriarchy and correct the tragic perversion of the meaning of Genesis 3:16 which is used to support the pervasive oppression of women that ensued.

Man's Rule over Woman

The first biblical reference to male rulership is in Genesis 3:16. It is not part of the first movement in God's epic story—**Creation.** Rather it portrays what happened and would happen *after* Adam and Eve's sin, an event that theologians often describe as "the fall." The first reference to male rulership is found in the chapter that kicks off the second movement in God's epic story: **Rebellion and Ruin.** Adam and Eve rebelled against God by breaking the one prohibition given them. Genesis 3:14–19 announced the beginning of the ruin that sin introduced into the world. In the context, those verses unquestionably must be understood as *descriptive* (how the fall changed Adam and Eve's lives and world), NOT as *prescriptive* (how God intended or commanded for people to be). Genesis 3:16 states, "To the woman he said, 'I will greatly increase your pains in childbearing; with pain you will give birth to children. Your desire will be for your husband, and he will rule over you.'"

Note that the context of the first reference to male rulership is a description of the tragic elements of sin's curse. As part of that curse (Gen. 3:14–24) snakes will crawl on their bellies, Satan's offspring will war against the woman's, childbirth will be painful, the cursed ground will require painful labor and sweat to reap its produce and to deal with its thorns, everyone will die and return to dust, women will seek to control men, and men will rule over them. None of those are *commands* to obey, but rather are tragic *consequences* which will be experienced in this new world—the world ruined by human rebellion against God.

In Genesis 3:16, men are no more commanded to rule over women than anyone is commanded to make snakes crawl, to make childbirth painful,

to plant thorns so farming will be difficult, to force men to perspire while working, or to put everyone to death so their bodies can decay and return to dust.

Consider how humans expend immense effort and resources in trying to reverse or end the results of the fall. Pharmacology and medical professionals do their best to minimize pain in childbirth. Agricultural and horticultural sciences constantly work to maximize food production and minimize the exhausting human efforts required to bring fruits, vegetables, and grains to harvest. Every effort to enhance herbicides to control unwanted plants is a constant war against the curse. Many billions of dollars are spent every year to extend life and to delay the inevitable march to the grave. Costly embalming and the use of coffins and vaults to hinder the return of the body to dust are part of our culture. Although no one seems to be working to get snakes off their bellies, most everyone agrees that humanity must unite to try to overcome these detrimental effects of the fall and the curse. Isn't it tragic so many, even among Jesus' followers, fail to see that the war of the genders is equally damaging to God's creation and creatures! That women vie for control and men use their power to rule over them is as awful as the pain of childbirth, the recalcitrance of the ground to produce food, and the unstoppable march toward physical death and the decay of the body. Patriarchy, the rule of men over women, is a result and an expression of human rebellion against God's will, not a beneficial expression of their Creator's good and loving design. Shouldn't mankind, especially the people of God, be expending the same (or more) efforts to end patriarchy, even as they do the other damaging effects of the Fall?

It would be difficult to overestimate the significance of this point. Genesis 3:16 has been one of the key texts misused by complementarians to prove that God intended for men to rule over women. The misrepresentation of this text as a divine *command* rather than an evil *consequence* of sin is a horrible perversion of what the Bible actually says! It is an incendiary and dangerous falsehood that has done immense damage throughout history. This tragic misinterpretation has greatly contributed to the gender bias that has often skewed the way interpreters have translated and understood other Bible passages. It has given support to unbiblical restrictions about church ministry prohibiting at least 50% of church members from participation in roles for which God gifted them and thereby hindering the effectiveness of Christianity in the world. It has helped to fuel the exit of many from the church and cemented unbelievers in their rejection of Christianity because of the oppression and exploitation of women which this misinterpretation appears to validate. And it has also encouraged husbands to rule over their wives. Many men have even taken this as an excuse or reason to bully and abuse their wives.

Think of it! **Not since the Garden of Eden has anyone ever seen or experienced the world apart from male domination and female subjugation.** Adam and Eve are the only humans in all history who experienced a relationship, however short-lived, in which neither exercised authority over the other. It was marital paradise! Ever since sin entered the world and our first parents were expelled from the Garden, patriarchy has prevailed in virtually every culture throughout history.[109] People cannot even imagine anything else. Consequently, for the majority of people throughout time, males leading and females submitting has seemed "normal," perhaps even "right." No wonder so many Christians and churches accept patriarchy in marriage and church as a positive thing. They are used to it. It is all they have known. It is bad enough this consequence of sin's curse is so pervasive even among Christians, but what is far worse is that so many Christians have been so horribly deceived into thinking that patriarchy is a good thing that benefits women, and that they defend this perversion from the Scriptures. It is a masterstroke of Satan, the ultimate deceiver, destroyer, abuser, and oppressor.

Perhaps this explains why many contemporary Christians and churches can be so incensed about the oppression and exploitation inherent to slavery, human trafficking, and racism at the same time they embrace and defend the oppression and exploitation of women—all the while vigorously denying that their position and practice are evil and abusive. A little like the proverbial "frog in the kettle," many Christians assume that the "temperature" of restrictive

---

[109] In recent history, the position of women has been slowly changing in the Western world (sometimes designated "the free world"), due at least in part to the influence of Christianity's emphasis on the equality of all people as God's image-bearers regardless of ethnicity, age, or gender, and the related emergence of nations built on the valuing of "human rights" and the belief that "all men are created equal." Global progress has been mixed and far too slow even in the USA where gender disparity is still evident in the gender wage gap and the "glass ceiling" limiting women in business, politics, and churches. The recent "#MeTo" movement reveals that sinful men who impose their will on vulnerable women is a far too prevalent reality.

gender roles in the church is a healthy and good thing rather than a deadly and evil boiling up of sin's curse as predicted in Genesis 3:16. Throughout much of the church, at least until relatively recently, patriarchy has been proclaimed and practiced as God's will and plan—even as beneficial for women. But, a proper understanding of Genesis 3:16 explodes any such assertion that patriarchy is normal, right, or beneficial. The nearly universal pervasiveness of patriarchy in the world and in the church is what God said would happen in a fallen world in the dysfunctional relationships of sinful men and women.

To say that patriarchy is normal or right is like saying that cancer is normal and right. NO! Sickness and death are the result of sin's curse. Patriarchy is no more what God desired or designed for the original perfect creation than are crime, war, cancer, sickness, and death. Forcing the curse's consequences on women isn't beneficial or beautiful; it is destructive and ugly. Patriarchy flows out of the fall, not out of creation.

Consider then the *origin* of the battle of the sexes as predicted by God during His catalog of the tragic consequences of the entrance of evil into the no-longer-perfect world: "Then He said to the woman, I will sharpen the pain of your pregnancy, and in pain you will give birth. And you will desire to control your husband, but he will rule over you'" (Gen. 3:16 NLT).

What is Woman's "Desire" for Her Husband?

In the use of the two key concepts ("desire" and "rule"/"master") Genesis 3:16 and 4:7 are parallel texts using precisely the same Hebrew words. This is very helpful in determining the meaning of the words as used in a key gender role passage.

VERSES (emphasis added)	"DESIRE"/"DESIRES"	"RULE"/"MASTER"
Genesis 3:16: "Your **desire** will be for your husband, and he will **rule** over you."	תְּשׁוּקָה , teshuqah	מְשַׁל, mashal
Genesis 4:7: "If you do what is right, will you not be accepted? But if you do not do what is right, sin is crouching at your door; it **desires** to have you, but you must **master** it."	תְּשׁוּקָה, teshuqah	מְשַׁל, mashal

As the chart reveals, the word translated "desire" in Genesis 3:16 regarding what the woman will experience regarding her husband is the same as sin's "desire" to *master* Cain in Genesis 4:7. Even as sin "desired" to *control* Cain unless he "mastered"/*ruled* it, so sinful women will "desire" to *control* sinful men but they will "*rule*" over them. The beautiful unselfish love and mutual submission that had characterized Adam and Eve's pre-fall relationship and that made any hint of hierarchy totally unnecessary is now replaced by a constant struggle to manipulate and to control. But as a consequence of sin's curse, the woman's desire for ascendency will be overpowered, mastered by the man's imposition (sometimes through violence) of his "rule" over her.

Perhaps male domination is effectuated in part due to man's greater physical strength and aggressiveness, though these are not asserted in the text.

What is crystal clear in the text is that sin launched the universal gender wars with the result that in the sinful, fallen culture, men will assume or forcefully impose their "rule" over women. This was not God's creation design. It is one of the first and worst results of sin and the curse. Patriarchy, man's rule over woman, is not God's plan; it is Satan's perversion of God's plan. Patriarchy is not God's creation, it is sin's curse. How tragic that complementarian churches adopt and promote the perpetuation of this evil as if it were good. The prophet warned, "Woe to those who call evil good and good evil" (Is. 5:20).

The War is On

How awful! God assigned Adam and Eve to rule His friendly and cooperative creation together as equal partners (Gen. 1:26) but now sin's curse included not only the creation's resistance to their rule (Gen. 3:17–19) but also their relational division, struggle, and conflict even as they attempt to exercise their more difficult rule over a newly recalcitrant creation (Gen. 3:16-19). No longer loving partners united in fulfilling God's creation mandate, now they struggle to selfishly dominate, manipulate, and exploit each other—a battle sinful males most often win. Through the ensuing millennia, patriarchy has been the persistent symbol and reminder of sin's influence on gender relationships. Perpetuating patriarchy is not a way the church displays faithfulness to God's will and Word. It is a tragic illustration of how Satan's strategy has penetrated and compromised the church and how worldliness has been baptized into orthodoxy. Husbands assuming authority over their wives is rebellion against God's will—not obedience to it.

This evil relational division and oppression did not stop with the gender wars. "Humans, who were created to rule together in unity, became divided in hostility and embedded in patterns of oppression, which, according to the creation account, started with male and female and extended throughout history to include other groups such as Jews, gentiles, slaves, and free persons (1 Cor. 12:13; Gal. 3:28; Col. 3:11)."[110] What begins in the most basic unit of society, marriage, spreads throughout the largest units, nations, spawning international conflict and war as one nation seeks to control, exploit, and dominate another.

Genesis 3:16b is a predictive warning about what relationships between sinners would be like in the sin-broken world. God described how fallen men and women will struggle for domination resulting in the stronger male ruling

---

[110] Westfall, *Paul and Gender,* 70.

over the female. This reveals that *male domination is a result and expression of human sinfulness* and will affect relationships and cultures until the new creation which will finally be achieved because of the wounding of Eve's offspring (Gen. 3:15). In the new creation, sin's curse will vanish ("No longer will there be any curse," Rev. 22:3). No longer will Satan fight against God. No longer will death reign over humanity. No longer will the ground fight back against those who till it. No longer will women seek to control men. No longer will men rule over women. God's original creation plan will be realized. What began in the first two chapters of Genesis will be restored in the last two chapters of Revelation.

Some suggest the *law of first mention* as a sometimes-helpful tool for understanding the Bible. The first time something is mentioned in Scripture, especially in Genesis (the book of *"beginnings"*), establishes something important about its significance throughout the Bible. Every later reference to patriarchy in Scripture is a reflection of its origin here—it is the product and expression of human sin.

Therefore, based on Genesis 3:16, the rule of males over females *should be understood as sinful oppression rather than as a divine assignment*. Sadly, this is so much a part of this sin-broken world that the rulership of males over females sometimes feels natural and right to those who have been immersed and enculturated in patriarchy. I suggest that this subconscious feeling of *rightness* is not only the product of sinful gender bias but also perpetuates gender bias even in the way some have translated,[111] read, and interpreted the Scriptures.

Complementarians sometimes object to using words such as *rule, domination, oppression* or even *patriarchy* to describe their position, preferring *head, headship,* or *leadership*. While I comprehend this preference for what they perceive to be gentler and more palatable words, I find a number of problems with the substitution: (1) the concept of *head* or *headship* is never mentioned in Genesis 1–3; (2) the translation of *mashal* as "rule" in Genesis 3:16 seems to be indisputable; (3) *rule* and *domination* are nearly synonymous and could be interchangeable translations,[112] even though to some complementarians the latter may sound more negative; (4) a sense of aversion to vocabulary that is a linguistically appropriate expression of

---

[111] The effect of gender bias in Bible translations will be discussed later.

[112] Brown Driver and Briggs first definition of מָשַׁל is: *"rule, have dominion* over, Gn 3:16."

biblical truth should perhaps be a *wake-up call* as to what their position in fact is and what others quickly perceive it to be; and (5) as will be discussed later, the complementarian understanding of *head* in a leadership or authority sense is probably not the correct meaning in the very rare occurrences (only two) where it is applied to the relationship of men and women (1 Cor. 11:3) or of husbands and wives (Eph. 5:23).

"Wait!" I can hear someone objecting. "What about Ephesians 5:22ff, 1 Timothy 2:11ff and other passages about women submitting to men and not taking authority over them?" Those passages will be carefully addressed in chapters 7 - 10 and shown to be in harmony with what Genesis 1–3 teach about God's creation design of gender equality and about patriarchy being an evil result of the fall. Clear Bible passages should inform our interpretation of challenging ones, not vice versa. A correct and compelling interpretation of those highly debated submission Scriptures will not contradict or cancel the very clear teaching of Genesis 1–3. Correctly understood, those passages will be harmonious in their interpretation and application.

Additional evidence for gender equality is revealed by what the Scriptures teach about gender roles in the New Creation. What should gender roles be like among Christians who, because of the third movement of God's big story, **Redemption**, are the "first fruits" (James 1:18; Rev. 14:4) of the world to come? How should and will the genders relate to each other in the final movement of the eternal story, **Restoration**, when sin's curse is gone?

The New Creation

A correct interpretation of all of Paul's New Testament writings regarding gender roles requires an understanding that Paul "is deeply interested in (1) how Jesus Christ fulfilled the purposes God intended for humanity at creation, (2) how Jesus reversed the effects of the fall, and (3) how God has and will complete his purposes for humanity including male and female"[113] (Gen. 3:15; Gal. 4:4, 5).

Jesus' death, resurrection, and ascension inaugurated His *new creation* in which original creation values, including absolute equality regardless of ethnicity, social status, and gender, are reaffirmed and are to be fully restored. Paul

---

[113] Westfall, *Paul and Gender*, 61.

announced this in Galatians 3:26–28: "You are all sons of God through faith in Christ Jesus, for all of you who were baptized into Christ have clothed yourselves with Christ. There is neither Jew nor Greek, slave nor free, male nor female, for you are all one in Christ Jesus." This is totally consistent with the lifting of the *curse* in the new creation (Rev. 22:3)—the curse that specifically includes women attempting to control men and men ruling over women (Gen. 3:16).

Jesus' redemption and restoration of the creation are the lens through which 1 Timothy 2:15 should be understood. It indicates that "the childbearing [της τεκνογονιας, *tays teknogonias*]," that is, the birth of Christ, the offspring of Eve (Gen. 3:15; Gal. 4:4, 5), is the means through which "women will be saved," that is, saved from the results of the fall, including subjugation to male domination and exploitation (see additional discussion of 1 Timothy 2:11–15 in chapters 9 and 10).

The new creation values of absolute gender equality and mutual submission are unequivocally exemplified in Ephesians 5:21: "Submit to one another out of reverence for Christ," and are affirmed repeatedly throughout 1 Corinthians 7 where husbands and wives have equal voice in marital and life decisions (verses 2-5, 8-16,32-34, 39, 40). In that chapter, Paul again and again affirms mutuality rather than hierarchy for Jesus' post-ascension male and female followers. These new creation values are to be practiced by Jesus' followers whenever possible while waiting for the full realization of them in the "renewal of all things" when Jesus returns (Matt. 19:28; Acts 3:23). 1 Corinthians 7 provides a helpful context underlying the temporary concessions called for in Ephesians 5:21–6:9 and other passages.

The legacy of the fall is female manipulation and male domination. The promise of the new creation is mutual complementation and submission. The fall produced selfish exploitation. The new creation will restore absolute equality expressed in loving cooperation, deference, and supportiveness. The fall equals paradise lost. The new creation equals paradise restored. It will be the *"renewal of all things"*[114] assured by Jesus; the *"restoration of everything"*[115] promised by the prophets and the apostolic preaching. The broken world of

---

[114] "Jesus said to them, "I tell you the truth, at the renewal of all things, when the Son of Man sits on his glorious throne, you who have followed me will also sit on twelve thrones, judging the twelve tribes of Israel," Matthew 19:28.

[115] "He must remain in heaven until the time comes for God to restore everything, as he promised long ago through his holy prophets," Acts 3:21

the fall will be replaced by the perfect world of the original creation. The new creation will be heaven on earth; God's kingdom come and His will done on earth as in heaven—what Jesus' followers pray for daily (Matt. 6:10).

Imagine a world where no one seeks to manipulate, control, use, oppress, dominate, subjugate, exploit, and master another! Imagine a world where love rules relationships as it did in the Garden of Eden. No wonder the gospel is "good news!" The Gospel is not about going to heaven forever when we die. It is about living forever in the new heaven and earth (Rev. 21, 22) after a temporary stay in heaven for those whose death precedes the Lord's return (1 Thess. 4:13-18). The Gospel is not about leaving earth to go up to heaven forever, it is about bringing heaven down to earth where we will enjoy it forever. The Gospel is not only about forgiveness of sins and freedom from condemnation for those who believe; it is about the restoration of all things, the fixing of all that sin broke, the final elimination of oppression and exploitation and injustice, and the realization of the new world that everyone longs for and dreams about, where everyone lives happily ever after.

The End of Sinful Hierarchy

Paul's declaration in Galatians 3:28 is sensational: "There is neither Jew nor Greek, slave nor free, male nor female, for you are all one in Christ Jesus." It announces the elimination of ethnic, socio-economic, and gender hierarchies. It is, however, interpreted differently by complementarians and egalitarians. Some complementarians insist that it has no bearing on the issue of gender roles in the church or marriage but is rather related only to equal access to salvation. This position means that the verse does not relate to racism, the institution of slavery, marital roles, or to gender roles in the church. At the core of this view is what appears to be an alarming devaluation of what it means to be "one in Christ" as Galatians 3:28 beautifully affirms. It seems to restrict salvation to an individualistic rescue from sin and hell so as to be forgiven and allowed into heaven. As wonderful as that is, soteriology is so much bigger than that!

Salvation is the magnificent and multifaceted rescue of selfish sinners, not only from judgement and banishment from eternal life, but also from divided relationships into a radically transformed new life of love, hope, unity, harmony, and the fruit of the Spirit as salvation progressively produces Christ-like character. Salvation transforms relationship and obliterates the walls of separation that Satan and sin erected to destroy unity and to divide people by ethnicity, social status, and gender.

Galatians was one of the earliest (49-50 A.D.) of all the New Testament writings, preceded only by James. It was Paul's first. Both because it was a letter to the churches throughout the large region of Galatia (modern Turkey) and was doubtless circulated among many churches, the new creation values enunciated in Galatians 3:28 would have had *foundational influence* as Christianity spread and matured. Later letters, such as 1 Corinthians and 1 Timothy, would have been understood against the backdrop of this ethnic-, status-, and gender-liberating and equalizing revelation.

Contextually, the erasing of former distinctions and hierarchies portrayed in Galatians 3:28 is related to the new covenant initiation rite of baptism—a great equalizer of the genders. Paul wrote, "You are all sons of God through faith in Christ Jesus, for all of you who were baptized into Christ have clothed yourselves with Christ. There is neither Jew nor Greek, slave nor free, male nor female, for you are all one in Christ Jesus" (Gal. 3:26–28).

Circumcision, which, in a patriarchy-permeated world, gave Jewish males an exclusive and superior role under the Old Covenant, was replaced by baptism that is administered to males and females alike, as well as to both Jews and Gentiles, rich and poor, masters and slaves, adults and children—thus eliminating any superior or oppressive status under the New Covenant. God erased the divisions that permeated the fallen world (superior/inferior, insider/ outsider, powerful/powerless, oppressor/oppressed, master/slave) and replaced them with total equality of relationships and roles in the new creation.

Commenting on Galatians 3:28, N.T. Wright observes: "We sometimes think of circumcision as a painful obstacle for converts, as indeed in some ways it was, but for those who embraced it, it was a matter of pride and privilege. It not only distinguished Jews from Gentiles; it marked them in a way that automatically privileged males. By contrast, imagine the thrill of equality brought about by baptism, an identical rite for Jew and Gentile, slave and free, male and female."[116]

---

[116] N. T. Wright, *Surprised by Scripture* (New York: Harper One, 2015), Kindle, 66.

Consider the implications of Galatians 3:28:

> "The distinctions within humanity that formerly indicated a
> person's value no longer hold sway because of God's work in
> Jesus Christ. Before his conversion to the way of Jesus, Paul
> regarded everyone according to their social status, assigning
> them a value according to ethnicity and gender. No longer
> is this the case. Now that Christ has come to unite his
> people, ethnic and gender differences are subsumed under
> the primary identity of membership in the body of Christ.
> Because of this, there can be no prioritizing of males or
> females; roles of responsibility and leadership in the home
> and the church are available to all. Any moves that denigrate
> or lessen the value of women are illegitimate."[117]

Although he does not apply Galatians 3:28 specifically to ministry roles, feeling that not to be the *primary* focus of the passage, N.T. Wright, responding to a pamphlet about gender roles, calls attention to a frequent mistranslation of the passage—the faulty translation *"male nor female"* (NIV) rather than the more accurate, *"male and* [καὶ, *kai] female"* (ESV). This change from the other couplings in the original Greek ("Jew nor [οὐδὲ, oude] Greek ... slave nor [οὐδὲ] free") cannot be unimportant:

> First, a note about translation and exegesis. I notice
> that on one of your leaflets you adopt what is actually a
> mistranslation of this verse: neither Jew nor Greek, neither
> slave nor free, neither male nor female. That is precisely what
> Paul does *not* say; and as it's what we expect he's going to say,
> we should note quite carefully what he has said instead, since
> he presumably means to make a point by doing so, a point
> which is missed when the translation is flattened out as in
> that version. What he says is that there is neither Jew nor
> Greek, neither slave nor free, *no 'male and female'*. I think
> the reason he says 'no male and female' rather than 'neither
> male nor female' is that he is actually quoting Genesis 1, and

---

[117] Timothy Gombis, *Paul: A Guide for the Perplexed* (New York: T & T Clark, 2010). 119.

that we should understand the phrase 'male and female' in scare-quotes."[118]

The quotation certainly appears to be from Genesis 1:27 which says, *"So God created man in his own image, in the image of God he created him; male and female he created them.*

> What Paul seems to be doing in this passage, then, is ruling out any attempt to back up the continuing male privilege in the structuring and demarcating of Abraham's family by an appeal to Genesis 1.[119]

The structure of Paul's vision expressed in Galatians 3:28 highlights how the total equality and partnership of the genders apart from hierarchy as described in the original creation (Gen. 1:27) is completely restored in the new creation (Gal. 3:28).

While Galatians 3:28 does not erase all differences between ethnicities, classes, or genders, and does not have ministry roles as its specific focus, the following observations seem to be a very natural and appropriate application—the chart exposes how complementarians and egalitarians would have to respond to the assertion of Galatians 3:28:

Questions on the application of Gal. 3:28	Complementarian answers	Egalitarian answers
Can a Gentile be an elder in the church?	Yes, of course!	Yes, of course!
Can a slave be an elder in the church?	Yes, of course!	Yes, of course!
Can a woman be an elder in the church?	No!	Yes, of course!

What seems to be the obvious, though shocking application of Galatians 3:28, was that "in Christ" there is now space in the church

[118] Wright, *Women's Service in the Church*, http://ntwrightpage.com/2016/07/12/womens-service-in-the-church-the-biblical-basis/
[119] Ibid.

- for a Gentile believer to become a church leader and for a Jewish believer to follow their leadership,
- for a believing slave to become a church leader and for their master or former master to follow their leadership, and
- for a woman to become a church leader and for her husband (and other men) to follow her leadership.

Put that way, how shockingly inconsistent is it to approve the first two conclusions in the chart but to deny the third?

This exposes the inconsistency and latent hypocrisy of the complementarian position. Virtually no complementarian would object to a Gentile holding a position of authority in the church over a Jew (or substitute any other ethnicities), e.g. as a pastor or elder, nor to a slave holding such a position of authority over a master in the church (though in our contemporary Western culture the whole institution of slavery is now seen as despicable and passé). While not completely parallel, is it not completely acceptable for an hourly employee to serve as a church elder with his employer/boss or business owner contentedly following their leadership in the church? However, still today, most complementarians would strongly object to a woman holding a position of authority over a man in the church, e.g. as pastor or elder. How is it that institutionalized racism, classism, and sexism are not seen as equally despicable and passé?

Because Galatians (c. 50 A.D.) was written before 1 Corinthians (c. 55 A.D.) and 1 Timothy (c. 64 A.D.), and Paul's letters were frequently circulated to churches in other cities (Col. 4:16), it could be argued that the Corinthians and Timothy (in Ephesus) would have been aware of what Paul previously wrote to the Galatians. Galatians was a regional letter to multiple churches "next door" to Ionia in which Ephesus was located. Both were in what is now Turkey. Paul's third missionary journey, several years after he wrote Galatians, took him through Galatia and on to Ephesus and Corinth. Thus, it is probable that the gender-role instructions for the Corinthians (1 Cor. 14:33–35) and for the Ephesians (1 Tim. 2:11–15) would have been read and understood in light of and in harmony with the new creation principle Paul had earlier and unequivocally asserted in Galatians 3:28 and doubtless taught in his personal visits to the churches.

Practically speaking, if based on a wrong interpretation of Genesis 3:16, husbands conclude that God wants them to **"rule"** over their wives, how could that potentially affect their marriage, their children, and their lives outside of their marriage? The following list is only suggestive and not fully developed. It is important to understand that these are *potential vulnerabilities* not *actual* or *certain results* of the husbands-are-supposed-to-**rule**-their-wives assumption. For better or for worse, none of us always act consistently with our beliefs and every individual and marriage have their own unique dynamics. Thankfully, sometimes we are better than our beliefs and, sadly, sometimes we are worse. Although these are reasonably possible vulnerabilities for the husband-is-the-**ruler** position, many Christian husbands minimize these by implementing the directives of Ephesians 5:25-33 built around the command to love their wives. Nevertheless, here is a thought-provoking, if perhaps worst case, list of vulnerabilities when the husband believes that God has appointed him to **rule** over his wife:

1. The husband may develop a spirit of entitlement about his role and how his wife is to respond to him.
2. The husband may conclude that the bottom line is that "It's all about me"—my plan, my wishes, my desires, my perspective, my analysis, my dreams, my agenda, and my decisions.
3. The husband may believe that his wife exists for his benefit—to fulfill his plans and desires. Consider the possible relationship of these attitudes and the #MeToo movement.
4. The husband may believe that in planning and decision-making, he doesn't need to be concerned about discovering his wife's feelings, desires, plans, agendas, insights, experience, opinions, or cautions.
5. The husband may see no need to discuss, listen to, or consider his wife's ideas and thoughts.
6. The husband may believe he doesn't have to take time to seek out or deal with his wife's input, perspective, dreams, visions, or disagreements.
7. The husband may see no need to seek a compromise when his wife disagrees with him.
8. The husband, when he and his wife aren't on the same page about something, may see no need to be patient about, to delay, to spend

time praying about, or to seek further information and counsel about a decision.

9. The husband may assume he has the right to make any and all decisions and that whatever he decides is right.

10. The husband may miss the opportunity to make better decisions, experience better results, and develop a better relationship with his wife.

11. The husband may look at his wife and expect her to respond as his implementor, assistant, underling, or servant.

12. The husband may expect that his wife will not disagree, discuss, argue, have a bad attitude about, oppose, or undermine his decisions.

13. The husband may believe that God is on his side and that he is merely obeying God when he "rules" over his wife in any and all decisions.

14. The husband may believe that he needs to insist that his wife submit to his "rule" and that if necessary he should force her to do so.

15. The husband may fail to develop skills in mutual decision-making and conflict resolution and therefore does not illustrate these to his children.

16. The husband may see no need to practice mutual submission as Ephesians 5:21 commands.

17. The husband may see no need to practice mutuality as 1 Corinthians 7 orders and illustrates.

18. The husband may see no need to develop team- or shared-leadership[120] in his marriage.

19. The husband may miss opportunities to develop and to share self-sacrificing love (Eph. 5:22-23).

20. The husband may never learn or appreciate that "it is not good for the man to be alone" (Gen. 2:18) and may never fully benefit from God's provision of a "suitable helper" in his wife.

---

[120] Team or shared leadership isn't everyone doing "what is right in their eyes" as in the time of the Judges (21:25). Team leadership is working together rather than independently or autonomously with both bringing to the table their own abilities, experience, expertise, values, resources, and desires—all for the benefit of both. It is what the Three Persons of the Trinity practiced for eternity past and what Adam and Eve practiced in the Garden of Eden.

21. The husband may fail to help his wife and his children reach their full, God-given, potential.

22. The husband may pass on to his sons and daughters an unbiblical model of marriage and of God's creation design for males and females.

23. The husband may carry the full burden of responsibility for every decision and has to be an expert in everything and always be right.

24. The husband may never understand or learn that in Christ, the sinful barriers which separate people by race, social stature, or gender have been removed (Gal. 3:28).

25. The husband may never learn that men ruling over women is sin's curse (Gen. 3:14-19) not God's command.

26. The husband may believe that because men are to rule over women, it would be sinful to have a woman president, senator, mayor, judge, police officer, supervisor, employer, boss, pastor, elder, college professor, probation officer, manager, etc.

27. The husband may fail to experience the kind of marriage Adam and Eve had in the perfect Garden of Eden, experiencing only marriage as it has existed after sin and the fall.

28. The husband may fail to provide the world with a picture of relationships in the New Creation (Gal. 3:28) and a sign of the "restoration of all things" and the values of Jesus' future kingdom on earth.

29. The husband may misrepresent the Gospel and the character and plan of God to the world.

30. The husband may never experience the "oneness" God designed for marriage

Fortunately, as stated above, many of these vulnerabilities are worst case scenarios and are not fully realized in a marriage where the husband believes he is commanded to "rule" his wife but also to "love" her. Unfortunately, many of us have witnessed first-hand husbands who epitomize some or many of these tragic dynamics.

In Summary

It is helpful to understand how the gender wars began. They were and are the tragic consequences of sin's ruinous entrance into God's perfect creation. Rather than being God's creation plan, Gen. 3:16 reveals that men ruling over women is the tragic result of sin. Patriarchy was never God's desire, plan, or mandate. It is an evil consequence brought about by Satan and sin. Patriarchy is wicked whether practiced in society, marriage, or the church. Women attempting to manipulate and control men, and men assuming authority over them are both expressions of sinful rebellion against God's beautiful plan for the genders. But in the part of the Big Story in which we now live God responds to the world as it is, not to the world as it someday will be. Therefore, at times, the Scriptures call for a temporary accommodation to patriarchy in oppressive cultures to maintain peace and to advance the Gospel. But this will be fully eradicated from Jesus' kingdom when new creation values fill the earth after Jesus returns. Whenever feasible, as they wait and pray daily for His kingdom to come and His will to be done on earth as in heaven, Jesus' followers and His church are to reject sinful patriarchy and practice gender equality, thereby creating beautiful *signs* of Jesus' now-and-future kingdom.

One stanza of Adolphe Adam's beloved Christmas carol, O Holy Night, is a beautiful reminder of our responsibility and hope:

> Truly He taught us to love one another;
> His law is love and His gospel is peace.
> Chains shall He break, for the slave is our brother,
> And in His name, all oppression shall cease.
> Sweet hymns of joy in grateful chorus raise we;
> Let all within us praise His holy name.
> Christ is the Lord!

FOR DISCUSSION

1. Read Genesis 1:26–31 and 2:23–25. What do these verses teach about the relationship God planned for men and women regarding the environment in which they lived?

2. Adam and Eve enjoyed the only perfect marriage in all history, though it apparently lasted for only a short time. What do you think their perfect marriage was like and how was it different than marriages today?

3. Read Genesis 3. Briefly describe all the ways Adam and Eve and their world changed because of sin and its curse.

4. Genesis 3:16 describes the beginning of the gender wars that have affected every culture in every time since. One aspect of sin's curse is revealed when women "desire" to manipulate or control men. What are some specific ways women try to manipulate and control men (their husbands or other men)?

5. As a part of sin's curse, Genesis 3:16 prophesied that men will "rule" over women. Was this part of God's original plan? Why or why not? How do men attempt to assert rulership over women (and husbands over their wives)?

6. "No one today has ever seen or experienced a world without patriarchy." Do you agree with this statement? Why or why not? Knowing that men have assumed authority over women in virtually all places since the fall, how do you think this has affected the debate about the role of women in the church and how people interpret the Bible?

7. Read Galatians 3:28. How does being "in Christ" change the way Christians relate to each other regarding ethnicity, social status, and gender? What are the implications of that for leadership in the church in those three categories? How can Christians display these new creation values today as previews of the coming Kingdom of God on the earth?

8. What are the implications of Galatians 3:28 for how the genders will relate to each other in the future new creation?

5

The Concession Passages:
Submission—a Personal Tipping Point

Have you ever become frustrated as you tried to follow supposedly simple instructions for putting together a toy, a piece of furniture, or some equipment? How difficult could it be to assemble an adjustable basketball goal to put up in my driveway for the enjoyment of my grandchildren? I've learned from experience that I shouldn't just assume that I could figure out how to do it on my own. I really should read the directions first, then follow them step by infuriating step. This proved to be a challenge to my patience and sanity as I sorted through a thousand large, small, and very small parts (that's an exaggeration!) and read instructions that seemed written by someone who had absolutely no gift for putting the cookies on the lower shelf. But, I was making what I thought was stellar progress because the partially assembled contraption on my garage floor was increasingly looking like the picture on the box and the floor model I had seen at Meijer.

Then it happened. I hit a major impasse. My inability to follow the next step described by the instructions exposed the fact that I had used the wrong nuts and bolts in a much earlier stage of the project. My attitude deteriorated rapidly as I realized that the only solution was to dis-assemble nearly everything I had painstakingly done for the last couple of hours and start over again using the correct bolts in the correct places. Who would have thought that less than a half inch difference in the length of several bolts would matter much? Although I proved that the time alleged on the box to be required to assemble this was woefully inadequate, I still had a sense of pride as I finally raised the backboard and rolled the entire sports masterpiece into place on the edge of our driveway. As my grandchildren happily engage with me in games of "horse," "twenty-one," "around the world," or "one-on-two," they have no idea how stupid their grandfather felt about his assembly skills.

Did you know that constructing a sermon series can parallel my basketball goal adventure? At least that was what happened in what turned out to be a momentous turn of events part way through a series I was preaching on a section of the book of Ephesians (5:21-6:9). While researching the passage I would deal with in two weeks, I hit the wall when I realized that what I was seeing in the text exposed that I had really messed up in how I handled one of the first messages which I had already completed in the series. The exposition of the later paragraph built on the foundation of the earlier ones. The only way to fix the situation was to admit that what I had taught in one of the earlier sermons had been seriously flawed. If I was going to effectively finish putting the series together to cohesively present what Paul intended, I had to go back and make significant adjustments in what I had already done. It happened like this . . .

In my gender-roles journey, a significant tipping point came as I studied what I now call the **concession passages.** They include the familiar New Testament Scriptures that address gender roles in *marriage* including apostolic instructions for wives to submit to their husbands. Two of the passages also instruct children and parents/fathers (Eph. 6:1-4; Col. 3:20, 21) and four also address the responsibilities of slaves to their masters (Eph. 6:5-9; Col. 3:22-4:1; Titus 2:9, 10; 1 Pt. 2:18-21).[121] My reason for calling these important texts *concession passages* will become evident below. Included in the gender role *concession passages* are the following instructions concerning marriage:

> **Ephesians 5:21–33:** Submit to one another out of reverence
> for Christ. Wives, submit to your husbands as to the Lord.
> For the husband is the head of the wife as Christ is the head
> of the church, his body, of which he is the Savior. Now as
> the church submits to Christ, so also wives should submit
> to their husbands in everything. Husbands, love your wives,

---

[121] Similarly, 1 Timothy 6:1–2, which addresses one side of the slave/master relationship but lacks any reference to wives and husbands or children and parents.

just as Christ loved the church and gave himself up for her to make her holy, cleansing her by the washing with water through the word, and to present her to himself as a radiant church, without stain or wrinkle or any other blemish, but holy and blameless. In this same way, husbands ought to love their wives as their own bodies. He who loves his wife loves himself. After all, no one ever hated his own body, but he feeds and cares for it, just as Christ does the church—for we are members of his body. "For this reason a man will leave his father and mother and be united to his wife, and the two will become one flesh." This is a profound mystery—but I am talking about Christ and the church. However, each one of you also must love his wife as he loves himself, and the wife must respect her husband.

Colossians 3:18 19: Wives, submit to your husbands, as is fitting in the Lord. Husbands, love your wives and do not be harsh with them.

Titus 2:4, 5: Then they can train the younger women to love their husbands and children, to be self-controlled and pure, to be busy at home, to be kind, and to be subject to their husbands, so that no one will malign the word of God.

1 Peter 3:1–7: Wives, in the same way be submissive to your husbands so that, if any of them do not believe the word, they may be won over without words by the behavior of their wives, when they see the purity and reverence of your lives. Your beauty should not come from outward adornment, such as braided hair and the wearing of gold jewelry and fine clothes. Instead, it should be that of your inner self, the unfading beauty of a gentle and quiet spirit, which is of great worth in God's sight. For this is the way the holy women of the past who put their hope in God used to make themselves beautiful. They were submissive to their own husbands, like Sarah, who obeyed Abraham and called him her master. You are her daughters if you do what is right and do not give way to fear. Husbands, in the same way be considerate as you live with your wives, and treat them with respect as the weaker partner and as heirs with you of the gracious gift of life, so that nothing will hinder your prayers.

A common theme in each of these four Scripture passages is the responsibility assigned to wives to *submit* to their husbands. These commands are the backbone of the complementarian vision for a Christian marriage and are often referenced as providing strong support for the complementarian stance on gender roles in the church. Although nothing in these texts applies these marital role directives beyond marriage, complementarians typically believe that they also reveal God's created gender roles for males and females in and beyond of marriage. They believe there is something about the genders inherent in God's original creation of male and female that equips men for leadership over women not only in marriage but also in the church. Some complementarians go even farther to apply this hierarchal designation to gender roles throughout society concluding that women should not have authority over men in business, education, government, etc.

In reality, if these hierarchical roles are gender-based as part of God's creation design, it would seem that *all* complementarians would have to apply them to *all* aspects of life including business, government, education, athletics, the arts, etc. When many complementarians do not advocate such far-reaching application, one must question why. If there is not any textual evidence for *limiting* their application to marriage and the church, perhaps complementarians need to do some serious soul searching to discern whether it is evidence of hypocrisy or of fear or of an inner witness from God's Spirit contrary to the idea that no woman should be in leadership over a man in any realm.

In contrast to the complementarian stance on gender roles, chapter 3 argued that God's creation intent as clearly revealed in Genesis 1, 2 gives absolutely no support to the view that created design equips males to lead and females to submit. On the contrary, as presented in chapter 3, the Genesis account of creation repeatedly emphasizes the inherent identity, unity, equality, and partnership of the genders. The gender differences enable them to complement each other but do not prepare or outfit one to have authority over the other.

The purpose of this chapter is to take a deeper look at the *concession passages* to see if the foundational complementarian assumption is correct— that is, that these texts contain a timeless mandate (based on created gender differences) for wives to submit to their husbands, and by implication, for women to be restricted from leadership positions in the church and beyond.

First, two questions will be valuable for framing one's interpretation of the passage:

(1) Does Paul's command for slaves to obey and to submit to their masters (Eph. 6:5; Col. 3:22; 1 Pt. 2:18; Titus 2:9) represent God's approval of slavery?

(2) Does Paul's command for wives to submit to their husbands (Eph. 5:22; Col. 3:18; Titus 2:4, 5; 1 Pt. 3:1) represent God's approval of patriarchy?

Virtually all contemporary Christians would give an unequivocal and resounding *"no"* to the first question and might well add that what Paul commanded for masters (Eph. 6:9, et al) effectively undermines the institution of slavery—at least that it prohibits the kind of abuse that was all too prevalent. Why is it then that virtually all complementarians would answer *"yes"* to the parallel question regarding the institution of patriarchy (husbands having authority over wives)? This is despite Paul's instructions to husbands (Eph. 5:25–33) that undercut the institution of patriarchy even as the parallel instructions to masters (Eph. 6:9) appear to undercut the institution of slavery.

Three Parallel Relationships

These considerations highlight the importance of the parallel nature of the three relationships in Ephesians 5:2–6:9 and Colossians 3:18–4:1. Unfortunately, adding chapter and verse numbers to the Bible text (about 1500 years after the New Testament was completed) breaks up the three relationships so they are not quite as obvious as they should be. Considering that the passage addresses three parallel relationships is a **KEY** to properly interpreting this unified passage. In the two closely parallel passages (Ephesians and Colossians) written at the same time, Paul gave practical instructions to the first century Christians in Ephesus and Colosse most of whom currently lived in one of the three relationships: wives and husbands, children and parents/fathers, and slaves and masters. Today virtually all churches, at least in the West, have only two of these relationships represented in their congregations, thankfully missing the component of slaves and masters which was very prevalent in the first century.[122]

In each of the three relationships, the first party addressed (wives, children, and slaves) was responsible to submit to or obey the second party (husbands, parents/fathers, and masters) and the second party was instructed how they were to act toward the first. The historical background was the culturally pervasive Greco-Roman household codes which assumed absolute, unquestioned, unilateral authority for males as husbands, fathers, and masters. The apostle's instructions about roles in marriage has traditionally been understood by complementarians as a timeless principle, and, although the passage says nothing about gender roles in church, they see the marital roles as providing evidence to support limiting to men the holding of positions of authority in the church. This expansion from marriage to church flows out of the previously discussed belief that the marital roles are based on created differences that fit males to lead and females to follow.

Recognizing that there are three parallel relationships raises the question, "If God approves of women submitting to their husbands as a timeless, creation-based dynamic, then doesn't it follow that God approves of slaves submitting to their masters (hence giving divine approval to the institution of slavery) as a timeless, creation-based dynamic?" Virtually no interpreter would agree with that. So how do we deal with this conundrum? What are we missing?

---

[122] This is not intended to minimize the appalling extent or horrific evil of the ongoing human-trafficking in the United States but assumes that these must remain in the shadows as they are repudiated and criminalized in our culture and, if discovered in the church, would be vigorously rejected. In modern America slavery is repugnant. Throughout the ancient world it was acceptable, legal, and valued by nearly everyone except the slaves.

There's Something More Here than Meets the Eye

The traditional complementarian understanding of Ephesians 5 and 6 has been so prevalent that most interpreters ignore or overlook at least **four important tip-offs** within the text which indicate there might be significantly more to the passage than appears on the surface and that is assumed in the traditional handling of the text. The first three tip-offs are text-based and the fourth is practice-based. They reveal that the simplest and supposedly the most obvious reading may not be the correct one.

(1) The first **tip-off** is the seemingly contradictory command at the head of the passage that requires every believer to submit to every other believer: "Submit to one another out of reverence for Christ" (Eph. 5:21). Both the grammatical structure and the position of the mandate for mutual submission reveal its importance for a correct understanding of the entire passage as it applies to and governs all three parallel relationships. Grammatically, "Ephesians 5:18–23 forms one sentence in the Greek, and the instructions to wives in v. 22 are grammatically dependent on the mutual submission in v. 21 because of the ellipsis (omission) of the verb 'submit' in v. 22."[123]

It would be difficult to overemphasize the importance of the fact that there is *no verb* in Ephesians 5:22 in the original Greek text. It literally reads: "Wives to your husbands as to the Lord." The word *submit* is not in the verse. It is supplied in our translations from the verb in the previous verse (21): "Submit to one another out of reverence to Christ." Verse 22 is not a stand-alone verse. It is a *subcategory* of verse 21. Wives submitting to their husband is the first illustration of the mutual submission commanded for all Christians in the previous verse. *Verse 21 is the controlling text that governs the interpretation of what follows.*

This is of paramount importance because preaching and teaching about marriage from Ephesians 5 invariably starts with verse 22 as if it could be understood independently from the controlling text, verse 21. The passage is not about wives submitting. It is about mutual submission for all believers with marriage being the first of three spheres of application.

In other words, Paul's instructions regarding a wife's submission to her husband cannot be interpreted apart from and in subservience to the

---

[123] Westfall, *Paul and Gender*, 22.

prior command for mutual submission between a husband and his wife. The location of the command for mutual submission at the beginning of the instructions for the three parallel relationships suggests that it does not merely apply to the first relationship, but to all three of the relationships. Had Paul intended for it to apply only to the marital relationship, he could easily have clarified this. Therefore, the submission of Christian parents/fathers to their children is in a precedential position to the submission of children to their parents/fathers. The submission of Christian masters to their slaves takes precedence over and helps to define the submission of slaves to their masters.[124] This is stunning! It is an earthshaking challenge to the traditional complementarian understanding of the three relationships. Ephesians 5:21 could be seen as a practical application of Paul's announcement (written ten years earlier) in Galatians 3:28 of absolute equality in the new humanity that Jesus' death and resurrection inaugurated: "There is neither Jew nor Greek, slave nor free, male nor female, for you are all one in Christ Jesus."

This precedential command for mutual submission is striking because it appears to stand in stark contrast to the orders issued within the specifics of each of the three relationships. Someone might even suggest that it contradicts them. It's easy to imagine a wife saying to her husband, "What do you mean I'm supposed to submit to you? You're not my boss. The Bible says that you're supposed to submit to me before it tells me to submit to you! You go first!" Imagine a slave confronting his master, "Weren't you listening to Paul's letter when it was read in church last Sunday? You're supposed to submit to me." And, what could it possibly mean to suggest that parents must first submit to their children? Obviously, there is something deeper addressed in this text.

(2) The second **tip-off** that something more than the traditional interpretation is going on in this passage is the unexplained change in the second of the three relationships from "parents" (verse 1) and "father and mother" (verses 2, 3) to only "fathers" (verse 4). When addressing children, the parties without power, Paul directs them to "obey your parents" and to "honor your father and mother." But when he speaks to the parties with power, it is "fathers" excluding "mothers" (Eph. 6:4). Why did he not stay with "parents" or "father and mother" when he gave directions to the second party? Why were mothers omitted? Were these changes simply for variety

---

[124] This reveals the basis of Paul's instructions to slave-owning Philemon (Philem. 15-21).

of expression or is there something much more significant and essential as related to the parallelism of the three relationships? This is especially significant for interpreters who are committed to the doctrine of *verbal plenary* inspiration[125] of the Scriptures. It seems unlikely that the change of terms could be dismissed as simply stylistic.

(3) The next **tip-off** is the jarring disparity of the third relationship (slavery) in comparison with the other two (marriage and family). The first two relationships are God-ordained, inherently love-based by design, and intended by God to be for the lifetime mutual benefit of all parties: wives and husbands, and children, and parents. But the third relationship is none of the above. It was not ordained by God, is by its nature not love-based, and is clearly not beneficial to one of the parties—the slaves. This is not to deny that a few highly exceptional instances existed in which a slave was loved by their master and received benefits from the relationship. This appears to have been the case in the story of the centurion who compassionately sought Jesus' help for his suffering servant (Matt. 8:5ff). Also, the Old Testament law provided for an about-to-be-released slave to *voluntarily* remain in slavery when they perceived the benefits from the relationship outweighed those of obtaining their freedom (Ex. 21:2–6; Deut. 15:16, 17). But, such relationships, even in the Bible, were rare. And, given the choice, very few slaves even of kindly masters would voluntarily remain in slavery, unless, perhaps there was some desperate or unique circumstance in play. Would any master be willing to trade stations with their slaves? Would any slave not leap at an opportunity to trade places with their master?

No parent has ever hoped their child would become a slave. No one aspires to become a slave. No one's life dream is to enter into the bondage of slavery. If a child answered the question, "What do you want to be when you grow up?" by saying, "A slave," everyone would be horrified and vociferously object. No one would ever voluntarily surrender their freedom apart from highly exceptional and desperate extenuating circumstances. The very nature of slavery is at best demeaning and dehumanizing. It robs one of dignity, respect, freedom, and self-determination, and eliminates any pursuit of personal agendas and dreams unless and only as long as they match the desires or whims of the master. It would be hard to conceive of a relationship more disparate than slavery compared to the other two relationships in the

---

[125] The belief that God inspired every word of the Scriptures.

triad. What is the significance of this disparity for how the passage should be interpreted? This disparity becomes even more jarring when one recalls that Paul is addressing three relationships that, as the structure of the passage reveals, are *parallel*.

In what way is the third relationship parallel to the first two? What is similar about wives, children, and slaves? As previously noted, the three relationships share identical structure by first addressing the party without power (wives, children, and slaves) and second, the party with power (husbands, fathers, and masters). Put another way, in each of the relationships the first party is called on to submit to the authority of the second and the second is instructed as to how to appropriately treat the first. This parallel structure coupled with the stunning difference between the first two relationships and the third should cause every interpreter to ask, "What does marriage have to do with slavery?" and "What does parenting have to do with slavery?" In order to correctly understand and apply these instructions involving parallel relationships, some unifying theme or principle must be identified that *applies to all three*. Interpreters must first determine why Paul places slavery in such close juxtaposition with marriage and family. The same issues apply to Paul's nearly identical teachings in Colossians 3:18–4:1.

Related to this, it is highly significant to note that **every passage in the Bible which directs wives to submit to their husbands is either followed by or preceded in the close context by directions for slaves to submit to or obey their masters.** In Titus 2 and 1 Peter 2, 3,[126] two of the three parallel and oppressive relationships addressed in Ephesians 5, 6 and Colossians 3 are similarly addressed.

---

[126] "In the same way" (1 Pt. 3:1) specifically connects the verses about wives to the preceding verses about slaves. 1 Peter changes the order addressing slaves before wives. Between the two relationships, Peter honored the suffering of slaves by comparing it to Jesus' suffering (2:21-25) and after addressing wives, honored their submission by comparing it to Sarah's submission to Abraham (3:5, 6).

PASSAGE	WIVES ARE TO SUBMIT TO THEIR HUSBANDS	SLAVES ARE TO SUBMIT TO OR OBEY THEIR MASTERS
Ephesians	Wives, submit to your husbands as to the Lord (5:22)	Slaves, obey your earthly masters with respect and fear, and with sincerity of heart, just as you would obey Christ (6:5)
Colossians	Wives, submit to your husbands, as is fitting in the Lord (3:18)	Slaves, obey your earthly masters in everything (3:22)
Titus	Then they can train the younger women . . .to be subject to their husbands (2:4, 5)	Teach slaves to be subject to their masters in everything (2:9)
1 Peter	Wives, in the same way be submissive to your husbands (3:1)	Slaves, submit yourselves to your masters with all respect (2:18)

This is important because if the submission of wives to husbands is a timeless mandate from God then so is the submission of slaves to masters—a tacit approval of the institution of slavery. Virtually no interpreter today would affirm that! There's obviously something more in this passage than initially meets the interpreter's eye.

(4) The fourth **tip-off** that the text is dealing with something more than may appear on the surface concerns how the slave-master portion is typically preached and taught today—not as presenting commands for actual *slaves* and *masters* as the text specifies, but as directions for contemporary *employees* and *employers*. That is obviously not the same! This arbitrary decision to replace valid interpretation with invalid or partly valid application for preaching and teaching is made for obvious reasons: (a) in most parts of the world today, congregations have lots of employees and employers but no slaves and masters, and (b) almost everyone wants to distance themselves from any suggestion that the Bible condones the institution of slavery.

While few would question that there may be some practical *applications* to workers and their bosses today, that manufactured application totally ignores an essential element of what is being considered, that is, a relationship that is evil, inhumane, demeaning, dehumanizing, degrading, and oppressive. The comparison of the slave/master relationship to the boss/employee relationship is an impossibly big stretch. Typically, in preaching the passage, no one offers a text-based or hermeneutical explanation as to why this *application* is substituted for the obvious *interpretation* of the text that concerns actual slaves and their masters. This common application ignores the structure of the passage and depends on the three relationships NOT being parallel.

While some employees may jokingly describe themselves as "slaves," the fact is that the worst modern employee/employer relationship in the Western world bears *no* resemblance to the first century slave/master relationship. Why then do nearly all modern interpreters deal with the passage in this way—as if it were talking about someone who works at Walmart or the hospital? It is understandable that we want to avoid the criticism that suggests that the Bible is an evil book because it promotes slavery. It appears that the institution of slavery is so patently offensive that commentators, teachers, and preachers seamlessly substitute "employee" for "slave" and "supervisor" for "master" as if this swap were not an arbitrary rewriting of the biblical text. The absence of any warrant in the text to interpret the first two relationships literally and then to interpret the third by changing the essential nature of the two parties should set off loud alarm bells that something important is going on in the passage overlooked in the traditional approach.

These four challenges to the overly simplistic and surface complementarian understanding of the text should cause every serious and sincere Bible student to reexamine the traditional interpretation of the passage with an open mind:

(1) the leadoff command for mutual submission,
(2) the unexplained shift from *"parents"* to *"fathers"* in the second relationship,
(3) the jarring juxtaposition of severely disparate but parallel relationships, and
(4) the common contemporary practice of substituting the employee/employer relationship for the slave/master relationship.

The Interpretive KEY

The **key** to resolving all four of these challenges in a way that is faithful to the text is to recognize that Paul's commands were <u>temporary concessions for believers who lived in an oppressive culture</u>. These accommodations were necessary on a temporary basis for preserving peace and promoting Gospel witness.

Paul's commands for submission and obedience were not *timeless mandates* based on creation design or intent. Slavery was absolutely not God's original plan for anyone, nor was domineering, exasperating (Eph. 6:40, or abusive control by husbands or fathers. The oppressive dynamic inherent to slavery is obviously the result of the entrance of sin into God's perfect creation even as the rule of men over women (patriarchy) was clearly the result of the entrance of sin into God's perfect creation (Gen. 3:16). Both are expressions of sin's curse, not creation's intent. Sin has corrupted all humans, all relationships, and all institutions in this sin-ruined creation.

The backdrop to the passage, domination by the three power-possessing parties (husbands, fathers, and masters), is evident when one looks at Paul's instructions to them and asks, "What was the existing problem in Ephesus which motivated Paul to give these three sets of similar instructions?" One would assume that the problem was behaviors that were the <u>opposite</u> of what Paul commands for husbands, fathers, and masters, that is: exploitation, selfishness, harshness, lack of consideration and respect, bullying, and injustice. Clearly, these three relationships were parallel regarding authoritarian domination by the parties with power.

This relational corruption is pervasive for everyone living in the present broken world between the fall and the future new creation. Sin-corrupted relationships reveal the pervasive and painful clash of values that persist in the time between the original creation and the future restored creation. The "in between" time—the period in which we now live and during which we long for the arrival of the new, restored creation—is characterized by dysfunctional relationships. In this age, all relationships are dysfunctional—just in different ways and to different degrees. To be sure, the beauty of the original creation at times shines through the brokenness of sin's consequences and gives us glimpses of how it was supposed to be. <u>Beauty and brokenness</u>

characterize us, our relationships, our cultures, and our environment, though some relationships are more beautiful or broken than others.

These corrupted values are obvious in the third relationship—slavery. But how does this relate to marriage and parenting? The answer is that throughout the *in-between time* including the past world of the New Testament and still today in many cultures and circumstances, patriarchal and hierarchical oppression were and are the prevailing societal norms. Husbands and fathers were and are all too often restrictive and abusive in their domination of their wives and children. In biblical times, authoritarian husbands and fathers were accepted as normal. This prevalence of male authoritarianism explains why in the second relationship Paul shifted from "parents" to "fathers." "Parents" weren't the power-possessing parties. "Fathers" were. All three parallel relationships exhibited the dynamic in which one party possessed all the power and all too often wielded it in a selfish, heavy-handed, or even tyrannical and abusive manner.

The *concession passages*, including Ephesians 5:22–6:5 and Colossians 3:18–4:1, instruct believers on how to live in peace while living under the curse, and how to live to display the attractiveness of the Gospel while living in a milieu of ugly oppression and inequality. A similar purpose of exhibiting the beauty of the Gospel under unjust persecution is expressed in 1 Peter 2:12, "Live such good lives among the pagans that, though they accuse you of doing wrong, they may see your good deeds and glorify God on the day he visits us." Also, there are many references in Acts and the New Testament letters about making accommodations for the sake of peace and order (1 Cor. 14:33, 40; Rom. 14:19; 1 Tim. 2:2,11, 12) and for the sake of Gospel witness (Acts 15:19; 16:3; 1 Cor. 9:19–23; 1 Tim. 6:1; Titus 2:5, 10; 1 Pt. 2:18, 19).

My Personal Epiphany

This game-changing understanding of a central, unifying theme in the *concession passages* emerged during my personal gender roles journey a few years ago while I was preaching through Ephesians 5:21–6:9 in a sermon series entitled **"Back Down: Winning through Surrender."** In my first sermon, I had already presented the traditional complementarian approach to Paul's mandate for wives to *"submit"* to their own husbands. I included the standard *disclaimers* that the husband was supposed to lead with love and a self-sacrificing spirit. My handling of the passage was pretty much the same as I had previously done through nearly fifty years of preaching, teaching, and premarital counseling. Before preaching my next sermon in the series that focused on the responsibilities of husbands, I was studying ahead on the passage about slaves and masters when I was suddenly struck by how I was again, as in the past, pretty much ignoring any serious reference to <u>actual slaves and masters</u> in my presentation, and was already planning my sermon around the theme of how a contemporary Christian <u>employee</u> should respond to their <u>boss or supervisor</u>, and how that contemporary Christian boss or supervisor should treat those who work for them.

Somehow, I had never considered how this approach totally ignored what the text was actually talking about (slaves and masters) and how doing so bypassed any effort to identify a consistent, unifying theme for the three relationships. If these were in fact three *parallel* relationships, then how I interpreted the slaves and masters segment had to be thematically consistent with and related to how I interpreted the wives and husbands segment as well as the children and fathers segment. What right or justification did I have to impose this alteration of the text? To maintain integrity in my approach to the Scriptures, I was forced to take a fresh and open-minded look at the entire passage before I could further attempt to understand the inter-related individual parts.

In this process, I not only discovered what I now believe to be the **key** to understanding Paul's directions for all three relationships, but also to understand how his opening line, "Submit to one another out of reverence for Christ," (Eph. 5:21) fits perfectly with his otherwise apparently contradictory commands for wives, children, and slaves to submit to and obey their husbands, parents, and masters. Which is it? Should husbands submit to wives (and vice versa) as Ephesians 5:21 required, or are wives exclusively to submit to their husbands as Ephesians 5:22 previously appeared to command? When I recognized that the passage was obviously built on the foundation of mutual submission and structured around these three parallel relationships each involving powerless and power-possessing parties, one of which involved the institution of slavery, I was forced to take a new look at the passage, as much as possible free of presuppositions and bias.

I had to acknowledge that while some contemporary *application* of

Ephesians 6:5–9 to employees and employers could be appropriate, it was a huge leap away from an *interpretation* regarding those whom the text was actually addressing. Without finding any textual support that allowed me to quickly pass over exegetical *interpretation* in order to replace it with barely comparable contemporary *application,* I had subconsciously been avoiding the unthinkable—that Paul's instructions could be, as many pre–Civil War Southern pastors passionately affirmed, a tacit approval of the horrific institution of slavery. If Paul commanded slaves to obey their masters and masters to treat them less abusively but FAILED TO CONFRONT the underlying evil of one human enslaving another both of whom were made in God's image, how was that not an approval of the institution of slavery? That unacceptable conclusion had seemed to be the only alternative to the typical employee/employer ploy. I was forced to ask myself, **"What does slavery have to do with marriage?"**[127]

Pursuing the answer to that question eventually opened my eyes to the harmonizing dynamic that connected the three parallel relationships, that is, **in a sinful and abusive culture, oppressed believers sometimes have to make temporary behavioral concessions in order to preserve peace and to promote rather than hinder the spread of the Gospel.** In addition to resolving the slavery-related issues ("How are the three relationships parallel?" and "Does the passage endorse slavery?") this interpretive recognition also reconciled the command for mutual submission (God's original plan and timeless desire) with the otherwise incongruous one-sided commands for the powerless to submit to the powerful—a provisional accommodation to living in a fallen world.

My subsequent study confirmed this recognition of Paul's teachings as *temporary concessions* to oppressive rulership in marriage, parenting, and slavery to preserve peace, order, and Gospel witness. This new understanding enabled me to harmonize statements within these passages that had seemed contradictory as well as to mollify interpretations that were often

---

[127] That question, "What does slavery have to do with marriage?" became the title of one sermon in the series as I shared my new interpretive discovery which now seemed so obvious in the text. Here is a link to the text of the sermon ("What Does Slavery Have to Do with Marriage?") in which I first tentatively presented this interpretive breakthrough: https://drive.google.com/file/d/0B_pt9hSBqOQgSE1NdzlPMTl6UEk/view?usp=sharing.

embarrassingly offensive to many reasonable people. For example, I have sometimes cringed in my spirit as I observed weddings, thinking about the common reaction by non-believers listening to the reading (or sermonizing) of Ephesians 5:22ff regarding wives submitting to their husbands. Many undoubtedly have seen it as an incredible, shocking, or even a revolting anachronism—a real "turn off" for Christianity and the church. This included not just unbelievers but also many Christians. They struggle to harmonize a small number of Bible passages that appear to promote patriarchy with what they perceive to be the very different spirit that permeates the creation account, the life and teachings of Jesus, and the spirit and instructions of the New Testament letters. But until my recognition of the *concession principle*, I had no alternative understanding to these uncomfortable readings that were often a hindrance that prevented people from exploring Christ or the Christian faith.

So, wives don't have to submit to their husbands? What should a Christian marriage look like? How should a wife respond to an abusive husband? These questions will be addressed later in this chapter. First, let's see if the *concession principle* has any confirming support elsewhere in the Scriptures.

Early Church Accommodations

Like a kitten with newly opened eyes, I began to see evidence of the *concession principle* in other Scriptures. Stackhouse refers to this as "the principle of *accommodation*" and states that

> God works within human limitations—to transform the world according to his good purposes. To be blunt, God works with what he's got—and with what we've got. When faced with our shortcomings and sin, God doesn't just erase us and create a whole new situation. Instead, God graciously pursues shalom in the glory and the mess that we have made. The living water of the Holy Spirit very rarely comes like a tsunami, forcing everything it encounters to submit to its will. Instead, God's Spirit graciously, humbly, and wisely, pours over the extant topography of the social landscape, conforming himself to the contours he encounters. As he

does so, however, like an irresistible flow of water he reshapes the landscape by and by, eventually making the crooked ways straight and the rough places plain (Isa. 40:3–4).[128]

While waiting for the full realization of the new creation order, Gentiles were sometimes temporarily directed to make concessions regarding the Jewish ceremonial law in order to minimize an offence to Jewish people that could hinder their acceptance of the Gospel. For example, Acts 15:19–35 describes the Jerusalem Council's letter to Gentile converts prescribing a few limited accommodations to Jewish sensibilities: "It is my judgment, therefore, that we should not make it difficult for the Gentiles who are turning to God. Instead we should write to them telling them to abstain from food polluted by idols, from sexual immorality, from the meat of strangled animals and from blood. For Moses has been preached in every city from the earliest times and is read in the synagogues on every Sabbath" (Acts 15:19–21). The temporary nature of these concessions is made evident by clear teachings in the New Testament letters indicating that both Jews and Gentiles were now free from adherence to the Old Testament ceremonial law.

Summarizing the decision made by the Jerusalem Council, James indicates that an evangelistic purpose dictated their conclusion to encourage temporary concessions to the Jewish Law: "It is my judgment, therefore, that we should not make it difficult for the Gentiles who are turning to God" (Acts 19:15). Think of this! If the same principle enunciated by the Jewish Council were applied in contemporary culture regarding gender roles, it seems evident that it would call for the *inclusion* of women in teaching and leadership roles in the church today at least in the "free world." Unlike the oppressively patriarchal culture of the first century, today's secular culture in the West reacts very negatively to patriarchy and anything that even hints of the oppression of women. A *stained-glass ceiling* which limits women in the church becomes, for many, an impenetrable barrier deterring them from pursuing any interest in the church or Christianity. Today patriarchal restrictions "make it difficult for the Gentiles who are turning to God."

It seems as if the contemporary secular culture has embraced some *new creation values* regarding women while much of the church still holds them at arm's length and stubbornly holds on to *fallen creation values* regarding

---

[128] Stackhouse, *Partners In Christ,* 52.

male rulership that is an evil consequence of sin's curse (Gen. 3:16). How sad if with regard to gender roles Jesus' influence has been more quickly adopted by the godless secular culture than by many of His professed followers and His church. Applying James' words to the gender roles debate, "we should not make it difficult for the Gentiles that are turning to God" by imposing highly offensive gender restrictions that characterize fallen culture (Gen. 3:16) rather than the new creation (Gal. 3:28).[129]

Another illustration of the principle of accommodation is found in Romans 14 where Paul instructs mature believers to avoid causing immature believers to sin by eating food that had been offered to idols or by failing to observe Jewish holy days. Even within that text and elsewhere in the New Testament Paul made it clear that these were neither permanent nor necessary requirements (Rom. 14; 1 Cor. 8; Gal. 2–6; Col. 2; etc.). Rather, these concessions regarding "disputable matters" (Rom. 14:1) were temporary, transitional, and not permanently binding or applicable. In fact, to continue to practice those temporary accommodations at some point becomes sin because it is no longer necessary for the sake of the Gospel but now promotes values contrary to those of Jesus' new covenant and kingdom and oppresses those whom the Gospel has set free as the Book of Hebrews makes clear.

Concessions to Hard Hearts

Another illustration of concession to fallenness is found in Jesus' teaching on marriage and divorce in Matthew 19:4–6 in which Jesus quoted from Genesis 2. While acknowledging that concessions for divorce were made for *hard-hearted* sinners under the Jewish law, His teaching from Genesis 2 *gave no support to any hierarchy in gender roles*. Rather Jesus not only asserted the *unity and oneness* of male and female in God's design, but He also granted the right of divorce to women (see Mark 10:11, 12, the parallel passage) which was a shocking egalitarian permission in that oppressively patriarchal culture where women normally had no legal rights at all. Jesus further affirmed that concessions because of hard hearts were not God's

---

[129] An obvious exception to this might be in a fundamentalist Islamic culture where the marital concessions of Ephesians 5 might still be an important strategy for peace and evangelism.

design "from the beginning." Jesus' clarification of God's original creation intent in Matthew 19:8 pointed His followers to a higher standard than the concessions permitted under the Jewish law as an accommodation to hard-hearted depravity.

A common theme in Jesus' teaching was the reimaging of Old Testament laws in ways that ultimately moved past (1) making concessions to the problem of hard hearts, (2) perpetuating the mandates for strict isolation from intermingling with the surrounding pagan cultures, and (3) adhering to voluminous and sometimes ridiculously complex extra-biblical, man-made traditions that had been added to and piled on top of the Mosaic law. These frequently perverted God's ultimate purposes. Illustrations from Jesus' teachings include previously mentioned divorce regulations (Matt. 19:1–12, Mark 10:1–2), as well as dietary laws (Mark 7:19), and Sabbath restrictions (Mark 2:27). Similarly, in a number of Old Testament laws relating to women we see illustrations "of God's accommodation to something he does not like, namely, patriarchy, and thus also his simultaneous amelioration of it."[130] These provide an anticipatory context for the temporary concessions the Apostolic Letters present.

Living Between the Fall and the New Creation—for the Sake of the Gospel

Living in the time some theologians describe as *"already/not yet"*[131] requires Jesus' followers to discern when their conduct must reflect the *"not yet"* (the world is still broken) and when it can and should portray the *"already"* (Jesus has begun to make all things new). Complementarians are vulnerable to not having enough "already" in their convictions and conduct, while egalitarians run the risk of being insensitive to the "not yet."

Whenever possible, in less oppressive or prejudiced settings and cultures,

---

[130] Stackhouse, *Partners in Christ,* 81.

[131] Heb. 2:7, 8 provides an illustration of the "already/not yet" dynamic with regard to the Father's placing of everything under the authority of Jesus: "'You made him a little lower than the angels; you crowned him with glory and honor and put everything under his feet.' In putting everything under him, God left nothing that is not subject to him. Yet at present we do not see everything subject to him."

believers should live out new creation values as a *sign* of the now-and-future kingdom of God (Ezek. 11:19; 36:26; 2 Cor. 5:17; Eph. 5:21; Gal. 6:15; Philem. 14–21). While post-fall, *not-yet* concessions may sometimes be necessary in a spiritually divided home (1 Pt. 3:1–7), *already* new creation values of equality and mutuality should be modeled between Spirit-controlled Christian husbands and wives (Eph. 5:18–21). New creation values should be practiced by believers committed to pleasing the Lord through mutuality in their marriage (1 Cor. 7:2–5, 32–34). Hopefully this will be emerging in an increasing percentage of marriages as well as male-female relationships and roles in the church (Gal. 3:28; 1 Cor. 11:5; and, rightly interpreted, 1 Cor. 14:26–40 and 1 Tim. 2:1–15).

Would I be correct in assuming that the more spiritually mature and Christ-like both husbands and wives are, the more egalitarian their marriage typically is in actual day-to-day practice regardless of how they might understand Ephesians 5? On the other hand, who could disagree with the observation that the less Christ-like a husband is, the more likely it is that he will abusively expect, demand, or force unquestioned submission by his wife? Fifty plus years of observing and counseling husbands and wives would absolutely affirm those conclusions.

A Christian marriage ought to be a beautiful island of new creation mutuality in a turbulent ocean of fallen-world oppression; an oasis of equality, deference, and loving partnership in a desert of patriarchy, subjugation, and selfish exploitation. The church ought to be a vivid and beautiful illustration of what it means for a community of people to live out new creation values under the wise and loving rule of God. Egalitarian practice is a *sign* of the now-and-future kingdom of God.

Stackhouse gives a thought-provoking summary:

> "To put it more pointedly: when society was patriarchal, as it was in the New Testament context and as it has been everywhere in the world except in modern society in our day, then the church avoided scandal by going along with patriarchy, even as the Bible ameliorated it and made women's situation better than it was under any other culture's gender code. Now, however, that our modern society is at least officially egalitarian, the scandal (ironically enough)

is that the church is *not* going along with society, not rejoicing in the unprecedented freedom to let women and men serve according to their gifts and callings without an arbitrary gender restriction. This scandal of keeping women subordinate to men impedes both the evangelism of others and the edification—the retention and development of faith—of those already converted. I am arguing that today we need to drop patriarchy because contemporary Western society has become ready to accept homes, churches, and secular institutions that welcome women into all roles, including leadership."[132]

Back to the Three Relationships

Having identified the *concession principle* as a KEY to rightly interpreting the three *parallel* relationships of Ephesians 5 and Colossians 3, it will be valuable to look now at each relationship in more detail. In the first century, in all three relationships, the first party was considered the property of the other: wives were owned by their husbands[133] even as children were owned by their fathers,[134] and slaves by their masters. In all three, the first party was the powerless oppressed and the second was the powerful oppressor. In each of the three parallel relationships the *powerless party* is commanded to submit to and/or to obey the *party possessing power*. Significantly, as with husbands,

---

[132] Stackhouse, *Partners in Christ,* 71, 72.

[133] Contra God's ideal for marriage portrayed in the mutual ownership expressed in the Song of Solomon. See 8:2, "My lover is mine and I am his," and 6:3, "I am my lover's and my lover is mine."

[134] The father's ownership and absolute authority over his children under the Old Testament law is illustrated in Genesis 19:8 where Lot had the power to offer his virgin daughters to a violent gang of men to be gang raped, and in Exodus 21:7–11 where an Israelite father had the authority to sell his daughter into slavery. Because we are so far distanced from that degree of abusive patriarchy, this is (and should be) shocking to us. In the latter we could easily miss that the controlling regulations Moses added were radically protective of such a daughter compared to the practices of the Canaanite nations around them. While this does not resolve all the obvious problems these texts afford to contemporary Bible students, it certainly casts light on Ephesians 6:1–4 and the oppressive power possessed by fathers.

the other two power-holders, fathers and masters, are NOT told to exercise authority over the powerless, but to act in ways that are radically different than was the norm for their roles in that culture. They are to act in ways which would totally disable authoritarianism and transform the relational dynamics infusing both parties with mutual respect, thoughtfulness, and deference.

Note in the chart below what each party is called on to do in Ephesians 5 and 6:

THE PARTIES	THE POWERLESS	THE POWERFUL
Wives/ Husbands	Submit, respect, love	Love, give themselves up for, do not be harsh, be considerate, treat with respect
Children/ Fathers	Obey, honor	Do not exasperate, do not embitter, bring them up[135]
Slaves/Masters	Obey, respect, try to please, not talk back to, not steal from	Treat them in the same way, do not threaten, provide what is right and fair

Are those in positions of power simply being told to be better husbands, fathers, and masters while those in powerless positions are ordered to meekly submit to their often-oppressive authority? No! To avoid chaos and division and to not hinder the advance of the Gospel, the powerless were to temporarily maintain behaviors that would be acceptable in that abusive culture. At the same time, an overriding mandate for mutual submission anticipated how relationships must come to be redefined as Jesus' now-and-coming kingdom took hold in believers and churches. Apart from the command for mutual submission, the instructions to the *powerless* paralleled what that abusive culture expected, while the instructions to the *powerful* were absolutely NOT what the culture expected or embraced. "Paul places the responsibility and obligation for sociological transformation in the Christian community upon those who have power, while he reverses the culture's negative evaluation of those without power."[136] The commands for husbands, fathers, and masters

---

[135] While not at all a literal translation, the Message captures the spirit of Ephesians 6:4: "Fathers, don't exasperate your children by coming down hard on them. Take them by the hand and lead them in the way of the Master."

[136] Westfall, *Paul and Gender,* 102.

were nothing less than revolutionary—harbingers of the coming new age that Jesus inaugurated and with which He will one day fill the earth.

Now let's consider each of the three parallel relationships more specifically against the backdrop of the concession principle.

Wives and Husbands

How then does Paul envision and command wives and husbands to relate to each other in the concession passages? As noted, the answer is not as simplistic as the traditional complementarian understanding assumes. For example, not just the relationship between wives and husbands, but all three parallel relationships are introduced under guidance of the heading of Paul's stunning command for everyone to submit to each other: *"Submit to one another out of reverence for Christ"* (Eph. 5:21).

A simple observation about the placement of this command is actually quite profound: *Ephesians 5:21 comes before Ephesians 5:22*. Before wives are commanded to submit to their own husbands, both are commanded to submit to the other. In other words, husbands are commanded to submit to their wives before wives are singled out to submit to their husbands. Likewise, fathers must practice submission with their children and masters with their slaves before the weaker parties are directed to obey them. In the Kingdom of God, the values and expectations that characterize relationships in the kingdoms of this world are turned upside-down. Fallen-world hierarchies are transformed by New Creation realities in which "There is neither Jew nor Greek, slave nor free, male nor female, for you are all one in Christ Jesus" (Gal. 3:28).

Nevertheless, it is unquestionable that the text calls on wives to "submit to your husbands as to the Lord" (Eph. 5:22). But, as will be shown, this command does not in and of itself constitute an innate, inherent, or indefinite justification for the unilateral submission of wives to their husbands. It is important that in all three relationships, the commands to submit or to obey are not followed up by a mandate for the power-possessing parties to impose or force the authority/submission dynamic on the disenfranchised parties. In other words, the submission is a *voluntary response to the Apostle's directive*, not a forced response by the husband's demands. Nor does the command for wives assume or reflect either creation-based or gender-based hierarchy. Had Paul intended those, the command for mutual submission ("submit to one another") in Ephesians 5:21 would make no sense.

Many complementarians would assert that a wife's stated responsibility to "submit" to her own husband is because he is her "head" (Eph. 5:22, 23), which, they suggest, implies the husband's *authority* over his wife. Notably *only two verses in the entire Bible* refer to the male or husband as "head" (1 Cor. 11:3 and Eph. 5:23) and in those two passages there is not even a whisper of a command for men or husbands to assume the position of leader or to impose ruling authority on women or wives. In fact, in the later passage, the husband-head is required to also submit to his wife. What the Ephesians 5 passage *does* teach for husbands (as do Col. 3 and 1 Pt. 3) is their responsibility to love, sacrifice themselves for, care for, be considerate of, treat with respect, not be harsh with, and to become one flesh with their wives. There is not one directive or even the slightest hint that husbands should take charge, lead, boss, command, rule, direct, manage, oversee, call the shots, be where the buck stops, act as CEO, exert authority over their wives, or that they should assert *any* kind of hierarchical position over their wives.

Further, it is very important to recognize that the assumption that *"head"* implies *authority over* is strongly challenged by many Bible scholars. They assert that a far preferable understanding of the meaning and significance of the concept of "head" in many Scripture passages and specifically in 1 Corinthians 11 and Ephesians 5 is *source* rather than *boss*. This will be discussed in greater detail in the next chapter. When Ephesians 5:23 calls Christ the "Head" of the church, it immediately describes what kind of Head He is: "Christ is the head of the church, his body, of which he is the Savior." He is the **Savior-Head** of the church, that is, He is the *Source* of her salvation.

What is indisputable in this text is that the husband is never told to make his wife submit to him, nor is he directed to take any action to assume or impose a leadership role. A wife is to submit to her husband because he is her head [source], but he is never commanded to do anything to assert a role of leadership over her or to force her submission. On the contrary, every behavior commanded for the husband is identical with those Christian virtues that the New Testament requires of *all believers* toward each other regardless of gender or role: love, self-sacrifice, generosity, kindness, and respect. Further, the husband is to become "one" with his wife (Eph. 5:28–30; Gen. 2:24) and to respond to her as his partner and fellow "heir" (1 Pt. 3:7).

In Ephesians 5:21–33, rather than being commanded to assume or demand authority over their wives, husbands are commanded to submit to them (Eph. 5:21), to sacrificially love and honor them as Jesus did His Bride (Eph. 5:25–27), and to love them as their own body (Eph. 5:28–33). These radical, counter-cultural, relational transformations would have been reprehensible to the average first century non-believing husband. For that matter, new or immature Christians would likely also have struggled with them. Hence the *concession principle* was necessary. Had Paul encouraged wives to demand their newly reaffirmed rights (Gal. 3:28), chaos, conflict, and division would doubtless have ensued. Rather than responding with loving submission as Ephesians 5:21 mandated, many husbands (probably both unbelievers and immature believers) would have retaliated with abuse, violence, or divorce. Rather than promoting "family values," Christianity would have been viewed as a marriage-wrecking, destabilizing, and destructive societal influence. The behavior of *rebellious* wives would turn people away from Jesus and the Gospel.

Understanding this cultural backdrop to the New Testament letters, it is readily understandable that the apostles would encourage the adoption of temporary concessions to be practiced in that oppressive culture to promote peace and to "make the teaching about God our Savior attractive" (Titus 2:10).

Clearly, promoting the Gospel was a motivation behind the Apostle Peter's instructions for wives. He was concerned as to how their unbelieving husbands could be "won over without words" by the beauty and winsomeness of their submissive actions and attitudes:

> Wives, in the same way be submissive to your husbands so that, if any of them do not believe the word, they may be won over without words by the behavior of their wives, when they see the purity and reverence of your lives. Your beauty should not come from outward adornment, such as braided hair and the wearing of gold jewelry and fine clothes. Instead, it should be that of your inner self, the unfading beauty of a gentle and quiet spirit, which is of great worth in God's sight. For this is the way the holy women of

the past who put their hope in God used to make themselves beautiful. They were submissive to their own husbands, like Sarah, who obeyed Abraham and called him her master. You are her daughters if you do what is right and do not give way to fear (1 Pt. 3:1–6).

In an oppressive culture or marriage, submission was an evangelistic strategy—not only for wives as stated in 1 Peter 3:1, 2, but also for slaves as affirmed in Titus 2:9, 10 ("Teach slaves to be subject to their masters in everything, to try to please them, not to talk back to them, and not to steal from them, but to show that they can be fully trusted, so that in every way they will make the teaching about God our Savior attractive").

These concessions could be an appropriate evangelistic strategy today in a strict Islamic or other strongly patriarchal culture. A woman who is a new believer might not survive asserting her equality let alone gain an opportunity to win her husband to her newfound faith in Christ. Rather, her potential success in witnessing to her Muslim husband would be enhanced by the concession strategy of 1 Peter 3:1–6.

Paul's personal adoption of the concession principle in his own lifestyle and teaching to advance the Gospel appears throughout his letters. For example, in 1 Corinthians 7–10 he emphasizes all of the "rights" he willingly surrenders if by so doing it will promote the Gospel and win more people to Christ. He is willing to forgo marriage (7:1–8, 28–35; 9:5), give up certain foods (8:1–18; 10:23–33), forfeit compensation for ministry (9:3–15), surrender his freedom from servanthood and Jewish/law requirements (9:19, 20) as well as from Gentile "not-under-lawness" (9:21), and not assume the principles and privileges of being strong in knowledge (8:1 with 9:22).

In the following statements, sense the depth of Paul's passion and willingness to make personal concessions for the sake of the Gospel in order to win as many people to Christ as possible:

> But we did not use this right. On the contrary, we put up
> with anything rather than hinder the gospel of Christ . . .
> Though I am free and belong to no man, I make myself a
> slave to everyone, to win as many as possible. To the Jews I

became like a Jew, to win the Jews. To those under the law I became like one under the law (though I myself am not under the law), so as to win those under the law. To those not having the law I became like one not having the law (though I am not free from God's law but am under Christ's law), so as to win those not having the law. To the weak I became weak, to win the weak. I have become all things to all men so that by all possible means I might save some. I do all this for the sake of the gospel, that I may share in its blessings . . . So whether you eat or drink or whatever you do, do it all for the glory of God. Do not cause anyone to stumble, whether Jews, Greeks or the church of God—even as I try to please everybody in every way. For I am not seeking my own good but the good of many, so that they may be saved (1 Cor. 9:12, 19–23; 10:31–33).

Remember that the pervasiveness of patriarchy is the reason gender role accommodations were necessary to not hinder the Gospel. Throughout the Roman Empire, the position and roles of women varied from place to place but the persistent default expectation in marriage was for patriarchal dominance. The Greco-Roman ideal continued to be for traditional female stereotypes.

This long-standing expectation was illustrated in the Old Testament Book of Esther when Vashti, King Xerxes' queen, defied his authority, thus threatening the patriarchy that was viewed (at least by men who possessed the power) as a foundational value in that culture. This called for drastic measures to ensure the perpetuation of male domination:

"According to law, what must be done to Queen Vashti?" he asked. "She has not obeyed the command of King Xerxes that the eunuchs have taken to her." Then Memucan replied in the presence of the king and the nobles, "Queen Vashti has done wrong, not only against the king but also against all the nobles and the peoples of all the provinces of King Xerxes. For the queen's conduct will become known to all the women, and so they will despise their husbands and say,

'King Xerxes commanded Queen Vashti to be brought before him, but she would not come.' This very day the Persian and Median women of the nobility who have heard about the queen's conduct will respond to all the king's nobles in the same way. There will be no end of disrespect and discord. Therefore, if it pleases the king, let him issue a royal decree and let it be written in the laws of Persia and Media, which cannot be repealed, that Vashti is never again to enter the presence of King Xerxes. Also let the king give her royal position to someone else who is better than she. Then when the king's edict is proclaimed throughout all his vast realm, all the women will respect their husbands, from the least to the greatest" (Esther 1:15–20).

This should not be surprising as patriarchy has been a dominant cultural value since the curse of sin first imposed man's rule over women (Gen. 3:16). While never God's intent, patriarchy has been globally pervasive throughout history since the fall. Thus, until very recently, virtually no society, other than the church, has experienced anything other than male domination, making anything else difficult even to imagine let alone to practice.

Solomon's romantic and erotic love song/poem appears to give a rare Old Testament glimpse of the beautiful potential of love and mutuality in marriage. For example, the King's bride, a commoner, twice makes a stunning claim of mutual ownership in their relationship: "My lover is mine and I am his . . . I am my lover's and my lover is mine" (Song 2:16; 6:3). These statements are breathtaking in a culture where wives were the *property* of their husbands, having *no personal rights*—even more so the wives of a King. But in the Song of Solomon, we see a preview of the new creation value of mutuality in marriage, similarly stated by Paul in 1 Corinthians 7:4: "The wife's body does not belong to her alone but also to her husband. In the same way, the husband's body does not belong to him alone but also to his wife."

The traditional ideal for marriage and the submissive role of women rose in significance in the Roman Empire in the event that a religious cult was under scrutiny. "When a cult was considered dangerous, the activities of women and the authority of their husbands came under public scrutiny, and what might be acceptable behavior in their first century context could be represented as dishonorable deviations from the rhetoric of the Greco-Roman ideal. In this way, the feminine and masculine Greek stereotypes and Roman ideals were used as primary weapons to attempt to control, discredit, or disable a dangerous cult or sect."[137] No wonder Paul and Peter directed wives to submit to their husbands as a temporary concession for the sake of peace and the promotion of the Gospel. The fledgling Jesus movement was under cynical scrutiny by the often intolerant and oppressive government, constantly measured against the hierarchical norms of the Greco-Roman culture.

It must be noted again that even in a culture where temporary concessions to fallen humanity were appropriate, believing husbands, fathers, and masters were commanded to replace oppression with mutual submission, exploitation with love, cruelty with kindness, and repression with respect, thus modeling the values of the *new humanity* inaugurated by Jesus' death, resurrection, and ascension. Among Christians, post-fall values should be strategically phased out as new creation values are adopted to display the *"first fruits"* and *"signs"* of the coming Kingdom of God on earth. This is true in all three relationships, but especially striking in the third, slaves and masters. Later in this chapter, it will be demonstrated that Paul's letter to Philemon anticipated the day when all Christian masters recognized the need to free their slaves and welcome them as equals in God's family.

Do these Gender Roles in Marriage Also Apply in Church?

Although no Scripture reference suggests a direct correlation between gender roles in marriage and gender roles in the church, the two are frequently treated as associated or parallel either from a complementarian or egalitarian perspective. At the same time, some interpreters deal with them as unrelated and advocate gender hierarchy in marriage but not the church. Others, such as relatively strict complementarians regarding church roles, sometimes function more like egalitarians in their marital relationships than in the church.

Even if one assumed that the gender roles in marriage laid out in Ephesians

---

[137] Ibid., 17.

5 should be applied to gender roles in the church, this would not translate into across the board gender-based restrictions for ministry or leadership today, given the *concession principle* and the consequent realization that Ephesians 5 kind of submission by wives was a *temporary* accommodation to a fallen and abusive culture. Paul did not teach that marital gender roles were based on any innate difference in men and women, nor did he prescribe a permanent continuation of the temporary concessions he called for in Ephesians 5. I believe that God's intent for absolute gender equality and lack of any gender-based hierarchy or restrictions should ideally be applied today in both marriage and church.

After Jesus' ascension, while awaiting the full realization of the new creation, Christians today live in the in-between time when the values of old and new creation are often in juxtaposition and conflict. Even as the whole creation "groans" under the curse while awaiting the future "liberation" from sin's curse, so all of society's oppressed "groan" while awaiting the coming "glorious freedom of the children of God" (Rom. 8:19–21). Oppressed people everywhere, including women in complementarian churches, understand the groaning produced by the "bondage" of the curse while they wait for the "freedom" of God's new world. Thus, an important backdrop to the New Testament letters is the need for believers to learn how to practice new creation values while still living in the broken-by-sin old creation. Jesus' followers are to model new creation values whenever possible in the home, church, and society (Gal. 3:28; Eph. 5:21; and 1 Cor. 7, a chapter containing many references to mutuality in marital gender roles[138]).

However, in oppressive cultures and marriages, believers may still need to make <u>temporary concessions</u> regarding gender roles to promote peace, order, and positive Gospel witness (1 Cor. 14:33a, 40; Rom. 14:19) and in order to not to bring reproach on the Gospel (1 Tim. 6:1; Titus 2:5). Westfall writes "Paul did not support traditional Greco-Roman gender roles for the church, even though he maintained the appearance of traditional gender relationships

---

[138] For example, 1 Corinthians 7:4 ESV where Paul says, "For the wife does not have authority over her own body, but the husband does. Likewise the husband does not have authority over his own body, but the wife does." This is a <u>stunning egalitarian statement</u> in which husbands and wives have identical authority over each other in regard to sexual intimacy.

in order to protect the church's reputation and enable its outreach, much like the practice of Christian missionaries in Islamic cultures."[139]

In summary, consider these very practical questions and answers:

QUESTION	ANSWER
Does this mean that Christian wives do not need to submit to their husbands?	No. Ephesians 5:21 teaches mutual submission. All Christian wives are commanded to submit to their husbands even as all Christian husbands are commanded to submit to their wives. Also, some wives may need to give unilateral submission to a patriarchy-oriented husband in order to maintain peace and Gospel witness, at least until he becomes an obedient follower of Christ, repents of his sin-based patriarchy, and commits to submitting to her and loving her as Christ loves the church.
So, what would an ideal Christian marriage look like if mutual submission were practiced as Ephesians 5:21 commands and it was unnecessary to practice temporary accommodations to sinful patriarchy?	It would look a great deal like Adam and Eve's perfect relationship in the Garden of Eden prior to sin and the curse. The love, respect, and deference by both would create beautiful unity, harmony, joy, and partnership with no need or desire for one to manipulate, exploit, control, or dominate the other. They could enjoy the uninhibited intimacy described in Genesis 2:25 that resulted from total openness and acceptance, having nothing between them—no clothes, cover up, secrets, hiding, holding back, pride, fear, embarrassment, shame, jealousy, selfish motivations, competition, hierarchy, or rank.

---

139 Westfall, *Paul and Gender*, 5.

140 "The man and his wife were both naked, and they felt no shame."

Imagine the personal satisfaction and fulfillment for a husband and wife in such a marriage. Imagine how such a marriage would make the Gospel attractive to non-Christian observers. Imagine the beautiful picture of Christ and the church such a marriage would make. Imagine what an anticipation-generating *sign* it would be pointing to Jesus' coming Kingdom. Oh, that Jesus' church would be filled with couples whose unselfish love for each other would produce such marriages to the glory of God.

Rather than taking the other two parallel relationships in the order in which Paul presents them, we will first look at the slave/master relationship and then the parent and father/child relationship.

Slaves and Masters

As mentioned earlier, my study of the three relationships in Ephesians 5 and 6 forced me to ask the question, "What does slavery have to do with marriage?" The only passages in Scripture in which women are commanded to submit to or to obey their husbands include instructions to slaves in the immediate context. It was a Eureka moment in my gender-roles studies because it forced me to face my shallow comprehension of and inaccurate teaching about a very familiar text. Recognizing that the *concession principle* was central to properly understanding and applying these verses about three *parallel* relationships turned the lights on for me. It allowed me to interpret and apply the text about the three relationships in a consistent and cohesive way, not only in Ephesians 5 and 6, but in the other similar passages in the New Testament letters.

The *concession principle* is easy to recognize regarding the institution of slavery. In the secular culture the often-brutal institution of slavery was deeply entrenched. Slavery was also practiced in Israel although the law of Moses strictly regulated it in ways that, though offensive and cruel sounding to our twenty-first century Western values, were, in biblical times, a radical shift toward compassion in a culture where savage oppression was often taken for granted.

Not all slaves were treated horribly in ancient Rome, and over time reforms slowly but inconsistently emerged—probably because of the influence of Stoicism and Christianity, both of which taught that all people were equal. Nevertheless, overall, the institution of slavery was pervasive and horrendously inhumane.

> Slaves were considered property under Roman law and had no legal personhood. Unlike Roman citizens, they could be subjected to corporal punishment, sexual exploitation (prostitutes were often slaves), torture, and summary execution. The testimony of a slave could not be accepted in a court of law unless the slave was tortured—a practice based on the belief that slaves in a position to be privy to their masters' affairs would be too virtuously loyal to reveal damaging evidence unless coerced . . . Estimates for the prevalence of slavery in the Roman Empire vary. Estimates of the percentage of the population of Italy who were slaves range from 30 to 40 percent in the 1st century BC, upwards of two to three million slaves in Italy by the end of the 1st century BCE, about 35% to 40% of Italy's population. For the Empire as a whole, the slave population has been estimated at just under five million, representing 10-15% of the total population of 50-60 million+ inhabitants.[141]

To a lesser degree, the institution of slavery continued to be practiced within Judaism in New Testament times.

Multiple references in the New Testament affirm that slavery was practiced by some Christians in the first century. Imagine the chaos that would ensue if Jesus' Apostles commanded all Christian masters to immediately free their slaves and preached to slaves the potentially incendiary message that in Christ they were equal and should be released. Most would view this as financially and socially disastrous. No wonder the New Testament promoted a transition plan. Otherwise Christianity might have been viewed as responsible for promoting devastating societal chaos and undermining long-accepted cultural norms and institutions. If slaves had begun to assert their equality, demand their freedom, or launch massive rebellions, fingers would have pointed at Christianity and the church as the instigators, and the

---

[141] "Slavery in Ancient Rome," Wikipedia, https://en.wikipedia.org/wiki/Slavery_in_ancient_Rome

advance of the Gospel could have been severely hindered if not eradicated. In that time, individuals and religious sects were measured against the standard of the pagan culture's traditional values.

Imagine if the abolition of slavery were a primary emphasis in the proclamation of the Gospel. How many pagan slave owners would be attracted to this new faith that would cause an upheaval to their economic and social stability?

If we think that a full-out attack on slavery in the first century would have gone well, think of the resistance to the abolition of slavery in the supposedly *enlightened* and freedom-loving United States (including many Christians), whose Declaration of Independence stated: "We hold these truths to be self-evident, that all men are created equal, that they are endowed by their Creator with certain unalienable Rights, that among these are Life, Liberty and the Pursuit of Happiness." Despite these lofty words in our founding document, remember the war that resulted from efforts to end slavery—a war that divided the nation, devastated the Southern economy, threatened to destroy the union, pitted brothers against brothers, and resulted in the death of approximately 625,000 soldiers.[142] The number of wives, children, parents, and siblings affected by that many deaths was staggering including negative economic and social results for over 150 years. Long after the Emancipation Proclamation, the systemic racism that has affected generations up to the present speaks to the lingering results of the institution of slavery in our own country. Horrific Jim Crow laws enforcing segregation and negatively impacting education, social interaction, commerce, transportation, housing, economic progress, etc., for African Americans in the United States were perpetuated into the 1950s. The practice of "redlining"[143] and other kinds of systemic racism continue to negatively impact economic status and potential, school funding and quality, etc. Even today overt and latent racism continue to divide and inflame our culture[144] and arguably had significant influence on

---

[142] Translated into a percentage of the current population of the U.S.A. this would represent about 6 million deaths.

[143] Redlining was the systemic denial of mortgages and other services, usually based on race, which produced segregated communities and neighborhoods and negatively impacted home ownership and real estate values for decades with negative economic impact continuing for generations into the present.

[144] Sadly, this evaluation includes many professing Christians as well.

the last two presidential elections in the United States. Just because a change is the right thing to do doesn't eliminate potential far-reaching repercussions resulting from its implementation, nor does it eradicate all vestiges of the evil. The bitter wages of sinful actions and institutionalized evil are often paid out for generations far beyond the cessation of the unrighteousness policies and actions.

Therefore, the abolition of slavery, as urgently as it was needed in New Testament times, called for a more nuanced and strategic approach than simply demanding that all believers immediately overturn the institution. Slavery, rather than the Good News about Jesus, would have become the lens through which everyone viewed the new religion spreading across the Empire. It would have been a lightning rod inviting the wrath of the Empire (and a large percentage of its populace) to rain down on the already persecuted church.

Rather, Paul called for adherence to temporary concessions for submission by Christian slaves at the same time that he demanded the compassionate, respectful treatment of those slaves by their Christian masters (Eph. 6:9; Col. 4:1). This was a radical departure from the frequently inhumane cultural norm. Even more radical was the overarching precedent command in Ephesians 5:21 that required Christian slave owners to "submit" to their slaves. Nevertheless, for the promotion of peace and the advance of the Gospel,[145] slaves who were followers of Jesus were also to submit to their masters. This did not free Christian slave owners to justify and perpetuate the evils of slavery. Rather, believers who were slave owners, however more or less oppressive, were all to treat their slaves with kindness and respect, not threatening them, but treating them in the same way they hoped that their Master/God would treat them (Eph. 6:9). Ultimately, Christian masters were challenged to free their slaves as Paul wrote in his letter to Philemon.

The *concession principle* permeates Paul's instructions throughout 1 Corinthians 7. Near the beginning of the chapter Paul states that his counsel to the Corinthian believers is based on "concession" rather than "command" (7:6). He applies the concession principle to slavery and to other relationships and life-circumstances regarding which one situation would most likely be perceived as desirable and advantageous over the other. These

---

[145] "All who are under the yoke of slavery should consider their masters worthy of full respect, so that God's name and our teaching may not be slandered" (1 Tim. 6:1).

include: marriage versus singleness, sexual fulfillment versus abstinence, remaining married versus divorcing, circumcision versus uncircumcision, freedom versus slavery, marital fulfillment versus virginity, happiness versus mourning, buying power versus loss of possessions, ownership versus borrowing, and the availability of resources versus the inevitability of losing them.

In each of these, Paul emphasizes that the apparently preferable and desirable circumstance should sometimes be *voluntarily conceded* based on one or more of a dozen guiding principles he enunciates in the chapter:

(1) God desires all Christians to value living peacefully (7:15);

(2) acceptance of God's sovereign assignment and calling can mitigate circumstances perceived to be adverse (7:17);

(3) those who lack self-control should sometimes forgo (concede) options that would otherwise be advantageous (7:2, 5, 9, 37);

(4) obedience to God is more important than freedom from difficult circumstances (7:19);

(5) stability is often a value higher than disruption that may result from the selfish or premature pursuit and achievement of a personal preference (7:17, 20, 24, 26);

(6) one's relationship and devotion to God is more important than any human relationship or earthly circumstance (7:22–24, 32–35);

(7) freedom of choice may include more than one valid and good option even though they may not appear to be equally advantageous (7:21, 25, 28, 35–39);

(8) choosing a more difficult and less satisfying option may produce positive evangelistic benefits (7:14, 16) and may be assuaged by consequent spiritual gains (7:22, 23);

(9) it is possible for a believer to be content and not "troubled" despite ongoing adverse circumstances, (7:21);

(10) what is broadly perceived to be the better and preferable status sometimes produces significant hardship (7:28);

(11) inherently stressful circumstances sometimes minimize the advantages of what would otherwise be assumed to be the best opportunity (7:26); and

(12) eschatological perspective about the eternal compared to the temporal and life's transitoriness minimize the advantages of having preferable circumstances (7:29–31).

As noted, Paul specifically applies this counter-intuitive *concession principle* to **slavery** (7:20–24). He reveals that for a Christian, the disadvantages of slavery are ameliorated by their status as "the Lord's freeman ... bought with a price." He states:

> Each one should remain in the situation which he was in when God called him. Were you a slave when you were called? Don't let it trouble you—although if you can gain your freedom, do so. For he who was a slave when he was called by the Lord is the Lord's freedman; similarly, he who was a free man when he was called is Christ's slave. You were bought at a price; do not become slaves of men. Brothers, each man, as responsible to God, should remain in the situation God called him to (1 Cor. 7:20-24).

Thus, it is evident that the underlying theme of 1 Corinthians 7 is that Jesus' followers, in order to pursue higher kingdom values, are sometimes called on to concede and sacrifice what would normally be considered to be their right and to be personally desirable or advantageous. This is the same principle that plays out in the *concession passages* regarding wives and husbands, children and fathers, and slaves and masters.

Over time, new creation values abolishing the oppressive institution of slavery should and would be adopted by believers. The beginning of this strategic transition may be seen in Paul's contrasting commands to groups of slave-owning Christians in the churches at Ephesus (Eph. 6:5–9) and Colosse (Col. 4:1) compared to his specific appeal to Philemon, an individual slave owner who was part of the church in Colosse (Philem. 15–21). Ephesians, Philippians, Colossians, and Philemon were written by Paul simultaneously (about 60 A.D.) from a Roman prison and hand-delivered to the three churches and to Philemon by Epaphras and Onesimus.[146]

---

[146] Colossians 4:16 seems to indicate another Pauline letter was delivered at the same time to the church in Laodicea. The letter was not preserved so is assumed to have not

Paul commanded the groups of slave-owning church members to treat their slaves well, whereas He strongly pressured Philemon to set his slave Onesimus free. Paul's close personal relationship with Philemon emboldened him to abandon the concession principle and to call on his friend to display New Creation values immediately rather than merely being a nicer slave owner.

This seems evident when one compares Paul's general, accommodating instructions for masters in Ephesians 6:5–9 and Colossians 3:22–4:1 with his specific and pointed directions to slave owner Philemon regarding Onesimus, his recently converted, runaway-but-now-returning slave (Philem. 8–21). In Ephesians 6:5–9 and Colossians 4:1 Paul called on masters to treat their slaves as they would want God to treat them but fell short of specifically requiring them to set their slaves free. However, in Philemon 8–21, consider Paul's no-holds-barred pressure for Philemon to treat Onesimus as his brother and no longer as his slave.

Paul's letter to Philemon was not a private communication he could read in the confidentiality of his home and then determine his response apart from any scrutiny or accountability from others, or apart from how his reaction might set an example for the other slave owners in the Colossian church. No! The letter was written "To Philemon our dear friend and fellow worker, to Apphia our sister, to Archippus our fellow soldier and to the church that meets in your home" (Philem. 1, 2, emphasis added).

This letter was delivered to the church in Colosse at the same time as the letter we now know as the biblical book of Colossians. It would be reasonable to assume that the larger letter to the church was read aloud to the congregation first, followed, likely in the same gathering, by the reading of the shorter letter to Philemon. Imagine the reaction of Christian slaves and masters (including Onesimus and Philemon) sitting in the congregation as they first listened to the reading of Colossians 3:22–4:1 (the concession passage) and then to Paul's very specific and powerful instructions and request calling for Philemon to free Onesimus. Was there an audible gasp at such an outrageous idea that a slave should be set free and elevated from bondage to brotherhood? This dynamic not only affirms the temporary nature of the concessions made

---

been inspired by the Holy Spirit and intended to be included with those books and letters which make up the New Testament Scriptures.

due to the slavery-permeated culture, but also the reality of the new creation values that believers should adopt rapidly.

Scot McKnight observes the stunning implications then and now:

> My contentions today are that you can't read this letter, or you can't sit in Philemon's home and hear this letter being read and not . . .
>
> **See Philemon put in the dock.** As I read this letter over and over I kept (and still keep) thinking, 'Man, Paul put this man in a corner in front of everyone.' He did. Paul had to.
>
> **Think that those with privilege and power are called to change the culture.** Paul didn't ask Onesimus to go back and challenge Philemon. Nor did he empower him to go back and start a revolution. Paul went to the powerful with a challenge: *power is in your hands to change the household and I'm challenging you to embody the challenge with Onesimus.* We hear a lot about white privilege today, and I'd expand that to economic privilege and power privilege. To the expanded group of privilege Paul says, 'It starts with you. Now.'
>
> **Know that Onesimus' life is dependent on what a Christian man chooses to do.** In my work on Philemon I often pondered this: 'Poor Onesimus, poor in two ways—economically and in power—is totally dependent on the decision of Philemon.' Let us not forget that those in power are sometimes, and more often than even that, *the only ones* who can change the culture. Onesimus the slave was dependent in this letter-culture of Paul and Philemon on the decision of Philemon. Feel for Onesimus. Feel for every slave in that household. Feel for every slave in Colosse.
>
> **Realize that leaders like Paul have a call to establish a kingdom culture in the church.** Let's get behind Philemon, the slave owner. It is Paul, a man who is not from Colosse

and has never been there. Paul, however, was a gospeler in the Roman empire. Paul was an apostle. Paul's co-worker Epaphras started that church in Colosse. Paul *saw his call come to fruition in the challenge of this little letter*: welcome the man back, he said. Even more, turn him into a brother in the household. That's kingdom culture taking root in embodied form in Colosse.[147]

Because Colossians and Philemon were most probably read aloud in the Colossian church gathering, all eyes would have been on Philemon. When he followed Paul's instructions and set Onesimus free, the pressure of his example would be on every Christian slave owner in the church. It could not be more apparent to them that Paul intended Philemon to set the stage for the subsequent release of all the slaves in the Colossian church.

An additional step away from concession toward elimination of slavery may be seen about four years later (c. 64 A.D.) in Paul's strong assertion regarding slave traders in 1 Timothy 1:9–11. There Paul condemns those who bought and sold slaves in company with the most despicable sinners such as parent-killers, murders, adulterers, homosexual pedophiles,[148] etc. A final New Testament condemnation of slavery is the announced judgement of Babylon in Revelation 18:10-13. Among the sins which will bring about Babylon's doom is slave-trading ("cargoes of . . . bodies and souls of men").

It would be important to not minimize the horrors of first century slavery by the Ephesians 5, 6 comparison with a marriage or family in which the husband and/or father was abusive—as if the three parallel relationships were equally oppressive, exploitive, and cruel. For example, if given the choice

---

[147] Scott McKnight, "You Can't Read Philemon and Not . . ." (Patheos/Jesus' Creed, 11/27/2017): http://www.patheos.com/blogs/jesuscreed/2017/11/27/can-read-philemon-not/?utm_medium=email&utm_source=BRSS&utm_campaign=Evangelical&utm_content=245

[148] The Greek word Paul used was not a general reference to homosexuality, but to homosexual *prostitution* and/or to the horrifically common practice of *pedophilia* or *pederasty*. Swanson, J. (1997). Dictionary of Biblical Languages with Semantic Domains: Greek New Testament (electronic ed.). (Oak Harbor, 1997), Logos Research Systems, Inc. "ἀρσενοκοίτης (arsenokoitēs), . . . **male homosexual**, one who takes the active male role in homosexual intercourse (1Co 6:9), specifically interpreted as male homosexual pedophilia.

between the first century status of a wife and the status of a slave, the selection would not be difficult. Nevertheless, the oppressive slave/master relationship in Ephesians 5, 6 and Colossians 3, 4 is clearly presented as parallel to the patriarchal wife/husband and domineering child/father relationships in those passages.

All three relationships as commonly enacted in the first century robbed fellow humans made in God's image of their freedom, self-determination, and of the full expression of their God-given abilities, inclinations, interests, and dreams. Though they were probably significantly different in degree, the three culturally defined institutions—slavery, family, and marriage—were not different in kind. Neither wives, nor many adult children, nor slaves were free to pursue God's calling or the employment of their gifts unless their husband, father, or master allowed it. Freedom for self-determination was disallowed for all. Their day-to-day agendas and many of their life choices were governed by another who had ultimate authority over them. The fact that wives and children typically had more freedoms and less abuse than many slaves doesn't change the nature of the relationships. In all three relationships,[149] Paul called for temporary concessions that ultimately give way to the restoration of creation values in which hierarchy had no place. At the same time, he prioritized his command for the new creation value of mutual submission in all three relationships (Eph. 5:21), thereby prohibiting all Christian husbands, fathers, and slave masters, from perpetuating the cultural norm of selfish and abusive male domination.

Incidentally, perhaps recognizing the implications of three parallel relationships in Ephesians 5, 6, some complementarians argue that first century slavery in the Roman Empire was not always as cruel and totalitarian as in some other times and places. While this may be true in some situations, to think this somehow ameliorated the evil and oppression of the institution of slavery is both ignorant and insensitive. The fact that some slaves were given more freedoms and opportunities than others and in rare situations a few slaves had a choice whether or not to continue in slavery, doesn't mean that any modern complementarian would volunteer to enter a similar relationship as a slave. No rational free person would surrender themselves

---

[149] The child/father relationship, while typically similar in the totality of the father's control and lack of loving nurturing and too often in the existence of abuse and exploitation, was nevertheless different in other ways. These will be discussed below.

to the ownership and authority of a master no matter how kind or permissive they might be. In the best slavery situation, it was still slavery. It was an institution in which a human of equal worth, made in the image of God,[150] enjoyed only those choices and benefits allowed by their master. Their owner maintained the absolute right of control and the unquestioned ability to significantly or completely limit that opportunities or freedoms might be permitted until they arbitrarily changed their mind. A nice slave owner still controlled and firmly held onto the loaf of bread even if they sprinkled a few more crumbs to their slaves than others did.

Today, virtually all Bible students, teachers, and pastors would vehemently assert that Ephesians 6:5–9 should not be interpreted as tacit or overt approval of slavery then or now. Yet, complementarians argue with equal vehemence that Ephesians 5:22–33 should be understood as a tacit approval of patriarchy. This hypocritical disconnect is why the majority of pastors and Bible teachers ignore what the text actually asserts for slaves and masters and instead apply these verses as teaching about contemporary employee-employer relationships—as if Paul were addressing modern labor-management issues. Interestingly, while all Christians would agree that slavery is an unmitigated evil, few can point to any text-based justification for this hermeneutical shift to employees/employers that substitutes concepts alien to the author's original intent or to the recipient's cultural setting. Nor can they point to anything in the text which justifies condemning slavery while continuing patriarchy in marriage.

It is important, in our self-perceived enlightened humanitarianism, that we not forget that "in America this consensus is officially less than 150 years old, and the racism that legitimized slavery has not been eradicated to this day."[151] Because of our contemporary understanding of all people being created in God's image, of Jesus' liberating example and teachings, and of prejudice-busting New Covenant values, virtually no one today would use the concession passages to endorse the perpetuation of slavery, yet many use them to endorse the perpetuation of patriarchy. Arguably, regarding Ephesians 5:21–6:9 and Colossians 3:18–4:1, we should be as shocked and

---

[150] Colossians 3:10, 11 asserts that in the "image" of the "Creator . . . there is no slave or free."

[151] Stackhouse, *Partners in Christ,* 73.

offended by patriarchal husband/wife relationships and by abusive father/ child relationships as we are by the evils of slavery.

Remember that prior to the Emancipation Proclamation, those who enjoyed the benefits of owning slaves were the last to let go of that evil institution, defending it with scores of Bible passages that, they claimed, "supported" their view. They were even willing to destroy the Union and to shed the blood of family members and hundreds of thousands of others to retain their power. Is it possible that some who today enjoy the benefits of complementarianism in the home and church (men) cannot recognize the subconscious biases that influence their biblical interpretations and fuel their efforts to defend an institution that, like slavery, robs fellow humans made in God's image from freely pursuing the employment of God's callings, gifts, and abilities to serve without limitation? Could it be that our long-held biases prevent us from seeing that gender-based ministry and leadership restrictions in the church are evil just as slavery?

Children and Fathers

When I first began to consider that an essential key to interpreting Ephesians 5:21–6:10 was to recognize that Paul's mandates were temporary concessions for believers living in oppressive parallel relationships, my biggest problem was how the middle relationship, children and parents, fit this dynamic. It was jarring to think of parents as oppressors. It was relatively easy to argue that the temporary concession principle might apply to first century marriage and slavery, but more difficult to conceive how it might relate to the relationship between children and fathers (Eph. 6:1–4). Would anyone suggest that honoring and obeying parents is now outmoded by applying new creation values? Therefore, some would argue that the children/ parents relationship stands against interpreting the entire passage as dealing with oppressive or abusive relationships.

Arguably, the second of these relationships is inherently different from the others because it was and is temporary rather than normally life-long as are the other two. However, this is a very Western family construct. In the first Century, as in many cultures today, the autocratic authority of fathers, even over their adult children, is assumed. Extended families often lived together or in close proximity and the father exercised significant control over them all.

Further, unlike wives and slaves, prior to adulthood, children's dependent relationship on their parents is related to their immaturity and need to grow up physically, mentally, emotionally, and socially. Unlike the other two relationships, even in a father-dominated extended family, there is a kind of expiration date for the relationship as conceived in the passage, that is, when the child reaches adulthood, marries, and leaves father and mother (Gen 2:24). At that point, the father's authority was at least partially transferred to the new husband.

Further, the relationship is unique compared to marriage and slavery because it was and is an <u>essential</u> relationship. Not everyone must or does get married and even fewer live in slavery. But everyone must have parents to exist and depends on them through the developmental years of childhood and adolescence. Granted, the parent-child relationship is sometimes unnaturally terminated by the death of or abandonment by the parents or is surrendered in favor of adoption by eager substitute parents, but none of those negate the necessity of parents in order to birth and nurture children. The point is that in this second relationship, even the most abusive control by fathers has a built-in termination time when the children come to maturity and are no longer under the rule of their father in the same way. God's plan from the beginning was that grown children "leave father and mother" (Gen. 2:24). Even sinless Jesus was "obedient" to His mother and step-father (Luke 2:1) until His time had come (John 2:4) and He had to be "in His Father's house" (Luke 2:49).

Nevertheless, none of these observations concerning the uniqueness of the middle relationship alters the fact that it is *parallel* to the other two. Like them, it involves a powerless and powerful party and the former is sometimes abusively dominated by the latter.

Authoritarian Fathers

For twenty-first century Western audiences, the idea that many first century fathers were autocratic and even exerted domineering and oppressive control of their adult children is unfamiliar and perhaps shocking. In our culture where child abuse is a crime, an abusive father is an ugly exception to the norm and few dominate their adult children. Thankfully, in our Western culture most people assume that fathers, though imperfect, will be loving, sensitive, and protective regarding their children. When discipline is necessary it is expected to be lovingly administered to benefit the child.

A familiar Old Testament story gives a chilling illustration of the absolute and oppressive control that could be exercised by a father in ancient times. Genesis 19 reveals the absolute and shocking control assumed by a patriarchal husband and father over his wife and daughters. Lot, considered a "righteous man" (2 Pt. 2:7, 8), valued the protection of his male guests above guarding the purity and safety of his own virgin daughters. He was more willing to give his daughters over to a mob of evil and violent men to be gang-raped than to violate cultural norms for giving hospitality to strangers. Lot's daughters must have been at least teenagers if not young adults, yet neither they nor Lot's wife had any say in this shocking and potentially life-scarring proposal because they were under the absolute and unquestioned authority and control of their husband and father.

While there have always been good fathers, the first century Greco-Roman father-child relationships were pervasively patriarchal, frequently oppressive, and often life-long.

"Under Roman law, the father possessed absolute paternal power (*patria potestas*), not only over his wife and children but also his children's children and even his slaves, in fact, anyone who lived under his roof."[152] Legally, a father was free to abusively discipline his children, arrange their marriages, sell them into slavery, or even kill them if unwanted. A father's authority over his children was unlimited.

Until maturity, a child had no rights. Galatians 4:1 affirms the powerlessness and complete lack of status of children in biblical times. In the context that follows (4:3–7) we see Paul's teaching about believers' bondage before they were set free by the Gospel into a beautiful and intimate relationship with God. They now call Him "Abba," "Daddy." Paul's teaching about our deliverance from slavery to freedom and intimacy was built on his characterization of the *oppressed* position of children in that culture: "What I am saying is that as long as the heir is a child, he is no different than a slave,

---

[152] "Roman Family," online Ancient History Encyclopedia, http://www.ancient.eu/article/870/

although he owns the whole estate. He is subject to guardians and trustees until the time set by his father" (Gal. 4:1, 2). Paul wrote this knowing his assumptions were indisputable in that culture, that is, that at least in some ways children were no different than slaves and were without freedom until their father decided otherwise.

"In household codes, which explained the proper relations of all members of a household with the head of the household, minor children were subordinated just as slaves were; only after leaving the home did a child achieve freedom in practice . . . Under Roman law, the status of the minor still under a guardian was roughly that of a slave."[153]

"Ancient Rome was a man's world. In politics, society and the family, men held both the power and the purse-strings—they even decided whether a baby would live or die . . . The paterfamilias had the right to decide whether to keep newborn babies. After birth, the midwife placed babies on the ground: only if the paterfamilias picked it up was the baby formally accepted into the family. If the decision went the other way, the baby was exposed—deliberately abandoned outside."[154]

Even among God's Old Testament people, it was assumed that fathers owned their children and exercised absolute control over them. For example, Exodus 21:7–11 assumes that fathers have the right to and will at times sell their own daughters into slavery ("When a man sells his daughter as a slave," Ex. 21:7 ESV). While this raises serious questions beyond the scope of this writing about how modern readers should understand and interpret such Scriptures, it is a shocking reminder of the absolute authority of fathers in the culture of that time. The fact that Moses' restrictions offered some protections for the daughter-turned-slave in that abusively patriarchal culture doesn't make the whole idea any less repugnant today, but it casts light on the background of Ephesians 6:1–4 and the potentially abusive authority that fathers had over their children.

It is important to remember that in the present age (from the Fall to the

---

[153] Craig Keener, *The IVP Bible Background Commentary: New Testament* (Downers Grove: Intervarsity Press, 1993), on line version in LOGOS Bible Program, in loc. Galatians 4.

[154] "The Roman Empire in the First Century," Internet article by the Public Broadcasting Service (PBS) taken from their video series, (Family Life), http://www.pbs.org/empires/romans/empire/family.html

Restoration), God deals with the world as it is, not as He would want it to be. There are many illustrations throughout the Scriptures in which God imposes laws or instructions restricting evil without eliminating it, or that seem intended to move society in a better direction incrementally. These steps in the right direction are achievable and realistic improvements or create more tolerable circumstances for fallen people living in a fallen world—for example, Mosaic laws relating to making interest-bearing loans, the eventual return of lost property to original owners, regulations regarding slavery, etc. In the New Testament, Jesus enunciated concessions allowing divorce because of the hardness of peoples' hearts (Matt. 19:3–12). These were contrary to God's plan and intentions for marriage "from the beginning." In the age to come everything will be put to right. God's people work toward that goal but live in the realm of "already/not yet."

Thus, when we interpret Paul's commands for children and fathers, we must not base it on our twenty-first century Western model of the family or on the expectation (however realistic or not) that fathers will be loving, reasonable, and sensitive to their children's needs, feelings, desires, and opinions.

This Relationship Is Parallel to the Other Two

To support interpreting the children and fathers segment (Eph. 6:1–4) as the second of three parallel, oppressive relationships are these three observations:

First, the oppressors in Paul's second relationship were not <u>parents</u> but rather were <u>fathers</u>. Paul's instructions to children, the powerless party in Ephesians 6:1–3, addressed their behavior toward their "parents," whereas in Ephesians 6:4, Paul, as with husbands and masters, spoke to the party possessing all the power in the relationship, that is, to "fathers." In all three relationships, the oppressed parties were addressed first and then the oppressors.

Although there were exceptions, in that culture it was the norm for fathers to exercise absolute, autocratic, and often abusive control over their children even when they were adults. One illustration is the prevailing custom of fathers selecting their children's mates and determining the time of their marriage. Neither children nor mothers enjoyed the positive status they usually do in our Western culture. In the three parallel relationships of Ephesians 5:21–6:10, wives, children, and slaves were all the disposable property of men—their husbands, fathers, or masters. Not all wives, children, and slaves were treated abusively. There were loving and kind husbands and fathers even as there were some masters who were more benevolent than others. However, that did not diminish their total authority or modify what was the norm in these three parallel relationships—a rigid and often oppressive hierarchy.

Second, as with his directives to husbands and masters, Paul's instructions to fathers were extremely radical in that very hierarchical culture—"do not exasperate your children" (Eph. 6:4) and "do not embitter your children or they will become discouraged" (Col. 3:21). Exasperation and embitterment were the normal result of sinful, domineering fathers. Paul called for a kind of respect, sensitivity, and compassion totally atypical in that world. "The training and instruction of the Lord" represented a radical, counter-cultural role for most first-century fathers—even as it would in many cultures today.

Third, as with the other two relationships, if children attempted to forcibly impose ideal new creation values into their unbelieving or spiritually immature family dynamics and if they participated in a revolt against autocratic fathers, chaos and violence would ensue and the fledgling Christian movement would doubtless have experienced crushing persecution more quickly and extensively. However, with the somewhat more temporary nature of the children/fathers relationship, the option of rebellion could more strategically be replaced with a more winsome approach—a temporary concession to oppressive relationships for the promotion of peace and harmony and to present a Gospel that was palatable and attractive rather than incendiary.

Additionally, it should be observed that if one assumes that the Ten Commandments express timeless values, then honoring one's parents (Ex. 20:12) is a lifetime responsibility, while obeying one's parents is limited to childhood (Eph. 6:1, 2) prior to leaving to establish their own family unit (Gen. 2:24).

Perhaps also, though difficult to imagine, "obedience" might be an unnecessary command for Spirit-filled, humble, peace-loving, and teachable children. The relationship of children and parents under the new creation should more closely resemble what it <u>would have looked like</u> (to the degree we can guess) under the original creation had the Fall not robbed us of a glimpse of sinless, loving and unselfish fathers, mothers, and children.

In any case, the command to obey expires when a grown child "leaves father and mother" to enter into a new relational priority, marriage (Gen. 2:24).

Everybody Submit to Everybody Else

It must be remembered that another important dimension regarding the three parallel relationships is the introductory *heading* at the beginning of the passage that calls for all parties to submit to each other (Eph. 5:21). What would it look like for husbands, fathers, and masters to submit to their wives, children, and slaves? Specifically, in this part of the discussion, what would it look like for fathers to submit to their children? Does Paul's command mean that children should be allowed to do whatever they wish and that their parents should submit to their every whim? Think about it—no more vegetables, banned television shows, limited time on electronic devices, homework, chores, clean underwear, required room cleanings, baths, bedtimes, or curfews. Instead, bring on the candy, junk food, unlimited video games, all-night television marathons, skipping school, messy rooms, profanity and crude language, disrespecting authorities, and whatever else feels good at the moment. It would resurrect the dynamic of the Book of Judges: "In those days Israel had no king; everyone did as he saw fit" (Judg. 21:25). Is that what Paul called for in Ephesians 5:21? Of course not! Paul commanded fathers to bring up their children "in the training [discipline] and instruction of the Lord" (Eph. 6:4).

Rather than submitting in the sense of unquestioned, servile obedience, a parent's submission would involve *placing the needs of their child ahead of their own*.[155] This kind of submission would be revealed in a parent unselfishly prioritizing their child's interests and feelings above their own. A parent

---

[155] Children innately know that their parents should love them in such a way that the parent sets aside their own desires and needs for the sake of their children. When a parent selfishly prioritizes themselves over their child, it promotes confusion, sadness, depression, disrespect, anger, bitterness, and rebellion.

practices submission when they set aside their own plans, agendas, and the things they would really enjoy doing in order to give themselves to caring for their child—listening to them rattle on about nonsense, helping them with their homework, reading them a story that they could recite from memory, playing Candyland for what feels like hours, ignoring knee pain to give them a horsey back ride on the floor, cheering madly on the sidelines of endless athletic competitions, concerts, and plays, or cleaning up their vomit and comforting them when the flu strikes in the middle of the night. It includes parents letting go of their rights, expectations, privileges, opportunities, and dreams to pursue the best interests of their children—these are expressions of parental submission to their children.

Deferring their own pleasure in order to pursue the pleasure of their child demonstrates a parent's submission. Spending a lot of money on a child's needs and wants rather than on the parent's desired hobbies, activities, and luxuries is an illustration of a parent's submission. Every decent parent knows what it is to surrender what they want to do to do what their children need them to do—this is submission. To submit is to surrender one's selfishness and self-serving demands and to replace them with loving words and actions on behalf of another. Further, to submit to someone is to respond to them with respect, honor, and deference—to treat them as having worth and value. In other words, children are not the father's *property* as the cultural norms suggested and so could be used, abused, or discarded at will.[156] They are God's fellow image-bearers to be selflessly trained and taught with love and respect. These examples are also suggestive of what a husband's submission to his wife and a master's submission to his slave could look like.

Because Jesus had inaugurated the now-and-future Kingdom of God and the New Creation, Spirit-filled (Eph. 5:18) husbands, fathers, and slave masters are to grow in their development of "the fruit of the Spirit [which] is love, joy, peace, patience, kindness, goodness, faithfulness, gentleness and self-control." (Gal. 5:22, 23). When those relational qualities are practiced there is no longer any need for the temporary, fallen-world hierarchical concessions Paul required in Ephesians 5:22–6:9. All must happily submit to each other (Eph. 5:19–21) so that ultimately there would be no need to perpetuate the legacy of the fall in which one party ruled over another.

---

[156] This also applied to wives who in that culture were similarly seen as the "property" of their husbands.

A Shocking But Proper Response to the Teaching Regarding Three Parallel Relationships

I am now convinced that a correct interpretation of the *concession passages* should lead us to being as horrified over the perpetuation of patriarchy in marriage as nearly everyone is already repulsed by life-scarring child abuse by wicked fathers and by the evil institutions of slavery and human trafficking. It is my conclusion these three post-Fall perversions of God's original plan for relationships are evil—even if many sincerely but wrongly attempt to justify one of them (patriarchal marriage) as if it expressed faithfulness to the Scriptures. This suggestion may be shocking, but I believe it is absolutely consistent with a proper interpretation of the concession passages. **While its dynamics are rarely as horrific as slavery, a male-dominated marital relationship is as evil as slavery.** Remember that at one time slavery was defended by many who claimed the support of Scripture. We must not perpetuate that error with regard to patriarchy.

Conclusion

Because many complementarians base their positions on gender roles in marriage and in the church on the same faulty foundation—supposed creation-designed, gender-based hierarchy—to some extent the two either stand or fall together. Understanding the dynamic behind the *concession passages* and anticipating what will be presented regarding the *prohibition passages* in chapters 7 - 10, it is my assertion that, however sincere some may be in defending patriarchy in marriage and gender-based restrictions in the church, those views are contrary to Scripture. Their inadequate, flawed, and biased interpretations must be confronted, repented of, and rejected. Humble requests for forgiveness will be an important first step in righting the wrongs done to women in marriage and in the church. I say this as one who spent the vast majority of my fifty plus years of ministry sincerely promoting those incorrect views. I now ask for forgiveness for my bias-protected erroneous hermeneutics and the wrongs they perpetuated against my wife and many other women along with thousands of congregants I wrongly taught.

FOR DISCUSSION

(1) Read Ephesians 5:21. If all you had was this verse, what conclusions would you draw about how Christians are to respond to each other? What would happen in a church if all the members practiced this command? What would it look like in a marriage if both husbands and wives practiced it? Do you think most Christian marriages exemplify this practice? Why or why not?

(2) Read Ephesians 5:22–24. What did Paul tell wives to do? How does this fit with the prior command in verse 21?

(3) Read Ephesians 5:25–33. What did Paul tell husbands to do? Which of Paul's commands for husbands are basically the same as what the New Testament requires of all Christians in their relationships with each other? Does Paul specifically tell husbands to "take the lead" in the marriage or to insist that their wives submit to them? Why or why not?

(4) Read Ephesians 6:5–9. What would you say to someone who insisted these verses show that God is not opposed to the institution of slavery?

(5) Describe the "concession principle" this chapter suggests is the key to interpreting the three parallel relationships. How does this principle help deal with the three relationships consistently? Even if the commands in this passage are temporary concessions, what are some circumstances in which a Christian should still follow them to keep peace and promote the Gospel?

(6) In a culture where women's rights are very much "in" and patriarchy is very much "out" how can Christians respond so it draws people to Jesus and the church?

6

What Does It Mean to Be the "Head"?

Because the coin landed **heads** up as he had called it, Fred, the **head** of the frat house, moved to the **head** of the line. When the group followed behind him to the beach, Fred could better observe the **head** of the river where the water splashed over the **heads** of two swimmers. Twenty feet from the shore, one observer with a level **head** who had been at the **head** of her class, slurped the **head** off her cold beer, then began working at the **head** of the picnic table chopping up a **head** of lettuce with the sharp **head** of an ax. Jake, a pot**head**, came out of the river to look for the outdoor toilet. "Where's the **head**?" he yelled. When it was time to eat, the swimmers raced out of the water to **head** for the food like a hungry **head** of cattle lumbering toward the feeding trough. Sally, running with a full **head** of steam, **head**ed off the others and, by a **head**, won the race to the table. Everyone knew her athleticism as she, on the varsity soccer team, often skillfully **head**ed the ball into the net. Her victory in the sprint to the food went to her **head** until Mindy went over the cook's **head** to get the privilege of going first in line. This injustice brought things to a **head** leading to a **head**y debate. Later what happened at the picnic was noted in the **head**line of the newsletter. The byline stood out due to the red ink from the printer **head**. The newspaper was available at the **head** of the hour at midday on Wednesday.

This nonsensical story illustrates there is more than one way to use the word *"head"* in the English language. The usages in the biblical languages may not be quite as plentiful or diverse, but similar variation exists. Therefore, it is essential to take a careful look at the range of ways the Bible uses the word *head* especially regarding the role of men and women in marriage and the church. This is an essential consideration in the gender-roles debate, particularly in what I designate as the *"headship passages:"* 1 Corinthians 11 and Ephesians 5.

Ephesians 5:22–24 is perhaps the best known and most used Bible passage to argue that God intended for men to be the leaders and women to be their followers. Those verses are front and center in many weddings and in sermons on marriage and in debates about gender roles in marriage and the church. Foundational to the complementarian position is the assertion that wives are to submit to their *husbands because* Ephesians 5:23 declares: "the husband is the head of the wife as Christ is the head of the church, his body, of which he is the Savior" [emphasis added].

With that pronouncement hanging in the air, we can almost hear the defense attorney confidently concluding his opening statement with, "I rest my case. Headship makes it a slam dunk!"

"I object," opposing counsel almost shouts as he jumps to his feet. "My worthy opponent has made a gigantic and totally unwarranted assumption. He assumes that 'head' means 'boss.' Evidence will prove beyond any reasonable doubt that his assumption is completely false. In this case, 'head' does NOT mean 'boss,' it means 'source.'"

The jury is in place (that's YOU, the reader). Let the trial begin. Please carefully consider the actual evidence without bias or prejudgment.

Does "Head" Mean "Boss"?

Complementarians assume that when Paul talks about the husband being the "head" (κεφαλή, *kephalē*), of the wife (Eph. 5:23), it can only mean he is her boss and that he has authority over her. This should be obvious, they argue, because, our physical bodies are controlled and directed by our heads—specifically by our brains that reside inside our heads. Is this traditional complementarian understanding of "head" as signifying *authority* an appropriate interpretation of what "head" means in the relevant Bible passages? Is it possible that modern interpreters inappropriately force twentieth and twenty-first century authority-related understandings of "head" back onto those Scriptures?

This chapter will explore the various meanings of "head" in the Hebrew

Old Testament (רֹאשׁ, *rosh*) and also in the Septuagint[157] and Greek New Testament (κεφαλή, *kephalē*) and will consider which one or ones are appropriate in the two New Testament "head" verses that relate to the gender roles controversy, 1 Corinthians 11:3 and Ephesians 5:23. That's right—*only those two* verses in the entire Bible use the word "head" with any specific connection to gender roles. However, they are significant passages for discerning God's intent for gender roles in marriage and the church.

First, how the word "head" was used in Bible times is not necessarily the same as how the concept is commonly understood in contemporary Western culture. Of course, when referencing the round (sort of) part of our body that sits on top of the neck, today's usage parallels ancient usage. But, consider the modern science-based understanding of brain function that drives the idea of the physical/anatomical *head* as the control center that directs all the functions of the body. This modern understanding was not available for many centuries after the New Testament was written. They did not understand the relationship of the head to the body as we do. Similarly, the concept of a corporate head—the power-brokering CEO in the business world—portrays a meaning unfamiliar in Bible times. Ancient world readers would be baffled by both of these twenty-first century concepts.

"Our problem when we approach the Old and New Testaments is that the function of the central nervous system was not known to the ancients; they were unaware of the fact that we think with our brains. For them, thought was not located in the head but in the body, in the diaphragm or the heart . . . We must be on our guard against thinking that Paul, for example, means by 'head' what we would mean if we used the term, or that he sees the relationship between head and body the same way as we do. He may, he may not . . . We must think hard about what the ancients had in mind when they spoke about head and body."[158]

It is my assertion that projecting male authority and female subordination

---

[157] The Septuagint is the Greek translation of the Old Testament completed in the second or third century B.C.E. It is sometimes referred to by LXX which references the tradition that it was translated by seventy Jewish scholars. Because of its age, it gives helpful insight into the meaning of Greek words close to the time of the New Testament.
[158] Marg Mowczko, *"Leon Morris on 'Head' (kephale) in the New Testament"* Marg Mowczko blog (October 27, 2013), http://margmowczko.com/leon-morris-on-head-in-the-new-testament/

based on biblical references to man as the *"head"* relies more on modern extra-biblical ideas imposed on the Scriptures than on the actual usage of the term in the Bible. "This is partly because 'head' is a metaphor for authority in Latin, English, and German"[159] while its meaning in the Bible is more dissimilar, diverse, and nuanced than that.

"Head" in the Old Testament

In the Old Testament, "head" is very infrequently used to designate a leader or person in charge. Other uses are far more common. Westfall reports that the biblical semantic range (all the meanings a word has in various contexts) of "head" includes: (1) the part of the anatomy on top of the body (including eyes, ears, nose, hair, etc.); (2) a synecdoche for the whole person; (3) a metaphor for "source;" and (4) a metaphor for "leader, ruler, person in authority."[160]

By far the most common OT usage of "head" refers to the part of the physical body on top of the neck and externally composed of the face, ears, and hair. In that ancient, prescientific age, no one would have suggested that the physical head exercised authority or control over the body. Similarly, the word is used to refer to the "head" of a stalk of grain, the part that sits on top of the plant. No one would have assumed that the "head" of the grain had authority over the stalk. Rather it is a reference to a segment of the whole in its spatial location atop the entity. There is absolutely no hierarchical implication in this usage.

Interestingly, the first biblical use of "head" (other than a derivative used in the opening verse of Genesis—see below) is in Genesis 2:10 where it speaks of one river flowing out of Eden and dividing into four "heads." The point of the river's division constituted the "head-waters" for four rivers; the sources or beginnings out of which each river flowed: "And a river went out of Eden to water the garden; and from thence it was parted, and became into four heads" (Gen. 2:10, KJV). Indisputably, any suggestion of hierarchy or authority is totally absent from this first usage of the concept. Today people commonly speak of the *head* or *headwaters* of a river, clearly referring to the

---

[159] Westfall, *Paul and Gender,* 87.
[160] Ibid., 38.

source or beginning of the river. Similarly, people today speak of moving to the *head* of a line—talking about the *beginning* or *source* of the line from which the rest of the line proceeds. There are no hierarchical or authority implications in these usages.

Two other familiar Old Testament passages illustrate a comparable use of *rosh* or a derivative to convey the meaning of source or *beginning* from which everything else flowed:

- "In the beginning (רֵאשִׁית, *roshith*) God created the heavens and the earth" (Gen. 1:1), and
- "The fear of the LORD is the beginning (*rosh*) of wisdom" (Ps. 111:10).

Obviously, in both of these familiar texts, *rosh* conveys absolutely no hint of hierarchy or authority. Rather it clearly portrays the idea of the beginning or source out of which other things came or followed.

But what about the many uses of "head" (*rosh*) in the Old Testament that obviously mean "ruler"? Don't they prove that in the two New Testament references to "head" regarding gender roles, the word should be understood as referring to one with authority over another? Actually, not! The overwhelming linguistic evidence from the Old Testament relevant to the gender roles debate does NOT support understanding "head" as a term that normally means to have *authority over* another.

The Septuagint, the Greek version of the Old Testament, is the most ancient translation of the Hebrew Old Testament. It was begun in the third century B.C. and completed before 100 B.C. Jesus and the other New Testament writers cited this version over 300 times (far more than the Hebrew text). It is a rich source for discerning how Greek words were used in biblical literature in the few hundred years before and in the time of Christ and the apostles. There are 171 instances in the Septuagint where "head" means *authority*. However, all but six do not use the Greek word *kephalē* which is the word used in in every relevant New Testament passage in which "head" appears. Instead, 165 times the Septuagint uses ἄρχων (*arxon*) which always means "ruler, leader, one who governs." This Greek word (*arxon*) is never used in the New Testament in any relevant "head" passage. Westfall observes, "It seems that most of the translators of the Septuagint knew that *kephalē* does not usually mean leader, ruler, or authority."[161]

Even in the six passages where it could be so translated (Judg. 11:11; 2 Sam. 22:44; Ps. 18:43; Is. 7:8, 9; and Lam. 1:5), it may be poorly translated (cf. the other 165 references) or it may illustrate the convergence of the concepts of *authority* and *source*. Westfall notes about these six references, "They may reflect a foundational and symbiotic relationship between an ancient king and his people (present and future) or territory. We find that κεφαλή often occurs in contexts of authority and preeminence because the function of being the source of identity and life can be the basis of authority or preeminence in the culture."[162] The notion of *leader* intersects with and is not exclusive from the idea of *source*. Individuals, armies, tribes, and nations looked to their leaders as the source of what they needed for life including national identity, stability, unity, order, laws, justice, provision, protection, and guidance.

One of the six Septuagint passages (Judg. 11:11) where *rosh/kephalē* is supposed to mean "ruler" is sometimes cited as evidence that *kephalē* in the New Testament should likewise be understood as *having authority over*. But a closer look at what the verse actually says exposes the weakness of that argument: "the people made him [Jephthah] head and commander over them" [emphasis added]. It is crucial to note that "head" (Hebrew = rosh; Greek = *kephalē* in the Septuagint) is used side-by-side with "commander" (Hebrew קָצִין, *qa-sin*; Greek = *hegiomai* in the Septuagint). Obviously, there is a distinction between the two terms, otherwise one is unnecessary and redundant. The second word (*hegiomai*) indisputably means "ruler, chief, commander, dictator, man in charge." Therefore, "head" must have conveyed a somewhat *different* concept—most likely the idea that in choosing Jephthah as their "head," they expected him to be the "source" to whom they looked to provide the needs of the nation (e.g. provision and protection), one of which was to be their "commander," which is represented by a different Hebrew word, *qa-sin*.

Westfall cites two illustrations of how *rosh* is used in the Old Testament: "The Jewish new year is celebrated as *Rosh Hashanah*, 'the *head* of the year'.

161 Marg Mowczko, *"Kephale and 'male headship' in Paul's letters,"* Marg Mowczko blog (September 18, 2011),
, http://margmowczko.com/kephale-and-male-headship-in-pauls-letters/
162 Westfall, *Paul and Gender,* 81.

The first day of the year is not 'in authority over' the rest of the year. Rather the year 'flows from' that first day. In the Old Testament 'The fear of the Lord is the *head* [*rosh*] of wisdom' (Psalm 111:10). English translations usually read, "the fear of the Lord is the *beginning* of wisdom.'

These quotations and observations indicate that the metaphorical concept of "head" in the Old Testament (Septuagint, *kephalē*), aside from its most common literal usages referring to the anatomical part of the physical body, is used most often to convey the concept of *source* or *beginning* even as in English we speak of the *head* of a river or moving to the *head* of a line.

Adam, the "Head" of the Human Race

This meaning (beginning/source) fits very well with the frequently mentioned theological concept of Adam as the *head* of the human race. Although the Bible never uses the word "head" with regard to Adam, theologians frequently refer to him as the *head* or *federal head* of the race to describe how he brought sin and death to the entire human race in contrast to Jesus who brought righteousness and life (Rom. 5:12–21). 1 Corinthians 15:21, 22, 45–49 states:

> "For since death came through a man, the resurrection of the dead comes also through a man. For as in Adam all die, so in Christ all will be made alive . . . So it is written: 'The first man Adam became a living being'; the last Adam, a life-giving spirit. The spiritual did not come first, but the natural, and after that the spiritual. The first man was of the dust of the earth, the second man from heaven. As was the earthly man, so are those who are of the earth; and as is the man from heaven, so also are those who are of heaven. And just as we have borne the likeness of the earthly man, so shall we bear the likeness of the man from heaven."

"Adam is the head of humanity because he is the source of biological life. Adam is not given supremacy, honor, authority, or reverence by humanity; rather, the relationship is one of identity derived from its origin, to which Paul gives a negative appraisal. Jesus replaced Adam as the head because Jesus is the spiritual life-giving source that fills the church, and the church forms an organic union with him (Eph. 1:22; 4:15–16; Col. 1:18). This relationship reflects the Greek meaning of 'head.'"[163]

Understanding *rosh* as *source* is essential background for interpreting the two *headship passages* in the New Testament with regard to gender roles in marriage and the church. 1 Corinthians 11:3 and Ephesians 5:23 are both rooted in Genesis 1, 2 and its portrayal of the creation of Adam and Eve. Adam was created directly by God. Eve was created from Adam. He was the *source* of her existence even as God was the *source* of Adam's creation. Eve was formed from Adam's rib (Gen. 2:21, 22)—thus he was the *source* from which she was made.

It is clear that in the Old Testament, the vast majority of references to "head" concern the physical head of a human, animal, or stalk of grain. Other key passages use "head" to mean *source*. Of those which could legitimately be understood as *leader* or *ruler*, only a tiny fraction (a mere 3.5%) are represented by *kephalē* in the Septuagint and in every one of those the meaning overlaps with *source*.

Even more significant, there is not one reference in the Old Testament that calls a husband the "head" of his wife, or to a man as the "head" of a woman, or that uses "head" in any way that might suggest gender-based hierarchy. **Not even one!**

"Head" in the New Testament

But what about "head" (*kephalē*) in the New Testament? How does its usage there cast light on how it should be translated in the two gender role passages, 1 Corinthians 11:3 and Ephesians 5:23?

First, in the Gospels and Acts, every reference to "head" refers to the anatomical head of a physical body or to the head of a stalk of grain. None of these imply authority. Jesus never spoke of men as "head" over women or as having authority over them. Never! **Not even once!** His silence speaks volumes.

When we move to the letters, we discover that at least thirty-one references to "head" are literal heads of physical bodies (human or animal) and not more than twelve are metaphorical such as Christ being the "head

---

[163] Westfall, *Paul and Gender,* 85, 86.

over everything" (Eph. 1:22) or the husband being "the head of the wife" (Eph. 5:23). The metaphorical references are found in 1 Corinthians 11:3, 4, 5; Ephesians 1:22;[164] 4:15; 5:23; Colossians 1:18; 2:10, 19.

Margaret Mowcsko, a prolific writer, theologian, and early Christian and Jewish studies scholar writes cogently about the meaning of the Greek word for "head" (*kephalē*):

> One compelling piece of evidence that *kephalē* did not usually mean 'leader' in Koine Greek is that the LSJ [The Liddell-Scott-Jones Greek Lexicon], one of the most exhaustive lexicons of Ancient Greek, does not include any definition of *kephalē* that approximates 'leader' or 'authority'...
>
> Paul's main point in the passage [Colossians 1:16–18]... is to show that Jesus is the creator, source, origin, and beginning of everything in the universe. This includes Jesus being the source and 'author' of the Church. Paul used the word *kephalē* (head) in this context—the context of source and origin . . . Unfortunately, many Christians have simply presumed that 'head' means authority' in 1 Corinthians 11:3 and Ephesians 5:23, and many churches continue to teach this misguided interpretation.[165]

Those two verses, the only ones that specifically speak of the word "head" in relation to gender roles, are important in the complementarian/egalitarian debate and will be considered below. First, we should consider each of the *metaphorical* references to "head" in Paul's letters which are:

- 1 Corinthians 11:3, 4, 5—these will be addressed in the next section.

---

[164] Ephesians 1:10 NIV uses the word "head" in its translation, but most versions do not use the word "head" (e.g. ESV, NASB, NRSV, KJV, NKJV, NLT, The Message). In that verse, the Greek word is ἀνακεφαλαιώσασθαι which means to "bring together, gather together, unify, sum up."

[165] Mowczko, "*Kephale and Male Headship,*", http://margmowczko.com/kephale-and-male-headship-in-pauls-letters/

- Ephesians 1:22, 23—"And God placed all things under his feet and appointed him to be **head** over everything for the church, which is his body, the fullness of him who fills everything in every way." While this is one of a very few passages where "head" (*kephalē*) seems clearly to convey the idea of *authority,* the meaning of "head" as *having authority over* and as the *source* converge and overlap. Paul states that Jesus "fills everything in every way," most likely indicating that He, the "head" is the *source* of all the blessings with which He fills the church. "Christ, the Head of the body, *fills* (*for Himself*) the church with blessings."[166] Compare Ephesians 4:10–12 which similarly speaks of Christ filling the "universe" and then describes Him as the *Source* of those spiritual gifts that equip the church for its mission ("apostles, prophets, evangelists, pastors and teachers").
- Ephesians 4:15, 16—"Instead, speaking the truth in love, we will in all things grow up into him who is the **head**, that is, Christ. From him the whole body, joined and held together by every supporting ligament, grows and builds itself up in love, as each part does its work." This use of "head" appears to be a clear illustration of its common meaning of *source.* Christ the "head" is the *Source* of the body's life, structure, unity, growth, and service. Significantly, these verses are only a few paragraphs before the crucially important gender-roles *headship* passage in Ephesians 5:23 and thus provide defining context for that comparable use of "head."
- Ephesians 5:23—this will be discussed extensively below.
- Colossians 1:18—"And he is the **head** of the body, the church; he is the beginning and the firstborn from among the dead, so that in everything he might have the supremacy." In the context of this verse it is clear that "head" conveys the idea that Jesus is the Source of everything in the universe—its Creator, Originator, and the One who began it all.
- Colossians 2:9, 10, 19—"For in Christ all the fullness of the Deity lives in bodily form, and you have been given fullness in Christ, who is the **head** over every power and authority . . . He has lost connection

---

[166] J. F. Walvoord and R. B. Zuck, eds. "Ephesians," *The Bible Knowledge Commentary: An Exposition of the Scriptures* (Vol. 2, 621), (Wheaton: Victor Books), Logos Bible Program.

with the **Head**, from whom the whole body, supported and held together by its ligaments and sinews, grows as God causes it to grow." Westfall observes:

Colossians 2:9–10 is one example of the close association between authority and source . . . This passage is cited by Schreiner as an unambiguous example of 'head' as 'authority' (cf. Col. 2:15). However, the point of Colossians 2:10 is that Christ is the source of the believer's fullness in the same way that he is the head (source and sustainer) of every ruler and authority. This meaning is made clearer because Paul has already emphatically made this point in Colossians 1:15–17, which explicitly includes the powers in 2:10 . . . Therefore, the reference to Jesus as the head of rulers and authorities may sound like it means the assumption of authority over them, but both the point of the passage and the close context indicate that it actually means that he is their source—that is, their creator.[167]

These observations make it clear that in Paul's writings, "head" (*kephalē*) frequently conveys the meaning of *source.* Even in the rare occasions in which it can mean *authority,* that sense is often closely connected to and inter-related with the idea of source which is comparable to previously discussed Old Testament uses. Against that definitive background, we must now consider the only two passages in the Bible in which headship has any possible connection with gender roles.

"Head" in 1 Corinthians 11:3–10

Before looking in more detail at the specific meaning of "head" in 1 Corinthians 11:3 and then later in Ephesians 5:23, it is important to note a significant difference between the two passages. The latter (Eph. 5) speaks of the head of a body as stated in verse 23 ("Christ is the head of the church his body"), whereas the former (1 Cor. 11:3) does NOT have the head of a body

---

[167] Westfall, *Paul and Gender,* 81, 82.

in view. The head of a body is <u>not</u> the underlying metaphor. Notice that verse 3 lists three parallel "head" (*kephalē*) relationships:

- "the head of every man is Christ"
- "the head of the woman is man"
- "the head of Christ is God."

Clearly, in the third statement of the triad, Christ is <u>not</u> God's body. That would approximate the ancient modalism heresy.[168] In the first statement in the triad, every man is not Christ's body. While the church is frequently identified as the "body of Christ," that is not what the text is saying. "Every man" is <u>not</u> a believer or part of Jesus' church, hence not part of His body. The obvious assumption then is that the second relationship in this literary triad is <u>like the other two</u>. Consequently, in this passage, the idea is <u>not</u> that the man is the head of woman who is his body. That IS the underlying metaphor in Ephesians 5:23 as specifically stated in verse 23, but it should not therefore be imposed back on 1 Corinthians 11:3.

This is important because a complementarian understanding of "head" in Ephesians 5:23 is often projected on 1 Corinthians 11:3, thus concluding that both passages designate males as having authority over females— <u>generally</u> (all males, not just husbands) in 1 Corinthian 11, and maritally in Ephesians 5. Whether or not this understanding of the meaning of "head" is correct (I will demonstrate that it is NOT), it is inappropriate to impose it from the Ephesian triad back onto the very different Corinthian triad which has nothing to do with the themes of Ephesians 5:21–6:5: marriage, parenting, and slavery, or with the marital metaphor of head and body. Regardless of whether the <u>meaning</u> of "head" is different or the same, the <u>metaphor</u> clearly is different. Paul's reference to "head" in 1 Corinthians 11:3 (written about 55 A.D.) may well inform the reference written five years later in Ephesians 5:23 (about 60 A.D.), but it seems unreasonable to suggest that the meaning of "head" in Ephesians can legitimately be projected back onto the earlier use in

---

[168] Modalism denies the Trinity. It teaches that the Father, Son, and Spirit are not distinct Persons, but are different modes in which God functions. For example, during the incarnation, Jesus, in a body, was the current mode or expression of God. At Pentecost, God assumed a different mode—a spirit, the Holy Spirit.

Corinthians. The head of a body concept simply does not fit in the parallelism of the literary triad in 1 Corinthians 11:3.

Although the metaphor of the church being Christ's body is very common in Romans, 1 Corinthians, Ephesians, and Colossians, there are only two references to Christ as the *"head"* of His body, the church: Ephesians 5:23 and Colossians 1:18. That is *not* the metaphor in 1 Corinthians 11:3. Rather, 1 Corinthians 11:3 is an unambiguous use of "head" with the meaning *source*. In the triad:

- Christ is the <u>source</u> of every man (every "human" or "person" could be a valid translation[169]); He is the Creator as John 1:3, 4 states: "Through him [the Word, Jesus] all things were made; without him nothing was made that has been made. In him was life, and that life was the light of men."

- The man (Adam) is the <u>source</u> of woman (Eve)[170] for she was made from his rib. His rib was the source of her existence as Genesis 2:21, 22 beautifully relates: "So the Lord God caused the man to fall into a deep sleep; and while he was sleeping, he took one of the man's ribs and closed up the place with flesh. Then the Lord God made a woman from the rib he had taken out of the man, and he brought her to the man."

- And God is the <u>Source</u> of the Incarnate Christ—not His Creator as if He had a beginning and was not eternal. Rather, Jesus is the "Son of God"—conceived in Mary's womb by God the Spirit and

---

[169] ἀνήρ (an-air), means a human being, a person.

[170] Although he could be speaking more generically, based on the grammar and the parallelism with what precedes and follows, it seems most probable that Paul had Genesis 1, 2 in mind and was talking about Adam and Eve—"the man" is ὁ ἀνήρ—the definite article particularizes the noun—"the man" referring to the first man, Adam, and "woman," γυναικὸς, which is anarthrous, that is, without a definite article, refers to the first woman, Eve. The majority of English translations translate this as referring to man and woman (likely Adam and Eve). A few translate it as referring to a married couple, e.g. "the head of a wife is her husband" (ESV) and "the head of a woman is her husband" (RSV). However, even if it were a generic reference to a wife and her husband, it seems that the meaning of "head" as *source* is still required because of its position in the middle of the triad in which the other two seem unquestionably to convey that understanding of "head."

announced in Psalm 2:7, "I will proclaim the decree of the Lord: He said to me, 'You are my Son; today I have become your Father.'" Jesus is the Father's "only begotten" Son (John 3:16, KJV)—in that sense, the Father is the source of the Son.[171]

One could easily substitute the word *source* for "head" in each of its three uses in verse 3: "Now I want you to realize that the SOURCE of every man is Christ, and the SOURCE of the woman is man, and the SOURCE of Christ is God."

Biblical scholar N.T. Wright agrees with the *source* understanding of "head" in 1 Corinthians 11 stating that "a good case can be made out for saying that in verse 3 he is referring not to 'headship' in the sense of sovereignty, but to 'headship' in the sense of 'source', like the 'source' or 'head' of a river. In fact, in some of the key passages where he explains what he's saying (verses 8, 9 and 12a) he is referring explicitly to the creation story in Genesis 2, where the woman's source was the rib of the man."[172]

This meaning is consistent with the meaning of "head" as *source* in virtually all of the other non-literal uses in Paul's letters as has been discussed.

In spite of all these indications that "head" should be understood as *source* in 1 Corinthians 11 (except when it is a literal, anatomical reference), many complementarians argue that in 1 Corinthians 11:3–10 headship speaks of authority AND that it applies beyond husbands and wives to males and females in general.

However, this passage is not about a chain of command or an organizational chart showing who is the boss. As already noted in verse 3, a more appropriate understanding of "head" in its non-literal uses in 1 Corinthians 11:3–5 is *source* rather than *authoritative leader*. Verse 3 is in a paragraph (1 Cor. 11:3–13) in which Paul uses the word "head" (κεφαλή/ *kephalay*) fourteen times in eleven verses. In these verses Paul plays on the literal meaning of "head" as part of our anatomy (eight times) and its metaphorical meaning as *source* (five times). In the midst of the discussion (11:8), he clearly confirms that the metaphorical meaning is *source:* "For man

---

[171] Theologians and ancient creeds refer to this as "the eternal generation of the Son." A more thorough discussion of this concept and the debates regarding it are beyond the scope of this study.

[172] Wright, *"Woman's Service in the Church."*

did not <u>come from</u> woman, but woman <u>from</u> man" (emphasis added)—an unmistakable reference to Adam as the *source* of Eve's creation. God used the dirt for Adam's construction (Gen. 2:7) and God used Adam's rib (Gen. 2:21, 22) as the *source* of Eve's.

There is an additional huge problem with the erroneous complementarian interpretation of "head" as *authority* in 1 Corinthians 11. That misinterpretation is inappropriately used as evidence for the prohibition of women in general from leadership over men in general. The practical problem is that very few who hold this view are willing to apply or impose it consistently in all settings. If the complementarian interpretation is correct, then gender restrictions should be applied throughout society, precluding women from <u>any position of authority</u> over men in business, manufacturing, government, education, sports, the arts, etc. Therefore, if men are present, there should be no female employers, supervisors, union stewards, managers, administrators, CEOs, governing boards members, committee chairpersons, team leaders, principals, college professors, coaches, symphony conductors, art curators, movie or theater directors, mayors, city commissioners, police officers, judges, congress members, ambassadors, presidents/vice presidents or cabinet members. Christian businessmen should be admonished to restrict women from positions of supervision, management, or team leadership, and Christian employees should wrestle with the rightness of working in a company that does not require these gender-based restrictions. Almost no complementarians are willing to go that far, instead most limit their gender role assignments and limitations to marriage and the church.

If complementarians believe that 1 Corinthians 11 asserts male headship beyond marriage (assuming that "head" implies *authority*), then it seems like gross inconsistency to extend it only to marriage and church and not also to all other societal venues. This is especially true if it is believed that men and women, <u>by God's creation design</u>, are made respectively to be leaders and followers. The complementarian interpretation of 1 Corinthians 11:3 would make it sinful rebellion against God's order for women, in any setting, to lead men.

Those complementarians who say that because Paul made provision for women to pray or prophesy it would also be permissible for them to serve in all of those other positions of leadership assuming that they serve under the authority of an appropriate male. If this is the case, what is the visible "sign of authority" (head covering, long hair, or contemporary substitute) that clearly shows everyone that they serve under the authority of a man? This is the typical complementarian understanding of the head covering's significance. If this is not required, on what textual basis is it eliminated and how is it that a woman in leadership demonstrates that she is under a man's authority?

Perhaps the reluctance of most complementarians to make this broader application for all men having authority over all women is less based on hermeneutics than it is probably an indication (a) of the subconscious corrective work of the indwelling Holy Spirit, (b) that they are responding appropriately to their own subconscious aversion to such broad gender restrictions, or (c) they are consciously or subconsciously more willing to compromise their convictions than to face the ridicule, rejection, and opposition which they know would result from making such a broad application of an all-men-have-authority-over-all-women position. There is a good deal of egalitarian pressure because there is an almost unanimous agreement in the Western culture outside the church that gender role hierarchy is repulsive and oppresses women. One must decide if the failure for Christians to support the all-men-have-authority-over-all-women concept is a massive compromise with evil or a "Copernican" revolution against a deeply and broadly held error.

It is important to assert that such broad restrictions for women seem radically out of sync with the overarching teachings of Scripture about the equality, worth, gifting, and abilities of women, and with the numerous positive illustrations in the Bible of women in leadership roles even in highly patriarchal cultures (see chapter 11).

All that said, five observations should be noted about the suggestion that 1 Corinthians 11:1ff extends the male-headship-understood-as-rulership concept beyond marriage to church and society at large as a timeless requirement:

(1) Within the text, Paul seems to discount any such conclusion when he immediately counters in verse 11, 12: "In the Lord, however, woman is not independent of man, nor is man independent of woman. For as woman came from man, so also man is born of woman. But everything comes from God."[173]

---

[173] Myers, A.C., The Eerdmans Bible dictionary (Grand Rapids: Eerdmans. 1987), 470. One might conclude that this "simply portrays the order of creation (i.e., 'head' as source) . . . man and woman are interdependent, with man the initial cause of woman and woman the instrumental cause of man."

(2) Rather than Paul's argument supporting the restriction of a woman's role in the church, within the paragraph Paul clearly affirms and assumes that women will lead church worship by praying and prophesying (verse 5). No one claims that verse 5 refers to a woman praying or prophesying exclusively to herself either in her mind or so softly that no one else (especially no men) could hear her. When a woman prophesied in the gathering, it is assumed that all others present (both male and female) ceased other activity to listen to her. At least in that moment, she was "leading" the worship and the worshipers.

In this passage it is clear that Paul made no distinction in the ministry roles or activities of men and women, but only in their outward physical appearance[174] while leading through prayer or prophecy. In the passage both women and men are assumed to minister in the same ways.

(3) Some would argue that the woman's head covering (or long hair as a substitute) is a "sign of authority" on her head (verse 10). They assume, with no support within the text, this is an indication of submission to *male* authority rather than to *God's* authority. Others have argued that the covering is a sign of the woman's authority to pray or prophecy publicly. In any case, the reference to "because of the angels" (1 Cor. 11:10) has been a great puzzle to virtually all interpreters. Perhaps, as in 1 Timothy 5:21 it is a reminder that angels observe our worship and thus should motivate us to worship appropriately. However, it is difficult to see how the mysterious angel reference can be used definitively to support any interpretation of the passage. It is my opinion that the covering is a sign of submission to God's authority. Regardless of one's understanding about angels in this text, it does not support contemporary gender-based restrictions because: (a) appropriately covered women were allowed to lead, and (b) nearly all interpreters today understand the head covering as a time- and location-necessitated cultural issue that is neither perpetuated into nor replaced in our contemporary culture.[175] The long hair commanded for men under a Nazarite vow (Numbers 6:1–5) is an obvious indication that 1 Corinthians 11:14—"Does not the very nature of

---

[174] Paul's requirements for head coverings may either be a response to a specifically local issue—see point (3)(b), or a further illustration of the *concession principle* presented in chapter five. Nearly all contemporary interpreters agree that the head covering directives are neither universal nor timeless.

[175] Westfall, *Paul and Gender*, 26ff: See extensive discussion of "the practice of veiling.".

things teach you that if a man has long hair, it is a disgrace to him"—is NOT a timeless value for all men everywhere.

(4) Most interpreters would freely acknowledge that 1 Corinthians 11:2–16 is a very complex and difficult passage to interpret with no consensus of a satisfactory way to explain or harmonize its numerous conundrums. Few Bible interpreters would disagree with the statement that important Bible positions should not depend on obscure, much-debated passages.

(5) If "head" is understood as *source* rather than *boss*, then in this passage any argument for patriarchy is lost. Simply reading the text substituting the word "source" for each reference *to* "head" will reveal how fitting that understanding is. This understanding seems further confirmed by two explanatory statements within the immediate context: "For man did not come from woman, but woman from man . . . For as woman came from man, so also man is born of woman. But everything comes from God" (1 Cor. 11:8, 12).

Therefore, any use of 1 Corinthians 11:3 as evidence supporting male authority over women based on a complementarian understanding of *headship* seems dependent on a very tenuous and insubstantial foundation.

But what about Ephesians 5:23? Doesn't Paul's comparison of the husband being the head of the wife in the same way that Christ is head of the church argue powerfully that husbands have authority over their wives who are commanded to submit to their leadership? If that is true, doesn't the principle carry over to gender roles in the church?

"Head" in Ephesians 5:23

Complementarians argue for authoritative male headship in marriage based primarily on Ephesians 5:22–33, Colossians 3:18–19, Titus 2:5, and 1 Peter 3:1–7. All four passages call on wives to submit to their husbands while only the first actually uses the word "head" regarding the husband. Ephesians 5:22–24 states: "Wives, submit to your husbands as to the Lord. For the husband is the head of the wife as Christ is the head of the church, his body, of which he is the Savior. Now as the church submits to Christ, so also wives should submit to their husbands in everything."

The complementarian view assumes that in this passage "head" must be understood in terms of having authority over another. But on what evidence is this assumption made? What is the lexical, etymological, and contextual evidence for this interpretive assumption? If such evidence is absent, is it possible that the assumption is based on unquestioned and unproven patriarchal tradition or on subconscious bias?

Before addressing whether the complementarian definition of "head" as representing an authority role can be correct, it should be noted that Ephesians 5:23 is the ONLY passage in the Bible that designates the husband as the wife's "head." 1 Corinthians 11:3 calls man the "head" (*source*, see Gen. 2:21, 22) of woman, but as demonstrated earlier in this chapter, it is *not* talking about marriage or the home. Regarding Ephesians 5:23, one writer opines, "It amazes me that the Church has developed a strong and pervasive doctrine of 'male headship' based on this one Bible verse. Note that nowhere in Scripture does it teach that the man is head of the house or family."[176] In fact, it is notable that 1 Timothy 5:14 assigns the *head of the house* role to the wife, not to the husband, literally designating her as the "house despot" (οἰκοδεσποτεῖν, *oikodespotein*): "So I counsel younger widows to marry, to have children, to manage their homes and to give the enemy no opportunity for slander."

Significantly, not one of the marriage passages in which wives are instructed to "submit" to their husbands calls on those husbands to "be the leader," to "assume authority," to "rule over," or to "manage" their wives or, for that matter, over *any* woman outside of marriage. On the contrary, the Ephesians passage opens with a command for mutual submission (Eph. 5:21) and follows with instructions to husbands, not to assume rulership, but rather to practice self-sacrificing love even as Christ did for His Bride, the Church. A key to understanding the three parallel relationships in Ephesians 5:21–6:5 is the *concession principle* presented at length in chapter 5.

So, What Kind of *"Head"* is Paul Talking About?

In addition to the extensive evidence presented earlier in this chapter that "head," unless a literal anatomical reference, most often means *source*, it should also be noted that Ephesians 5:23 immediately clarifies what kind

---

[176] Mowczko,"*Kephale and Male Headship*," http://newlife.id.au/equality-and-gender -issues/kephale-and-male-headship-in-pauls-letters/.

of "head" is under consideration: "For the husband is the head of the wife as Christ is the head of the church, his body, of which he is the Savior." Jesus is the *Savior-Head*. Jesus, the "head" of the church, is "the Savior" of His body on earth, the community of believers called the church. The savior concept is further defined in the paragraph by Jesus' example that husbands are ordered to follow: "Husbands, love your wives just as Christ loved the church and gave himself for her to sanctify her by cleansing her with the washing of the water by the word" (Eph. 5:25, 26). The headship of the husband, like Christ, is expressed in his being her savior by sacrificing himself for her so she might reach her full potential. Jesus is the *source* of the church's soteriological rescue and all the blessings that that includes. The husband is to be the *source* of his wife's rescue/salvation from the ways sin would diminish and limit her perfecting and her potential.

The husband then, like Jesus, is to be the *source* of her salvation—not of her soteriological salvation (only Jesus can provide that), but rescuing her from life's hardships, perhaps even from sin's curse, which includes the fall-induced evil of patriarchy (Gen. 3:16) and all forms of oppression—domestic, spiritual, mental, emotional, physical, and societal. Rather than imposing his "rule" over her (an evil expression of sin's curse, Gen. 3:16), the savior-head-husband sacrifices himself, dying to his own agenda and demands, to pursue what is best for her, and to love her as himself, as his own body. What is startling is, following Christ's example, that the husband is to care for his wife's needs "in terms of domestic chores normally performed by women: giving a bath, providing clothing, and doing laundry (including spot removal and ironing) (5:26, 27) . . . this is a brilliant description of servanthood."[177] Far from these verses advocating male domination in marriage, it is a powerful call for mutual submission and servanthood and for the elevation of other above self.

The fact that "head" in Ephesians 5:23 is not about authority or leadership, either of the husband or of Christ, does not at all diminish Jesus' authority over His church. That is assumed throughout the New Testament.[178] He is

---

[177] Westfall, *Paul and Gender*, 94.

[178] The emphasis on Jesus' authority is illustrated in that in the book of Acts He is called "Savior" twice but "Lord" more than 100 times. In the New Testament, Jesus is called "Lord" 618 times, but "Savior" only 15.

Lord and King. But in this passage, "head" is not about taking authority but about being the source from which his wife's needs are provided.

Paul does not tell husbands to be the leaders in the marriage or to exercise authority over their wives. He commands husbands to love their wives sacrificially; to care for them and nurture them. They are to do this just as Jesus laid His life down for His bride, the church. They are to love and care for their wives as Jesus cares for the church. The husband is to be the sustainer and source *(kephalē) of his wife's nurture just as Christ is the Sustainer and Source (kephalē)of nurture for the church.*

If the husband is the head and the wife is the body, then clearly, they are one, suggesting the "one flesh" of Genesis 2:24 and Ephesians 5:31. Indeed, the two are so essentially and inseparably connected that it is as if they are no longer two but one identity. 1 Corinthians 12 extensively develops the metaphor of the church as a body. The only reference to the "head" in that discussion clearly emphasizes that it is not separate, over, or in charge of the body, but ONE with the body, and not superior in any way: "As it is, there are many parts, but one body. The eye cannot say to the hand, 'I don't need you!' And the head cannot say to the feet, 'I don't need you!'" (1 Cor. 12:20, 21). Obviously if, in Paul's thinking, the head is no more valuable or important than the feet, then to build the complementarian case on portraying the head as the *boss* with authority over the body is completely inappropriate. Regarding Ephesians 5,

> "This passage provides the key for tracing Paul's adoption and adaption of the Greek word κεφαλὴ as he transfers the characteristics of a progenitor to both the husband and Christ in his relationship to the church (Eph. 5:31 // Gen. 2:24). Since the husband is his wife's source, he is her head, but since they are one flesh, she is his body instead of his seed. This breaks down the Greco-Roman philosophy about hierarchy and the separation between the genders in favor of an organic unity and biological interdependency. The interdependency that Paul explains involves how the husband continues to be the source of his wife as a head ... Besides the evidence that man is the source of woman in the creation account, the wife is depicted by Paul as dependent

on the husband for her life support (food, clothing, nurture, protection, and love) in the same way that the body is dependent on the head for food, water, air, and the senses of sight and hearing."[179]

Further evidence that in Ephesians 5:23 "head" should be understood as *source* is in the extended context of Paul's letter to the Ephesians. An earlier reference to Jesus as the church's head is found in Ephesians 4:15, 16, "Instead, speaking the truth in love, we will in all things grow up into him who is the Head, that is, Christ. From him the whole body, joined and held together by every supporting ligament, grows and builds itself up in love, as each part does its work." Notice how well that passage fits Paul's assertion regarding Jesus and the church if the word *"Source"* is substituted for "Head" in the passage: "We will in all things grow up into him who is the SOURCE, that is, Christ. From him the whole body, joined and held together by every supporting ligament, grows and builds itself up in love, as each part does its work." What follows is a beautiful description of how the cohesion, support, growth, and building up of the body flow to the church from Jesus, the Source.

Precisely the same dynamic is evident in the parallel sections of Paul's concurrent letter to the church in Colosse. As in Ephesians, prior to his presentation of the three parallel relationships, Paul talks about Jesus' headship of the church in terms that reveal that He is the *Source* of the church's support and strength: "He has lost connection with the Head [SOURCE], from whom the whole body, supported and held together by its ligaments and sinews, grows as God causes it to grow." (Col. 2:19).

The concept of savior and source is further illustrated in the larger context of Ephesians. In Ephesians 1:3–14, Jesus is the Source of an astounding list of blessings for the church. In Ephesians 4:11–14, He is the Source of the church's spiritual gifts and callings. He even shares and assigns the leadership of His church to those who are part of the body. Think of it! "As his body, believers are completely identified with Christ and his human status; he made them heirs of God and joint heirs with himself (Romans 8:17). The analogy between Christ and the husband should lead men to share authority, status, power, and resources, and bring freedom that is comparable to what their head, Jesus Christ, provided for them and intends for the rest of His body. Men should

---

[179] Westfall, *Paul and Gender,* 94, 95.

love women and treat them literally like themselves, not just as they imagine they would want to be treated if they were women."[180]

In Ephesians 5:28 Paul adds yet another dimension to his *head-love*. Husbands are not merely commanded to love their wives AS MUCH AS or IN THE SAME WAY AS they love their own bodies. We all work hard to take care of our own bodies. Rather, he calls on them to love their wives because they ARE their own bodies. Wife-love is self-love. In appropriately loving his wife, the husband loves <u>himself</u>: "In the same way husbands ought to love their wives as their own bodies. He who loves his wife loves himself." The husband is to love his wife as his own body—that is, he is to love her as his body because THAT IS WHAT SHE IS—HIS BODY—indivisibly one with him. She is not under or below him. She IS him. Head and body are one inseparable unity. Separate them and they are DEAD! A beheaded body immediately ceases to live. Cut off the head from the body and every part and system of both immediately shuts down and dies. Neither head nor body can survive, let alone thrive, without dynamic and essential union with the other. Like Eve, she is "bone of his bones and flesh of his flesh" (Gen. 2:23). It would be difficult to conceive of a stronger assertion of equality, identity, and total partnership than this.

It seems patently obvious that "head," rather than conveying a twenty-first century *CEO* picture as the complementarian view suggests, instead the biblical data communicates the picture of *source* and *savior.*

But What about the Relationship of <u>Submission</u> to Headship?

If all this is so, why does Paul appear to link the wife's *submission* to the headship of her husband in Ephesians 5:22–24? Doesn't that argue for understanding "head" as having *authority* over another?

First, it must be noted that verse 22 immediate FOLLOWS and is inseparably connected to verse 21, "Submit to one another out of reverence for Christ." The wife's submission to her husband is the first practical application of the prior command for mutual submission between all believers regardless of gender, position in family (children or parents), social status (slaves or masters), ethnicity, or any other distinction. Remember, as previously noted,

---

[180] Ibid., 95.

that the word "submit" is not present in the original Greek of verse 22. The word "submit" is assumed/supplied from verse 21. There is no marital submission (verse 22) apart from mutual submission (verse 21) and mutual submission *takes precedence over* marital submission.

If the wife's submission to her husband is a gender-based requirement designed by God from creation for all time, and if, as complementarians like to assert, it is beneficial to the wife, why would Holy Scripture include this contradictory command for mutual submission? Clearly the wife's submission in verse 22 does not trump or replace the immediately prior and proximate command for mutual submission in verse 21. Rather the wife's submission is one illustration of what all believers are to render to each other. In the context of these three parallel relationships, the command for wives to submit to their husbands is a temporary concession in a fallen, oppressive culture in order to preserve peace and promote the Gospel, not a timeless command for gender-based submission (see chapter 5).

Second, the cultural setting of the passage is the Roman system of patronage in which wives, children, and slaves depended on their husbands, fathers, and masters as the *source* for all of their basic needs, even as citizens depended on those who governed them. That was the role of the husband in the Greco-Roman world. The wife's identity, position in society, financial provision, property, inheritance, housing, food, clothing—all were provided by her husband. He was her life-sustaining source—her "head." "The Greco-Roman cultural values convincingly explain how the husband is the source of the wife's life, not only in the creation account (Gen. 2), but also as practiced in the first century world (Ephesians 5:23) because of the very real dependence of women on their husbands."[181] No wonder Paul likens the husband's headship to Jesus' headship. Jesus is the Source and Provider of everything the church needs. Understanding of "head" as *source* in Ephesians 5:23 is completely appropriate both for husbands and Jesus. Based on the benefits that flowed from their first party source, the second parties were to respond to them with submission, taxes, respect, and honor (Eph. 5:22–24; Rom. 13:1–7; 1 Pt. 2:13–3:7).

Third, it must also be noted that in Ephesians 5 and 6 Paul's commands to husbands, fathers, and masters, utterly undermine the oppressive hierarchy that was commonplace and accepted in those three relationships. Rather

---

[181] Ibid., 22.

than assuming authority over them, Christians in the power position were commanded to respond to those who, in that culture, were under their authority, by submitting to them (5:21) and by loving and serving them (5:25-31). Jesus' followers were to operate according to different norms and values than those of the pagan culture in which they lived as illustrated by Romans 12:10 (ESV): "Love one another with brotherly affection. Outdo one another in showing honor." Believers were to relate to each other as equals.

Near the end of the passage, Ephesians 5:29 supports the view that a central purpose of the passage was to address the abusive authority by males prevalent in that culture (husbands, fathers, and masters). The husband's love of wife-as-his-own-body is sharply contrasted with the unnatural idea of *hating or abusing* one's own body: "For no one has ever hated his own body but he feeds it and takes care of it, just as Christ also does the church." Self-love[182] is healthy. Self-abuse is a sign of some serious, unhealthy issue.

All the parts of the passage fit together harmoniously when viewed through the lens of "head" meaning *source* and the instructions for the three parallel relationships interpreted as calling the powerless party to make temporary accommodations while living in an oppressive culture so peace might be maintained and the spread of the Gospel unhindered.

A Reminder Concerning Gender Roles in the Church

Regardless of how "head" and *headship* are understood or whether the instructions in these passages are intended as timeless requirements, local prescriptions, or as temporary concessions it is essential to recognize that nothing in Ephesians 5 applies wives' submission beyond their relationship to their own husbands. Again, neither in Ephesians 5 or Colossians 3, or in any other Scripture, is there any stated or implied application of these marital roles to men in general or to the church or to societal roles such as government, education, law enforcement, military, or business. It is a huge, unsubstantiated hermeneutical leap to argue for restricting women from church leadership based on these marriage-related *headship passages* in which there is absolutely no supporting textual evidence. Rather Ephesians

---

[182] Self-love not in the sense of narcissism or self-centeredness but of appropriate self-care.

5:22 (ESV, NASB95, KJV), specifically instructs wives to submit to "their own (τοῖς ἰδίοις, *tois idiois*) husbands," NOT to men in general or to men in the church or in any other setting.

Despite the total absence of any biblical connection between supposed male leadership in marriage and their ascendency in the church, many complementarians assert that the one assumes or requires the other. This is a crucial point. Even if one accepts the marriage passages as teaching male authority and female submission not as a temporary concession but as a timeless mandate in marriage (which view I vigorously oppose as contrary to what the text actually says), it is still absolutely unwarranted and unjustified based on anything in the text to transfer that same hierarchical dynamic to the church.

The bottom line is that the two key headship passages do NOT portray men and husbands as authoritative heads, but as source and savior heads. The implications for the church and marriage could hardly be greater!

Now You've Really Opened a Can of Worms

As if it weren't enough to challenge traditional gender role restrictions in the church, now I have also challenged traditional gender roles in the institution of Christian marriage. It seems like an old adage may speak to such insanity: "Fools rush in where angels fear to tread." But now I've done it. Pandora's Box has been opened and it's too late to stuff these theological demons back inside.

I have to recognize that had someone hit me with "both barrels" just a few short years ago, I might have written them off or quickly dismissed them as having gone over the edge. Parachutes anyone?

Although it is not the purpose of this book to introduce confusion and instability into marriages—God knows they already face immense stresses and pressures in this family unfriendly culture—there didn't seem to be any way to address the issue of gender roles in church without including a somewhat thorough consideration of the key New Testament marriage passages. Many will bring them up to use as big guns in the complementarian-egalitarian wars.

It is my prayer and sincere hope that to the best of my readers' ability, they will not allow the magnitude of interpretive and behavioral change I have advocated in the first 50% of this book to cause them to simply dismiss this study out of hand. Too much is at stake and *rightly interpreting the Sacred Scriptures* is too important to not give what I have written sincere and serious consideration. I plead with my readers to set aside known or subconscious bias (is that even possible?) as well as unthinking acceptance of what one may have always been taught so as to thoughtfully engage with <u>what the Bible actually says regarding gender roles in the church and in marriage</u>. I think that most of my readers would agree that it doesn't ultimately matter how difficult or disruptive it may be, discerning what the Scriptures actually teach and then aligning one's life is far more important.

For every follower of Jesus, conversion involved a radical rejection of personal sin, a perverted world view, and countless ways of thinking and behaving that had to give way to a whole new way of perceiving, believing, and acting as a new and stumbling follower of Christ. We call that "repentance." That wasn't the end of our transformation. It was only the beginning. The entire Christian life is one of being transformed by the renewing of our minds (Rom. 12:1, 2)—unless we are reprehensibly apathetic, ungrateful, lazy, self-deceived, foolishly stubborn, and backslidden (or maybe not even truly converted, but just fooling ourselves). We must NEVER assume that we've got it all right and need not reexamine the Scriptures to see where we might need to bring our beliefs, convictions, relationships, and conduct into conformity with God's plan for us.

Will you accept the challenge however painful the process of study (and possible life-change) may be? I can assure you that whether we need to reaffirm and hang on to our current understandings about gender roles in the church and in marriage or to make a radical shift in our understanding and practice, discovering and doing God's will is a wonderful adventure with eternally positive ramifications.

But, I need to warn you, there are more theological demons ready to leap out of Pandora's Box. Now we need to move to "Ground Zero" in the gender roles debate—the two *prohibition passages* that are the strong fortress of complementarian convictions. 1 Corinthians 14:33–35 and 1 Timothy 2:11–15 are the passages that, on the surface, seem to mandate silence and submission for women in the church and that ban them from leading men. Are you ready to have your theological world rocked? Let's move on. What I'm about to share may feel like the enactment of the theological "nuclear option." The question is, what does the Bible say?

FOR DISCUSSION

(1) For each of these sentences, come up with a short definition for the word "head":

    a.   Since Billy ran into the front door, his "head" hurt.

    b.   Tom and Sally had a big argument about who should be the "head" of their house.

    c.   The teacher rewarded Janet by sending her to the "head" of the line.

    d.   It took three hours to paddle the canoe up to the "head" of the river.

(2) Read Ephesians 5:23. Which of the different definitions of "head" in question (1) could fit this verse?

(3) What arguments could you come up with that in Ephesians 5:23 "head" means *having authority over* and how many can you come up with for it meaning *source of*?

(4) 1 Corinthians 11:3 says that Christ is the head of every man (human); man is the head of the woman; and that God is the head of Christ. What do verses 8 and 12 suggest about whether "head" in verse 3 should be understood as *having authority over* or as *source of*?

(5) Read Ephesians 5:25–28. How does Paul say that the husband-head is supposed to treat his wife?

(6) Read Ephesians 5:21–23. What do you think is the significance that before Paul commanded wives to submit to their husbands, he first commanded all Christians to submit to each other, including husbands to wives?

(7) Give five or more very practical illustrations of what mutual submission might look like in a Christian marriage today.

(8) If in Ephesians 5 "head" means "source" rather than "boss," what are some practical ways that should change the attitudes and actions of Christian husbands?

7

"Ground Zero" In the Gender Roles Debate

One day a couple of years ago when I walked across the street to grab our mail from our green mailbox, I quickly flipped through the stack to see if anything was truly interesting amidst the annoying pile of junk mail and catalogs filled with pictures of things we couldn't be happy without. In the stack I spotted one letter that our postal carrier had uncharacteristically put in the wrong mail box. It was addressed to our next-door neighbor. I had taken a couple of steps toward his mailbox twenty yards down the street when my attention was drawn to the return address on the envelop. It read: "THE WHITE HOUSE, 1600 Pennsylvania Avenue NW, Washington, DC 20500."

"Wow!" I thought to myself. "It looks like our neighbor just got a letter from the President of the United States." Then I noticed that our neighbor's name and address were hand-written." This looked like a personal letter.

In a moment of near insanity, curiosity overcame my better judgment and would not allow me to dwell on the potential <u>consequences</u> of what I was contemplating: a federal offence; FBI agents surrounding my house; my face on the six o'clock news as I was stuffed into the back seat of a federal agent's black car with my hands cuffed behind my back; then disappearing from society without a trace. I told myself that I could employ my untested skills in steaming open the fancy envelope so I could read the letter, then reseal it and covertly place it in my none-the-wiser neighbor's mailbox.

Back in my house with the shades drawn, I unfolded the personal letter I had carefully extracted from its envelop. The letter was hand-written on expensive linen stationary with the familiar picture of the White House at the top. Turning to the end of the letter I saw that it was written on behalf of then President Barak Obama by his personal assistant, Reggie Love—a man believed by many to know the president better than anyone outside of his immediate family.

As I read down through the letter, I was keenly aware that the letter was not written to me, but with nearly every sentence I learned something new about the president as well as something I didn't know about my neighbor.

Although much of what the President's assistant wrote to my neighbor had little to do with me, I couldn't help but be impressed by the very personal and wise counsel the President, through his assistant, gave my neighbor regarding a situation very much like something I was dealing with in my own life. Although the letter wasn't to me, I determined that I would follow the President's advice as if it had been.

The New Testament Letters Are Somebody Else's Mail

Now perhaps you've already guessed that I've been telling you a crazy, imaginary story to illustrate a very important point—when you read someone else's mail, it's possible to learn a great deal about the author and the recipient, and sometimes even things that you could apply to yourself. That's what we need to remember when we're reading the twenty-two letters in the New Testament of the Bible (Romans through Revelation). They are letters written to specific individuals and groups of people who lived in the first century. When we read those ancient letters, we are actually reading somebody else's mail. That's essential to remember as we interpret and apply them. Almost all of the letters tell us the name of the author and identify to whom they were written, whether to a specific congregation in an ancient city, to a group of people scattered throughout a region, or even to an individual like Timothy, Titus, or Philemon.

When I was a teenager, we used to sing a chorus at church and in youth group that went like this (aren't you glad you can't hear me singing?):

> Every promise in the Book is mine,
> Every chapter, every verse, every line;
> All the blessings of His love divine,
> Every promise in the Book is mine.

The song was fun to sing and was an encouraging affirmation of the personal value of the Bible, but it was WRONG! God promised Abraham a son when he was eighty-five years old (Gen. 15:4). His wife Sara was seventy-five. If that promise is mine, I better warn my dear wife, Gloria, who is not as old as Sara was, but is definitely past the "let's have a baby" stage. God promised the enslaved Israelites that He would take them back to the Promised Land (Ex. 3:16, 17). Should I pack my suitcase? Holy Land here I come! That's silly! Those promises were made to someone else. They aren't "mine" as the chorus declared.[183] When I read the Bible, I need to be aware of to whom the passage I'm studying was written. Just like I learned a lot about the president and my neighbor from reading his letter, I can always learn from those parts of the Bible not addressed to me as Romans 15:4 and 1 Corinthians 10:6 teach regarding the Old Testament: "For whatsoever things were written aforetime were written for our learning, that we through patience and comfort of the scriptures might have hope . . . Now these things were our examples, to the intent we should not lust after evil things, as they also lusted." But while I can always learn from them, precisely how I should interpret and apply any Scripture is very much dependent on an awareness of to whom it was written and what circumstances may have prompted the original communication.

Benjamin Corey gives a helpful reminder about the importance of discerning authorial intent and the circumstances of the recipients in biblical interpretation— key factors in studying the New Testament letters:

> You're reading books and letters where the primary/original meaning is what the author intended the original audience to understand.

---

[183] Two classic illustrations of Christians incorrectly claiming someone else's promise are: (1) 1 Chronicles 7:14 ("If my people . . .). The promise was given to God's chosen nation Israel and the "land" God promised to heal if they repented was the Holy Land, not the USA. Of course, we can learn from the verse, but we cannot legitimately claim it as God's promise to twenty-first century Christians in the USA; and (2) Jeremiah 29:11 ("For I know the plans I have for you . . . "). That beautiful promise was to the Israelites whose 70-year exile in Babylon would soon end and God would take them back to and prosper them in the land promised to Abraham. The promise teaches us comforting truths about the character and trustworthiness of God, but the specific promise is not ours.

I remember learning in Sunday School that the Bible was "God's love letter to us." It's a cute idea but is less than helpful because we're not the original audience, and that matters.

The reality is that these are sacred books, stories, and letters, where the *primary/original* meaning is the meaning the *original* author intended to convey to the *original* audience– and we're neither of those parties. It's almost like trying to understand an inside joke; until you understand the relationship between the sender and receiver of a message, and the context of what's being discussed, it's easy to walk away with all sorts of broken understandings of what was really being communicated. This makes things like understanding ancient culture, customs, and general history, a critical aspect of understanding the Bible.[184]

This is important to remember as we read Paul's first letter to the Corinthians and another to young pastor Timothy in Ephesus. While we can learn and apply a great deal from those letters, we must interpret them in light of who wrote them, to whom they were written, what the historical and cultural backgrounds were, what the circumstances were that occasioned the letters, and what the author's purposes were in writing them.

Obviously, the letters teach us a great deal about the authors and the recipients, about God, and about what it meant for them to follow Jesus in their unique historical and cultural settings. Of course, there are many truths and lessons we can learn for ourselves and what it means for us to follow Jesus today, but those must be discerned in concert with our understanding of the original intent of the author regarding the people and circumstances addressed.

"But that sounds like a lot of work," someone objects, "Can't I just read

---

[184] Benjamin L. Corey, "5 Things You're Reading, When You're Reading the Bible," *The Official Blog of Benjamin L. Corey* (blog), March 13, 2017, http://www.patheos. com/blogs/formerlyfundie/the-things-youre-reading-when-youre-reading-the-bible/?utm_source=PatheosNL&utm_medium=referral&utm_campaign=Progressive +Christian&utm_source=[!]%20Newsletter&utm_medium=email&utm_ campaign=NL%20Progressive%20Christian&utm_content=49114

my Bible?" Sure, but Proverbs 2:1-5 reminds us that the pursuit of wisdom in the Scriptures requires diligent effort:

> My son, if you accept my words and store up my commands within you, turning your ear to wisdom and applying your heart to understanding, and if you call out for insight and cry aloud for understanding, and if you look for it as for silver and search for it as for hidden treasure, then you will understand the fear of the Lord and find the knowledge of God.

Frequently the effort you put into something determines the benefit you get out of it.

Reading Someone Else's Mail about Gender Roles

When it comes to the gender roles debate, a strong case can be made that the traditional interpretation of the key gender role passages in Paul's New Testament letters (1 Cor. 14 and 1 Tim. 2) does not reflect the kind of serious hermeneutically-driven analysis which biblical interpretation demands including giving careful attention to the recipients and the context.

For example, Westfall writes a scorching critique of the sloppy interpretive methods too often employed to arrive at the traditional complementarian regarding the "ground zero" gender role texts.

> There has been a major problem with a lack of consistent methodology in the interpretation of the text. Traditional readings of texts on gender are not based on hermeneutics that are consistently applied to passages addressing or concerning gender, nor are they consistent with hermeneutics that we generally apply to other texts to determine what a text originally meant. Within the tradition of interpretation, the passages that concern gender have not been understood in the contexts of the discourses in which they occur, the biblical theology of the Pauline corpus as a whole, the narrative of Paul's life, a linguistic understanding/

analysis of the Greek language, or an understanding of the culture that is sociologically informed. The support of the traditional readings assumes the strength of their position, and the analyses of the text are therefore argumentative and assume the conclusions.[185]

[She asserts that] the traditional interpretations of 1 Tim. 2:12 and other passages on gender are based on information, assumptions, and inferences that are imposed on the text, part of the interpreter's embedded theology, and/or the direct and inevitable outcome of how the understanding of the passage has been taught, preached, and discussed in various venues by teachers, preachers, parents, and companions. Consequently, the traditional assumptions have been combined with an inspired status of being 'what God says.' These assumptions have been combined with atomistic readings that are removed from the biblical situation, time, and culture.[186]

These are very serious accusations. If she could be correct, the complementarian position *must* be carefully re-examined. Such a serious accusation from a credible Bible scholar should not be lightly dismissed, but rather calls for an unbiased (to the degree that is possible) investigation of the validity of her claims by applying the commonly accepted hermeneutical practices to the relevant gender-roles texts.

Therefore, as we approach the two primary passages in the Bible regarding gender roles in the church, 1 Corinthians 14 and 1 Timothy 2—indeed, the ONLY passages which address this issue directly—we must give careful attention to appropriate interpretive dynamics. We cannot simply jump into the passages as if they directly and simplistically address our twenty-first century culture and churches. To do so would show gross disrespect for what the Bible says about itself, and to ignore the important statements about why and to whom those letters and particular passages were written. Remember, the Bible is trustworthy. Human interpretations of the Bible may not be.

---

[185] Westfall, *Paul and Gender,* 3.

[186] Ibid., 2.

In my imaginary story, I learned a lot about my neighbor and about President Obama by reading my neighbor's mail, and I also gained personal insights and conclusions for myself from it. But I understood that I must not treat my neighbor's letter as if it had been written to me personally regarding my own unique circumstances. The same is true of Paul's letters including those written to the first century Christians in Corinth (1 Corinthians) and Ephesus (1 Timothy). This recognition is essential to correctly interpret and apply these gender-role texts.

Therefore, it's essential to answer very important questions: What was going on in the churches in Corinth and Ephesus which occasioned these teachings? What happened that Paul needed to correct? Were they local problems in the first century not applicable to us today, or were they timeless issues (and solutions) affecting all Christians everywhere?

How one understands 1 Corinthians 14:33-40 and 1 Timothy 2:11-15 is really the tipping point in the gender roles discussion. These are *control texts*. "While we believe that all of the Bible is inspired by God, there are some texts of the Bible that clearly dominate our interpretation and reception of the others."[187] Apart from these two texts, the hierarchical position in the church gender role debate would be greatly diminished or more probably would disappear. In fact, the complementarian position in the Western church hangs on a slender thread of how four Greek words in these two passages have been translated into English. Unfortunately, the unclear and/or misleading they are translated in most English Bible versions[188] has exerted huge influence on their interpretation as well as on how other Scriptures have been understood and applied. This will be addressed below.

The following three observations suggest that gender restrictions in the church cannot be supported by the two key gender role passages when they are properly translated and understood.

(1) **If one assumes that the Scriptures, rightly interpreted, do not contradict each other, then comparing these key Scriptures with other biblical passages clarifies that they <u>cannot possibly</u> be**

---

[187] Stackhouse, *Partners In Christ*, 37.

[188] It appears that few have questioned these translations and done even the most basic exegetical research which would have exposed their flaws.

understood as an absolute prohibition of women from speaking or from teaching men in the church.

Any interpretation of these two passages must be harmonized with other passages such as 1 Corinthians 11:5ff in which Paul unquestionably recognizes the legitimacy of women speaking in church with men present—specifically praying and prophesying. 1 Corinthians 11:5 states that "every woman who prays or prophesies with her head uncovered dishonors her head." While praying and prophesying are not necessarily *official* leadership positions such as elder, it seems clear that anyone who prays or prophesies in a church service is, at that moment, *leading* the congregants in prayer or instruction/ teaching. Note that Paul assumes that women pray and prophecy in church. He does not restrict this as to audience. There is no suggestion this applies only to teaching or leading other women or children. Paul's only concern is whether they have their heads covered when they do it.

Today most Bible students on both sides of the gender role debate interpret the required head covering and hair length requirements in the passage as first century Corinthian cultural issues no longer binding or relevant today.[189] Paul's negative commentary regarding a man's long hair is consistent with similar negative attitudes in the Greco-Roman culture regarding men having long hair.

First and Second Corinthians seem to have been written primarily to Gentiles (see Acts 18:1-8 and 1 Cor. 12:2: "You know that when you were pagans you were led astray to mute idols"). In the first century Gentile culture, male head coverings were considered "dishonorable" (11:4). However, it was a somewhat common practice in pagan religions for men to pull their toga over their head during a religious ceremony. Obviously, believers would not want to duplicate this. Paul would likely not have said this if his audience had been primarily Jewish. Although wearing the yarmulke (skull cap) did not become fully normative for worshipping Jewish men until the Middle Ages, it was a widespread practice long prior to that time as a sign of respect and reverence for God.

If it were a timeless principle that men's hair should be short, how can one harmonize the requirement that someone adopting the Nazarite vow

---

[189] Rare exceptions may be found among certain very conservative Amish, Mennonite, and fundamentalist groups.

(Num. 6:1ff) must not cut his hair (remember Samson whose long hair was inseparably connected to his God-given supernatural strength).

Thus, it seems evident in 1 Corinthians 11 that Paul is addressing first century Corinthian cultural issues, not timeless requirements for all believers.

But, regardless of how one understands the head coverings, it is indisputable that Paul *assumed* that women would pray and prophecy in the Corinthian church. He does not raise even a whisper of objection to this ministry. His only concern is that their head be covered while they minister. This participation in worship by women was radically counter-cultural in a pervasively oppressive patriarchal environment. The permission this passage granted for the role of women in church was astounding and must not be minimized or contradicted by other less clear and more disputed passages which have been hotly debated for centuries by Bible students and scholars. Rather than being a misogynist as sometimes accused, the doors for ministry in church which Paul threw open for women reveal Paul to be shockingly egalitarian regarding gender roles especially considering the culture in which he lived.

This issue is more significant because the two apparently contradicting passages are in the same Book, separated by only a few chapters (1 Cor. 11 and 14). They might be easier to explain away if they were in different books of the Bible written by different authors to different people living in different times, places, and circumstances. But they were both written by the same author to the same recipients in the same place at the same time. Either Paul made an obvious error, had a serious mental lapse, or the apparent contradiction is the result of a *faulty interpretation* of one of the passages. While there are aspects of 1 Corinthians 11 which interpreters dispute, there is virtually no disagreement that verse 5 teaches that women are permitted to pray or prophecy in church.[190] On the other hand, the meaning of 1 Corinthians 14:33-35 and 1 Timothy 2:12-15 are greatly disputed. Therefore, it seems obvious that we must accept the clarity of 1 Corinthians 11:5 as establishing boundaries as to how the disputed passages can and cannot be interpreted.

---

[190] What is sometimes disputed is the meaning of the head covering and whether it is timeless or a local issue in first century Corinth.

What Are the Boundaries?

In light of 1 Corinthians 11:5, all those who believe in the unity and trustworthiness of the Scriptures must not interpret 1 Corinthians 14 and 1 Timothy 2 as absolute or total prohibitions against women speaking, teaching, or leading[191] men in church. This conclusion provides essential boundaries for how those passages can be interpreted—boundaries which eliminate any understanding which prohibits women from all speaking or leadership roles in church. It undermines the typical complementarian understanding of the two prohibition passages.

Complementarians attempt to address this argument in relationship to 1 Corinthians 14 in several ways. Some limit the scope of application of the demand for women to be silent. This results in a significantly watered-down gender restriction, perhaps, consciously or subconsciously, to limit its unpalatable offensiveness or impractical application. For example, "some evangelicals have allowed women to preach but only in foreign missionary situations (what I call **'the missionary exception'**). Others, allow women to participate in spiritual leadership, but only in so-called parachurch organizations, and not in congregations and denominations (what I call **'the parachurch parenthesis'**)."[192]

Many complementarian churches and Christian ministries "permit women to have even wide-ranging theological careers of speaking and writing, as long as they profess to be responsible to a man, whether husband or pastor or both (**the 'under authority arrangement'**)."[193] I wonder how diligently the specifics and accountability of this "under authority arrangement" are actually defined and monitored or if, in reality, it is a just a convenient or clever way to rationalize something a literal application of their position would not allow?

In most churches, regardless of their position on gender roles, the overwhelming majority of children's ministry teachers, leaders, and

---

[191] This is not an exegetical observation, but a practical one: when calling on a church member to pray in a service, the pastor will often say, "Fred, will you lead us in prayer?" The expression is a tacit acknowledgement that when one prays in church, they are in fact, *leading* the congregation. This would be even more obvious with prophecying.

[192] Stackhouse, *Partners in Christ,* 44, 45.

[193] Ibid.

"directors"[194] are female. Probably 95% of complementarian churches rationalize women serving as teachers and leaders by applying what might be called **the "teaching children concession."**[195] Significantly, a miniscule number of those churches have determined and monitor what they believe to be a biblically designated age at which a boy becomes a man and therefore must no longer sit under female teaching or authority. Do any supply ear plugs for the men also present as volunteer workers in the children's department when the children are being taught by a woman? Some of these churches would justify these anomalies by suggesting that the female children's teachers and leaders serve under the authority of the senior pastor or an associate pastor. Yet few, if any of them, demonstrate this "sign of authority" (1 Cor. 11:5–15) with some kind of head covering, whether a hat, doily, scarf, or burka, or with hair that meets some unspecified standard of what it means to be "long" (1 Cor. 11:5-16).

By the way, consider this: the predominance of female teachers of children in churches exposes a fallacy of thinking or a huge illustration of hypocrisy. Aren't children the most vulnerable and pliable recipients of instruction? Don't they represent the future of our churches (and the world)? If there is a gender-based problem with women serving as teachers, why are they the backbone of every church children's ministry?

Some would defend these *under authority* exceptions as applications of the "head covering" or "long hair" requirements of 1 Corinthians 11 by employing some contemporary substitution of a different symbol.[196] This

---

[194] In many churches, the job description for the "children's ministry director" are identical to that of a "children's ministry pastor" except for the gender of the office-holder. Which title is granted is determined solely based on the person's gender. Perhaps the inconsistency and potential hypocrisy of this verbal exercise should cause some to rethink their positions. Is it just a shell game? Guess which gender is under the "director" shell.

[195] This is most likely defended on the basis of 1 Timothy 2:12 "I do not permit a woman to teach or to have authority over a man," which will be discussed at great length in chapters 9 and 10.

[196] Some complementarian churches justify a woman teaching when she is "under the authority" of her husband and the male pastor, elders, or board (assuming those are all males). Precisely what it means for her to be under their authority doesn't seem to be well or consistently defined. More importantly, this imposes a different meaning on 1 Tim. 2:12 than even the complementarian view assumes. The complementarian

might be designated as **the substitute head covering allowance.** No one seems able to point to evidence in the text that allows for such a substitute symbol of authority, nor does there seem any specific visible symbol actually practiced today as a replacement for the long hair or hat. Apparently, the new symbol is secret or invisible— which hardly satisfies the purpose or definition of a "sign" of authority.

Complementarians like John Piper seem to rely on the "teaching children concession" as they prohibit women from teaching men, not only in church, but even from teaching them in seminary. As part of his argument in favor of that prohibition, Piper observes that a seminarian has "moved beyond the adolescent years of transition from boyhood to manhood."[197] Holding to the traditional complementarian position that the pastoral office is limited to biblically qualified men, Piper asserts that "The issue is whether women should be models, mentors, and teachers for those preparing for a role that is biblically designed for spiritual men."[198] Thus he asserts that women should not be allowed even to teach men in seminary who are preparing to be pastors. Those same pastoral candidates were doubtless taught the Bible by women throughout their most formative years, but apparently the fact that it was called "Sunday School" rather than "seminary" makes it okay. Let's hope that those female Sunday School teachers gave them a solid biblical foundation for the seminary to build on.

If Piper is correct then Priscilla should not have been involved in explaining to preacher Apollos "the way of God more adequately" (Acts 18:26). Scholars are virtually unanimous in their conclusion that she was the dominate teacher in the husband wife duo of Priscilla and Aquila, because, contrary to acceptable style in that patriarchal culture, her name is listed before her husband's five out of seven times in the New Testament). Perhaps she could be excused for such an egregious violation of complementarian

---

understanding of is not that a woman is forbidden to teach or have authority over a man UNLESS some factor allows it. The complementarian understanding of the text is that a woman is prohibited from teaching or having authority over a man. Period! No exceptions are given. I reject this entire complementarian understanding but want to call attention to the inconsistency of application by some who embrace it.

[197] John Piper, "Is There a Place for Female Professors at Seminary?" *Desiring God* (blog), January 22, 2018, https://www.desiringgod.org/interviews/is-there-a-place-for-female-professors-at-seminary

[198] Ibid.

gender role restrictions because she had not seen 1 Tim. 2:12-15. That Pauline letter would not be written for more than a decade after the events of Acts 18. However, any such rationalization is obliterated by the consistent complementarian insistence that the gender roles are *creation based*. Hence, someone who assumed the role of Apollos' "seminary professor" in order to teach him "the way of God more adequately" should certainly have been aware of the teachings of Genesis 1, 2. One must either condemn Priscilla, a New Testament heroine, or reexamine and reject the presupposition that patriarchal gender-based restrictions were God's plan from the beginning. History includes the names of many women in the line of Priscilla who have competently served as seminary professors and scholars and have helped to shape generations of male students for effective pastoral ministry.

Some interpreters attempt to harmonize the permissions of 1 Corinthians 11 with the apparent prohibitions of 1 Corinthians 14 by suggesting there were times for women to be silent and times they could speak. In this view, the "right times" would be defined by when it was or was not appropriate to practice one's legitimate freedom in Christ (Gal. 5:13, 14; 1 Cor. 8:12, 13; 10:23, 24; 1 Pt. 2:16) based on not scandalizing a society often not yet ready to receive women leaders. Although this could be a valid application of **the stumbling block principle** (1 Cor. 8:9; Rom. 14:13) or **the concession principle** (Eph. 5:21–6:9), it should be noted that it nevertheless assumes that women are free to teach and give verbal leadership whenever such circumstances are absent. The times when that principle would apply two thousand years later would certainly be far less common—especially in Western cultures. Perhaps such a concession would still be necessary in a radical Muslim setting.

Additionally, it should be noted that the stumbling block principle doesn't apply to someone merely *upset* by a woman in leadership based either on their understanding of Scripture or on their personal bias. In 1 Corinthians 8 it was intended as a safeguard against practicing one's freedom in a way that influenced someone to forsake their faith and return to the idolatrous practices of their old life. Today, nearly all Western cultures are becoming more welcoming to women leaders. An egalitarian understanding doesn't cause immature believers to forsake their faith. It certainly doesn't scandalize unbelievers. Rather it makes the Gospel more attractive to them. Obviously, this might be very different in a traditional Muslim community. In that setting, applying the concession principle might offer a valid strategy for maintaining peace and for not turning Islamic males away from the Gospel over the wrong issue. But, the principle no longer applies in the prevailing Western culture that largely rejects patriarchy. Quite the contrary, it is the complementarian position that is offensive, scandalous, and unnecessarily harms the reputation and witness of the church. If there is any validity in applying the stumbling block principle to the gender roles issue, it would be to the *complementarian* position, which actually is a stumbling block to many people who see it as oppressive to women and therefore as a reason to abandon their faith or for others to reject any thought of becoming a Christian. This is not an argument that secular culture's values should determine our theology, but of how the stumbling block principle should apply with regard to gender roles.

But the contradiction problem for complementarians is bigger. The contradiction problem goes beyond the apparent discrepancy between 1 Corinthians 11 and 14. The former assumes women will speak in church by praying, prophesying, or speaking in tongues. Any prohibitions related to gender must also harmonize with numerous passages about spiritual gifts in which no gift is designated as gender-specific or gender-restricted (1 Cor. 12:7ff; 14:3–5, 8–16, 24–33, 39f; 1 Pt. 4:10–11) as well as with the prophetic ministry of women at Pentecost (Acts 2:17–18) and numerous biblical examples of women who are honored for the numerous ministry and leadership roles they embraced (see chapter 11).

(2) **In these passages and their contexts, distinguishing between what was addressed to first century local issues and what was intended to be universally applied beyond the first century significantly affects how they should be interpreted and substantially undermines using them as timeless requirements for gender hierarchy in the church.**

Most of the New Testament letters were written to specific congregations in specific localities (e.g. the churches in Rome, Corinth, Galatia, Ephesus, Philippi, Colossae, Thessalonica, Sardis, Smyrna, etc.), to specific groups (Hebrews, scattered believers), or to individuals (Timothy, Titus, Philemon). The letters addressed specific circumstances, events, problems, or needs unique to each setting or individual. Although there are lessons and principles that often have universal application, it would be a mistake to fail to consider that some of what was written was intended for the original recipients and their unique local circumstances. For example, no one would take Paul's words to Timothy, "Stop drinking only water, and use a little wine because of your stomach and your frequent illnesses" (1 Tim. 5:23) as a biblically mandated health prescription for every pastor or Christian today with some kind of stomach ailment. While Paul's encouragement might be a valid argument against a mandate for total abstinence and his prescription could be healthy for some, it could also be detrimental for others, as for example, recovering alcoholics. Timothy's ailments called for an adjustment in his beverage intake. Paul's wine prescription was not a universal dietary mandate. The New Testament letters are not one-size-fits-all general letters the specific details of which apply in every respect to everyone in every time and every place. Remember the imaginary story at the beginning of this chapter about reading my neighbor's mail.

The two key prohibition passages, 1 Corinthians 14 and 1 Timothy 2 are part of Paul's letters to the church in Corinth and to Pastor Timothy in Ephesus. To some extent, they deal with local and unique problems in Corinth as illustrated in 1 Corinthians 1:11; 5:1; 6:7; 7:1, etc., and in Ephesus as stated in 1 Timothy 1:3ff, 19, 20; 2:9, etc. This is true of most of the New Testament letters (see, for example, Gal. 1:6ff; Titus 1:5, 10–12; and Philem. 8ff). While lessons and principles may be gleaned from all Scripture (Rom. 15:4), care must be given to distinguish between issues which were primarily or uniquely local and issues that require identical application in all times and cultures. The prohibition sections of 1 Corinthians 14 and 1 Timothy 2 relate to specific local issues, suggesting the need for caution regarding applying them universally. Remember, we are reading someone else's mail.

(3) **Correcting or enhancing the inadequate, misleading, or incorrect English translations of key Greek words in the two primary prohibition passages undermines the traditional complementarian understanding. A clear and correct translation of key Greek words erodes support for traditional gender restrictions in the church and brings the passages into harmony with the themes of their immediate and extended contexts. These corrections or improvements in translation support an egalitarian rather than a complementarian position.**

Translating from one language to another is always a challenging task made even more difficult when the original and target languages are not closely related. With ancient languages such as biblical Hebrew and Koine Greek[199] there is no one alive today from those times and neither language is spoken today in the form in which they were in Bible times. Millions of people in the world today speak Hebrew and Greek, but the contemporary spoken form of these languages is considerably different from when the Scriptures were written.

Even the English language today is significantly different than 600 years ago as illustrated by these lines from Chaucer's famous Canterbury Tales:

> But now passe over, and lat us seke aboute,
> Who shal now telle first, of al this route,
> Another tale;' and with that word he sayde,
> As curteisly as it had been a mayde,
> 'My lady Prioresse, by your leve,
> So that I wiste I sholde yow nat greve,
> I wolde demen that ye tellen sholde
> A tale next, if so were that ye wolde.
> Now wol ye vouche-sauf, my lady dere?'
> 'Gladly,' quod she, and seyde as ye shal here.

Obviously a mere 600 years of the evolution of English requires careful translation if we are to understand it. No wonder the ongoing study of Hebrew and Greek, not spoken in far more centuries than Chaucer's English, is essential if we are to correctly understand the Scriptures. Thankfully, both biblical Hebrew and Greek in their ancient forms are extensively studied today by linguists, historians, and especially by students and scholars of the Bible. Ongoing research continually provides important new understandings relevant to biblical interpretation. This helps to minimize the considerable *distance* that remains between the Bible's writers and contemporary translators and readers.

Bible scholars committed to orthodox Christianity are unanimous in their agreement that our English versions give us highly accurate and trustworthy

---

[199] Koine Greek was the common language of the street in New Testament times. This was in contrast to Classical Greek.

translations of the Old and New Testaments. While we do not possess any of the original texts, the quantity and quality of extant ancient manuscripts guarantees that we possess virtually identical versions of the *autographs* (the actual texts written by the Bible's authors). Readers of the English Bible translations should have confidence they are reading a trustworthy version of God's written message. However, Bible scholars would acknowledge that while the most common English versions are highly accurate, they are not infallible. God did not guarantee the supernatural preservation of the word-for-word integrity of every translation throughout history. Furthermore, the ongoing study of the ancient languages and texts through a number of scholarly disciplines continues to sharpen our understanding of the Bible, its words, grammar, etc. If there were one perfect English translation and no debate regarding how to translate many words and phrases, there would be no need for the plethora of ever-emerging new English translations and paraphrases, except perhaps for occasional updates to reflect changes in the English language. While credible Bible translations are very similar, differences are based on the opinions, theological orientation, and even the biases of the translators.

For the most part translation differences are minute and insignificant. No major doctrine is affected such as those articulated in the Apostles' Creed and accepted by all Christians everywhere. However, various subgroups of Christians often show preference for particular versions they apparently feel best support their expanded doctrinal statements including their denominational distinctives and debatable interpretations, or which include study notes supporting such. With a number of disclaimers, Scot McKnight gives his personal take on translation preferences by various groups including those of complementarians and egalitarians:

> The NIV 2011 is the Bible of conservative evangelicals.
> The NLT is the Bible of conservative evangelicals.
> The TNIV is the Bible of egalitarian evangelicals.
> The ESV is the Bible of complementarian conservative evangelicals.
> The NASB is the Bible of conservative evangelical serious Bible students.
> The NRSV is the Bible of Protestant mainliners.

The RSV is the Bible of aged Protestant mainliners.
The CEB is the Bible of Protestant mainliners.
The KJV . . . fill in the blank yourself.
The Message is the Bible of those who are tired of the politics
(and like something fresh)."[200]

We could add to that list the preferred English versions of groups such as Roman Catholics (Catholic edition of the RSV or NRSV, the Jerusalem Bible, or the Confraternity Version), and Jehovah's Witnesses (The New World Translation[201]).

A common challenge of translators is that there is sometimes no direct correspondence between a word in the source language and the target language. Grammar and syntax in various languages are different as are the uses of tense, voice, mood, and number. Words often have multiple meanings so the translator must discern which fits the context and conveys the meaning intended by the author for his specific audience. Translators must wrestle with using formal equivalence (word-for-word) versus dynamic equivalence (sense-for-sense) in their translation. It is not uncommon for words to have no one-word equivalent in the new language so it is necessary to use several words to convey its meaning and not risk misunderstanding or ambiguity. A simplistic one-word translation can be misleading if it fails to convey essential nuances of the original meaning.

Regarding the gender roles debate, crucial factors include:

- how to translate *"silence"* (σιγάω, *sigaō*) and "speak" (λαλεῖν, *lalein*) in 1 Corinthians 14, and
- how to translate "quiet . . . quietness . . . silent" (ἡσυχία, *haysuxia*) and "authority" (αὐθεντεῖν, *authentein*) in 1 Timothy 2.

How these words are translated propels the reader toward either a

---

[200] Scot McKnight, Jesus Creed (10/21/2014), on-line blog, http://www.patheos.com/blogs/jesuscreed/2014/10/01/the-politics-of-bible-translations/

[201] The Jehovah's Witnesses' New World Translation has been widely recognized as including misleading, inaccurate, and dishonest translations in order to promote their erroneous doctrine, as for example John 1:1, "In the beginning was the Word, and the Word was with God, and the Word was a god" (emphasis added). The translation of τὸν θεόν ("the God") as "a god" is not merely inaccurate and dishonest, it is heretical!

complementarian or an egalitarian understanding of the passages. In both cases the contexts are instructive in helping to determine which meaning is accurate. This is a pivotal concern in the gender roles debate which will be considered in great detail in the next chapters of this study.

In order to determine the meaning of a word in the Bible, consideration must be given to its etymology (its origin, development, and history), its semantic range (i.e. its entire scope of meanings in different contexts and times), usage in parallel passages, as well as its immediate context in the Scriptures. The contextual meaning of a word is closely related to the theme of the passage in which it is used, and to the history and culture of both the author and his audience.

Looking at a word as used in other texts that are comparable and somewhat contemporaneous can be immensely helpful in determining the best way to translate it. However, determining the meaning of a word that is a *hapax legomenon* can be especially challenging. This is a word that is used only once in a document so it's meaning can't be determined by looking at other uses in the same document. A key word in the gender roles discussion, *authentein,* is a *hapax legomenon* which is translated "authority" in 1 Timothy 2:12: "I do not permit a woman to teach or to have authority over a man; she must be silent." Not only is it used only one time in the entire Bible, it is also a comparatively rare word in ancient times outside the Bible. Its preferred meaning in 1 Timothy 2:12 is highly controversial, with opinions pretty much dividing along *party lines* in the gender roles debate. It would be hard to overstate the importance of the translation of *authentein* in the interpretation of this most important of all gender roles passages.

When one reads the scholarly literature, it is disappointing to discover that regarding whether the "authority" intended by Paul is positive or negative, the opinions expressed frequently sometimes appear to be less based on the available evidence than on which gender roles position the scholar holds. In other words, complementarian scholars generally argue that the "authority" in view is either neutral (leadership without implication of good or bad) or positive (good leadership), whereas egalitarian scholars largely see it as inherently negative (self-appointed, domineering, bullying leadership). While understanding that I too have personal biases in this debate (doubtless including subconscious ones), nevertheless when I carefully examine the evidence about the meaning of *authentein*, the meaning seems very clear—not even a close call. Which understanding is correct has gigantic implications for how the whole passage should be understood and applied regarding gender roles in the church.

These translation issues will be considered extensively in chapters 8 through 10. It will be demonstrated that the alleged inadequate, incorrect, or misleading translations of four key Greek words portrayed in nearly every popular and influential English translation of 1 Corinthians 14 and 1 Timothy 2 favor complementarian patriarchy. The misleading translations expose the possibility that hundreds of years ago a conspiracy to silence women in the church influenced the translation of key words. These misleading translations may have been born out of widespread patriarchal prejudice and practice that reflected the tragic, predicted result of sin's entrance into the world, that is that men will rule over women (Gen. 3:16).

I understand that for me to suggest misleading translations in our most trusted English versions of the New Testament is shocking to the max. Who am I to make such a bold and momentous accusation? Please consider carefully the evidence I will present.

Deep seated and widely held biases often function at a subconscious level. The resulting patriarchal-supporting and misleading translations have been passed on through generations of English language versions and paraphrases and they have significantly influenced the content of preaching and teaching to support complementarian patriarchy. Whether intentional or the unconscious reflection of long-standing fallen culture's gender bias and patriarchy only God can determine. But the nearly ubiquitous continuation of these biased and/or misleading mistranslations in subsequent English versions of 1 Corinthians 14:33–35 and 1 Timothy 2:11–12, has significantly influenced the imposition of teaching and leadership restrictions on women in the church and continually breathed life into complementarianism. The following demonstrates how this dynamic can perpetuate erroneous doctrine in the church:

Biased translations→Biased preaching/teaching→New biased translations→Continued biased preaching/teaching

---

In reality gender bias in translation[202] probably did not begin in the English translations but much earlier, for example in Jerome's very influential Bible translation, the Latin Vulgate (382 A.D.).

> In the 4th century A.D. the church became the state religion of the Roman Empire. It may be said of this merger that Christianity altered Rome. I think it may be equally said, however, that this merger altered Christianity, and not for the better. Gender bias in translation did not begin with the English language; it started in the fourth century, when St. Jerome helped to translate the Bible into Latin (the Vulgate). Words took on new meanings, and passages that might put women on equal footing with men were altered, in some cases subtly, in others more dramatically.

> In the Vulgate version we find the first change in the translation of "prostartis". Jerome was a man of his times; in other words, a very patriarchal Roman. He had a negative view of women and is quoted as saying, "a wife is classed with the greatest evils". Not a very Christian sentiment, but a very Roman one.[203]

In Romans 16:2 προστάτις (*prostatis*), referring to Phoebe, is translated "help"[204]—most likely influenced by Jerome's Latin Vulgate translation,

---

[202] More than one illustration of gender bias in translation is noted in an informative article on 1 Timothy 2:12: "Elizabeth A. McCabe has identified and documented evidence of gender-bias in English translations of the Bible. This does not apply exclusively to the word *authentein*. Greek words indicating that women held positions of authority in the church also appear to have been altered in translation. Women identified in Greek manuscripts as a *diakonos* (deacon) or *prostatis* (leader), are referred to as servants in some English translations, like the King James Version. This is inconsistent with the manner in which these words are typically translated regarding men." Wikipedia, https://en.wikipedia.org/wiki/1_Timothy_2:12#Meaning_of_authente.C5.8D. Recognizing that Wikipedia is not a recognized scholarly source, readers are encouraged to follow the footnote references to more scholarly sources.

[203] Ibid.

[204] *Prostatis* is translated "help" or "helper" in the NIV, NKJ, NLT, NASB, NCV, GWT, KJV ("succorer" an old word for helper). The ESV ("patron") and NRSV ("benefactor")

"*astiti*" meaning one who "assists." Romans 16:1, 2 says, "I commend to you our sister Phoebe, a **servant** of the church in Cenchrea. I ask you to receive her in the Lord in a way worthy of the saints and to give her any help [πρᾶγμα, *pragma*] she may need from you, for she has been a great **help** [προστάτις, *prostatis*] to many people, including me." The rendering of two words in this passage, "servant" and "help," are illustrations of potential gender translation bias.

Taking the second first because of the apparent influence of Jerome's mistranslation, notice that a reader of the English version of Romans 16:2 would likely incorrectly assume that the same Greek word is used twice and translated "help" both times. While that may be a valid translation of the first word (*pragma*) it is NOT a valid translation of the second (*prostatis*) which literally means to "stand in front of" or to "stand at the head of"—in other words, to be the leader.[205] How can one not strongly suspect gender bias in English versions which translate two totally different Greek words in the same sentence as "help" thereby implying that the second, *prostatis*, conveys "assisting" rather than "leading"? In 1 Timothy 5:17 the same word (*proistamai*), referring to an elder, is translated "direct the church" or "rule."[206] When precisely the same Greek word, used by the same author, is translated "help" when referring to a woman's service and "rule" when referring to a man's, the possibility of gender bias in translation must be considered. Paul did not commend Phoebe to the Roman Christians as a helper in her church, but as a leader.

The gender-bias plot thickens when one observes that, in the previous verse regarding Phoebe (Rom. 16:1), διάκονον (*diakonon*) is translated "servant" rather than "minister" or "deacon" thus failing to acknowledge her apparent official role in the Cenchrean church.[207] Paul calls her "a *diakonon* of the church in Cenchrea." It seems highly unlikely that he would have singled her out for such specific and unique commendation if she were one of many

---

are marginally better. I found NO English version that translated *prostatis* more accurately as "leader."

[205] In Romans 12:8, a closely related word, *proistēmi*, is translated "leadership," a spiritual gift with which one should "govern diligently."

[206] Elizabeth A. McCabe, "*A Reexamination of Phoebe as a 'Diakonas' and 'Prostatis': Exposing the Inaccuracies of English Translations,*" Society of Biblical Literature, https://www.sbl-site.org/publications/article.aspx?articleId=830.

[207] Ibid.

women who *served* in that church in a variety of capacities (as is the case in virtually every church). Rather, her role sounds more official, as confirmed in the next verse where she is called a "great" *prostatis*—one who stands in front to lead. Recognizing that the combination of these two Greek words strongly suggests that Phoebe was a "deacon" or "minister" **and** a "great leader" in the Cenchrean church, it appears to be a gender bias "double whammy" when most versions instead portray her as a "servant" (16:1) and "helper" (16:2).

It is true that the word *diakonon* can convey service on behalf of others ranging from a household servant or one who provides table service, all the way to one who carries out the work of a deacon or to another official church ministry including an apostle. Yet, the majority call her a "servant" (NIV, ESV, KJV, NKJV, NASB) while only a very few popular contemporary translations designate Phoebe as "a deacon" (NRSV, NLT), or "deaconess" (RSV) and NO English version I could find represents her as "a minister" or "an apostle." While the same Greek word is sometimes used referring to the service of men in terms of helpers, servants, or workers, it is also used in reference to the seven men assumed to be the first "deacons" (Acts 6), to the apostolic ministry of Jesus' twelve apostles (Acts 1:17, 25), and to Paul's ministry as an apostle (Acts 21:19; Rom. 11:13; 2 Cor. 4:1; 6:3; Col. 1:23, 25; and 1 Tim. 1:12). How is it that in the only New Testament passage where *diakonon* is used of a female, not one English translation renders it as "minister," though such a rendering is common in English translations when referring to at least a half-dozen men? Is it a foregone conclusion that a woman could not be a "minister" like men?

More importantly for this discussion, I believe that the prevalent English translations of the two key prohibition passages (1 Cor. 14:33–35 and 1 Tim. 1:11–15) include translation choices that very much appear to reflect gender bias. These apparently biased English translations of four key words are a central part of the essential interpretive foundation on which complementarian patriarchy in the Western church has been built and perpetuated. A correct translation of these words in these two central passages undermines the view that women are prohibited from teaching or leading men in the church. Correctly translated, these verses do not restrict women from teaching men or from serving as pastors or elders in the church.

Chapters 8 through 10 will address these issues in detail and provide evidence supporting the translation corrections illustrated in the following chart. This chart provides a simple preview of the issue by showing the words, their misleading translations, and a suggested enhanced translation. The enhanced translations illustrate the difficulty of attempting to capture the precise meaning of some Greek words without using multiple English words.

PASSAGE	GREEK WORD	MISLEADING NIV84 TRANSLATION	A MORE ACCURATE, EXPANDED, INTERPRETIVE TRANSLATION/ PARAPHRASE
1 Cor. 14:34	σιγάτωσαν from σιγάω (sigaō)	"women should remain silent"	"women should not talk endlessly in order that others can also have a turn"[208]
1 Cor. 14:34	λαλεῖν from λαλέω (laleo)	"women are not allowed to speak"	"women are not allowed to be talking non-stop"
1 Tim. 2:11, 12	ἡσυχία (haysuxia), used twice	"a woman should learn in quietness . . . must be silent"	"a woman should learn in a peaceable, serene, non-combative manner[209] . . . must be peaceable, serene, non-combative"
1 Tim. 2:12	αὐθεντεῖν from αὐθεντέω (authĕntĕō)	"I do not permit a woman to have authority over a man"	"I do not permit a woman to commandeer abusive control over a man"

Another very important textual issue with potentially earth-shaking implications for the gender roles debate is the stunning discovery that there is strong evidence from some of the most ancient and reliable extant New Testament Greek manuscripts as well as writings of the early church fathers that 1 Corinthians 14:34, 35 was not written by the Apostle Paul and was

---

[208] The meaning of sigaō is not perpetual silence, but temporary silence—a hiatus or pause in speaking to allow others to speak.

[209] The word haysuxia, peaceable, is the opposite of being argumentative or combative.

[210] This rare and unusual Greek word is used only here in the New Testament but its meaning is clearly established in its contemporary extra-biblical uses as will be demonstrated in chapter 10.

not part of the inspired letter he penned. Rather, those verses were a later interpolation, a scribal addition to the text.[211]

In his immensely helpful, scholarly study, *Man and Woman, One in Christ: an exegetical and theological study of Paul's Letters*, following a long, detailed presentation of the compelling evidence, Philip Payne summarizes: "1 Cor 14:34–35 is a non-Pauline interpolation, it does not carry apostolic authority and should not be used as such to restrict the speaking ministries of women, nor should it influence the exegesis of other NT passages."[212] While this highly important revelation will be carefully examined in the next chapter, it is important to note that even though my argument for an egalitarian understanding of the biblical data regarding gender roles in the church would be greatly enhanced by the credible conclusion that 1 Corinthians 14:34, 35 does not belong in the Scriptures, this study will proceed as if those verses were part of the original Corinthian letter. Because many people will not accept the proposal that these verses are spurious, it is essential to address their meaning for the gender roles debate. It is the assertion of this study that if those verses truly are Holy Spirit-inspired Scripture, when they are correctly translated and understood, they become a powerful support for the elimination of gender-based church ministry restrictions.

The next chapters will present compelling evidence for these assertions regarding misleading or faulty translations in 1 Corinthians 14 and 1 Timothy 2. These considerations are "ground zero" in the gender roles dispute. One's position stands or falls based on the meaning of these two highly controversial passages.

FOR DISCUSSION

1. Most Christians believe that the Bible never contradicts itself, yet Bible critics identify a number of illustrations of apparent

---

[211] Other New Testament passages virtually unanimously accepted by biblical scholars as possible interpolations include: Mark 16:9–20 and John 7:53–8:11. Most modern translations include a note at those passages such as "Some of the earliest manuscripts and other ancient witnesses do not include ... " See, for example, the NIV, ESV, NASB, NRS, etc. 1 John 5:7 is removed from nearly all versions except the KJV and NKJV.

[212] Philip B. Payne, *One in Christ, an exegetical and theological study of Paul's Letters* (Grand Rapids: Zondervan, 2009), 268.

contradictions. What should someone do when confronted with an apparent contradiction in Scripture? What are some ways that apparent contradictions can be resolved? What are a person's options if they cannot discover a good explanation for an apparent contradiction?

2. Read 1 Corinthians 11:5 and 1 Corinthians 14:33–35. In your own words, summarize the apparent contradiction between the two passages.

3. These apparent contradictions are especially significant because both passages are written by the same author, in the same book, separated by only two chapters. How do you believe the apparent contradiction between 1 Corinthians 11:5 and 1 Corinthians 14:33–35 can be resolved?

4. Glance through 1 Corinthians 11–14 and make a list of the topics covered. As you think about the focus of these chapters, which interpretation regarding the apparently contradictory statements seems more consistent with the *context* of the four chapters? Why do you draw those conclusions?

5. Often contradictions exist because one or both passages are not being interpreted correctly. As you think about the character of God and about what the rest of the Bible teaches, does one passage seem more consistent with what the Bible teaches about the character of God, about who receives spiritual gifts, and with the larger message of the Bible? Which of the two passages about gender roles in church seem more consistent with or more out of line with the following passages: 1 Corinthians 12:7–11; 14:26; Acts 2:16–18; 21:8–9; and Galatians11:28?

6. Read 1 Corinthians 14:26. Based on that verse, what do you think God values regarding participation in worship gatherings? Whether you hold to a complementarian or egalitarian understanding of Scripture, how would you like to see men and women serving in your church worship services as envisioned by this verse? What could you do to turn that vision into reality?

8

Women Are Not Allowed to Speak . . . Or Are They?

"Be quiet!"

The command seems rather simple and easy to understand. Right?

But the *context* of those words affects their meaning and significance. Consider if the same identical words, *"be quiet,"* were spoken in each of these settings:

- A mother whose baby <u>finally</u> fell asleep and the other children's noisy play threatens to wake her;
- A judge silencing a disruptive observer in the back of the courtroom who has no right to speak in the judicial proceeding;
- A librarian determined to keep her domain conducive to undistracted reading;
- A teacher whose second-grade pupils are <u>all</u> talking loudly at the same time . . . again;
- A bomb disarmer poised to cut what he hopes is the right wire knowing that a quick movement or a shaky hand could blow up the block;
- A father attending a funeral whose toddler in his lap is disrupting everyone around them;
- A teenager whose younger sibling's incessant talk tempts him to consider sibling homicide;
- A theater usher trying to quiet a couple whose escalating argument is interfering with people trying to watch the movie;

- A parent in a fancy restaurant whose children need to lower their voices to an appropriate volume for the high class setting;
- An employee whose all-too-brief lunch hour is being eaten up by an obnoxious talker at the next table who has never used a period in their life . . . only an endless supply of commas;
- A small group leader who has one member who isn't giving anyone else a chance to talk.

In each scenario, the words "Be quiet!" may be the same, but how and why they are spoken and understood may be quite different.

CONTEXT MATTERS!

Interestingly, in not one of these situations is the speaker calling for a permanent cessation of all talking in that setting. The context determines whether it's a call

- to not talk so loudly or incessantly,
- to pause so someone else can have a turn,
- to stop talking until something has been finished, or
- to not speak at all for a specified time. **CONTEXT MATTERS!**

Likewise, when Paul in 1 Corinthians 14 told women in the Corinthian congregation that they should "remain silent in the churches," that they "are not allowed to speak," and that "it is disgraceful for a woman to speak in the church," **CONTEXT MATTERS**. Similarly, in 1 Timothy 2 when Paul told Pastor Timothy that the women in his congregation in Ephesus "should learn in quietness" and "must be silent," **CONTEXT MATTERS**.

Therefore, in this chapter we will take a hard look at the CONTEXT of these two prohibition passages along with some other crucial issues to discover the meaning of these challenging verses.

Paul's instructions to the Corinthian church recorded in 1 Corinthians 14 are a pivotal point in the gender roles discussion. Along with 1 Timothy 2:11–15, these two prohibition passages are the foundation of the complementarian position—the *sine qua non*.[213] They are also *the only* Bible passages that speak directly to the possibility of restricting certain roles in the church based solely on gender:

- As in all the congregations of the saints, women should remain silent in the churches. They are not allowed to speak, but must be in submission, as the Law says. If they want to inquire about something, they should ask their own husbands at home; for it is disgraceful for a woman to speak in the church (1 Cor. 14:33–35).
- A woman should learn in quietness and full submission. I do not permit a woman to teach or to have authority over a man; she must be silent (1 Tim. 2:11, 12).

While these verses constitute the core of the complementarian case for gender-restrictions in church leadership, it is also true that these two passages, or at least the traditional interpretation of them, are a key reason many people, even some embarrassed followers of Christ, think that Paul was at best a product of his times in his patriarchal attitudes toward women, and at worst, either strongly biased against women or a nasty misogynist. A few even suggest that Paul was a woman-hater. They wonder if some painful experience or relationships earlier in his life deeply hurt and prejudiced him. Are they correct?

Has Paul Been Misunderstood and Slandered?

I believe that the traditional misunderstanding and misrepresentation of Paul's instructions regarding women have spawned this unfair and inaccurate caricature of the Apostle. Nevertheless, this complementarian interpretation is one reason some Christians have struggled to hang on to their faith and others have walked away from it. Some have not walked away from Jesus, but they have left the church they see as perpetuating the oppression of women contrary to the teaching and example of Jesus.

Although some might hope to resolve the accusation of misogyny against Paul by arguing that patriarchy is beneficial for women and others

---

[213] Latin: *"without which* [there is] *nothing."*

by proposing alternative views of the nature of the Scriptures and divergent theories regarding the doctrine of inspiration, this study, while recognizing the importance of those discussions, argues that any suggestion of gender bias against Paul and his writings is based on an *erroneous interpretation* of what he actually said. I would urge anyone who, because of the traditional understanding of Paul's gender role comments is considering rejecting Christianity or a traditional view of Scripture, to first reconsider what Paul actually wrote, rather than what inadequate or misleading translations and interpretations have suggested.

It is unnecessary to enter into a debate about the precise nature of inspiration to discern Paul's attitude toward women or his position regarding women teachers and pastors in the church. It is the assertion of this study that any biblical interpretation that portrays Paul as anything but a *radical first century advocate of total equality of the genders* and *the eradication of any gender-based hierarchy* has misunderstood and misrepresented him.

The problem is not human error in the writing of the relevant Scriptures, but rather is human error in the misleading translations of those writings and the erroneous interpretations they spawned. Tragically, the most popular and influential English translations of the Bible are inconsistent, unclear, and misleading regarding Paul's instructions about women in 1 Corinthians 14 and 1 Timothy 2. These misleading translations and resultant interpretations have opened the door for some to wrongly perceive Paul as gender-biased and anti-women.

It is the assertion of this study that Paul did not require restricting women from ministry roles based on their gender. We will consider five serious problems with the traditional complementarian understanding of 1 Corinthians 14:33–35 and, propose and defend what I believe is the best interpretation of these difficult passages. Some of these overlap with the treatment of 1 Timothy 2:12–15 in chapters 9 and 10:

(1) The traditional complementarian understanding does not adequately consider the historical, cultural, and local background in first century Corinth and Ephesus and their importance for interpreting Paul's letters.

(2) The traditional view proves far too much. Virtually no complementarian actually teaches or practices what their own interpretation of 1 Corinthians 14:33–35 requires.

(3) The traditional view blatantly contradicts what Paul wrote a few paragraphs earlier in the same Book, 1 Corinthians 11:5.

(4) The traditional view is based on inaccurate and/or misleading English translations of key Greek words in the text, and completely misses the theme and structure of the paragraph that includes the Corinthian gender role verses.[214]

(5) The traditional view overlooks the strong possibility that 1 Corinthians 14:33–35 was not written by Paul and inspired by the Holy Spirit but was a later addition/interpolation by a scribe.

Each of these will be fleshed out below.

(1) The Traditional Understanding of the Prohibition Passages Does Not Adequately Consider the Historical, Cultural, and Local Context

Remember, if the Scriptures are to be interpreted correctly, CONTEXT MATTERS. The historical, cultural, and local backgrounds provide essential insight into the context of these challenging and much-disputed prohibition passages. As was pointed out in the previous chapter, whenever someone reads the New Testament letters, it is essential to remember that they are reading someone else's mail. If we respect the Scriptures and what they actually say, then we must take them seriously when they state that they were written to a particular group of believers residing in a particular locality at a particular time in history. The stated recipients of 1 Corinthians were the believers who comprised the first century church in the ancient Greek city, Corinth. That is an important fact for understanding Paul's letter. The recipient of 1 Timothy was Paul's young protégé and apostolic representative in Ephesus.

---

[214] 1 Corinthians 14 and 1 Timothy 2 are sometimes referred to as the "clobber passages" because their traditional interpretation is often used like a club to demand restrictions against women in church ministry and to knock out any question to the contrary.

The circumstances in those two ancient cities are crucial considerations in order to correctly interpret the prohibition passages Paul addressed to them.

So, What Was Going On in Corinth (and Ephesus)?

The gender-role issue is only one of a long list of serious and specific problems that existed in the Corinthian church. No other New Testament church appears to be so problematic. These situations occasioned Paul's first letter including:

- divisions in the church (chapters 1–3);
- favoring one preacher over others (chapters 1, 3);
- the existence of gross immorality requiring excommunication (chapter 5);
- one member suing another (chapter 6);
- issues related to singleness and marriage (chapter 7);
- disputable matters involving convictions or preferences (chapter 8);
- the need to surrender rights for the sake of the Gospel (chapter 9);
- abuses at the Lord's Supper (chapter 11);
- important understandings and customs related to male and female participation in worship (chapter 11);
- the nature, distribution, and employment of spiritual gifts including parallel regulations for tongues speakers, prophets, and women (chapters 12–14);
- the problem of loveless ministry (chapter 13);
- the content of the Gospel (chapter 15); and
- confusion about Christ's resurrection and its implications for believers (chapter 15).

Paul had learned of these problems in several ways. He had been informed of some by report from a church family (1:11). He learned about others through the first century "rumor mill"—in other words, they were public information (5:1; 11:18). The rest had been communicated to him in an official letter from the church (7:1). Throughout 1 Corinthians Paul addressed these issues one-by-one.

These problems were part of the historical context behind Paul's letter.

They must be considered to interpret and apply the text appropriately. To whatever degree these issues were exclusive to Corinth or also existed in other churches cannot be determined with certainty. It would seem probable that many of Paul's teachings on spiritual gifts (1 Cor. 12 and 14), love (1 Cor. 13), the content of the Gospel, the resurrection (1 Cor. 15), etc., include important lessons for all Christians in every place and time and are common themes in his other letters. However, some of the specific regulations about abuses in using spiritual gifts may have been local problems in Corinth rather than pervasive in the New Testament churches since they are addressed only in this letter.

We recognize that over time copies of the New Testament letters were made and circulated among all the churches across the Roman Empire. Much like my imaginary scenario of a White House letter to my neighbor (chapter 7), every congregation would benefit from all the letters even while recognizing that they were sometimes reading someone else's mail in which not everything was written to them or fit their unique circumstances.

Other problems that prompted Paul's insights and likely had application beyond first century Corinth include:

- celebrityism—elevating one teacher over another (chapter 3),
- lawsuits—responding to one believer suing another regarding personal issues (chapter 5), and
- blatant immorality—dealing with unrepentant believers who continued to be active in the church (chapter 6).

But some of Paul's teachings appear to apply primarily to that time and place. For example, most interpreters agree that the head coverings of 1 Corinthians 11:3ff are not relevant or applicable for twenty-first century Christians, and that some of Paul's instructions about marriage were specifically given for the difficult season of persecution in which the Corinthian Christians found themselves (1 Cor. 7:26, "because of the present crisis").

The subject of gender roles is one *very small* segment of Paul's instructions about spiritual gifts in 1 Corinthians 12–14. An important underlying theme was the promotion of orderliness, appropriateness, and tranquility in worship gatherings. These values are the specific context for both of the prohibition passages: 1 Corinthians 14:33- 40 and 1 Timothy 2:11–15. In 1 Timothy 2 serenity *outside* the church is addressed in verses 1, 2[215] while serenity *inside* the church is discussed in verses 8–10 and 15. Paul commended the same values in Colossians 2:5 where he expressed his delight when he saw "how orderly" they were. Here in 1 Corinthians 14, Paul presents solutions to ways men and women were disrupting the peace and unity.

Ephesus, where Timothy served as Paul's apostolic emissary when 1 and 2 Timothy were written, had problems including outspoken and aggressive women who were disrupting the orderliness and tranquility of worship and were forcibly foisting themselves on the church as teachers and leaders. This will be detailed in later chapters along with the historical backdrop in Ephesus of female-dominated Artemis worship and proto-gnostic false teaching about Adam and Eve. Perhaps to a slightly lesser degree, the church in Corinth was facing some of the same concerns necessitating Paul's directions about women.

"Hey Honey," (Yelling across the Room) "What Did the Preacher Mean by That?"

A common practice in many ancient worship gatherings (and in some contemporary cultures) could also elucidate Paul's instructions and prohibitions in these two passages. Little is known with certainty about church buildings in the first and second centuries. Property ownership may not have been permitted and the church was very focused on using its resources to help the poor and to purchase freedom for slaves rather than to procure permanent facilities. Acts and the New Testament letters reference churches meeting in homes. Acts 19:9 speaks of a "lecture hall" Paul used for instruction. Wherever the church met, by the fourth century there are multiple references to the practice of separate seating for men and women in the church meeting places. This gender-separating practice was widespread as evidenced by positive references to it by early church fathers in Jerusalem (Cyril, 313-386), North Africa (Augustine, 354-430), and Turkey

---

[215] "I urge, then, first of all, that requests, prayers, intercession and thanksgiving be made for everyone—for kings and all those in authority, that we may live peaceful and quiet lives in all godliness and holiness" (1 Tim. 2:1, 2).

(Chrysostom, 349-407).[216] The Orthodox Church (among others) continues this practice today and claims it to be a 2000-year church tradition.

On this basis some argue that this separation of the genders in church was the background for 1 Corinthians 14:33-35. They suggest that as the chatter from the women's section grew in volume, it would become necessary for the leader to call out, "Will the women please be quiet!"—resembling Paul's admonitions for the women to be silent. Then, if the women began to interact about their questions or call out loudly across the room to their husbands regarding their questions, the leader might have responded like Paul, "If you have questions, ask your husbands at home." This portrayal, they suggest, is consistent with Paul's concern for orderliness in the gatherings.[217]

Although I do not think this explanation is at all necessary to understand 1 Corinthians 14:33-35, it certainly adds an interesting and helpful insight, though it may feel a bit like gender stereotyping. But, whether or not this particular cultural scenario underlies both 1 Corinthians 14:33–40 and 1 Timothy 2:11–15, what seems undeniable in the latter (1 Tim. 2), is, as was previously mentioned and will be demonstrated in more detail later, that the church in Ephesus where Timothy ministered faced a serious problem with outspoken, argumentative, aggressively assertive, and self-promoting women. It will also be demonstrated concerning 1 Corinthians 14:33–35 that at least some of these same problems were the backdrop for Paul's directions to the Corinthian church. It would be foolish for interpreters to not consider this background as they wrestle with the meaning of these prohibition texts. Context matters!

These gender-related issues were not unique to Corinth and Ephesus in the first century as demonstrated by Paul's reference to "all the congregations of the saints" in 1 Corinthians 14:33, and by Jesus' warnings to the sister church in Thyatira (Rev. 2:20ff[218]) where a woman, "Jezebel," was not only guilty of promoting false teachings, but apparently also of inappropriate

---

[216] John Habib, *"The Early Church Tradition of Separate Seating: Ancient Practice, Not a Cultural Anomaly,"* Blog: Orthodox Christianity Meets World (12/3/2014).

[217] N.T. Wright is one who finds this scenario attractive for understanding 1 Corinthians 14. Wright, "Women's Service in the Church."

[218] "Nevertheless, I have this against you: You tolerate that woman Jezebel, who calls herself a prophetess. By her teaching she misleads my servants into sexual immorality and the eating of food sacrificed to idols" (Rev. 2:20).

self-promotion[219] as implied by the fact that the church seemingly had not authorized her role, but nevertheless "tolerated" it.

This much seems crystal clear: in Corinth there were a number of people, both males and females, who were disrupting and monopolizing the church gatherings by their non-stop talking. Among those who needed to be reined in were some tongues speakers without interpreters, prophets not giving others a turn, and some women talking non-stop. Order had to be restored and maintained. Paul capped off his instructions about spiritual gifts (chapters 12–14) by reminding his friends that "everything should be done in a fitting and orderly way" (1 Cor. 14:40). Paul's solution for these three groups of over-communicators was wrapped up in a single word—"silence"—but not *permanent* or *absolute* silence, but rather *temporary* silence—a pause to promote participation by others.

To interpret and apply the two prohibition passages without considering the local problems they were intended to correct would be the height of interpretive folly. Therefore, at least two hermeneutical concerns exist: (1) How do our interpretations and applications fit with the specific local problems the texts addressed? (2) In what way do the passages have universal application or were they written just for a particular time, place, and people?[220] To fail to enter into this hermeneutical exercise would be naïve, unwise, or irresponsible.

---

[219] "You tolerate that woman, Jezebel, who calls herself a prophetess . . . " (Rev. 2:30, emphasis added).

[220] 1 Corinthians 7 gives at least three situations which applied specifically to Corinth, or at least, primarily to the first century Roman world, but which do not have relevance to the average Western Christian today: Paul encouraged the Corinthian Christians to remain in the same circumstance as when they came to faith with regard to: (1) circumcision (7:18–20), (2) slavery (7:21–24), and (3) remaining single rather than seeking to be married (7:25–28). In at least this third circumstance, the instructions were specifically "because of the present crisis" (7:26), which most interpreters understand as the season of intense persecution which affected first century Christians in some regions more than others.

(2) The Traditional Understanding of the Prohibition Passages Proves Too Much

The two prohibition passages are not merely the ONLY verses in the entire Bible that directly address the question of gender role restrictions in church but are without question THE MOST ESSENTIAL consideration in the debate. The traditional, complementarian understanding of what seems, on the surface, to be the most obvious meaning of these two texts, is that women are prohibited from speaking, asking questions, or from teaching or leading men in the church—thus excluding them from serving as teachers of men, preachers, pastors, elders, or other leaders over men. Eliminate these two passages and the complementarian position would be greatly diminished if not irreparably damaged, dismantled, or destroyed. Show them to mean something different than their traditional understanding and the complementarian position potentially collapses like a house of cards in a tornado.

So, What if NOBODY Does What it Says?

There is a very serious problem with the traditional complementarian interpretation of 1 Corinthians 14:33–35, that is, its advocates fall far short of accepting, teaching, and practicing what their understanding requires—that women must be totally silent in church, not even speaking to ask a question about something they don't understand. Almost *no churches anywhere* demand such absolute or perpetual silence by women in church. If the interpretation is correct, why does virtually NO ONE practice it?

Imagine walking into a church gathering where no women spoke—to each other or to anyone else. Prior to the service, women would be seen standing silently off to the side, in small quiet circles with other muted women, or perhaps standing quietly among the men but not participating in the conversations with even a single word. If you dropped off your baby and elementary child it would be noticeable that primarily men were "manning" the nursery and children's ministries except for some totally silent female helpers. When the service began two things would quickly become obvious: first, it would sound like an all-male choir because no

230

women's voices would be heard singing, and second, no woman would sing in a choir or praise team, make an announcement, read Scripture, lead in prayer, share a prayer request, give a testimony, sing a solo, or preach. After the service it would again be apparent that only male voices could be heard greeting or fellowshipping. If you were not accustomed to the dynamic, it would be awkward when you greeted a woman with "Good morning. How are you?" and in response received only a silent nod and smile. Such would be the church that actually obeyed what the traditional interpretation of 1 Corinthians 14:33-35 demands. Silent women! Have you ever been to such a church?

"Come on, Bill," I can hear someone objecting. "That's ridiculous! Nobody would expect women to be that silent." Okay then, where is the evidence in the text that there are any exceptions to the required silence? Given the complementarian interpretation, *there is no allowance for anything except total silence on the part of women* when they are in the congregation of the church. Just because obeying the complementarian interpretation sounds impossible or ludicrous doesn't give anyone permission to ignore what the text, according to their interpretation, actually says: "As in all the congregations of the saints, women should remain silent in the churches. They are not allowed to speak" (1 Cor. 14:33, 34, emphasis added), and "she must be silent" (1 Timothy 2:12, emphasis added).

Respectfully, it's time to "put up or shut up." Either show where the text allows exceptions[221] to being silent and not allowed to speak at all in the church congregation or else start practicing what you preach! Where are the many thousands of churches around the world where the complementarian interpretation is actually practiced? Where is even one? Apart from those two options—either identify textual exemptions or silence women—the only remaining option is to see if there is a legitimate alternative to understanding the passage.

As everyone would have to acknowledge, modern churches simply could not function without the involvement of women teaching in children's ministries as well as helping in music ministries, hospitality

---

[221] For example, does the text say, "once the actual service begins," or "during the sermon," or "once everyone has been seated and the pastor or male leader starts leading the worship"? The answer is clear: the text gives no such escape routes from demanding total silence by all women.

ministries, compassion/caring ministries, etc., all of which require *speaking.* Complementarians typically restrict women only from positions of teaching adult men, preaching to the entire congregation, or holding the office of pastor, elder, deacon, or board member. While those distinctions might possibly be argued from 1 Timothy 2:11–15 (the next chapters will demonstrate that such an interpretation is unwarranted and inaccurate), it *cannot* be argued from 1 Corinthians 14:33–35. The traditional complementarian interpretation of 1 Corinthians 14:33–35 identifies no text-based exceptions or loopholes that allow women to speak in church under any circumstances. Nothing in the 1 Corinthians 14 text suggests that the required silence refers only to teaching or to leadership roles when men are in the audience.

Rather, if one holds to the perpetual silence view, then women should not be allowed to teach women or children, give announcements, participate in music ministry, read Scripture, share a missionary report, talk during any church-based ministry, or even converse with another woman in the congregation. After all, **silence is silence!** The fact that no church obeys this "clear" command apparently reveals that the subconscious Spirit-led scruples of the church reject implementing the traditional complementarian understanding. The actual practice of the church at large totally rejects the imposition of absolute silence. Apparently, the collective conscience of the church leads to the adoption of a more egalitarian *understanding* or at least a more egalitarian *practice* of the passage.

To emphasize this point, it should be noted that if one does not accept the premise of this chapter that women may speak but must pause to give others a turn (male or female), then the alternative isn't merely that women cannot teach or be pastors, but that women cannot talk at all. Period! No exceptions! Total silence! Wow! Can you imagine? Who does that?

One Bible scholar indicates that the inconsistencies of the complementarian view were a key factor in his reluctant conversion to an egalitarian view. He now asks his detractors to wrestle with the same questions he had to honestly face:

> If someone believes that Paul meant what he said about
> women in church as a universal statement, then why don't

they practice it consistently? Why don't they forbid all women in every context, at every church, at all times, to speak a word in church; and require all women in every context, at every church, at all times to go home and ask their husbands about anything they don't understand in church?

Why is it okay for a woman today to share a testimony or talk about a ministry she serves in—in front of the entire congregation at a service gathering? And even further— why is it okay for a woman to lead the church in worship— to stand in front of the congregation and sing and quote Scripture and offer spiritual encouragement if she's not supposed to speak? Why are women allowed to raise their hands and ask questions in settings where men are present instead of waiting to ask their husbands at home? Why don't husbands make their wives wear a head covering when they pray?[222]

You can't have it both ways.

(3) The Traditional Understanding of the Prohibition Passages Contradicts 1 Corinthians 11

Further, as discussed, the typical complementarian limitations on women based on 1 Corinthians 14 and 1 Timothy 2 stand in stark contradiction of Paul's undeniable approval of women praying or prophesying in church, if, in the Corinthian setting, they are appropriately adorned with a head covering (1 Cor. 11:1–16[223]). Regarding 1 Corinthians 14, N. T. Wright asserts:

---

[222] Kat Armas, "Both Can't Be True" (11/16/2017), Jesus Creed: http://www.patheos.com /blogs/jesuscreed/2017/11/21/both-cant-be-true/?utm_medium=email&utm_ source=BRSS&utm_campaign=Evangelical&utm_content=245

[223] "Every woman who prays or prophesies with her head uncovered dishonors her head" (1 Cor. 11:5).

"What the passage cannot possibly mean is that women had no part in leading public worship, speaking out loud of course as they did so. This is the positive point that is proved at once by the other relevant Corinthian passage, 1 Corinthians 11.2–11, since there Paul is giving instructions for how women are to be dressed while engaging in such activities, instructions that obviously wouldn't be necessary if they had been silent in church all the time. But that is the one thing we can be sure of in this passage."[224]

However, even more significant is the discovery that the complementarian position depends on what turns out to be an inconsistent, unclear, inadequate, or misleading translation of keywords in these texts, and a frightening disregard of the clear theme and structure of the immediate context. Was Paul talking about a temporary and purposeful pause in speaking or a continued state of silence? Remember, CONTEXT MATTERS! This will be discussed below.

(4) The Traditional Understanding of the Prohibition Passages Is Based on Inadequate and/or Misleading Translations of Key Greek Words and Completely Misses the Theme and Structure of the Paragraph

It is a serious problem when one holds to an interpretation that no church does or can implement and that is contradicted by a clear passage just a few chapters earlier. Hanging on to such a view is even more problematic, given the *bombshell discovery* that, in the most popular and influential English translations, keywords in <u>both</u> of the prohibition passages have been translated in a manner that, in the most generous representation, is inconsistent, unclear, inadequate and/or misleading. It is crucial to discern a less easily misunderstood and more perspicuous translation of these key Greek words so that contemporary application is faithful to the author's intent.

---

[224] Wright, *"Women's Service in the Church."*

As noted, one part of the translation difficulty is that frequently in moving from one language to another, the precise meaning simply cannot be expressed by a single word or even a couple of words. This is certain: arriving at a correct understanding of the two prohibition passages is <u>the definitive issue</u> regarding Paul's teaching about women's roles in the church. The inconsistent, unclear, or misleading translations and consequent interpretations and applications of these two key texts have been pivotal in marshalling and maintaining support for the complementarian viewpoint.

The first translation issue concerns the Greek word σιγάω (*sigaō*) which is used three times in a ten-verse, thematically unified paragraph found in 1 Corinthians 14:26–35. Its repeated use helps to identify the structure and theme of the entire chapter. The contexts in which *sigaō* is used in other New Testament passages also shed defining clarity on its precise meaning.

Sigaō means *"to be silent, to hold one's peace."* Although the tense, voice, and mood of *sigaō* in each of the three verses is <u>identical</u>,[225] how it is translated, for example in the NIV, is not consistent. The translation virtually requires the English reader to assume that *three different words* were used by Paul rather than one. Other translations don't accurately reveal the actual meaning of *sigaō*. The result is misleading for the gender roles debate and has contributed to the adoption of the complementarian position by many people. These observations become evident in the following chart:

Text	Form of σιγάω (*sigaō*)	The tense, voice, mood, person, and number of the verb	Translation in the New International Version (1984)
14:28	Σιγάτω (*Sigatō*)	Present active imperative third person singular	"keep quiet"
14:30	Σιγάτω (*Sigatō*)	present active imperative third person singular	"should stop"
14:34	Σιγάτωσαν (*Sigatōsan*)	present active imperative third person plural	"remain silent"

---

[225] The only difference in the three uses of *sigaō* is that in 14:28 and 30 it is third person singular and in 14:34 it is third person plural.

What about other English translations? Do they do better? Do they make it clear that Paul used the same Greek word three times and translate it appropriately?

There are three very important issues regarding the translation of "silent" (*sigaō*) in 1 Cor. 14:26–35: **CONSISTENCY, CLARITY,** and **ACCURACY.**

In seven of the most popular and influential English translations, <u>not one</u> accomplished all three interpretive goals in the way they rendered this identical and crucially important word. How these seven versions translated *sigaō* and scored on these three issues is detailed in the two charts below.

Translation of silent/ σιγάω in 1 Cor. 14:26–35	NIV	ESV	KJV	NKJV	NASB	NRSV	NLT
Tongues speakers	keep quiet	keep silent	keep silence	keep silent	keep silent	be silent	be silent
Prophets	should stop	be silent	hold his peace	keep silent	keep silent	be silent	stop
Women	remain silent	keep silent	keep silence	keep silent	keep silent	be silent	be silent

Translation of silent/ σιγάω in 1 Cor. 14:26–35	NIV	ESV	KJV	NKJV	NASB	NRSV	NLT
INCONSISTENT: identical words in the same text are translated differently	X	X	X				X
UNCLEAR: the translation doesn't distinguish between a temporary, purposeful pause in speaking and a continuous state of silence	X	X		X	X	X	
MISLEADING: the translation gives an inaccurate impression of the actual meaning of the word	X	X	X	X	X	X	X
CONSISTENT, CLEAR, AND ACCURATE: identical words are translated identically using language that clearly and accurately conveys the correct meaning							

So how did the seven English versions do?

- Regarding **CONSISTENCY**, only three versions appropriately translate *sigaō* identically in its three parallel uses in the paragraph that forms a thematic unity: the NKJV, NASB, NRSV.
- All seven versions flunk the **CLARITY** test because how they translate *sigaō* fails to communicate that the word speaks of a temporary and purposeful pause in speaking rather than implying a continuous state of silence. In the case of *prophets* (14:29-33), only three, the NIV, KJV and NLT, translate *sigaō* in a way that could

possibly (not certainly) be understood as a temporary pause ("stop," "hold his peace," "stop"). Not one of the seven gets it right in the verses addressing *women* (14:33-35).

- In my opinion, all seven versions miss the **ACCURACY** goal because they use "keep" or "be" along with "silent" which could easily be misconstrued as calling for a continuous state of silence. One, the NIV, is the most egregious regarding accuracy as "remain silent" (used only regarding women) strongly suggests a continuous state of silence that is a complete misrepresentation of its lexical and contextual meaning.[226]

Because the correct meaning of *sigaō* is clear (see below), is affirmed by the theme of the passage, and is confirmed by its use in other texts, it would be extremely difficult to not wonder if pervasive gender bias, whether conscious or unconscious, was strongly at work in the choices made by the scholars who produced these Bible translations.

The influence of these inconsistent, unclear, and misleading translations of one of the two most significant passages in the Bible about gender roles in the church is immeasurable!

One can only imagine how different the discussion, and more importantly, the practice in churches might have been if the translation of this central passage had been consistent, clear, and accurate in conveying that the silence required in this three-scenario paragraph, in each case, was *temporary*, and that Paul's unambiguous assumption was that each of the parties (tongues speakers, prophets, and women) would RESUME SPEAKING as soon as an interpreter was present or when other prophets and individuals had opportunity to have a turn participating. Remember that the underlying theme in this three-scenario paragraph is orderliness in church worship.[227] Chaos could be avoided simply by taking turns. Sometimes everything we need to know was taught in Kindergarten.

---

[226] Remember the "CONTEXT MATTERS" illustration at the beginning of the chapter.

[227] See the conclusion of the passage in 1 Corinthians 14:40: "But everything should be done in a fitting and orderly way." Orderliness is also a central theme in 1 Timothy 2—a recognition which is essential for a correct understanding of that passage—the second of the only two and the most important Bible passages which speak directly about gender roles in the church.

Below is an expanded translation/paraphrase which conveys the meaning of *sigaō* consistently, clearly, and accurately.

Verse	Expanded translation/paraphrase to accurately portray the meaning of "silent" (*sigaō*) in 1 Corinthians 14
14:28	"If there is no interpreter, the tongues speaker should defer[228] speaking in the church and speak to himself and God *until there is an interpreter*"
14:30	"if a revelation comes to someone who is sitting down, the first prophet should defer speaking *until the other has an opportunity*"
14:34	"women should defer speaking in the churches *when it is necessary in order to give others an opportunity*"

Now let's flesh this out in more detail.

Three Parallel Problems Disrupting Worship

In 1 Corinthians 14:26–35 the three uses of *sigaō* appear in one thematically united paragraph that addresses three parallel situations in which the goals of participation and orderliness in worship were stressed. It would be very difficult to overemphasize the importance of recognizing the *unifying theme and structure* of these nine sequential verses to interpret them correctly.

In verse 26, Paul envisioned participation by **everyone** present: "What then, brothers? When you come together, each one has a hymn, a lesson, a revelation, a tongue, or an interpretation" (emphasis added). Obviously, if only a few participants—worse, only a few *male* participants—dominated the service, the goal of broad participation would be thwarted. Further the orderliness of the service would be at risk if some were attempting to exercise their spiritual gifts but were shut out by the insensitivity or selfishness of others who dominated. Imagine the chaos as one monopolized the floor while others kept trying to break in. In each case, the way to encourage participation and to prevent inappropriate disruption of worship was the implementation of temporary "silence" (*sigaō*) respectively by three groups:

---

228 To defer is to put something off to a later time.

tongues speakers, prophets, and *women.* Clearly, how *sigaō* is interpreted must be consistent in all three closely proximate and parallel uses. To interpret the first two in the same way and the third differently would demand very obvious textual indicators requiring such a change. No such indicators are present, therefore, the third instance of *sigaō* must be interpreted consistently with the first two.

In the first two instances, it is unmistakably clear that <u>perpetual</u> silence is NOT what is required by *sigaō.* Rather, in the first instance (14:27, 28) the tongues speaker must be silent (*sigaō*) only <u>unless or until</u> there is someone available (of either gender) to interpret: "If there is no interpreter, the speaker should keep quiet in the church and speak to himself and God" (14:28). The intent for a *temporary pause* rather than for *perpetual silence* could not be more clear. If the church is to be strengthened (14:26) in an orderly environment, up to three tongues speakers are allowed "one at a time" (14:27), but they must *temporarily* stop speaking (*sigaō*) in the absence of an interpreter. No one understands this first of three parallel uses of *sigaō* to be a *permanent* ban on speaking in tongues in the church! After all, a few verses later Paul mandates, "do not forbid speaking in tongues" (1 Cor. 14:38).

Similarly, in the second parallel scenario (14:29–33) the mandated silence for prophets is NOT *perpetual* but is only a *temporary* pause to give a speaking opportunity to others (male or female[229]) who also have a prophetic message to share: "And if a revelation comes to someone who is sitting down, the first speaker should stop [*sigaō*]." In other words, Paul directs them to *"suspend speaking in order to give someone else a turn to speak,"* or to *"pause and be silent long enough to defer to someone else who also desires to speak."* If there is no one else with a revelation to share, the first one may *continue* speaking. The issue is speaking "in turn" (14:31). No one interprets this second use of *sigaō* to permanently restrict prophets from speaking in church!

Disregarding the significance of these three parallel uses, when they come to 14:34, many complementarians conclude that Paul was mandating *perpetual* silence for women in church when he wrote that "women should <u>remain silent</u> [*sigaō*] in the churches" (emphasis added). The unfortunate reality is that in 14:28 and 30 the translations in their contexts are recognized

---

[229] In addition to a number of Old Testament examples of prophetesses, in the New Testament, women were permitted to prophecy according to Acts 2:17, 18 and 1 Corinthians 11:5.

as portraying a *temporary* cessation of speaking with tongues speakers and prophets, but with women in 14:34, the translation is designed and/or perceived to imply *perpetual* silence. This unwarranted, ongoing restriction violates and perverts the theme and structure of the paragraph, disregards the cohesion of the three parallel scenarios, and misrepresents the identical meaning of *sigaō* in these side-by-side usages. This misrepresentation of the meaning of the text has had momentous implications in the gender roles dispute. When one looks at the theme, structure, and identical vocabulary, it is very difficult to not suspect gender bias by the **NIV's 104 male translators and editors (not even one female scholar)**[230] in the misleading way the passage has been translated and interpreted.

Not all complementarians arrive at their misinterpretation of this passage because of personal gender bias but nearly all complementarians have almost certainly been influenced in adopting their complementarian understanding of 1 Corinthians 14:33–35 by the faulty or inadequate English translations of the text. If they took a serious look at the Greek text, they could *not* legitimately arrive at the complementarian understanding of the passage.

Thus, in the third parallel scenario (14:33–34), most translations, without any evidence in the text that this usage of *sigaō* is different from the first two, translate it in ways that are easily understood as if Paul were mandating a perpetual silence for women in the church. Most English versions, like the NIV, appear to support this unjustifiable change: "As in all the congregations of the saints, women should remain silent in the churches. They are not allowed to speak, but must be in submission, as the Law says" (emphasis added). This inconsistent, unclear, and potentially misleading translation has had momentous influence on the gender roles debate. To more accurately and consistently translate the meaning of *sigaō* regarding women, the English versions would need to portray the temporary nature of the silence required in all three scenarios: for tongues speakers, prophets, and women. This might require using more than one English word to adequately convey the precise meaning when translating from Greek to English.

To promote participation and to preserve orderliness and peace in worship, Paul directed women to defer by politely suspending their talking

---

[230] A list of the translators and editors for the original and 1984 revision of the NIV included **104 men and no women.** "The NIV Committee on Bible Translation," http://www.bible-researcher.com/niv-translators.html

until others also had an opportunity to participate. In all three parallel uses of *sigaō* Paul did not call for perpetual silence but for a *hiatus* in speaking so others might also contribute. This proper understanding of the text is devastating for the complementarian position. It should be further noted that 1 Corinthians 14:34, 35 has ABSOLUTELY NOTHING to do with whether or not a woman can be a pastor or teacher of men.

The focus in each of these three scenarios is on a considerate and respectful deference to others, not on perpetual silence. It is grounded in the law of love: to love one's neighbor as themselves; to submit to and to give preference to them. It calls for putting a hold on one's continued speaking until others have also had their say. Nonstop talkativeness selfishly excludes the participation of "each one" employing their gifts as Paul envisioned for the Corinthian church in 14:26.[231] Paul did not mandate that women never speak in church. Rather he regulated their participation to prevent a few from monopolizing the gathering.

What parent at the dinner table has not called on one of their children to "Stop talking!" Perhaps the non-stop chatterer had become annoying and disruptive for the whole family. Maybe the child was monopolizing the conversation so their eager siblings or dinner guests had no opportunity to share their stories from the day, or possibly the child was talking in order to escape eating the required "two bites" of vegetables. But the point is that the parent is not forbidding the child from ever again speaking during meals. The call to "be silent" is a temporary directive to create peace, to allow others to participate, or to encourage completion of another important responsibility (eating). Likewise, Paul's call for women to "stop talking" in church, was never intended as a permanent muzzle on all females. All three groups, tongues speakers, prophets, and women, needed, at times, to *"stop talking."* It was like a judge calling for "order in the court" to quell the disruptive talking that hindered the orderly conduct of the proceedings.

Thus, it is evident that 1 Corinthians 14:26–35 portrays three parallel scenarios in which deference to others is required in order to not allow individual tongues-speakers, prophets, or women, to selfishly monopolize the service and limit maximum participation. Paul's vision for the worship

---

[231] "What then shall we say, brothers? When you come together, everyone has a hymn, or a word of instruction, a revelation, a tongue or an interpretation. All of these must be done for the strengthening of the church" (1 Cor. 14:26).

gathering was that one or a few individuals would not dominate the service to the exclusion of others. He wrote that "All these must be done for the strengthening of the church" (14:26b)—not for the elevation or exaltation of a vocal few.

Though not a perfect parallel, perhaps Paul's three scenarios that limited participation could be compared to a common model in the church today in which a few professionals or highly gifted and/or trained volunteers *perform* from the platform while the vast majority of attendees are minimally-participating spectators. If Paul's vision for *"each one"* to use their gifts to edify the church (1 Cor. 14:26) is to be accomplished, provision must be made for broader involvement in and around the worship gatherings as well as in much smaller and more participatory venues such as small groups or classes. The use of the gifts for edification should not be viewed as taking place only during the structured order-of-service-driven time. Rather, before and after the service as believers "come together" to fellowship, the plethora of gifts should be active. Some churches regularly include an extended "fellowship" or "family time" in every service giving everyone present an opportunity to mingle and minister to each other in an informal and very personal exercise of each one's spiritual gifts. Exercising the gifts of encouragement, helps, prophesy, etc., should occur one-on-one or one-on-three as well as one-on-one hundred or one-on-five thousand.

Paul's instructions in 1 Corinthians 14: 27-35 were not intended to eliminate or marginalize a particular gift or gender. Rather, he called for speaking "in turn" in order to prevent domination by a few. This, as eloquently stated in 1 Corinthians 13, is *the way of love*, "the most excellent way."[232] Love, not self-assertion or self-promotion is to be the prevailing value in the employment of spiritual gifts. The solution to the Corinthian problem was not to silence all tongues speakers, prophets, or women, but to regulate their participation out of love for others and for the edification of the whole church. Tongues speakers, prophets, and women were instructed to learn, in twenty-first century idiom, to "hit pause." They were not commanded to be endlessly silent.

In summary, whether 1 Corinthians 14:26–35 supports the complementarian or egalitarian viewpoint hinges on the understanding of the meaning of *sigaō* in the three parallel scenarios about encouraging maximum

---

[232] "And now I will show you the most excellent way" (1 Cor. 12:31b).

participation and maintaining orderly worship. A complementarian conclusion requires disregarding the theme of the passage, disrupting the flow of the paragraph, and arbitrarily changing the meaning of *sigaō* from a *temporary* curtailing of one's speaking to defer to others, to permanently imposing silence on women as a class in church gatherings.

But, it is not merely the context that should guide one's understanding of the meaning of *sigaō*. It is also how the word is used in other New Testament passages—a study that confirms the meaning just presented.

Do Other Texts Confirm These Shocking Revelations?

In every other New Testament usage, *σιγάω* (*sigaō*) or *σιγὴ* (*sigay*) convey the meaning *"to temporarily stop speaking, become silent, or hold one's tongue."* It means to *pause silently* in response to something that was or was not happening. In every instance, it is assumed or stated that after the hiatus, the speaking would or did resume. The word is never used in the New Testament to portray unending silence as is evident in the following passages (in each the translation of *sigaō* or *sigay* is underlined):

- "And when the voice had spoken, Jesus was found alone. And they kept silent and told no one in those days anything of what they had seen" (Luke 9:36 ESV)
- "Those who led the way rebuked him and told him to be quiet, but he shouted all the more, 'Son of David, have mercy on me!'" (Luke 18:39)
- "They were unable to trap him in what he had said there in public. And astonished by his answer, they became silent" (Luke 20:26)
- "Peter motioned with his hand for them to be quiet and described how the Lord had brought him out of prison" (Acts 12:17)
- "The whole assembly became silent as they listened to Barnabas and Paul telling about the miraculous signs and wonders God had done among the Gentiles through them" (Acts 15:12)
- "Having received the commander's permission, Paul stood on the steps and motioned to the crowd. When they were all silent, he said to them in Aramaic . . . " (Acts 21:40)
- "Now to him who is able to establish you by my gospel and the proclamation of Jesus Christ, according to the revelation of the

mystery hidden[233] for long ages past, but now revealed and made known through the prophetic writings . . . " (Romans 16:25, 26a)

- "When he opened the seventh seal, there was silence in heaven for about half an hour" (Revelation 8:1)

Based on these and every other use of *sigaō* and *sigay* in the New Testament, it is clear that the three uses in 1 Corinthians 14 should be translated in the same way—not as referring to a permanent ban, but as a temporary and purposeful silence with the assumption that speaking would be resumed whether by tongues speakers, prophets, or women.

It is evident then that the difference between the misleading translations and the correct understanding of *sigaō* in 1 Corinthians 14:34 is very much like the difference between an elementary classroom teacher saying *"James, when you are in my classroom, you are not to talk at any time for the rest of your life,"* and saying, *"James, you've said enough. Stop talking until everyone has had a turn."*

There's a Difference Between Saying Something and Non-Stop Talking

This linguistic and contextual understanding of *sigaō* is consistent with the two uses of λαλεῖν (*lalein*)—the *present* infinitive of λαλέω (*laleō*)—that immediately follow in 1 Corinthians 14:34, 35. An expanded translation of the present tense could be, "they are not allowed to be continually speaking" (emphasis added) and "it is disgraceful for a woman to be continually speaking in the church" (emphasis added). This implies something very different than the muzzling demand suggested by the verbiage of most translations: "not allowed to speak" (14:34) and "disgraceful to speak" (14:35). "Thereby the apostle seeks to transform the noisy confusion of the Corinthian worship into a harmonious masterpiece that will glorify God and edify the church."[234]

The proper translation of these two key Greek words, *sigaō* and *lalien*, has huge implications for the gender roles debate. The inconsistent, unclear, and/or misleading translation of both words has been used to support

---

[233] "Hidden" means "kept silent about."
[234] Grenz, *Women in the Church*, Kindle, Loc 1358.

the complementarian position while the more accurate translation is unmistakably more consistent with the egalitarian view and completely undermines the complementarian restrictions on women in church.

But Why Does Paul Place Limitations on Women as a Class?

Another objection to Paul's teaching in 1 Corinthians 14:33–35 raised by some is, "As he regulates participation, why does Paul address women as a class? They are the only group of the three (tongues speakers, prophets, and women) for whom *gender* is the defining characteristic. Isn't this offensive and bigoted? Isn't this a degrading expression of gender bias against women?" This objection is understandable from the perspective of a twenty-first century Westerner. But, 1 Corinthians was not written to a twenty-first century Western congregation. There are four factors which address the objection to Paul imposing this restriction on women as a class: (a) the cultural context, (b) the concession principle, (c) the local and regional problem, and (d) the conflicting manuscript evidence.

(a)   The Cultural Context

Gender bias against women is, as it should be, a highly sensitive and super-charged topic today. The first century was a very different cultural setting. It was pervasively patriarchal. What seems shocking and reprehensible in our contemporary culture would not have been at all shocking in that highly patriarchal world. In that time, synagogues forbade women from speaking in public. This may have been more cultural than religious as Plutarch, a Greek philosopher and writer around the same time as the writing of Paul's letters, wrote that the speech of a virtuous woman, like her arm, "ought not to be for the public and she ought to be modest and guarded about saying anything in the hearing of outsiders since it is an exposure of herself . . . For a woman ought to do her talking either to or through her husband."[235] Clearly, the verses addressing women in 1 Corinthians 14:33–35 would not have been received by the first century recipients of the letter as they would be today.

Further, when Paul addressed women as a class in the other prohibition

---

[235] Payne, *One in Christ,* 218.

passage, 1 Timothy 2:9–15, he had first addressed men as a class in a similarly less than flattering manner (1 Tim. 2:8): "I want men everywhere to lift up holy hands in prayer, <u>without anger or disputing</u>" (emphasis added). Some might argue that Paul was guilty of negatively stereotyping men in this characterization. Others would insist that Paul was addressing ways the peaceful worship atmosphere in Ephesus was imperiled by both men and women in different but equally problematic ways. Both genders needed to be called out regarding their particular disruptive behaviors in the Ephesian church, as tongues speakers, prophets, and women needed to be in Corinth (1 Cor. 14:27-35). In the first century these gender-based correctives would not have been viewed as being offensive or gender-prejudiced in the same way as they might today and it is doubtful that any of Paul's original readers would have assumed he was talking about every man and every woman when he addressed these gender-specific concerns.

(b) The Concession Principle

Paul's words might also be another illustration of the need to make temporary concessions to an oppressive culture for the sake of keeping peace and advancing the Gospel as was previously demonstrated in chapter 5.

(c) The Local and Regional Issue

As referenced earlier (and will be addressed more later), more than one of the New Testament churches had an extensive problem involving some women who attempted to monopolize the worship gatherings, were insensitive to the desire of others to participate, spoke incessantly, were disruptive, were teaching false doctrine, or were aggressively commandeered teaching and leadership positions through which their bullying tactics produced division and chaos. These problems in Corinth (1 Corinthians) and in Ephesus (1 Timothy) elicited Paul's church-specific instructions even as the circumstances in Thyatira prompted Jesus' exhortations in Revelation 2:20: "Nevertheless, I have this against you: You tolerate that woman Jezebel, who calls herself a prophetess. By her teaching she misleads my servants into sexual immorality and the eating of food sacrificed to idols." Jesus rebuked the church for tolerating the dangerous false teachings of a self-proclaimed prophetess. It is probable that at least in Ephesus there were a number of women who had been influenced by the female-dominated Artemis cult (Acts 19). If a similar female-promoted false teaching spread in a church today, a corrective pastoral letter might use similar gender-specific language for that situation.

Understandably if someone today in a pastoral letter to a church made a similar negative gender characterization about women as a category, for example to the Refreshing River Church in Chicago,[236] it would undoubtedly be portrayed by some as highly offensive and an indication of serious gender-bias. However, if that specific congregation had a unique situation involving ministry-dominating ladies in the congregation,[237] the pastor's letter would be totally understandable as addressing a *local* issue rather than women as a class. It's my guess that the members of Refreshing River would be very much aware of the issue and appreciative that it was being addressed. Remember, CONTEXT MATTERS. It seems highly probable that first century Corinth had a *local* problem with *three* classes of protagonists: tongues speakers, prophets, and women. After all, no similar instructions are given in any other New Testament letter regarding *any* of those three groups.

(d)   The Conflicting Manuscript Evidence

The objection against Paul's restrictions for a whole class of people (women) would instantly vanish if these verses were discovered to not be Paul's Holy Spirit-inspired words, but rather were a later addition to the text (an interpolation) by unnamed scribal copyists. Despite very strong evidence supporting that viewpoint summarized later in this chapter, the egalitarian conclusions presented throughout this book are not dependent on it. Rather the author's arguments have been presented as if these controversial verses were written by Paul in the original copy of his first Corinthian letter and belong in the Scriptures. That is not because I believe that the evidence for 1 Corinthians 14 being a non-inspired interpolation is weak and unconvincing, but because it will be, for many, such a controversial idea that they might

---

[236] This is an imaginary church.

[237] Think of Paul's plea to two ladies in the church at Philippi, Euodia and Syntyche (Phil. 4:2, 3).

dismiss the entire egalitarian case as if it depended on this one shocking revelation. It does not!

Actually, the manuscript of this book was more than 80% complete when I became aware that there was anyone who seriously questioned the textual integrity of these verses and who presented credible evidence that 1 Corinthians 14:34, 35 does not belong in the Scriptures. When my study indicated how convincing the evidence is, I knew that I had to include a summary of it even though it is by no means necessary for the egalitarian case. This very important topic will be addressed near the end of this chapter.

The fact that the manuscript evidence against 1 Corinthians 14:34, 35 is so strong raises a question on why so few Christians, pastors, seminarians, and Christian leaders, even know about this textual issue. It's difficult not to wonder if it could be because of a bias-driven cover-up, or at least an arbitrary decision that it is either unimportant or too shocking and divisive to reveal. At the same time, this ignorance should serve as a reminder that we need to read and research beyond the familiar sources produced within our theological or denominational tribes.

Regulating the Q & A Time in Church

Returning to Paul's teaching in 1 Corinthians 14, another important question is "Why did Paul tell women to get their questions answered at home by their husbands rather than simply asking them in the church gathering?" It was pointed out earlier in this chapter that a common first century practice in synagogues and churches was for men and women to sit on opposite sides of the room. If women shouted their questions across the room to their husbands, it would definitely be disruptive.

Further, the nuances of the Greek construction behind the English translation and how these instructions fit into the theme of the larger context clarify these instructions.

In 1 Corinthians 14:35,[238] Paul directs that if women want to learn, that

---

[238] "If they want to inquire about something, they should ask their own husbands at home; for it is disgraceful for a woman to speak in the church" (1 Cor. 14:35).

is to "inquire"[239] about something, they should "be asking [ἐπερωτάτωσαν, *eperotatosan*, a *present* active imperative indicating *continuing, progressive* action] their own husbands at home." The present tense suggests that Paul's concern was that asking one question after another should be reserved for home, rather than repeatedly interrupting the public service with a stream of disruptive questions.[240] This is not a prohibition against asking an *occasional* question in church. That would have been more clearly conveyed by an aorist infinitive (completed action).

Thus, Paul's requirement should be understood not as an absolute prohibition of women ever asking a question but as an avoidance of repeatedly disrupting the time of instruction or selfishly crowding out the participation of others. This is consistent with Paul's theme in addressing tongues speakers, prophets, and women: *do not dominate the service in such a way that others also cannot freely participate.*

What? Women Can Learn?

In that first century culture it was a radical departure for women to be treated as fellow disciples along with men or to even be deemed as capable of, let alone permitted to be, *learning* God's truth in public as question-asking disciples. Paul's teaching and assumptions both in 1 Corinthians 14:35 and 1 Timothy 2:11 were profoundly counter-cultural. Paul undoubtedly learned this from Jesus, as for example, in His shocking praise of Mary when she left the traditional women's role in the kitchen to sit at Jesus' feet in the disciples' men-only club (Luke 10:38ff).[241]

For Jesus to welcome Mary into the circle of His disciples was stunningly contrary to the prevailing cultural mores of the day. "Women were only allowed to receive very little education on religion and the main religious instruction in the home was given by the man and not the woman. They

---

[239] μαθεῖν (*mathein*), aorist active infinitive of μανθάνω (*manthano*), meaning to be taught, to study, to be instructed, to come to understand.

[240] This would be especially disruptive if men and women sat separately in the gatherings and/or, as one commentator suggested earlier in this chapter, if there were linguistic challenges faced by many women.

[241] "Only one thing is needed. Mary has chosen what is better, and it will not be taken away from her" (Luke 10:42).

could not be disciples of any great rabbi, they certainly could not travel with any rabbi."[242] Jesus blatantly violated these cultural norms as His teaching ministry constantly included women among his hearers, warmly received Mary into His circle of disciples (Luke 10:38–40), honored her for choosing to be there, and even depended on women's support as part of His traveling entourage (Luke 8:3).

Paul's teaching in the prohibition passages as well as his frequent allusion to women as partners in his ministry (Rom. 16, etc.) appears to follow Jesus' example in His revolutionary inclusion of women among His close ministry associates.

The same theme and word (*manthano*, «*a disciple/learner"*) are in view in 1 Timothy 2:11 ("a woman should learn"). In both passages, the concern was that women, while speaking or learning, were not to take over the service in their eagerness to be taught or to employ their gifts, nor were they to dominate the service by continually talking or asking questions, especially if these were practiced in a combative and argumentative manner (1 Tim. 2:11, 12, ἡσυχία, *haysuxia*—see chapters 9 and 10). These behaviors would violate the values of broad participation, orderliness, peace, and appropriateness which underlie both 1 Corinthians 14:26–40 and 1 Timothy 2:1–15. But don't miss it! Paul said, "Let a woman learn" (1 Tim. 2:12). Is it possible that God intended for women to learn but then to keep it all to themselves or only to teach other women and children? Where does the Scripture suggest any such stifling assignment?

More Reasons Why Some Things Should be Done at Home

Perhaps another reason Paul wanted wives to direct their questions to their husbands at home arose from his concern that the out-of-control, non-stop talking and disruptive questioning in Corinth not only might disrupt worship gatherings but also could be *embarrassing, belittling,* and *emasculating* to a husband in a pervasively patriarchal culture. Such a husband could be demotivated to come to the gathering if he felt that his overly-talkative wife might publicly embarrass him—even more so if he were an unbeliever or an

---

[242] "Women in Ancient Israel," Bible History Online: http://www.bible-history.com/court-of-women/women.html

immature Christian. In contrast, if a wife respectfully brought her spiritual questions to her husband at home, it might motivate him to step up and seek the answers. It would allow him to be her spiritual hero. At risk of engaging in stereotyping, I would suggest that most husbands long to be their wife's hero. Their desire and need to be looked up to by their wives is insatiable. Hence Ephesians 5:33 emphasizes the importance of a wife "respecting" her husband.

While the too-talkative-in-church-embarrassing-her-husband dynamic may have been a somewhat unique or special problem in Corinth and Ephesus, it is probably common to some extent in some other cultures and times—especially in patriarchal settings. Although I have served in a pastoral role in six churches for fifty plus years, I am grateful to have rarely experienced this problem. However, I remember a particular woman who exhibited a propensity for dominating church meetings with her unending comments and questions. Her husband stayed in the background and was typically silent and non-participatory in her presence. But in her absence, as in a men's group, he came out of his self-imposed and/or overly-talkative-wife-inspired shell and participated by offering wise and appropriate observations and questions. Clearly his wife's verbal domination precipitated his silent shrinking into the background. She often gave good input but her over-communication stifled her husband's involvement and robbed the church of his wisdom.

In another congregation where I was the senior pastor, during a short but very painful season of conflict, there were a few women who, while not the only perpetrators, played a very significant role in spreading slander and division which resulted in much harm. Perhaps both of these situations might have been different if the spirit of 1 Corinthians 14 had been followed in the first instance and of 1 Timothy 2 in the second. Thankfully, in the six churches where I have had some pastoral role, the vast majority of women have been wonderful, godly workers and leaders whose influence for the kingdom was outstanding!

A command comparable to 1 Corinthians 14:35 regarding doing something "at home" is found in 1 Corinthians 11:20–34, where Paul commands the Corinthians to "eat at home" rather than at the church gathering ("If anyone is hungry, he should eat at home," 11:34). The context is clear that Paul did not forbid all eating in church gatherings in perpetuity, or in church *buildings* as a handful of denominations have assumed leading to the construction of separate fellowship halls and kitchens disconnected from the building which houses the sanctuary. Rather Paul prohibited selfish insensitivity to others by consuming so much food and drink at the communion love feast that there was nothing left for others to eat. Eating was not the problem. Selfish overeating and especially robbing others of the opportunity to participate was. In the same way in 1 Corinthians 14, the problem was not that women spoke or asked questions in church, but that some women in Corinth (and Ephesus) were selfishly talking too much and some were dominating the Q & A time, thus selfishly robbing others of the opportunity to participate and/or embarrassing their husbands. That is not the way of love (1 Cor. 13).

An Appeal to the Law—But Which Law Is It?

Another challenging interpretive issue in 1 Corinthians 14 is the phrase, "as the law says" (14:34). This is an equally difficult statement for both complementarians and egalitarians. Discerning the source of the reference is challenging because there is *not one* Old Testament passage in which women are commanded to be submissive to men, where women are required to be silent in worship, or where women are directed to ask their questions to their husbands at home. Really? Wow! That is very significant! There are a number of illustrations of women verbally participating in or even leading God's people in worship or governance as for example Miriam in Exodus 15; Deborah in Judges 4; Huldah in 2 Kings 22 and 2 Chronicles 34; Noadiah in Nehemiah 6; and Isaiah's wife in Isaiah 8.

The best understanding of the reference to "the law" seems to be that it recalls Genesis 3:16b which is found at the beginning of the "five books of the Law" (Genesis through Deuteronomy). This turning-point verse describes male rulership over females as one of the tragic results of sin in the now fallen world which will henceforth be oppressively patriarchal ("he will rule over you").[243] Therefore "the law" doesn't mandate female submission and male rulership. It identifies the origin and pervasiveness of sinful, gender-based hierarchy throughout history and the consequent need to make temporary

---

[243] See chapter 4 for a discussion of Genesis 3:16 demonstrating that it is descriptive and not prescriptive.

accommodations to patriarchy when essential to preserve peace and promote the Gospel.

Nowhere else in Paul's writings is there a similar reference where the source or text of the referenced law is not specified and/or obvious. The inconsistency and lack of clarity in this reference to "the law" can be easily understood if in fact it was NOT Paul's writing but a later addition by a copyist. This is not the only aspect of 1 Corinthians 14:33–35 incongruent with Paul's style, vocabulary, and theology. Therefore, we must consider:

(5) The Traditional Understanding of the Prohibition Passages Overlooks the Strong Possibility that 1 Corinthians 14:34, 35 Was Added to the Text Later by a Scribe and Isn't Part of the Inspired Scriptures

Why do these gender-restricting verses feel strangely problematic when compared to the rest of the Scriptures including Jesus' teaching and practice? Why in the traditional complementarian understanding are they overtly contradictory to specific teachings of Paul in other passages, notably three chapters earlier in the same letter (1 Corinthians 11:4, 5) which assumes women will speak in church by praying and prophesying? Could the answer be because these verses, as suggested by important evidence from ancient biblical manuscripts, are in fact *not* the inspired words of the Apostle Paul, but are a later scribal addition to the original text?

In his monumental study of Paul's letters (Man and Woman, One in Christ: An Exegetical and Theological Study of Paul's Letters) Philip Payne[244] addressed the question, "Did Paul forbid women to speak in church?" by asserting that "The central textual issue is whether these verses are an interpolation not in the original text."[245]

Payne's conclusion that these few verses do <u>not</u> belong in the Scriptures, while discussed in meticulous detail in 142 pages in the Kindle edition of

---

[244] Philip B Payne is a widely respected evangelical New Testament and textual criticism scholar and author (PhD from Cambridge) who served as an Evangelical Free Church missionary for seven years in Japan and has taught at Cambridge, Trinity Evangelical Divinity School, Gordon-Conwell, Bethel, and Fuller Seminaries.

[245] Payne, *One in Christ,* 216.

his seminal work (only one out of twenty-four chapters), is only one aspect of his massive study of all of the relevant passages in Paul's letters relating to man and woman in relationship to Christ. After an extensive presentation of evidence, he concludes: "The combination of all this internal evidence with the external evidence makes a powerful case that 1 Corinthians 14:34–35 is an interpolation." Interpolations are not uncommon in the New Testament as sometimes noted in footnotes and notations in the margins of English translations.[246] Payne observes that "most scholars who have published their analyses of the text-critical aspects of this passage have agreed that it is an interpolation."[247]

The case Payne builds that these verses should not be included in the Bible is both extensive and, in part, highly technical. While some of his arguments are very accessible, a good deal of his material about ancient biblical manuscript evidence is so technical it would be challenging for the average reader to fully comprehend because they lack a background in the important scholarly minutia integral to the study of textual criticism. Even so, the general meaning and significance of his arguments are readily discernable if the popular reader commits to eat the fish and leave the bones.

The first part of Payne's argument against including 1 Corinthians 14:34, 35 in the Bible involves seven external evidences each of which he develops in detail:

---

[246] An "interpolation" is a later edition to the biblical text, not part of the original writing by the inspired author. To illustrate: contemporary Bible scholars virtually all agree that the Trinitarian portion of 1 John 5:7 (see KJV) was not in the original text but was a very late forgery by a Medieval scribe and therefore no modern translation includes it (except the NKJ which follows the KJV). John 5:4 is another late forgery not included in any modern English version other than the KJV and NKJV). All modern versions recognize the controversy over John 7:53–8:11 and Mark 16:9–20 and while including them in the text, include a foot or marginal note respectively such as "the earliest manuscripts do not include . . . " or "some of the earliest manuscripts do not include . . . " Payne writes "Many who study the NT are unaware that the oldest surviving NT manuscripts differ, sometimes significantly, and various passages do not appear in the most reliable texts at all, which has led virtually all biblical scholars to conclude that some passages are interpolations" (Ibid., Payne, 226). Modern Christians are often unaware that the Shepherd of Hermas, an extensive book written a few decades after John wrote Revelation, was considered for decades to be part of the Scriptures by a large part of the church.

[247] Payne, *One in Christ*, 226.

(1) Probabilities regarding variations in surviving ancient manuscripts;[248]

(2) Highly technical observations about the precise markings in the margins made by scribal copyists in Codex Vaticanus, one of the oldest extant manuscripts of the Bible;

(3) Omission from an early and respected ancient codex;

(4) Apparent omission from the manuscript from which Minuscule 88 was copied;

(5) Omission from Clement of Alexandria's quotation of 1 Corinthians 14 (he was a respected second century church father);

(6) Omission by other apostolic church fathers as they quoted 1 Corinthians—"Even though 1 Corinthians was the most quoted epistle by Christian writers in the second century, none of the Apostolic Fathers cite 1 Cor 14:34–35."[249]

(7) The unusual number of variations in the ancient manuscripts within these two verses.

The second part of Payne's argument against including 1 Corinthians 14:34–35 in the Bible includes nine internal evidences:

(1) The glaring contradictions with Paul's assumptions stated in 1 Corinthians 11:5, 13;

(2) The ways that verses 34, 35 interrupt the flow of Paul's theme, logical argument, and symmetrical literary structure (a chiasm) in 14:26–40;

(3) The use of alien vocabulary in these two verses;

(4) The conflict with the instructional goals expressed in the chapter;

(5) The inconsistency of the phrase, "as the law also says," with Paul's theology, ethics, and literary practice;

(6) The subordination of a weak and oppressed social group uncharacteristic of Paul's championing of the downtrodden;

(7) The mimicking of the vocabulary of 1 Timothy 2:11–15 (written approximately 10 years later);

(8) The unprecedented command addressed to a category of people "in the churches;"

---

[248] Ibid., 229. Concerning this evidence, Payne quotes another biblical scholar (Fee) as stating, "I am now 99% sure that 1 Corinthians 14:34–35 is an interpolation."

[249] Ibid., 251.

(9) The obvious motive for interpolation, namely to silence women in church. "Every manuscript containing 1 Cor 14:34–35, or an allusion to it, comes from the [later] period of the church's reaction against women in leadership in Gnostic circles."

After answering the most common objections to this view, Payne concludes: "The thesis that 1 Cor 14:34–35 is an interpolation fits the external and the internal evidence far better than any other thesis. If 1 Cor 14:34–35 is a non-Pauline interpolation, it does not carry apostolic authority and should not be used as such to restrict the speaking ministries of women, nor should it influence the exegesis of other NT passages."[250]

Although the prospect of these verses not belonging in the Holy Scriptures may be unsettling to some, believers should recognize that ADDING to the Scriptures is just as possible and problematic as TAKING AWAY from them: "I warn everyone who hears the words of the prophecy of this book: If anyone adds anything to them, God will add to him the plagues described in this book. And if anyone takes words away from this book of prophecy, God will take away from him his share in the tree of life and in the holy city, which are described in this book" (Rev. 22:18, 19). Although this severe warning relates primarily to the Book of Revelation, because of its position in the last canonical book written (about 95 A.D.) some see it as a more sweeping warning about Scripture as a whole.

Although in my personal judgment, the assertion that these two verses are not inspired Scripture cannot be proven beyond all doubt, the evidence is strong enough that Bible students should be <u>very cautious if not hesitant</u> to use these three sentences to support a complementarian case. Without these two verses, the complementarian case is significantly weakened!

Nevertheless, the arguments of this book for an egalitarian understanding of the Scriptures do not depend on the probability that 1 Corinthians 14:34, 35 is a later interpolation. Rather, they are all based on careful exegesis of the relevant texts along with contextual insights that inform their interpretation.

---

[250] Ibid., 268.

In Summary

In 1 Corinthians 14:34, Paul asserts the importance of the women in Corinth avoiding non-stop talking or asking endless questions in church. These instructions had relevance "in all the [first century] congregations of the saints" (verse 33) because such *perpetual* talking would not only hinder broad participation but would also disrupt the essential orderliness of the gatherings. It would be divisive, offensive, and counterproductive in that fallen, male-dominated culture.

It is evident then, that when correctly translated and when the historical/cultural background and the immediate and larger contexts are considered, 1 Corinthians 14:26–35 does not support broad, ongoing gender-based restrictions in the church as asserted by complementarians. Correctly translated and understood, Paul's instructions are liberating and consistent with full participation by women in the life and leadership of the church as is asserted by egalitarianism.

FOR DISCUSSION

(1) One common stereotype today is that women are much more talkative than men. Do you think this is generally true or false? Why? What are some dangers in stereotypes? Are they ever accurate? How can you discern the appropriateness of a stereotype?

(2) In your experience, how do many men respond in church if women are dominating a conversation?

(3) In a culture where, right or wrong, many people assume that men are supposed to be the leaders and women are to submit, how do people respond when a woman, especially a wife, is outspoken or bossy? Why is this?

(4) When the New Testament was written, the culture was very patriarchal. Men were very dominant. How might it have affected the witness of the church had women strongly asserted themselves in the church and were not seen as submissive? How might this dynamic be seen in some contemporary cultures?

(5) In 1 Corinthians 14, Paul commanded prophets, tongue-speakers, and women, to not dominate the service by non-stop talking. Rather they were to pause so others could participate. In a contemporary worship gathering, class, or small group Bible study, what are some ways these instructions might be important to remember?

(6) Based on what you read in this chapter, how does it affect the way you look at the two prohibition passages (1 Cor. 14:33–35 and 1 Tim. 2:11–12)?

(7) Because of studying this chapter, what are two things you feel you should do to please God and help your church?

9

To Be Silent or to Be Serene,
That Is the Question

Imagine a giant tub stuffed with 23,145 <u>white</u> ping pong balls. Imagine there are nine <u>red</u> ping pong balls mixed in with all the white ones. That means you have 2,571 white balls for every 1 red ball. The red ping pong balls illustrate the number of Bible verses that reference gender role restrictions in the church—**nine** of them found in 1 Corinthians 11:5; 14:33–35 and 1 Timothy 2:11–15—compared to **23,145**, the total number of verses in the Bible.[251] If you lined up the white ping pong balls each representing a Bible verse, they would make a line *over three quarters of a mile* long. If you lined up the red ping pong balls representing all the gender roles verses, they would compose a line under *fourteen inches*, or <u>one half step out of a three-quarter mile walk</u>. **Seldom has so much been made of so little—nine verses out of 23,145!** The complementarian position that has severely limited the involvement of more than half of the church population in a majority of churches around the world for 2,000 years is based on a mere nine verses out of 23,145 that address the gender restriction issue with specificity in the English Bible. How did so little influence so much? Is this what God planned from the beginning (Gen. 1 2) or the tragic result of sin's curse (Gen. 3:16)? Does this help the church accomplish its mission or is it a masterstroke of Satanic strategy to hinder its effectiveness?

On the one hand, those numbers suggest that the complementarian

---

[251] Put another way, that's **161** words about gender roles in the church out of **783,137** words in the King James Bible (**.02%** of the Bible's words).

stance is not based on nearly as big an emphasis in the Bible as is suggested by the importance placed on it. On the other hand, because the issue potentially either liberates or eliminates at least half of all the members of every church in the world for service in primary teaching and leadership roles, then correctly understanding and applying those nine verses in 1 Corinthians 11:5; 14:33–35; and 1 Timothy 2:11–15 is imperative. Does it seem probable that God would place such a gigantic limitation on half of the church population supported only by nine hotly debated verses?

First Timothy 2:11–15, along with 1 Corinthians 14:33–35, represent **ground zero** in the gender roles debate. The most significant words in those passages are: "A woman should learn in quietness and full submission. I do not permit a woman to teach or to have authority over a man; she must be silent" (1 Tim. 2:11, 12). A simple, straightforward reading of these two verses seem on the surface to provide unassailable evidence supporting the complementarian view that the Bible prohibits women from teaching and holding leadership roles over men in the church. Is that understanding correct?

A Painful Caricature

Occam's Razor, the famous problem-solving maxim (*"the simpler solution is usually the better one"*), can be helpful but does not always pan out to be correct. A simple (or simplistic) traditional reading of 1 Timothy 2:9–15 often ignores the contextual and thematic dynamics of the passage. This has prompted some to characterize it in ways that others may find offensive, but that may painfully expose how the complementarian interpretation comes across to many people. For example, N.T. Wright has written sarcastically (this does not express his own view): "The whole passage seems to be saying that women are second-class citizens at every level. They aren't even allowed to dress prettily. They are the daughters of Eve, and she was the original troublemaker. The best thing for them to do is to get on and have children, and to behave themselves and keep quiet."[252]

Obviously this over-the-edge, unflattering caricature of the passage would only be adopted and promoted by an extreme and insensitive complementarian,

---

[252] Wright, *"Women's Service in the Church."*

by a sarcastic egalitarian, or by a cynic intending to discredit the Scriptures. However, rather than Wright intending to engage in hyperbolic and inflammatory rhetoric, his painful portrayal was most likely designed to help us understand how a significant number of people *outside* the church feel about what they perceive to be the gender bias and oppressive patriarchy taught by Scripture and embraced by many churches and Christians. For some outsiders, this sufficiently justifies rejecting Christianity and Christ. Perhaps Wright's sarcasm exposes the unreasonableness of a simplistic, traditional interpretation of the text by unmasking how shocking it actually sounds to many who haven't been pre-conditioned to accept patriarchy in the church. Is it possible that patriarchy is a "frog in the kettle" issue for many Christians—they've become used to it and fail to recognize the scandal it represents?

Sometimes it takes the shock of being mocked to help us to self-perceive. Many years ago, in my quite legalistic days, a young mom in our church asked if she could sing a solo in one of our services. I responded positively. "No," she countered, "I don't want to sing unless you listen to the song first and give your approval." I agreed and accompanied her to our sanctuary where she slid a cassette tape into her portable player to accompany her solo. It took only a few minutes for me to recognize that I was facing an awkward moment. The lyrics were good, the taped accompaniment was good, her voice was lovely, but one minor aspect of the style of her singing was contrary to my hyper-conservative "convictions" about *worldly music*. I attempted to gently but piously vocalize the "biblical principle" I felt she was violating.

For a few seconds she looked dumbfounded, then suddenly burst into laughter. Stunned, I realized that she thought I was joking. My musical "conviction," rather than being musically and theologically clear and convincing, was so utterly ludicrous to her that she assumed I had to be kidding. She couldn't believe that I was serious. My "biblical conviction" was so far out in left field she could not imagine that I actually believed it. Seeing how preposterous my position appeared to a reasonable, sincere, and godly person, was a small but important step in my spiritual journey away from at least one area of unbiblical legalism to embrace a much better application of the Scriptures. Her mocking laughter forced me to see how I was imposing unbiblical cultural biases onto my so-called "convictions" regarding music. I had unthinkingly accepted what I had been taught without testing the supposedly biblical basis.

Wright's sarcastic caricature of a complementarian understanding of 1 Timothy 2:9–15 could be a similar wake up call to some who are insensitive to how offensive, ludicrous, and preposterous their interpretation of this "ground zero" passage comes across to many, many people. To be sure, God's ways are higher than ours (Is. 55:8–9) and fallen people often rebel against God's ways. But, if many reasonable people, including Bible-believing Christians, find "His ways" offensive and outlandish, it should be a call to at least recheck one's understanding of the issues to be certain that "God's ways" have not be misrepresented. Perhaps sometimes God would distance Himself from what humans claim to be "His ways."

Considering that 1 Timothy 2:9–15 is the strongest, best known, and most used passage supporting the complementarian ban on women teaching or leading men in the church, it should give pause if a literalistic understanding seems to many people more like a complementarian's nightmare than their dream. If the passage asserts that women should not teach or have positions of authority over men in the church, then it also teaches that women should not wear fancy hairdos, jewelry, or expensive clothing, and that they should be *totally* silent in church. There is no justification within the paragraph to cherry pick only two of the prohibitions and throw out the others or assign them to the no-longer-applicable, first century cultural waste basket. When is the last time you heard a "no styled hairdos, rings, necklaces, bracelets, expensive dresses or shoes" sermon in a complementarian church? If you did (unlikely) what was the standard suggested for what "expensive" means—$10, $75, or $200? Aside from a few small and extreme sects there are virtually no evangelical churches who teach and practice all of these requirements for women. The apparent unacceptability and obvious inconsistency of this selective application should set off loud alarms that there is something else going on in this passage than the typically imposed limitations on women teaching or leading men asserted by complementarians.

This Is a Really Tough Passage

1 Timothy 2:11–15, is arguably THE most important Bible passage regarding the role of women in the church. Wright agrees: "I don't think I exaggerate when I suggest that this passage above all others has been the sheet

anchor for those who want to deny women a place in the ordained ministry of the church, with full responsibilities for preaching, presiding at the Eucharist, and exercising leadership within congregations and indeed dioceses."[253] This paragraph of Paul's instructions to Timothy, his young protégé and apostolic representative in Ephesus, is complicated and much-debated because in addition to the well-known section it includes several elements that baffle or challenge interpreters on both sides of the debate. Interpreters on all sides of the gender roles conversation have difficulty seamlessly connecting all the dots in this challenging paragraph.

One might wish that the passage at the epicenter of the debate would be so clear that every reasonable observer would be compelled to agree. Yet despite its importance both complementarians and egalitarians have significant difficulty interpreting all the parts of this passage harmoniously. This may be one of the "hard to understand" Scriptures that Peter asserted are "distorted" by some people to their own harm (2 Pt. 3:16)—a warning that calls us to humility and to extra diligent and careful exegesis. This text, along with the other applicable texts over which Bible scholars disagree, is a reminder that the gender roles issue is a very challenging topic in the Scriptures. Both sides of this debate should recognize that there is no unassailably clear position on either side that doesn't have some parts of texts that seem at least very difficult to harmonize. While these are not necessarily central to the gender roles debate, it is therefore evident that humility and a teachable spirit are appropriate when there is not broad agreement throughout Jesus' global church.

Theologian John Stackhouse Jr. wrote with regard to his personal struggle about biblical gender roles:

> Finally one afternoon . . . I underwent an explosive paradigm shift. Yes, we come—already!—to the promised key to the lock, the clue to the puzzle, the Answer to the Problem. I had been struggling with gender questions again, and had been reading on various sides of the issue. At the crucial moment I have described, I had been reading yet another explanation of 1 Timothy 2:11–15, easily one of the most obscure of the classic passages on this matter. And I remember quite clearly

---

[253] Wright, *Surprised by Scripture*, 78.

now—more than twenty years later—putting the book down on my lap and realizing this insight: nobody could explain this passage.

To be sure, I had been reading more than a dozen *attempts* to explain this passage. Some of them were ingenious; a few were even likely. But it struck me with paradigm-shaking force that no one could explain all the clauses in this passage with full plausibility. And I then began to think that this problem was true not only of expositions of this text, but of the whole gender question. No one I had read (and I had read quite a few) could put all of the relevant texts together into a single, finished puzzle with no pieces left over, no pieces manufactured to fill in gaps, and no pieces forced into place. I began to recall, with mounting excitement, how champions of one view typically ignored or explained away the leading texts of champions of other views. This phenomenon is what lawyers call avoiding or finessing the 'bad facts' of a case.

So I came to a principle of general theological method out of this wrestling with the particular issue of gender: We should not wait to come to a theological conclusion for the happy day in which we have perfectly arranged all of the relevant texts. Instead, we should look at all of the texts as open-mindedly as possible, and see whether among the various competing interpretations there is one that makes the most sense of the most texts and especially the most important ones. We should look, in basic epistemological terms, for the preponderance of warrants or grounds to believe p instead of q. If no such preponderance is evident, of course, then we should suspend making a decision. But if we do conclude that a preponderance is discernable, then we should acknowledge it—indeed, be grateful for it—and proceed to act on that basis.[254]

---

[254] Stackhouse, *Partners In Christ*, 30, 31.

The Problem of Unconscious Bias

I suggest that these difficulties are not only the result of genuine interpretive challenges in the passages but also arise from the subconscious gender bias that is virtually universal in this fallen world. Genesis 3:16 informs us that the struggle for control between women and men and the dominance of the stronger male gender is the tragic legacy of sin's entrance into God's previously perfect creation: "you will desire to control your husband but he will rule over you" (NLT). We are foolish and become vulnerable to deception if we do not acknowledge the subtle influence of our own subconscious biases.

Thus, in studying these verses, we must not only invest our very best efforts to diligently apply appropriate hermeneutical principles to our research and study, but also to sincerely attempt to identify our personal biases and to resist allowing them to influence our efforts to correctly handle the word of truth (2 Tim. 2:15).

Putting the Puzzle Pieces Together

With that in mind, hopefully with a sincere sense of humility joined with a mind open to consider contradictory arguments and evidence, it's been my goal to correctly understand this immensely challenging passage including its most perplexing assertions. My intensive study has brought me to a new appreciation for and understanding of 1 Timothy 2 which I now am convinced *strongly supports the egalitarian position*. What I now believe to be a compelling interpretation of the passage does not explain and harmonize every clause with an equal level of clarity and conviction (no position does). However, it is the assertion of this author that an egalitarian understanding of 1 Timothy 2:11–15 far and away best explains both what is clear and not so clear in this passage. I believe that it is the best way to fit all the pieces of the puzzle together to create an accurate, harmonious, and satisfying interpretation.

Context Matters

The traditional complementarian exegesis of 1 Timothy 2 fails to give appropriate consideration to the central theme of the chapter, relies on a faulty or misleading translation of two key words, and consequently is unable to successfully harmonize all parts of the passage with:

- the immediate context of 1 Timothy 2,
- the extended context of 1 and 2 Timothy and other related texts concerning the church in Ephesus such as Acts 19:1–41; 20:16–38, and
- the much larger contexts of the New Testament and the entire Bible.

At the outset of studying this crucial passage, it is important to be reminded of the over-arching purpose of Paul's letter. Remember, CONTEXT MATTERS. At the beginning of his letter Paul wrote: "As I urged you when I went into Macedonia, stay there in Ephesus so that you may command certain men not to teach false doctrines any longer nor to devote themselves to myths and endless genealogies. These promote controversies rather than God's work—which is by faith" (1 Tim. 1:3, 4). The Ephesian church was *under attack* by teachers promoting false doctrine. This was apparently an *on-going* problem as indicated by the present infinitive (ἑτεροδιδασκαλεῖν, *heterodidaskalein*) represented in the NIV by "not to teach false doctrines any longer" (emphasis added). Specifically, the false teaching involved the promotion of "myths and genealogies" that were producing disagreement and division in the church. Later in his letter, Paul again warns about "godless myths and old wives' tales" (1 Tim. 4:7). Some wanted to insert themselves as teachers (1 Tim. 1:7).[255] When he wrote his second letter to Timothy a couple of years later, the problem of false teaching persisted (2 Tim. 2:14, 16–18, 24–28; 4:3–4).

It is important to note that the false teachers that Paul commanded Timothy to ban were not necessarily only "men" as some potentially misleading translations suggest (e.g. NIV84, NASB95). Rather, they were "certain persons" as the ESV correctly translates the indefinite Greek pronoun, τὶς (*tis*).[256] The false teachers Paul warned against could have been either male or female or both. The reference to "old wives' tales" in 1 Timothy 4:7 makes it certain that at least some of the false doctrine originated with women.

---

[255] As will be discussed later, 1 Timothy 2:12 (correctly translated by the KJV) indicates a need to deal women who were usurping (assuming for oneself illicitly without required authorization) roles of domineering teaching and bullying leadership.

[256] See also *"certain people"* (NRSV) or *"some"* (KJV).

As will be further developed later in this chapter, these observations about the purpose and background of 1 Timothy are very important to correctly interpret Paul's instructions for both men and women in chapter 2.

Crucial Translation Issues in 1 Timothy 2

It is striking how few commentators call attention to the THEME of 1 Timothy 2 which is **living peacefully without disruption or conflict**. This theme is built on the three-fold use of the Greek word *haysuxia* in the chapter (verses 2, 11, 12). Unfortunately, it is easy to miss the thematic focus and structure of the chapter because of the inadequate and misleading translation of the three uses of *haysuxia*. Many versions, including the NIV, translate the same Greek word in different ways in the chapter making it much more difficult to discern the thematic structure of the passage unless the reader can read the Greek text.

The first KEY to interpreting this passage is a correct understanding of what *haysuxia* means in its three appearances in the chapter. The word means *"tranquil, serene, restful, at peace, free of disruption, free of conflict."* Tragically, when English versions use the words *"quiet"* or *"silent"* to translate *haysuxia*, they are misleading because they imply <u>verbal</u> quietness rather than <u>environmental</u>, <u>community</u>, or <u>relational</u> quietness, as in *"peaceful"* or *"serene."* The word **does not** communicate the idea of *"no talking."* It **does** convey the thought of *"no fighting."* It **is not** about verbal muteness but about a person or community being at rest, at peace, and undisturbed. It **does not** refer to a quiet mouth but to a quiet life.

Unfortunately, the majority of English Bible versions do not translate the word consistently in 1 Timothy 2 so that the unified thematic structure of the passage is hidden rather than obvious as it should be. No one reading the English translations could see how the repetitious use of *haysuxia* <u>organizes the chapter around a theme</u>. The following chart reveals the inconsistency with which the same word, *haysuxia*, is translated in a majority of the most popular and influential English versions:

Translation of ἡσυχία (haysuxia) in 1 Tim. 2	NIV	ESV	KJV	NKJV	NASB	NRSV	NLT
1 Tim. 2:2	quiet	quiet	peaceable	peaceable	quiet	peaceable	quiet
1 Tim. 2:11	quietness	quietly	silence	silence	quietly	silent	quietly
1 Tim. 2:12	silent	quiet	silence	silence	quiet	silent	quietly

This inconsistency makes it virtually impossible for the reader of many English versions to detect the theme of the chapter and how the parts interrelate around that theme.

The following chart, similar to the one in chapter 8 regarding the translation of *sigaō* in 1 Corinthians 14:26–35, reveals how all seven popular English versions fail in the crucial translation issues of **CONSISTENCY, CLARITY,** and **ACCURACY** regarding *haysuxia* in 1 Timothy 2:2, 11, 12.

- About **CONSISTENCY**, only three versions (ESV, NASB, NLT) are consistent in their translation of *haysuxia* but those three fail the other tests.
- Regarding **CLARITY**, only three versions correctly convey the meaning of *haysuxia*, as *"peaceable"* (KJV, NKJV, NRSV), conveying environmental and relational tranquility rather than verbal silence, but they do so in ONLY ONE of its three uses in the chapter. No one could recognize that the same word is used two more times.
- Those same three versions fail the **ACCURACY** test two out of three times due to their misleading translations of *haysuxia* as "silence" or "silent." The other four fail the **ACCURACY** test as they translate *haysuxia* as "quiet" or "silent" both of which suggest <u>verbal</u> silence rather than <u>relational serenity/peacefulness</u>.
- <u>Not one</u> of the seven most popular and influential English versions effectively translates the three uses of *haysuxia* in ways that are **CONSISTENT, CLEAR,** and **ACCURATE**. "Quiet, quietness, quietly, silent, and silence" all suggest to the modern reader that a person should either speak in a soft and barely audible voice or that they should not speak at all. This is absolutely NOT the meaning of *haysuxia* as will be demonstrated below.

These observations are visualized in the chart that follows:

Translation of ἡσυχία (*haysuxia*) in 1 Tim. 2:2, 11, 12	NIV	ESV	KJV	NKJV	NASB	NRSV	NLT
INCONSISTENT: identical words in the same text are translated differently	X		X	X		X	
UNCLEAR: the translation doesn't convey being serene, tranquil, peaceful, free of disruption, division, and conflict	X	X	2/3	2/3	X	2/3	X
MISLEADING: the translation gives an inaccurate impression of the actual meaning of the word	X	X	2/3	2/3	X	2/3	X
CONSISTENT, CLEAR, AND ACCURATE: identical words are translated identically using language which clearly and accurately conveys the meaning							

Thus in 1 Timothy 2:2, 11, 12, it is imperative to comprehend that *haysuxia* is not about being "quiet" in a verbal or auditory sense, that is, of speaking softly, not speaking, or being silent, but rather it is about being "quiet" in an environmental or relational sense, that is, maintaining a state of peacefulness, serenity, tranquility, and calm. The opposite of experiencing *haysuxia* is to be at war or to be involved in conflict and disputation. The quietness of *haysuxia* is freedom from disruption, disturbance, disputation, and debate. For example, if a news reporter said, "All is quiet on the Western front," they do not mean that no soldiers were talking on the battlefield. They mean that there was no war or fighting that violated the peace. That is the meaning of *haysuxia*. "Quiet" is about being serene, peaceful, and tranquil; about the opposite of being contentious or argumentative. **The word has nothing to do with being verbally silent.** For example, after arguing and yelling all day, Sam and Linda finally settled down and had a quiet (*haysuxia*) conversation. They talked, but it was a peaceful conversation without quarreling.

The Theme: Living Peacefully

The following chart reveals how 1 Timothy 2 is structured around the theme of **living peacefully without disruption, division, or conflict.**

TEXT	REALM	MANDATE	GREEK WORD
1Tim. 2:1, 2	OUTSIDE the church	EVERYONE is to pray so as to live **without conflict** caused by warring or persecuting governments	ἡσυχία *haysuxia*
1Tim. 2:8	INSIDE the church	MEN are to pray **without conflict**[257] precipitated by their angry or contentious spirits	Different words: ὀργή and διαλογισμός *orgay* and *dialogismos*
1Tim. 2:9–11	INSIDE the church	WOMEN are to learn **without conflict** resulting from their assertiveness, combativeness, or argumentativeness	ἡσυχία *haysuxia*
1Tim. 2:12	INSIDE the church	WOMEN are to teach and lead **without conflict** brought on by their self-promotion, assertiveness, combativeness, and bullying	ἡσυχία *haysuxia*

In this chapter Paul laid out a strategy for promoting peace and tranquility:

- First, he encourages Timothy to promote <u>prayer</u> for those who govern so everyone might enjoy living in a **peaceful environment** so they

---

[257] In verse 8 Paul does not use the word for quiet tranquility (*haysuxia*) but rather identifies two of the ways men destroy tranquility and which are the opposite of *haysuxia* in the church: angry or argumentative spirits.

could practice their faith and spread the Gospel without disruption (2:1–7).

- Then he encourages first men and then women in the church to <u>conduct themselves</u> in ways that would promote a **peaceful environment** free of argument or conflict.

- He did this by calling on men to <u>pray</u> without anger and disputation both of which destroy a **peaceful environment** by injecting animosity and contentiousness (2:8).

- Next Paul urges women to not <u>dress</u> in a manner that would be disruptive to the **peaceful environment** of the worship gathering by calling inappropriate attention to themselves by their fancy hair styles or their expensive jewelry and clothing (2:9, 10). This could indicate that rich women in the church were ostentatiously showing off their wealth to gain influence and to acquire teaching or leadership roles based on their economic or societal superiority rather than on their godly character, doctrinal knowledge, or pedagogic competence.

- Further as women <u>learn</u> in church, Paul indicates that they should do so without disturbing the **peaceful environment** through arguments, debates, divisiveness, or a rebellious spirit (2:11).

- Finally, as women <u>teach or lead</u> men in the church, Paul directs them to preserve the **peaceful environment** by not commandeering authority or by being argumentative, divisive, domineering, bullying, or abusive.

In other words, everyone in the church has a role in minimizing disruptive behaviors that upset the **peaceful environment** that should characterize Jesus' church. This advances the goals of promoting godly living (1 Tim. 2:1) and spreading the Gospel (1 Tim. 2:4).

Notice in this analysis of the text that Paul *assumed* that women would be formally discipled and that they would <u>teach and exercise authority over men (both of which were shockingly counter-cultural).</u> But he prohibited their doing either in a <u>manner</u> that would disturb the **peaceful environment** (*haysuxia*) and promote division. This understanding is confirmed in 1 Timothy 2:12 by Paul's use of a very rare word, αὐθεντέω (*authĕntĕō*), misleadingly translated in a neutral or positive fashion, *"to have authority over,"* when its primary meaning, demonstrated in numerous ancient extra-biblical uses, is to exercise a *negative* kind of authority—<u>autocratic,</u>

domineering, and <u>abusive</u>. The meaning of this word will be discussed more thoroughly in the next chapter. Obviously, exerting abusive authority would disrupt the **peaceful environment**.

With this understanding, 1 Timothy 2:11–15 is seen to be a <u>powerful affirmation of having no gender-based restrictions in church ministry</u> thus confirming that <u>women may serve in any capacity that men do</u>. Women may preach or hold the office of deacon, pastor, or elder. However, neither men nor women are permitted to conduct ministry in a manner that is disruptive, argumentative, divisive, or abusive which would disturb a **peaceful environment**.

Debunking Gender Stereotypes

It is important to note in 1 Timothy 2 that Paul has separate instructions for men (verse 8) and women (verses 9–12) calling both to peaceful and orderly behavior in their worship gatherings. He discourages them acting in ways that would be disruptive or would call distracting or self-promoting attention to themselves. In so doing, he may also have intended to discourage behavior which aligned with or perpetuated uncomplimentary gender stereotypes that would not have enhanced tranquility in the church.

> The first verse (8) is clear: the men must give themselves to devout prayer,[258] and must not follow the normal stereotypes of "male" behaviour: no anger or arguing. Then verses 9 and 10 follow, making the same point about the women. They must be set free from their stereotype, that of fussing all the time about hair-dos, jewelry, and fancy clothes—but they must be set free, not in order that they can be dowdy,

---

[258] A common contemporary gender stereotype is that women are much more likely to be distinguished by prayerfulness than men. Many years ago, when I proposed a "pastors' prayer partner" ministry for the men in our church, I was told that if I wanted to launch a successful prayer ministry I would need to recruit women rather than men. Clearly Paul did not encourage that stereotype. I was thrilled by the robust response by nearly one hundred men to this new ministry of intercessory prayer for the pastors of the church.

unobtrusive little mice, but so that they can make a creative contribution to the wider society.[259]

Thus, in verses 11 and 12 Paul intended to discourage women from behaving in ways that supported the negative feminine stereotypes of being overly talkative, argumentative, controlling, and bossy.

Nobody Takes It This Far

A similarly important observation regarding interpreting 1 Timothy 2 is that the traditional complementarian interpretation of these verses proves far too much.[260] As noted, *"quietness"* in verse 11 and *"silent"* in verse 12, have been incorrectly assumed by complementarians to mean verbal quietness and silence (no talking), which is NOT the meaning of *haysuxia*. But if this incorrect understanding of the text is assumed, the vast majority of complementarians nevertheless distance themselves from the practical applications it requires, not merely about hairstyles, jewelry, and expensive outfits, but more important they fail to insist that women should say nothing at all in church.

A consistent application of this interpretation of the text not only prohibits women from teaching or preaching in the presence of men (2:12) but also prohibits them from teaching children, teaching women, singing, praying, giving missionary reports,[261] making announcements, or even conversing with one another because "a woman should learn in quietness and full submission . . . she must be silent" (both "quietness" and "silent" translate *haysuxia, 2:11, 12b*). "Quiet" is quiet! Silent" is silent! As the word is understood by complementarians, it must mean to not talk at all. Perhaps a consistent application of these faulty understandings could permit women in church to help in the kitchen, nursery, or other ministry if they were mute—totally silent. NO ONE accepts this interpretation and application yet no one

---

[259] Ibid., Wright, "Women's Service in the Church."

[260] The same is true of the complementarian interpretation of 1 Corinthians 14:33–35 as was noted in chapter 8.

[261] This would be staggering as two-thirds of all vocational missionaries today are women!

provides solid textual evidence allowing for the ban to be applied only with regard to women teaching adult men.

But even if the prohibition is only applied in the more limited understanding of not teaching or leading men, then women should not be allowed to teach or lead in church any time men are present. Therefore, it would have to be determined at what age male children become "men." Does the Bible specify some age? Whatever the cutoff, at that age women should no longer teach them in Sunday School, youth group, vacation Bible school, etc. Is it at age twelve, sixteen, eighteen, twenty-one, or thirty? Is it at age thirteen when Jewish boys come of age (*bar mitzvah*) and are considered a man? What if a woman is teaching a ten-year-old class and an adult male is present as a Sunday School worker? Must he cover his ears or leave so he will not be taught by a woman? If someone thinks I'm being ridiculous in these questions, perhaps they ought rather to consider whether the complementarian understanding of the passage creates ridiculous distinctions in its common applications.

Additionally, in the complementarian view, no woman should ever lead or supervise men in either staff or volunteer roles or lead a task team or committee that includes men or whose decisions affect men by exercising authority over them. In a literal and consistent application of the complementarian understanding of 1 Timothy 2, it could even be argued that women should not be allowed to vote[262] on any church matter that affects men (whether in a business meeting or in a committee meeting) as they could thereby exercise authority over them by producing or helping to form a majority decision. If the vote of a woman or women produces a majority voting block regarding any governing decision or policy, have those women not exercised authority over men? Don't forget, if the complementarian position rests on the view that these restrictions are gender-based, then why shouldn't they apply to all male/female relationships throughout all aspects of society?

Of course, all this flows out of an incorrect understanding of the meaning

---

[262] After all, the complementarian view of inherent gender distinctiveness rests on a similar foundation to that of the patriarchal power which delayed women's suffrage (the right to vote) in the U.S.A. for 144 years (ratified in 1920). Christians and churches were divided over giving women the right to vote, but those who were at the forefront of that liberating movement are now recognized as heroic and on the side of right. This author believes that the same will be true regarding the movement to liberate women's roles in the church. In both issues, a correct understanding of the Scriptures supports the liberation and empowerment of women.

of *haysuxia*, but verbal silence is the meaning accepted and inconsistently applied by complementarians.

Where's the "Beef"?

While the vast majority of complementarians would not take the passage this far, it must be asked what textual evidence supports their limited obedience to Paul's commands or if instead they have accepted a compromised position for some reason other than exegetical? Perhaps the fact that a consistent practice of the traditional understanding of "quietness" and "silent" is virtually non-existent should cause people to ask why. If the church universally finds itself unable or unwilling to implement this straightforward understanding of the text from a complementarian standpoint, it should raise questions about the accuracy of that understanding.

Perhaps in the past there were churches that required total silence of women in the church, but it would be exceedingly difficult if not impossible to find any today at least in the Western world. When this norm is practiced in an Islamic setting, most Christians would criticize it as stifling, offensive, demeaning, and oppressive regarding women. Somehow, they fail to recognize that based on their interpretation of the passage, a literal application requires no less than what they find offensive in another religion.

If churches universally reject a consistent literal application of the text's directives, those churches are either disobedient or their interpretation is faulty.

This is an essential consideration for someone who at this point is saying, "I just take the Bible literally and the Bible says women are supposed to be silent. The Bible says it and that settles it for me." Wait a minute! You are NOT taking the **Bible** seriously. You're taking seriously what some translator (and/ or interpreter) **says** the Bible says. The translator stands between you and the text. It's kind of like kissing your wife through a proxy. What if the translator didn't correctly tell you what the Bible says? If you insist he did, then you must take the whole passage for what it literally says. That means you must demand that men always raise their hands when they pray; women must stop styling their hair, wearing jewelry, and wearing anything but cheap clothing; and women must not say a word at church—not a word. They must be totally silent at all times. You must be consistent with your view.

Complementarians must respond to the question, *"What is it in the text that allows them to significantly limit the scope of their gender restrictions?"* Rather than the improbable and unwise imposition of far more comprehensive and oppressive gender restrictions to totally silence all women, perhaps complementarians should sincerely consider whether the nearly universal compromises regarding women's participation in church suggest there must be a more appropriate way of translating and/or understanding these verses.

This book asserts that there is a much better way to interpret and apply 1 Timothy 2:11–15—a way that is faithful to the text, to the immediate and larger contexts, to the consistent evidence throughout the Scriptures, and to the clearly described values of God's original and new creations.

Remember the Ephesian Threat

To correctly interpret Paul's letter to pastor Timothy, it is very important to understand the contemporary circumstances behind it. The specific theme of 1 Timothy 2—keeping peace in the church—is related to the larger purpose of the letter to counteract the threat of false teaching. First Timothy 1:3–11; 4:7 and 6:3–5, 20, 21 all inform us that false teaching was a very serious problem in Ephesus as the following excerpts from those passages clearly reveal:

> As I urged you when I went into Macedonia, stay there in Ephesus so that you may command certain men not to teach false doctrines any longer . . . Some have wandered away from these and turned to meaningless talk. They want to be teachers of the law, but they do not know what they are talking about or what they so confidently affirm . . . Have nothing to do with godless myths and old wives' tales . . . If anyone teaches false doctrines and does not agree to the sound instruction of our Lord Jesus Christ and to godly teaching he is conceited and understands nothing. He has an unhealthy interest in controversies and quarrels about words that result in envy, strife, malicious talk, evil suspicion, and constant friction . . . Timothy, guard what has been entrusted to your care. Turn away from godless chatter and the opposing ideas of what is falsely called knowledge,

which some have professed and in so doing have wandered from the faith.

When Paul, approximately seven years before writing 1 Timothy, made what he assumed would be his life-concluding journey to Rome, he gathered the Ephesian elders in Miletus to warn them about the impending threat of false teachers both from *outside* and *inside* the church. He warned the Ephesian leaders there would be those who would attempt to deceive the Ephesian believers to gain personal followers: "I know that after I leave, savage wolves will come in among you and will not spare the flock. Even from your own number men [humans[263]] will arise and distort the truth in order to draw away disciples after them. So be on your guard!" (Acts 20:29–31). We also know from Revelation 2:20ff that in the church in Thyatira (not far from Ephesus) dangerous false teachings came from a woman teacher metaphorically named "Jezebel." These factors suggest both a local and regional vulnerability to false teaching in general but also specifically by women.

Paul *opened* and *closed* his letter to Timothy with instructions about confronting false teachers and teachings in Ephesus (1 Tim. 1:3, 4 and 6:20,21). These heresies were being taught by "certain men" [264] (1:3) and by "some[265] . . . [who had] wandered from the faith" (6:21)—apparently both men and women. Thirty years later, Jesus commended the Ephesian church for its diligent rejection of false teachers: "I know your deeds, your hard work and your perseverance. I know that you cannot tolerate wicked men, that you have tested those who claim to be apostles but are not and have found them false" (Rev. 2:2). Perhaps this protective behavior was in response to Paul's earlier warnings in 1 Timothy.

Both biblical and historical evidence indicate that the Artemis cult in Ephesus may also have been a major source of the kind of false teaching Paul

---

[263] ἄνδρες (*andres*) can be either "males" or "humans" of either gender.

[264] The word "men" is not in the Greek text. English translators added it after the indefinite pronoun (τις) which is an indefinite pronoun used in a gender-neutral manner, "certain ones," regardless of gender, as, for example in Mark 8:4; 9:30; 11:16; et al., or which can even be used specifically of a woman as in Luke 8:46.

[265] Paul used the indefinite pronoun (τις, tis) which is used of "humans" without regard to gender or can refer to a male or female. See footnote 193. The same is true in 1 Timothy 6:3 where Paul wrote, "If anyone [τις] teaches false doctrines and does not agree to the sound instruction of our Lord Jesus Christ and to godly teaching . . ."

warned Timothy about. Although an important backdrop to all of the New Testament was a culture where women were oppressed and marginalized, in contrast, many women in Ephesus may have lived in a more complex gender role milieu. While oppressive patriarchy permeated the larger culture and also existed in Ephesus (cf. Eph. 5:22-33, see chapter 5), there may also have been some mixed and sometimes contradictory gender issues in Ephesus where Timothy was serving—especially in the realm of religion.

In Ephesus, the world-renowned temple and the female-focused worship of the goddess Artemis were prominent and famous throughout the world. The production of silver Artemis shrines was an essential and passionately protected aspect of the city's economy (Acts 19:24–27). Artemis worship strongly influenced the psyche of the city as demonstrated by the fanatical mob riot described in Acts 19. The female goddess and her hundreds of priestesses most likely made the Ephesian culture uniquely friendly to prominent female teachers and prophetesses.

The significance of Artemis worship in Ephesus as a cultural backdrop to 1 Timothy could hardly be overemphasized. This is evident both in the biblical description of Ephesus in Acts 19 and in ancient secular literature and archeological discoveries. Scholars have calculated

> that of all the references to Ephesus in ancient Greek literature, fully one-third of the passages referring to Ephesus or things Ephesian refer to the goddess, her sanctuary, or her cult personnel. Devotion and affection for Artemis is portrayed especially in the Ephesus-centered novels by Xenophon and Achilles Tatius. It is also attested to in the numerous devotional inscriptions . . . [It is estimated] that we have approximately 6000 inscriptions from Ephesus.[266]

In addition to the influence of the Artemis cult in Ephesus, it seems evident that there was also the influence of a proto-Gnostic cult that advocated false doctrines regarding Eve including *myths* and perverted *genealogies* regarding the creation of her and Adam (cf. 1 Tim. 1:4, "myths and endless

---

[266] Marg Mowczko: *"1 Timothy 2:12 In Context: Artemis of Ephesus and Her Temple,"* Blog: Marg Mowczko (4/17/2013), http://newlife.id.au/equality-and-gender-issues/1-timothy-212-in-context-2/

genealogies"). These false teachings in Ephesus at the time of Paul's letters to Timothy is not only important regarding the self-asserting role of women in the church and the concern about false teaching, but also for the interpreting Paul's references to Eve in 1 Timothy 2:13, 14.

In her New Life Blog, Mowczko wrote:

> I have suggested that the heresy in Ephesus—which motivated Paul to write his first letter to Timothy—was an early kind of gnostic or syncretistic heresy (cf. 1 Tim. 1:3–7; 2:5; 4:1–4, 7; 6:20; etc.). I have also suggested that 1 Timothy 2:13–14 was written to correct some proto-gnostic teachings concerning Adam and Eve[267] . . . [she notes that] the ancient gnostic texts found in Nag Hammadi in Egypt in 1945 show . . . [that] Eve is sometimes described as Adam's teacher. She is also depicted as superior to Adam, as preceding him, and as giving life to him in some way.[268]

> Several ancient documents survive which contain corrupted versions of the Genesis 2–3 creation account. In these documents, Eve, or a powerful feminine force, gives life to Adam, and Adam is the one deceived. The various versions of these distorted accounts were taught by Jewish and Christian Gnostics and their forerunners.[269]

These diverse streams of false teaching related to women and to Eve converged on and were flowing through Ephesus at or near the time of Paul's writing 1 Timothy.

> The Ephesian church was wracked by the influence of false teachers who espoused a proto-Gnostic form of Jewish Christianity. They probably proclaimed a dualism that led

---

[267] Marg Mowczko, *"Adam and Eve in Ancient Gnostic Literature and 1 Timothy 2:13, 14,"* Blog: Marg Mowczko (3/9/2015), http://newlife.id.au/equality-and-gender-issues/adam-and-eve-in-gnostic-literature/

[268] Ibid.

[269] Marg Mowczko, *"An interpretation of 1 Timothy 2:12 that joins the dots of 2:11-15,"* blog: Marg Mowczko (8/30/ 2017): http://margmowczko.com/interpretation-of-1-timothy-212/

to either libertine or ascetic approaches to physical existence (1 Tim 4:1–8). These false teachers propagated myths and genealogies (1 Tim 6:3–5), as well as godless chatter (6:20–21). They were especially successful at influencing the women of Ephesus (2 Tim 3:1–9). Younger widows were plagued by sexual problems (1 Tim 5:6, 11–16). The women were weak in faith and susceptible to evil desires (2 Tim 3:6–7), and they were immodest in dress (1 Tim 2:9–10). Women were probably among the perpetrators of the old wives' tales (1 Tim 4:7) and myths (1 Tim 1:3; note the indefinite pronoun *tisin)* that competed with Christian truth ... Hence orthodox teaching—not the preservation of male headship—appears to be uppermost in Paul's mind as he writes his injunction concerning women.[270]

In other words, the Ephesian church faced a unique challenge involving women engaging in and/or being deceived by false teaching.

Further, as previously noted, the <u>immediate context</u> of this much-disputed gender role passage (1 Tim. 2:11–15) suggests that there were wealthy women in the Ephesian church who were attempting to draw attention to themselves or perhaps to gain dominance and influence by their ostentatious and costly grooming, jewelry, and attire (1 Tim. 2:8–10).

1 Timothy 2:11–15 should no more be understood as timeless and absolute prohibitions against women speaking or leading in church than the immediately proximate and related instructions in 1 Timothy 2:9 should be understood as a timeless and absolute prohibition against women styling their hair, using jewelry, or wearing expensive clothes. Gender-biased inconsistency in application bristles from typical complementarian teaching on this passage in that while women's ministry roles are restricted in many churches and denominations, there is virtually no similar restriction about hair styling, jewelry, or the cost of clothing worn to worship.[271] These observations are not

---

[270] Grenz, *Women in the Church*, Kindle loc 1478, 1487.

[271] The exceptions include a very small number of groups in which women all adopt plain hair styles (e.g. long and uncut) and clothing, and wear no jewelry, as in a small number of Fundamentalist Pentecostal denominations or conservative communities among the Amish and Mennonites. Those who impose gender-based ministry restrictions should

an argument in favor of restricting women regarding their appearance but highlight the inconsistent, incorrect, and perhaps hypocritical restriction of them from teaching and leading.

Together these factors suggest that Paul was addressing a specific, local problem of domineering female teachers in the church under Timothy's care. Their argumentative and controlling manner coupled with the false teaching they promoted disrupted the beautiful peace the church had enjoyed. Paul's instructions have timeless application but addressed a specific first century situation in Ephesus. They should not be interpreted apart from these essential background factors. Remember, CONTEXT MATTERS!

What the Words Really Mean

While these background observations are very important for a correct understanding of 1 Timothy 2:11–15, the exegetical considerations that follow, specifically semasiological considerations (the study of the meaning of words),[272] provide the most compelling evidence for an egalitarian understanding of the passage.

Discovering the correct meaning of key words in this definitive gender roles passage is absolutely essential. While this is the final and most compelling interpretive element, its correctness is validated by how well it fits with and responds to all of the essential interpretive elements and observations we have identified:

- the purpose of 1 Timothy,
- the structure and theme of chapter 2,
- the pervasive misleading translations in key English versions of the Bible,
- the inconsistencies in the traditional treatment and application of the passage, and

---

acknowledge that to be consistent in their interpretation and application of 1 Timothy 2, perhaps they should add these strict appearance restrictions as well.

[272] Semasiology (from Greek: σημασία, *semasia*, "signification") is a discipline of linguistics concerned with the question "what does the word X mean?". Wikipedia, "Semasiology," https://en.wikipedia.org/wiki/Semasiology

- the historical backdrop of the Ephesian Artemis cult and of early expressions of proto-gnostic heresies.

The Brightest Facets of the Complementarian Diamond Ring

If 1 Corinthians 14:33–25 and 1 Timothy 2:9–15 are the diamond ring of the complementarian position, then 1 Timothy 2:11–12 is the diamond: "A woman should learn in quietness and full submission. I do not permit a woman to teach or to have authority over a man; she must be silent." It would be impossible to overstate the importance of these twenty-eight words[273] for the gender roles issue. These two sentences as traditionally translated and understood are the indispensable cornerstone of the complementarian viewpoint. Some would suggest that apart from these two verses, the complementarian case is a non-starter. Without them it is dead in the water. Unquestionably, these two verses are absolutely central to the debate regarding whether there are gender-based restrictions for leadership in the church. Can you think of any other biblical teaching that forces significant restrictions on at least 50% of all church members every Sunday[274] as well as through the week that is based primarily on twenty-eight *words* of Scripture?

For complementarians, these two verses deliver the clearest, most compelling, and **the ONLY specific gender-based restrictions on church leadership**. Their influence on interpreting other passages, such as Genesis 1, 2, is huge, and, if the conclusions of this study are correct, completely unwarranted. However, it should be recognized that the subconscious influence of hundreds of years of patriarchal thinking and biblical assumptions will not necessarily be erased even for those who change from a complementarian to an egalitarian understanding of 1 Timothy 2. But then, patriarchy has dominated the world from nearly the beginning of human history—namely since the curse of Genesis 3:16.

To correctly understand 1 Timothy 2:11, 12 an accurate rendering of the precise meaning of two Greek words is essential:

---

[273] In the NIV84.

[274] Actually, every day: the ministry of the church is not confined to Sunday but spans the entire week.

(1) ἡσυχία *(haysuxia)* which in 1 Timothy 2 (NIV) is translated "quiet" (verse 2), "quietness" (verse 11), and "silence" (verse 12), and

(2) αὐθεντέω *(authĕntĕō)* which in the NIV and most other versions is translated "authority" (verse 12).

Are these translations accurate? Do they appropriately represent the meaning of those words? Does the translation fit the context and the theme of the passage? Is the translation consistent with how the words are translated in passages other than 1 Timothy 2? Has the translation of these words been influenced by gender bias?

Quiet Mouth or Quiet Circumstances?

Looking only at the English translations, one might assume that the Greek vocabulary in 1 Corinthians 14:33, 34 and 1 Timothy 2:11, 12 is similar or identical, because "silent" appears in the English translation (NIV) of both passages. However, in 1 Timothy 2:2, 11, 12, Paul used a totally different Greek word (ἡσυχία, *haysuxia*) than the Greek word (σιγάω, *sigaō*) he used in 1 Corinthians 14:33, 34. This identical translation is *very misleading* because the meanings of the two Greek words is significantly different.

As previously demonstrated, *sigaō* in 1 Corinthians 14:33, 34 conveys the meaning of <u>pausing in one's verbal speaking</u> to defer to others so they can also participate. In contrast, *haysuxia* in 1 Timothy 2:2,11, 12 communicates nothing about being verbally silent (neither temporarily nor permanently). Rather, as presented earlier in this chapter, the word conveys the idea of <u>being serene, tranquil, and peaceful or peaceable</u>. Thus, understanding the correct meaning of the three uses of *haysuxia* in 1 Timothy 2:11, 12 is absolutely essential to discern its implications for the gender role controversy.

Haysuxia is not at all about verbal silence, but rather is about environmental, community, relational, or behavioral tranquility. In 1 Timothy 2:2 *haysuxia* is about people enjoying *national or local tranquility* resulting from the wise rule of those who govern them. In 1 Timothy 2:11, 12 *haysuxia* is about women displaying *behavioral tranquility-promoting actions and words* while they learn, teach, or lead.

In the former (v. 2), Paul's intent in urging intercession for kings was not so their subjects would be able to <u>stop talking</u> (that would be ludicrous!) but rather that they would be able to live <u>in peaceful tranquility</u>, free from disturbance, war, persecution, conflict, and trouble. That is the meaning of *haysuxia*.

In the later (vv. 11, 12), *haysuxia* calls for a woman to have a peaceable rather than an argumentative and combative demeanor while she learns, teaches, or leads. The word *haysuxia* indicates a *quiet manner*, NOT a *quiet mouth; a serene and tranquil life* rather than *muzzled lips*. It refers to a spirit that promotes peace rather than conflict, disturbance, debate, and division. Correctly translated, this word organizes and advances the chapter's theme of *living peacefully without disruption or conflict. Haysuxia* creates the structure of the chapter which addresses serenity *outside* the church in verses 1-7 and *inside* the church in verses 8-15.

Regarding Paul's requirement for **women** to promote *haysuxia* in the church, there is a parallel warning (using different Greek words) for **men** in verse 8 where Paul declares, "I want men everywhere to lift up holy hands in prayer, without anger [ὀργή, *orgay*] or disputing [διαλογισμός, *dialogismos*]." No one understands verse 8 as prohibiting males from praying in church, but rather as prohibiting a *manner* of praying that manifested an angry and contentious spirit.[275] In this way it is parallel to the instructions for women that do not prohibit women from speaking, learning, teaching, and leading in church, but rather prohibits a *manner* of doing those things that manifested a contentious and domineering spirit contrary to Paul's deep desire for the Ephesian believers to live in peace without disruption or conflict. This of course, was not the end goal, but rather was a means to exalt the Lord Jesus and promote His gospel.

What About Other Scriptures Where *Haysuxia* is Used?

A comparison of other New Testament uses of *haysuxia* absolutely confirms this understanding of its meaning. In Luke 23:56 *haysuxia* is translated "rested" on the Sabbath. No one understands this as not talking for twenty-four hours. Rather the Sabbath was to be restful and peaceful, not

---

[275] Perhaps some of the men were engaging in angry, imprecatory-type prayers against those in government, against their persecutors, and/or against some who were perceived to have wronged them. These would disrupt the tranquility (*haysuxia*) Paul desires for the Ephesian church.

full of exhausting, disruptive labor. In 2 Thessalonians 3:11, 12 *haysuxia* has to do with "settling down" rather than being a "busybody." The problem was not that people weren't working to earn their own food because they were talking too much, but because they were inappropriately inserting themselves into people's business and causing disruption.

Paul's admonition in 1 Thessalonians 4:11, 12 again confirms this understanding: "Make it your ambition to lead a quiet life [*haysuxein*], to mind your own business and to work with your hands, just as we told you, so that your daily life may win the respect of outsiders and so that you will not be dependent on anybody." Living a "quiet life" did not mean a verbally silent life, but meant a tranquil, noncombative life. In Luke 14:4, Acts 11:18; 21:14; and 22:2 the verb form communicates *ceasing argument, debate, or disagreement.*[276]

In those few passages in which *haysuxia* conveys the idea of cessation of speaking, it is not that someone stopped talking or had silence imposed on them so that they then refrained from all speech. Rather it is that that they had been shouting, debating, or strongly disagreeing but now settled down and ceased their raucous yelling. (Acts 22:2) or argument (Luke 14:3, 4; Acts 11:18; 21:14). In the Acts 22 incident, the Jewish crowd abruptly ended the peaceful silence (*haysuxia*) as they began to shout, throw off their coats, and fling dust in the air. The point is not whether someone was talking, but the *manner* in which they were talking. *Haysuxia* marked the end of or temporary cessation of argumentative speech or disorderly and cacophonous rioting which disrupted peace and tranquility.

First Corinthians 14:34 addressed **how much talking** (quantity) was appropriate for women as they exercised their spiritual gifts in church (they were to allow others a turn to speak) while 1 Timothy 2:11, 12 addressed **what kind of spirit** (quality) was appropriate for women as they learned, taught, and led (they were not to be argumentative, divisive, or domineering). Neither passage prohibits women from talking, teaching, or leading regardless of the audience, male or female.

Paul is not placing a ban on females teaching or leading men but rather

---

[276] Grenz, *Women in the Church,* Kindle loc. 1487. "In the first century 'silence' (*hesychia*) was a positive attribute. It did not necessarily entail 'not speaking,' as is evident in Paul's use of the word earlier in the chapter (1 Tim 2:2; compare 2 Thess 3:12). Rather, it implied respect or lack of disagreement (as in Acts 11;18; 21:14)."

assumes both as legitimate while prohibiting a particular kind of teaching and leading—that which is disruptive, argumentative, and domineering.

Other Interpretive Issues in 1 Timothy 2

In addition to these crucial understandings about the meaning of *haysuxia* and *authĕntĕō*, it is important to notice the tense and connotation of the verbs, "to teach or to have authority over a man" (verse 12, emphasis added).

Regarding *tense,* both words are *present* infinitives that convey continuous, ongoing, or habitual behaviors.[277] Paul is not talking about a single instance of teaching or leading but of the continuing role of being a teacher or leader. Wuest indicates concerning the significance in 1 Timothy 2 is that "*didaxai* (διδαξαι, aorist tense), would be to teach, while *didaskein* (διδασκειν) (present 2:12), is to be a teacher."[278] Together the words comprise Paul's prohibition of a continuous or habitual peace-disrupting style of instruction and leadership apparently being practiced by some women at Ephesus. This needed to be curbed.

The *connotation* of the two verbs concerns whether they convey a positive or a negative meaning. The two infinitives are joined by the Greek connective, οὐδὲ (*oude*). "When οὐδὲ joins two activities, they both carry the same connotation, whether negative or positive"[279] (emphasis added). To teach (διδάσκειν, *didaskein*) is a neutral concept that may refer to any kind of teaching, either orthodox or heretical. Which is in view is determined by

---

[277] "In Greek, however, the present tense primarily tells us the *type* of action. The Greek present tense indicates **continued action**, something that happens continually or repeatedly, or something that is in the process of happening. If you say, for instance, "The sun is rising," you are talking about a process happening over a period of time, not an instantaneous event. The Greeks use the present tense to express this kind of continued action. In contrast, Greek uses the aorist tense to show simple action. An aorist verb simply tells you that something happened, with no indication of how long it took. Aorist is like a snapshot; present is like a video." "The Tenses Explained: Basic Meanings of Greek tenses," Ezraproject.com.

[278] K. S. Wuest, *Wuest's word studies from the Greek New Testament: for the English reader.* (Grand Rapids: Eerdmans, 1997), Logos at 1 Tim 2:11.

[279] Kostenberger, *Women in the Church,* Kindle page 100.

the context. On the other hand, to assume authority (*authĕntĕō*), or better, to *"usurp authority"* as the KJV accurately renders, is not a neutral concept in which the context determines its meaning. As will be argued, *authĕntĕō* nearly always has a strongly negative connotation. It is overbearing, controlling, domineering, and bullying authority which has been commandeered rather than appropriately assigned.

With others, I conclude that both terms (joined by *oude*) should be understood as having a <u>negative</u> connotation rather than positive. Thus, we see that not all teaching and leading of men was prohibited for women. Rather, only divisive, domineering, and abusive teaching and leading by women was prohibited. That spirit was also prohibited for men in 1 Timothy 2:8, "without wrath," as well as in the warning in 3 John 9ff for the abusive leader, Diotrephes. Once again, this linguistic understanding fits with and advances the central and unifying theme of the chapter: *living peacefully without disruption or conflict.*

But What about Being in "Full Submission"?

To correctly interpret 1 Timothy 2, one must take into consideration additional elements in the passage. Regarding Paul's requirement for "full submission" in verse 11, it should be noted in the context that having a yielding rather than willful, independent, or rebellious spirit is in view. A submissive attitude is especially important in an environment like Ephesus where abusive and domineering women were apparently disrupting the peace—the peace that is the goal of Paul's instructions in 1 Timothy 2. Perhaps it is even a reminder that no one is prepared to lead who is not first able to follow. Additionally, any understanding of "submission" in 1 Timothy 2:11 (written about 64 A.D.), must consider Paul's earlier instructions (written about 60 A.D.) to both genders in the same church in Ephesians 5:21: "Submit to one another out of reverence for Christ." The *same Greek word* is used in both passages as a verb in Ephesians (ὑποτάσσω, *hupotasso*) and a noun in 1 Timothy (ὑποταγή, *hupotagay*).

More importantly, with regard to "full submission" (1 Tim. 2:11), it is essential to recognize that Paul is talking about <u>how women are to learn</u> ("A woman should learn in quietness and full submission"); <u>not</u> about how women are to submit to their husbands or to male church leadership. Their demeanor while learning was to be characterized by being peaceful and not argumentative and by being humble and teachable rather than aggressive, self-seeking, or domineering. Genz notes, "With both of these statements, Paul is enjoining an attitude of receptivity."[280] They should submit to those who were sound in their teaching (male or female), rather than being "swayed" by false teachers, a problem Paul addresses again in 2 Tim. 3:6–8.

One commentator notes: "The concept of women being submissive has been greatly over-emphasized by many Christians, but submission is simply the opposite of rebellion. In verse 11 Paul is simply instructing a woman to learn in a quiet, respectable manner—the usual conduct of a good student—and not to be loud, offensive or rebellious."[281]

Further, rather than assuming, as complementarian commentators do, that Paul is talking about women fully submitting to their *husbands* or to *men* or to *male teachers* and *leaders,* it is at least equally reasonable to assume that Paul is talking about being fully submissive to *God* and to *the truth they are learning*. Women, like men, are not to learn the Scriptures merely for the sake of learning, to accrue knowledge, or to decide whether to obey those Scriptures, but rather are to learn in order to submit to the truth they received. Learning must lead to obedience. This understanding fits the context and seems to be the best understanding of Paul's intent.

It is essential to note that the text gives no distinct, clear, or indisputable indication (or even a hint) on the object of submission. Whether the submission is directed toward men, church leaders, God, or the Scriptures, is disputable. Therefore, to use Paul's reference to submission as lending support for a complementarian understanding of this text is unwarranted and unprovable. However, submission to God and His truth seems to be the most fitting understanding.

In 1 Timothy 2:9–15, Paul assumes that women will speak, learn, teach, and lead in the church, but all of these must be done without being immodest, obstinate, disruptive, rebellious, divisive, argumentative, self-promoting, or domineering.

---

[280] Grenz, *Women in the Church,* Kindle, Loc. 1496.

[281] Mowczko, "*1 Timothy 2:12 in Context: Phrase by Phrase,*" Blog: Marg Mowczko (4/17/2013), http://newlife.id.au/equality-and-gender-issues/1-timothy-212-in-context-4/

But If My English Bible Contains These Misleading Translations, Can I Trust It at All?

Because this study has exposed misleading English translations in crucial gender-role passages, it is important to address the question about the trustworthiness of those Bible versions. In exposing the very serious issue of misleading translations regarding gender roles in 1 Corinthians 14 and 1 Timothy 2, I have concern that I not thereby undermine the average Christian's confidence in their English Bible—especially the majority of believers who do not have any background in the Greek language or access to scholarly tools in order to conduct significant linguistic research.

First, it is important to know that translation errors in the English Bible are <u>extremely rare</u> —actually infinitesimal compared to the Scriptures as a whole and even more rare are examples where a doctrinal or behavioral issue is affected. In fact, although the misleading translations of four words are very significant in the gender roles debate, it is important to look at the big picture of the English Bible versions. These misleading translations regarding gender roles are all in six verses: 1 Corinthians 14:28, 30, 34, 35 and 1 Timothy 2:11, 12. That's six verses out of 23,145 verses in the Bible (.025%). The problem is with four words out of 783,137words in the Bible (.00051%).

This is not to suggest that there are no other misleading translations in the English Bible. But, perfection should not be our standard or expectation for any *copy* or *translation* of the Bible. Virtually all orthodox theologians believe that the doctrine of inspiration relates only to the original documents (the autographs). God never promised to perfectly preserve any or every later copy or translation. Therefore, inevitably, human frailty will cause some errors to creep in. The alternative is unthinkable—that every time any individual or group decided to prepare a new translation of the Bible, the Holy Spirit would have to supernaturally guide every choice of vocabulary, tense, voice, and mood so that every word of every new translation faithfully and perfectly portrayed God's intent in the same way as when He guided/inspired the original authors. The English Bible society estimates there are about 900 partial or complete paraphrases or translations of the English Bible.[282] Does

---

[282] *"Number of English Translations of the Bible"* (12/2/2009), on line article, American Bible Society News.

anyone really believe that divine inspiration extends to every word in all of them? If not, who determines which, how many, none, or all, are fully and perfectly inspired by God?

In other words, almost no one who has seriously considered the issue believes that divine inspiration extends to any or all English translations of the Bible,[283] let alone, to all complete or partial translations into the languages of the world (far over 3000 have been made). However, all reputable Bible scholars affirm that the most popular English translations are very accurate and trustworthy and that no orthodox doctrine as expressed in any of the major creeds of history is affected in the slightest by this minute number of disputed translations.

Of course, some versions are superior to others, especially those produced by a *group* of well-qualified and widely recognized biblical scholars (rather than a lone translator) who are committed to accuracy in translation rather than to the promotion of any denominational or personal agenda. Comparing several of the most reliable English translations is often an excellent study method especially for understanding difficult passages.

Christians can read their English language Bibles with a high level of confidence that despite the plethora of versions, even with all their nuanced and stylistic differences, the major doctrines of Scripture are unaffected. The exception to that statement would be a handful of versions dishonestly produced by individuals, sects, or cults to promote their heresies. Some of these demonstrate a willingness to produce deceptive and erroneous translations to promote their false doctrine.[284]

That is not to suggest that while the biblical teaching regarding gender roles in the church is not an "Apostle's Creed" level doctrine, it is therefore unimportant. It is immensely important for all the reasons expressed in this study. The number of misleading translations that occur in the six Bible verses

---

[283] A unique exception would be to a very small segment of Fundamentalism such as some "King James only" groups who believe that God miraculously and perfectly inspired that particular translation. This in the face of the virtually unanimous position of biblical scholars.

[284] For example, "the Word was a god" (John 1:1) in the Jehovah's Witnesses' New World Translation. This blatantly deceptive translation promotes their belief that Jesus is "a" god but not "the" God as the Greek article (τὸν θεόν) affirms, thus emphasizing His oneness and equality with the Father. All other translations render this as "the Word was God."

that deal directly with gender roles in the church is stunning—especially because there are so comparatively few comparable misleading translations in the rest of the Bible. Therefore, it seems impossible to avoid the suspicion that these misleading translations have been made and perpetuated under the influence of deep-seated though perhaps subconscious gender bias. This should sound an alert as to how pervasive and deep-seated gender bias is, even among wise and godly Christians, and should promote sincere introspection regarding how easily I could be subconsciously biased in my own study and understanding of the relevant Scriptures.

While looking at the big picture regarding these misleading translations, it is important to reaffirm that, as important as these issues are, one's position on gender roles in the church is not a test of orthodoxy. Whether one believes there are or are not gender-based restrictions on some church positions is very important but is not a core Christianity kind of issue.

Although the concern about undermining someone's confidence in their Bible is valid and important, it must not be allowed to stifle efforts toward bringing to light what God's Word *actually* says rather than what it may have been *misrepresented* to say. Getting the Bible right is too important to gloss over translation issues to preserve feeling comfortable or to avoid experiencing conflict.

All that said, it's important to note that the average Bible student with no training in the original languages could come to many of the same conclusions by using a major concordance such as Young's or Strong's to compare how identical Greek words are translated throughout the New Testament.

Those concordances would, for example, reveal that in 1 Timothy 2:1–12, *haysuxia* occurs multiple times within the same paragraph. In verse 2 no one would assert that when Paul used *haysuxia* he was urging intercession for kings so that everyone could live in a verbally silent society where no one talked! Clearly what Paul had in mind by *haysuxia* was that their prayers would result in a *peaceful environment, free of conflict and trouble*. This suggests how *haysuxia* should be understood in the rest of the chapter. Therefore, in verses 11 and 12, the comparison with verse 2 (as well as with other New Testament texts identified in the concordance such as Acts 22:2 and 2 Thess. 3:12) indicates that *haysuxia* is not about prohibiting women from talking in church, but rather is prohibiting them from a particular kind of behavior—that which violates the peaceful, conflict-free environment appropriate to God's holy assembly.

These conclusions, easily discoverable in Young's or Strong's Concordance, demonstrate that a Bible student need not have gone to Seminary or spent years studying the Greek language to discover these things. The use of readily available, non-scholarly study tools such as a good concordance would reveal the misleading translations in 1 Timothy 2:11, 12.

So Why Are There So Many Misleading Translations in These Few Verses?

With this revelation from other New Testament and contextual uses of *haysuxia*, one has to wonder why the English translators perpetuated a translation which is misleading at best, and more likely, biased, deceptive, or even dishonest. Why did the NIV translators, in the same paragraph, change from "quiet" and "quietness" (which at least could conceivably be understood as non-disruption rather than non-speaking) to "silent" which completely misrepresents the meaning (as is also evident in the other New Testament usages)? Compare the NIV translation below with a proposed expanded translation on the right:

1 Timothy 2:11, 12 NIV	1 Timothy 2:11, 12: more accurate, expanded translation/paraphrase
A woman should learn in quietness and full submission. I permit no woman to teach or to have authority over a man; she must be silent.	A woman should learn with a peaceful, non-combative spirit and be submitted to the Scriptures. I permit no woman to be teaching or to seize a leadership role in a forceful, domineering manner, but to be teaching and leading with a peaceful, non-combative spirit.

In my opinion, the misleading translations in these two key passages (1 Cor. 14 and 1 Tim. 2) are the result of deeply held (though hopefully subconscious) gender bias, perhaps even a long-continued conspiracy to perpetuate gender-based restrictions on women. Some or even most of those participating in this conspiracy may not self-perceive what they are doing. Tragically, this has strongly prejudiced the interpretation of other passages throughout the Scriptures and has both maintained the oppression and illicit restrictions placed on women in the church. For centuries it has robbed the church of at least 50% of the gifted teachers and leaders God has placed in the church.

In Conclusion

Paul's much debated instructions in 1 Timothy 2:8–15, rightly translated and interpreted, do not teach gender-based restrictions on women speaking, learning, teaching, or leading in the church. Rather, as part of the theme of the chapter (*living peacefully without disruption, division, or conflict),* these verses teach that both men (verse 8) and women (verses 9–15) in Ephesus must not disrupt the peace and order of the church either by engaging in angry, disruptive, argumentative, or divisive communication, nor by commandeering and exercising abusive authority over men (or anyone) in the church. The peace-promoting behaviors Paul ordered are in contrast with and in opposition to the pervasive influence of false teaching that included the Artemis cult and proto-gnosticism. The teaching of these verses is consistent with the assertion that women may serve in the church in any capacity that men do, including teaching, preaching, and being an elder or pastor.

FOR DISCUSSION

(1) Were you surprised by how few verses in the Bible (nine) actually talk about gender restrictions for church ministry? Why do you think many people believe the Bible says a great deal more about this subject?

(2) Realizing that only nine much-debated verses in the Bible discuss gender role restrictions in church ministry, why do you think so many churches take such a strong stand on this issue, prohibiting at least half of their members from being pastors, elders, and preachers?

(3) What are some things you learned from this chapter about the problem of false doctrine in Ephesus? How does this influence the way you understand 1 Timothy 2?

(4) In your English Bible, identify the three times in 1 Timothy 2 that *haysuxia* is used. Summarize the discussion about the meaning of *haysuxia* in 1 Timothy 2 (quiet mouth or quiet circumstances). Why is this important for the gender roles debate?

(5) Paul's goal in writing 1 Timothy 2 was to promote ***living peacefully without disruption or conflict.*** How does the theme help us interpret the verses about gender roles?

(6) How should Paul's teaching about peace, unity, and division, affect the way the gender roles issue is handled between Christians and in a church? Regardless of your position or your church's position on gender roles, how can you promote those values in your church?

10

Women: Pastors or Bullies— Which Was It?

In my childhood years at Lincoln Elementary School and into my pre-teen time at Soo Jr. High School in Sault Ste. Marie, MI, Franky Tomlinson (not his real name) was one of a couple of resident bullies. He was notorious for picking on kids who were younger and smaller than he. Looking back, I feel compassion for Franky because I now realize that his bullying was an attempt to make up for some painful deficits in his life. He was older and bigger than his classmates because of being held back in school. He probably sensed that he would never excel academically or athletically or perhaps in any other area that could be a path to recognition. In retrospect, I wish I had been more discerning and compassionate. Anyway, Franky gained attention and fed his hungry self-esteem by beating up vulnerable kids. I was several years younger than Franky and small for my age. Fortunately having my older and much bigger brother Terry around as we walked to and from school was like having my own private security detail. All my brother lacked was a dark suit and an earpiece.

I don't remember why, but one frigid Northern Michigan winter afternoon I was walking home from school alone. Out of the blue, Franky showed up and promptly begin to harass, threaten, and man-handle me. Suddenly, like Superman to the rescue, my brother appeared out of nowhere and deposited Franky face-down in a deep snow bank. The years may have enhanced the pleasant memory, but I recall, as Terry and I walked away arm-in-arm, looking back over my shoulder and seeing Franky's legs and feet sticking up in the air with his head and upper torso buried in the snow.

Nobody likes a bully. Many people can tell painful stories of their own experiences of being bullied. I am blessed to have very few. Thankfully in recent years the spotlight has been placed on bullies and bullying so public schools regularly provide staff training and student education to identify and eliminate bullying. Policies are in place to stop this unsavory school yard phenomenon.

Unfortunately, there don't seem to be many comparable training resources or sample policies available for dealing with church bullies. Many are in leadership positions and engage in what is called "spiritual abuse." One might guess church bullying isn't rare because, while editing this paragraph, I stopped to google "church bullies" and instantly had access to "about 944,000" sites I could explore. Sometimes the pastor is the bully and church members are the victims. Sometimes the church bully is an influential member and the pastor is the victim or one of the victims. The focus of half of one short New Testament letter is the exposure of a first century church bully named Diotrephes. The congregation must have been encouraged by the Apostle John's assurance that he planned to expose the bully and his controlling ways: "So if I come, I will call attention to what he is doing" (3 John 10).

The majority of church bullies I have personally dealt with or heard about were men. But not all of them. In the Bible, Jezebel wasn't a *church* bully. She was the most infamous queen of ancient Israel (1 and 2 Kings) in the eighth century B.C. Her husband's notoriety for evil was eclipsed by Jezebel's wickedness and bullying. Significantly, in His letter to the first century church in Thyatira, Jesus metaphorically assigned the name "Jezebel" to a self-appointed, influential woman in the church whose false teaching and sinful clout was wrongfully being tolerated. Jesus' scathing condemnation of this first century A.D. church bully stands as a warning to churches in all times and places: "He who has an ear, let him hear what the Spirit says to the churches" (Rev. 2:29).

"What does this have to do with gender roles in the church?" someone may be asking. The answer is, "A great deal!"

This Is a Really Big Deal

First Timothy 2:12 is without question THE MOST IMPORTANT verse in the gender roles controversy. It is the complementarian's *tour de force* alleged to support their position that women are prohibited from ministry involving teaching or holding a position of authority over men in the church—thus, among other things, eliminating women from holding the position of pastor or elder. Paul wrote: "I do not permit a woman to teach or to have authority over a man; she must be silent." No matter their personal feelings about that apparent gender-based restriction, many Christians feel conscience bound by this verse to support the complementarian view.

However, a careful examination of the context of 1 Timothy 2 and the meaning and etymology of key Greek words in verse 12 reveals that Paul's intent was *not* to prevent women from being church *teachers or pastors*, but rather was to preclude them from being *self-appointed* church *BULLIES*.

The meaning of *authĕntĕō* ("to have authority over") in 1 Timothy 2:12 is a central issue in the debate about women in ministry. It could be argued that the gender roles debate for some people is won or lost on the meaning of this **one word**. Complementarians understand *authĕntĕō* to be a reference to *ordinary* and *positive* leadership authority in the church and conclude that in this passage Paul prohibited women from having such authority over men. Therefore, complementarians believe that women should not serve as teachers of men in the church or in positions of authority such as elder or pastor. Egalitarians, on the other hand, assert that the very unusual Greek word *authĕntĕō* does not refer to *ordinary, positive* leadership authority, but rather to *abusive* and *bullying* authority *commandeered* by an individual rather than *commissioned* by the church. They believe that Paul's prohibition applies only to self-assumed, domineering teaching and authority and that he imposed no gender-based restrictions on normal ministry or leadership authority in the church. Consequently, egalitarians believe that qualified women are free to serve as teachers, elders, or pastors just like qualified men.

So, What Is the Real Meaning of "Authority"?

The KEY question is whether in 1 Timothy 2:12, *authĕntĕō* refers to ordinary and beneficial leadership, or if it refers to bullying authority hijacked without authorization. It is my conclusion that the latter is correct, that *authĕntĕō* in 1 Timothy 2:12 is negative and harmful to the peace and unity the chapter was written to protect. If this is correct, it absolutely undermines the complementarian understanding of the passage and affirms the opposite of any gender-based restrictions on ministry roles in the church.

Arguments supporting the interpretation of *authĕntĕō* as self-appointed, controlling, domineering, and aggressive authority include: (1) Paul's decision to *not* use the common words normally employed for church leadership authority, (2) the lexical definitions of the word, (3) comparative uses in extra-biblical literature, (4) contextual considerations in 1 Timothy, (5) the historical/cultural background of Ephesus, (6) contextual and theological considerations in the Scriptures as a whole, and (7) consideration of how this interpretation explains and harmonizes challenging aspects of 1 Timothy 2.

(1)   Paul Did Not Use the Ordinary Greek Words for Authority

Significantly, Paul does *not* use the usual and very common word for authority (ἐξουσία, *exousia*) which is what would be expected if he were referring to an ordinary church leadership position from which women were restricted. Nor does he use other common New Testament words for authority such as ἐπιταγή/*epitagē* and ἡγέομαι/*hēgeomai*. These three were all used in the New Testament regarding church leadership (see below). Although it would be a jarring departure from his theme in 1 Timothy 2, had Paul used any of these in 1 Timothy 2:12 it would be far more plausible to assume that ordinary church leadership roles, such as elder and pastor, were in view.

In addition to many references to *exousia*[285] (authority, rule, ruler, power) outside the church (e.g. Mt. 7:29; 8:9; 9:6, 8; 10:1; Lk. 12:11; 19:17; Acts 9:14;

---

[285]   There are approximately 100 uses in the New Testament.

Rom. 13:1-3; Eph. 2:2), Paul applies the word to church leadership in the following passages:

- "For even if I should boast somewhat more about our authority [*exousia*], which the Lord gave us for edification and not for your destruction, I shall not be ashamed— lest I seem to terrify you by letters" (2 Cor. 10:8, 9)
- "This is why I write these things when I am absent, that when I come I may not have to be harsh in my use of authority [*exousia*] —the authority [*exousia*] the Lord gave me for building you up, not for tearing you down" (2 Cor. 13:10).

Clearly *exousia* is used to indicate normal leadership authority in church. Paul chose NOT to use this word in 1 Timothy 2:12. If he had, the complementarian argument would thereby gain some credibility.

The following are illustrations of church leadership using the other two other previously mentioned common New Testament Greek words for authority:

- "These, then, are the things you should teach. Encourage and rebuke with all authority [*epitagē*]. Do not let anyone despise you" (Titus 2:15)
- "Obey your leaders and submit to their authority [*hēgeomai*]. They keep watch over you as men who must give an account. Obey them so that their work will be a joy, not a burden, for that would be of no advantage to you" (Heb. 13:17)

Again, had Paul used either of these words in 1 Timothy 2:12, the complementarian position would have some support. But Paul did NOT use either of these words. Rather, he chose a rare word whose most common meaning is negative referring to a domineering or even aggressive or violent wielding of self-appropriated authority. Paul's word in 1 Timothy 2:12, *authĕntĕō*, is not used any other time in all of Scripture[286] and is used infrequently in ancient Greek literature outside the Bible. Neither is there an

---

[286] Because *authĕntĕō* is a *hapax legomenon* (a word used only once in a book) there are no other biblical instances to which it may be compared.

extensive number of usages in extra-biblical ancient Greek literature. Most scholars are in agreement that the word is rare and that in extra-biblical literature it is most often used with an undeniably negative meaning. Unless Paul intended a negative meaning for *authĕntĕō*, it is difficult to conceive what would motivate him to bypass the common and positive (or neutral) words that he used a number of times elsewhere in his letters and instead chose a rare word that clearly had a negative, even violent or criminal meaning in many if not most of its uses. It seems that the obvious conclusion is that Paul made an intentional choice so that his words would be understood as restricting women from commandeering an unhealthy kind of authority rather than restricting them from being commissioned for any authoritative role in the church.

(2) The Lexical Definitions of the word

A lexicon is a catalog of words and their meanings, similar to a dictionary. Hubner cites eight standard Greek lexicons most of which convey the meaning of *authĕntĕō* as referring to autocratic, domineering authority. These lexicons designate the meaning of *authĕntĕō* as follows: "to assume a stance of independent authority, to give orders to, to dictate to;" "of one who acts on his own authority; hence have control over, domineer, Lord it over;" to "control, have authority over;" to "domineer, have authority over;" "to have full power over;" "dominate;" "domineer over."[287]

The Greek-English Lexicon, which focuses on the contextual aspect of words, likewise represents the meaning of *authĕntĕō* as "to control in a domineering manner . . . [example from 1 Tim. 2:12] 'I do not allow women . . . to dominate men' . . . 'To control in a domineering manner' is often expressed idiomatically, for example, 'to shout orders at,' 'to act like a chief toward,' or 'to bark at.'"[288] Further, lexical usages indicate that inherent to the meaning of *authĕntĕō* is that it refers to authority which is self-appointed

---

[287] Jamin Hubner, *"Translating αὐθεντέω (authĕntĕō) in 1 Timothy 2:12,"* Pricilla Papers, Vol. 129, No. 2 (Spring, 2015), http://www.academia.edu/24894103/Translating_ αὐθεντέω_in_1_Timothy_2_12

[288] Johannes P. Louw, and Eugene Nida, The Greek-English Lexicon, Logos Bible Program, Louw-Nida, 37.21.

or even commandeered, rather than commissioned, granted, or assigned appropriately.

Clearly those lexical definitions at the very minimum indicate that the pejorative understanding of *authĕntĕō* in 1 Timothy 2:12 is a strong possibility, but more likely, that its *normal* meaning is derogatory.

So, how did most English translations reject this negative lexical meaning of *authĕntĕō*? As with some other gender-biased mistranslations, this may have its roots in Jerome's very influential Latin Vulgate translation. Completed about 400 A.D. the Vulgate for many centuries was considered to be the premier Bible translation and became the standard against which future translations were compared.

> It was also Jerome who significantly—and for all time since—altered the meaning of 1 Timothy 2:12. This passage allegedly prohibits women from teaching or leading men in the church. Thanks largely to Jerome's example, a key verb here (authentein) has been translated 'to exercise authority'. In Jerome's time, it was rendered more in terms of 'having dominion over' or 'dominating' a man. Prior to this, the word more commonly referred to the instigation or commission of an act of violence, suicide or murder. In the Greek Septuagint, for example, a noun form of the word (authentas) refers to those who engaged in ritual violence in the worship of a false god . . . Prior to Jerome's translation, 1 Timothy 2:12 would probably not have been understood as a prohibition against female authority. It is more likely—given the most common usage of 'authentein,' the nature of Paul's concerns, and the context of the letter — that it is a prohibition against women teaching or instigating ritual violence against men.[289]

---

[289] Bob Edwards: *"Lost in Translation: A Look at 1 Timothy 2:12-15,"* The Junia Project (9/16/2013), http://juniaproject.com/translation-1-timothy-212/.

(3)   Comparative Uses in Extra-Biblical Literature

It would be helpful if interpreting comparative uses of *authĕntĕō* in extra-biblical literature would be so unmistakably straightforward as to not generate any controversy. Sadly, this is not the case. Although nearly all scholars acknowledge that extra-biblical usages of *authĕntĕō* range from "murder" to "authority," the agreement often ends there. Hubner opines about the extensive scholarly research, "Despite such painstaking work, there remains considerable disagreement about what the term means. Both egalitarian and complementarian evangelicals claim the research is in their favor."[290] It is disappointing to discover that arguments for translating it in a positive or neutral sense approximately equivalent to *exousia*, are most often asserted only by those who are *predisposed* in favor of and are defending a complementarian view. Arguments for a negative, pejorative understanding, are most often asserted by those who either embrace the egalitarian view or express no view in the gender-roles debate. This scholarly disagreement probably illustrates the pervasive influence of subconscious bias and adds to the confusion regarding the passage and illustrates the difficulty in arriving at a consensus view.

In a perfect world, anyone who studies the Bible and related ancient literature in a word study such as this would make every effort to identify and minimize the influence of their own personal biases. But when biblical scholars disagree about the meaning of *authĕntĕō* in extra-biblical texts, it is frustrating that the disagreement appears to be divided along "party lines" (complementarian versus egalitarian) as to whether it should be understood in a positive or pejorative way.

I attempted to read translations and/or the original Greek of nearly all of the most relevant extra-biblical uses of *authĕntĕō* in their original contexts. At risk of failing to recognize my own biases, from my own examination of those extra-biblical uses at a time when I was not yet settled on either position, it appeared to me that this party line division is very much out of sync with the preponderance of evidence clearly supporting a negative meaning for *authĕntĕō*. It appears to me that unless one is determined to force the evidence

---

[290] Hubner, "*Translating αὐθεντέω (authĕntĕō) in 1 Timothy 2:12,*" Pricilla Papers, Vol. 129, No. 2 (Spring, 2015), http://www.academia.edu/24894103/Translating_αὐθεντέω_in_1_Timothy_2_12

to fit a complementarian understanding, it obviously supports the conclusion that *authĕntĕō* is primarily about domineering and abusive authority.

It is my observation that as the scholars present their *case* regarding the extra-biblical usages of *authĕntĕō*, those who conclude that the pejorative understanding best represents the texts most relevant to 1 Timothy 2:12 seem to be the most straightforward and reasonable, whereas those who favor a more positive rendering of *authĕntĕō*, often minimize and attempt to explain away what seems obvious <u>even in their own English translations of the original sources.</u>

Surprisingly, one of the arguments that most convinced me of the pejorative meaning of *authĕntĕō* was a chapter written by a respected biblical scholar in which he argued in favor of a non-pejorative meaning of *authĕntĕō*) in 1 Timothy 2:12.[291] He argues extensively from the extra-biblical usages of the word in its various forms, focusing especially on those from 312 A.D. and after. I was surprised that as much weight was given to those late appearances of the word rather than to those in earlier centuries more proximate to the time of 1 Timothy. I was disappointed to observe what appeared to be circular reasoning, contradictory statements, dismissal of evidence which refuted his thesis, and even seeming to misrepresent what the ancient texts actually said. For example, he stated, "We are hard pressed to find a pejorative meaning anywhere" but went on in the *same paragraph* to specifically acknowledge a number of examples of pejorative usages.[292] His chapter contained numerous illustrations of *authĕntĕō* (in its various forms) where its meanings included: harassment, murder, violence, slaughter, massacre, crimes, initiating brazen deeds, ritual castration, taking precedence (as in stealing the limelight), acting on one's own, etc.

Stanley Grenz states that "Recent studies indicate that in the first century *authĕntĕō* was more likely to carry negative than neutral or positive connotations . . . At the time of Paul, the verb carried two closely related meanings: *'instigating or perpetrating a crime'* and *'the active wielding of*

---

[291] Dr. Albert Woters, emeritus professor of religion, theology, and Classical languages, wrote the chapter on "The Meaning of Αὐθεντέω" in the pro-complementarian scholarly volume, *Women in the Church: An Interpretation and Application of 1 Timothy 2:9-15*, Kostenberger, Andreas J. and Thomas R. Schreiner (Crossway: Wheaton, Third Edition, 2016).

[292] Ibid., 85.

influence (with respect to a person) or the initiation of an action . . . Timothy J. Harris concludes from his study of the occurrences of the verb close to the New Testament period that it meant *'to hold sway or use power, to be dominant.'* In itself it never meant 'to be an official' or "to be authorized."[293]

The understanding of *authěntěō* as negative or abusive authority is compellingly demonstrated in a scholarly paper by Cynthia Westfall on the meaning of *authěntěō* in 1 Timothy 2:12 may be found at the following link: http://www.jgrchj.net/volume10/JGRChJ10-7_Westfall.pdf.

Westfall's more recently released book, *Paul and Gender, Reclaiming the Apostle's Vision for Men and Women in Christ* (2016) is an exhaustive study of the gender roles issue in Paul's writings. The book strikes some balance between being popular and scholarly in its presentation, though some would probably say that the scale tips toward scholarly. Her discussion of the meaning of *authěntěō* is clear and compelling. She writes,

> Many outside the debate assume that αὐθεντέω is a technical term for 'being a pastor,' since it is the primary justification for excluding women from the office of pastor and from other leadership over men. However, out of the over three hundred occurrences of the verb in the TLG database,[294] no one has identified a case where it refers to any kind of benevolent pastoral care of an individual or group by a pastor or church official. Among the eighty-two occurrences of the verb that Scott Baldwin used to support the position that the word means 'to have authority,' there is no example of a male doing this to another person or a group of people in a ministry or church leadership context where the referent action had a positive evaluation in the context . . . In the Greek corpus, the verb αὐθεντέω refers to a range of actions that are not restricted to murder or violence. However, the people who are the targets of these actions are harmed, forced against their will (compelled), or at least their self-interest is overridden because the actions involve the imposition of

---

[293] Grenz, Woman in the Church, Kindle, Loc. 1548.
[294] The TLG database is a digital library which gives a comprehensive digital library of Greek literature from the 8th century B.C. to the present.

the subject's will over against the recipient's will ranging from dishonor to lethal force ... It is inconsistent with and in contrast to Paul's model of leadership as well as Jesus' model. Glossing this verb merely as 'having authority' and then interpreting it as if it describes servant leadership or pastoral care is misleading in the extreme.[295]

Westfall graciously gives some latitude to biblical scholars before the twentieth century who did not have the "sound lexicography and linguistic methodology [that are available today however] ... There is now ample evidence that was not available to the nineteenth century lexicons which we tended to depend on ... the database, search engines, and linguistic theories are now in place to move forward. The church has reached its age of accountability; it is time to assume responsibility (or liability) for excluding women from church leadership positions based on the word αὐθεντέω."[296] Stated more simply and straightforwardly, with the resources now available for biblical research which previous generations of interpreters did not have regarding the meaning of Greek words, **there is no longer any valid excuse for placing gender-based restrictions on women for any church ministry role based on Paul's instructions regarding authority (*authĕntĕō*) in 1 Timothy 2:12.**

To be blunt: it is my hopefully well-informed opinion, based on the consensus of a seeming majority of contemporary biblical scholars and the ancient language tools available today for Bible students, those who continue to claim that *authĕntĕō* refers to ordinary, beneficial church leadership authority appear to be either uninformed, incorrectly taught, deceived, ignorant, blinded by bias, or dishonest regarding Paul's instructions.

This understanding of the vocabulary of 1 Timothy 2:11, 12 (*authĕntĕō* and *haysuxia*) makes it abundantly clear that Paul was not forbidding women to be teachers or to hold positions of authority over men in the church. Rather he was forbidding women from being a particular kind of teacher or leader—one who was unteachable, independent, rebellious, self-exalting, combative, controlling, domineering, argumentative, and abusive.

---

[295] Westfall, *Paul and Gender*, 291–94.
[296] Ibid., 294.

(4)   Contextual Considerations

This understanding of *authĕntĕō* as authority commandeered and exercised in a *controlling, domineering, abusive, autocratic, authoritarian, and/or aggressive manner* is further borne out by considerations in the context.

The long-loved but linguistically outdated King James translation captured an important aspect of this meaning by rendering 1 Timothy 2:12 *"to usurp authority over the man"* [underline added]. To *"usurp"* means to take illegally or by force, to topple, to commandeer, or to overthrow. By using the word *"usurp"* the translators rightly discerned that the apostle's concern was not that women might be inappropriately commissioned for positions of teaching or leadership authority by the elders, but rather that women might wrongfully seize such positions apart from going through the ordination process the New Testament described regarding church leadership. That process involved the laying on of the elders' hands (Acts 6:6; 1 Tim. 4:14; 5:22; 2 Tim. 1:6) to ordain those who met stated character requirements (1 Tim, 3:1ff; Titus 1:5ff) and who were not new converts (1 Tim. 3:6; 5:22).

The English "usurp" is not in any Greek text, so it seems evident that the translators of the KJV correctly felt that this pejorative descriptor was necessary to accurately communicate that the non-permitted actions *were unilaterally initiated by the woman*. The authority envisioned was not inappropriate because of gender but was because such authority was inappropriately assumed by the individual. It would of course be equally wrong for a man to personally *"usurp"* authority over others. But in Ephesus, the proud home of the world-famous, female dominated Artemis worship, Paul called on Timothy to address what apparently was a gender-related problem in the church at Ephesus.

First Timothy 2:11, 12 describes one activity a woman *is required to* initiate, that is to learn in a noncombative/non-divisive manner with a spirit of submission to what she learns; and two related activities a woman *is not* permitted to initiate—to commandeer unauthorized and domineering teaching and leading positions and to carry them out in a combative/divisive manner.

As discussed in chapter 9, the two related activities, *to be teaching* and *to be assuming dominating authority over a man*, are joined by οὐδέ *(oude)* a connective of two related things—either both positive or both negative.[297] The two infinitives, *to be teaching* and *to be assuming dominating leadership*, form a hendiadys (from the Greek and Latin, "one through two") that involves two inter-related words connected by the conjunction *"and" (oude)*, therefore expressing a related concept. *"To be teaching"* does not take a genitive object but *"to be mastering or dominating"* does. Therefore, the second infinitive, *"to master or dominate a man (ἀνήρ/anēr,* man, genitive case)," informs the interpretation of *"to be teaching."* The two activities cannot be treated as separate and unrelated concepts which are *dissimilar* in their nature. The tone or flavor of the second infinitive ("to be mastering/dominating") determines the tone of the first ("to be teaching"). Thus, based on the meaning of *authĕntĕō*, Paul's ban on women teaching men in 1 Timothy 2:12 was not gender-based, but rather referred to a particular kind of teaching role—that which was self-appointed and domineering. This understanding is consistent with the contextual theme—how to maintain peaceful worship free of conflict and division.

The contrasting activity in 1 Timothy 2:12, introduced by ἀλλά, *(alla), that means* "instead of, on the contrary, rather,"[298] indicates that a woman, rather than engaging in the first two activities, instead is to promote *haysuxia*—that is, *to be keeping the peace and tranquility*[299] (the opposite of being combative or divisive). That is what Paul desired and encouraged for the church. Indeed, it is the BIG IDEA in the chapter.

Summarizing: in contrast with teaching in a domineering manner or with commandeered, aggressive, and adversarial authority over men, women, *as they teach and lead*, are to promote harmony and a peaceful atmosphere in the church. The contrast *(alla)* makes no sense if the teaching and assuming authority are both positive activities. This further confirms the negative meaning of *authĕntĕō*. The contrast is only meaningful if the teaching and assuming authority are both negative.

Thus, Paul is not prohibiting women from being authorized to teach or to hold an authoritative leadership position over men. He is prohibiting women

---

[297] Discussed later in this chapter.

[298] Arndt and Gingrich, *A Greek-English Lexicon,*37. "But" *(alla)* is an "adversative particle indicating a difference with or contrast to what precedes."

[299] See chapter 9 for an extensive discussion of the meaning of this key word *(haysuxia, tranquil, serene)* and how its three uses in 1 Timothy 2 frame the theme of the chapter, i.e. preserving peace free of disruption, division, and conflict.

from usurping those roles and carrying them out in a domineering manner. This would violate the serene and conflict-free environment that Paul called on all the believers to pray for (2:1, 2) and for both men (2:8) and women (2:8-12) to protect and promote. This is not only totally consistent with the theme of the chapter—*living peacefully without disruption, division, or conflict,* but also with the historical backdrop of 1 Timothy 2—the prevalence of domineering women in the Ephesian Artemis cult.[300]

It should further be noted that in this passage Paul did <u>not</u> instruct Timothy or the Ephesian elders to refuse to put women into leadership over men. That is what we should expect if it were his intent that women should not be ordained for pastoral ministry. It would have been crystal clear if Paul had simply instructed Timothy, "Do not lay hands on a woman" even as he prohibited the ordination of a new convert ("Do not be hasty in the laying on of hands," 5:22), an untested candidate ("must not be a recent convert," 3:6), or someone with a negative reputation with unbelievers ("must also have a good reputation with outsiders," 3:6). Clearly, Paul was not averse to mandating those restrictions regarding whom Timothy and the elders should not lay hands on for ordination. It was the elders' responsibility, not an ambitious woman's, to determine who should be commissioned for leadership by the laying on of hands.

What Paul prohibited in 1 Timothy 2:12 was *not* the ordination of women by Timothy or the elders but was for a woman to illicitly elevate herself, confiscating a teaching or leadership role—doing so in a unilateral, disruptive, and contentious manner. What Paul forbade was basically, a *hostile takeover* of the teaching or pastoral office, this in order to carry on a teaching and leading ministry that was domineering, and contentious, or that involved promulgating false doctrine. Church leaders were initially appointed by the apostles (Acts 14:23), by their personal representatives (Titus 1:5), and then by the elders of the churches (1 Tim. 4:14; 5:17). The New Testament never envisioned church leaders as self-appointed; as commandeering a leadership role without proper authorization. Church leadership is not up for grabs or subject to being hijacked by someone of either gender. In Ephesus, this was obviously a problem exhibited by some assertive and aggressive women.

Additionally, it should be noted that if Paul is understood in 1 Timothy 2:12 as forbidding women to teach altogether, it proves too much. Almost no one believes that women cannot teach other women and children. This would

---

[300] See (5) and (7) below.

contradict Paul's specific instructions in Titus 2:3, 4 that older women are to teach younger women. If Paul's intention in 1 Timothy 2:12 was a general ban on women teaching in the church, nearly every congregation in the world today is in violation. Such a ban would cripple children's and ladies' ministries everywhere.

On the other hand, if Paul is understood as disallowing only the teaching of men, then his order still stands in stark contradiction with:

- his stated assumption in 1 Corinthians 11:5 that women will pray and prophesy in church,
- his teaching in 1 Corinthians 12 and 14 that spiritual gifts are given to all believers regardless of gender (including the gifts of teaching and administration), as well as
- his favorable description of Pricilla's teaching of a male preacher (Apollos) in Acts 18:26.

An expanded paraphrase of 1 Timothy 2:12 will illustrate and summarize these conclusions based on the context and specific linguistic factors in the text: "I do not permit a woman to appropriate for herself the role of teaching in a domineering manner or to seize a leadership role in order to exercise domineering authority over *a* man, but rather, she should be display the opposite, a harmonious spirit as she promotes peaceful tranquility in the church."

Paul's teaching concerning women in church could be summarized as follows:

Paul DOES teach that a woman:

- must learn with a noncombative/non-divisive spirit (*haysuxia*),
- must be fully submitted to obey what she learns,
- must not teach with a combative/divisive spirit (the opposite of *haysuxia*),
- must not commandeer domineering authority (*authĕntĕō*) over men, and
- must not exercise authority with a combative/divisive spirit (the opposite of *haysuxia*).

Paul <u>DOES NOT</u> teach:

- that women cannot learn alongside men,
- that women cannot teach men,
- that women cannot be appointed (or ordained) to have authority over men.

In other words, a woman **is** to learn, teach, and lead, but must do all of those in a noncombative and non-divisive manner. She **is not** to commandeer unauthorized teaching or leading roles or carry them out in domineering or bullying way.

(5)   Historical and Cultural Background of Ephesus

Understanding the historical background in Ephesus is essential for interpreting 1 Timothy 2. Ephesus was the location of the church where Timothy served as Paul's representative. Some of the historical information comes from the New Testament texts written about Ephesus or to the Ephesian church including Acts 19, both of Paul's letters to Timothy, and Jesus' letter to the church in Ephesus in Revelation 2:1–7. Strong historical tradition places the Apostle John in Ephesus at the time of his death (Patmos, where he was exiled was near Ephesus) and that he had served as pastor there. Therefore, 1 John (90-95 A.D.) may also reflect conditions in Ephesus, including the prevalence of false teachers (e.g. 1 John 2:22-27; 4:1-6). Additional very helpful historical information comes from a variety of extra-biblical sources that provide helpful insights into the circumstances that may have prompted Paul's letters to Timothy and that provide the background for what he wrote.

Because the relevant historical and cultural background of Ephesus have been previously discussed in detail, they will not be addressed at length here. However, some historical observations will be considered below. Suffice it to say that the existence of false teachers and teachings including proto-gnosticism and the influence of the Ephesus-based, world-renowned Artemis worship call attention to Paul's need to curtail self-appointed, domineering and disruptive women from teaching and leadership roles in the church. These background insights serve to confirm the negative meaning of *authĕntĕō* in relation to the implications of Paul's theme in 1 Timothy 2, that is, *living peaceably without conflict and disruption*. This theme is built around the three uses of *haysuxia* (peaceable, tranquil, serene) in the chapter.

(6)   Contextual and Theological Considerations in the Scriptures As a Whole

Chapters 3 and 4 in this book are an essential foundation to later biblical discussions about gender roles. The absolute equality and oneness of the genders portrayed in the story of creation in Genesis 1, 2 as well as the understanding of the sinful origin and perpetuation of patriarchy resulting from the Fall described in Genesis 3 are the baseline and foundation for all later understanding of gender relationships and roles. These are consistent with the egalitarian interpretation of 1 Timothy 2:12.

Jesus' teaching and example regarding women are absolutely consistent with and determinative of the egalitarian position on women's roles in the church. These are discussed in various places in this book and lend convincing support to the egalitarian understanding of 1 Timothy 2:12.

Further, four factors from the larger context of the Scriptures provide affirmation and lend credibility to interpreting 1 Timothy 2 advanced in this chapter:

- Paul's teaching about women praying and prophesying (1 Corinthians 11) and exercising their spiritual gifts (1 Corinthians 12, 14—which affirms spiritual gifting to all believers and mentions no gender-based restrictions for any of the gifts);
- Paul's assertions about the elimination of ethnic, gender, and social distinctions in the new humanity (Gal. 3:28); his discussions of marital gender roles and headship (1 Cor. 7; Eph. 5, 6);
- Paul's references to women as his honored partners in ministry (Rom. 16, et al.);
- The ministry and leadership roles that women engaged in throughout the Scriptures (see chapter 11).

All of these provide affirmation and lend credibility to the interpretation of 1 Timothy 2 advanced in this chapter. They are powerful affirmations of the pejorative meaning of *authĕntĕō* and the egalitarian understanding of 1 Timothy 2. Each is discussed elsewhere in this book.

(7)   Satisfying Harmonization for Challenging Aspects of 1 Timothy 2

Have you ever been putting a puzzle together and had several pieces you couldn't make fit? No matter where you tried to place them, it wasn't right. Why couldn't you make them fit? Were some of the earlier placed pieces in the wrong spot? Did someone throw in some extra pieces from a different puzzle?

Several parts of 1 Timothy 2 are like that. Banning immodest clothing makes some sense, but what about the rest of the verse? Does verse 9 ban women from having their hair done, wearing jewelry, or dressing in anything not purchased at a thrift shop? Paul says, "I also want women to dress modestly, with decency and propriety, not with braided hair or gold or pearls or expensive clothes." What does that have to do with whether or not women can teach or lead?

Verses 13–15 also add some unique challenges. They just don't seem to fit in a harmonious way with the rest of the chapter. This is a problem for all interpreters whether their orientation is complementarian or egalitarian. Some seem straightforward enough, such as "Adam was formed first, then Eve," and "Adam was not the one deceived; it was the woman who was deceived and became a sinner." But the theological significance often imposed on those statements seems unwarranted if you notice it has no parallel or support in the original contexts in Genesis 1–3, is out of sync with other Scriptures, and is confusing in how it is frequently applied in the thematic context of 1 Timothy 2. Paul's assertion in verse 15 raises all sorts of questions: "Women will be saved through childbearing." Is this another means of achieving salvation—having a baby? Where does that leave childless wives and singles? What about men? Does impregnating a woman count toward salvation for a man? What is it about child-bearing that is salvific?

When it is recognized that Paul's prohibition in 1 Timothy 2:12 was not contrary to women teaching or becoming church leaders but was against women unilaterally grabbing positions of teaching or leadership to be exercised in a domineering and abusive manner, it becomes much easier to interpret the whole of 1 Timothy 2:12–15 harmoniously. My assertion is that the egalitarian understanding of 1 Timothy 2 provides the most satisfying harmonization of the elements in this chapter. Four of these will be addressed below.

First, verse 9 says: "I also want women to dress modestly, with decency and propriety, not with braided hair or gold or pearls or expensive clothes."[301] Complementarians frequently explain this verse in terms of modesty and humility (not calling attention to self through manner of dress, fancy hair dos, valuable jewelry, and expensive outfits) or frugality (not spending a lot of money on personal appearance), or they relegate its prohibitions to a first century cultural issue no longer applicable today. The suggestion these instructions were not timeless but intended only to address some first century issue we may or may not understand today prompted Haley Watson Kim to ask, "Well how come we care about the prohibition of women teaching but not women wearing gold jewelry?"[302] The pertinence of this question is evident in that nothing in the text suggests cherry picking some parts as timeless and others as no longer applicable.

In any case, these understandings do not seem to connect the instructions to any over-arching theme in the chapter unless it something very general such as "regulations for worship gatherings." This however fails to encompass the opening verses about praying for those in authority so as to live in peace (1 Tim. 2:1–7). On the other hand, when it is recognized that the theme for all of chapter 2 is **how to live in peace without conflict and division**, the entire chapter fits together. The threefold use of *haysuxia* in 2:2, 11, 12 ties the theme of tranquility and the absence of conflict together both in the *world* (2:1–7) and in *worship* (2:8–15).

As noted earlier in this chapter, Paul prohibited women from teaching and leading in a self-asserting, controlling, abusive, and divisive manner (2:12). His command against immodest and ostentatious appearance by women was apparently a response to wealthy women in the congregation seeking unwarranted prominence and/or influence by flaunting their riches. Rather than pursuing peace and tranquility, they aspired to inappropriate positions of teaching and leadership in which they could dominate and control others.

---

[301] Some important insights about this verse, including relevant cultural factors, were presented in chapter 9.

[302] Halley Watson Kim, *"How to be egalitarian with a complementarian spouse,"* The Junia Project (6/13/2017): http://juniaproject.com/how-to-be-egalitarian-with-a-complementarian-spouse/

Their appearance was not so much a sexually suggestive or egotistical "look at me" ploy but rather was designed to elevate themselves to secure influence and control. Their gussying up wasn't flirtatious but a power-grab.

Second, verses 13, 14 say: "For Adam was formed first, then Eve . . . And Adam was not the one deceived; it was the woman who was deceived and became a sinner." At first glance, many assume Paul is using the order of creation as an argument for why women cannot be teachers in church or hold a position of leadership authority. A deeper investigation reveals problems with that understanding and provides an alternative way of reading these verses much more in harmony with the chapter's theme—*how to live in peace in the world and the church.* Remembering the theme *clarifies* Paul's reference both to the order of creation ("For Adam was formed first, then Eve") and to Eve's culpability in the original temptation and fall ("And Adam was not the one deceived; it was the woman who was deceived and became a sinner"). Rather than these two assertions about Genesis 1–3 supporting patriarchy in the church, they were instead a much-needed call for the women of Ephesus to display humility, interdependence, and the ability to obey and to follow directions <u>whoever is leading</u>, rather than exhibiting self-assertive, domineering, and independent spirits while teaching or leading.

These controlling personality traits are unacceptable for both women and men (1 Tim. 2:8; 3 John 9, 10). They were especially offensive in women who lived in a very patriarchal culture or one where prominent women were offensively brash, combative, argumentative, assertive, and domineering. This understanding is consistent with Paul's immediately preceding assertion in verses 11, 12 that women were to learn, teach and lead with a peace-promoting and humble spirit.

Furthermore, to argue that Paul used the order of creation to support hierarchal patriarchy misses the point of the creation narrative. Man could not find his *equal* and the solution to his aloneness among the animals. His equal, his counterpart, his partner, and his soul-mate could only be found in the one taken from his side.

> The whole purpose of the narrative in Gen. 2:21-24 is to emphasize the equality and interdependence of man and woman, husband and wife. When the man looked at his new partner he exclaimed that she was 'flesh of my flesh

and bone of my bone'. How much more equal can you get? But to further emphasize the point, Gen. 2:24 says that when a husband and wife join in marriage they become one flesh. God's ideal at creation was that the husband and wife be equal, compatible, and rule over nature together (Gen. 1:26–28). Gender equality, or mutuality, is the godly ideal we should aim for. To say that Paul is using the creation order of male first and female second to create a chain of command is entirely missing the point of Genesis 2:21–24 which is of equality, affinity and unity.[303]

Grenz observes: "Paul declares that in Christ the creation order of woman coming *from* man is balanced by women giving birth *to* men (1 Cor 11:11–12),"[304] "In the Lord, however, woman is not independent of man, nor is man independent of woman. For as woman came from man, so also man is born of woman. But everything comes from God."

The creation story in Genesis 1, 2 gives no suggestion of hierarchy between the genders. On the contrary, they were both created in God's image (1:26, 27) which had nothing to do with gender. Gender isn't what distinguished them from the earlier creation of plants and animals who were not gender neutral but were also male and female. Further, Adam and Eve were given the creation mandate together (1:28–30). They were equal partners in this vocation. There was no hint that God assigned a leadership role based on gender. The complementarian suggestion that the order of creation presupposes or implies a hierarchical relationship of the genders was thoroughly debunked earlier in this study (chapter 3).

In addition, a strong case can be made that Paul was addressing a growing first century problem of false doctrine that may have had unique traction in

---

[303] Mowczko, *"1 Timothy 2:12 In Context,"* http://newlife.id.au/equality-and-gender-issues/1-timothy-212-in-context-5/

[304] Grenz, *Women in the Church,* Kindle Loc. 1591.

Ephesus[305]—a Proto-Gnostic heresy[306] that glorified Eve, asserted that she was Adam's teacher, *was created before him*, and that she was superior to him.[307] Westfall states:

> We also know of an early recorded myth that (1) reversed the role of male and female in the order of creation and deception in the fall, (2) possibly could be dated as early as the second century CE, and (3) was part of gnostic literature that originated in oral tradition . . . Thus, there is sufficient evidence to suggest that there might have been a myth circulating among the women in first century Ephesus that reversed the accounts of the creation and fall, and perhaps it was antecedent to the gnostic oral tradition.[308]

On a similar note, Grenz observes:

> The Gnostic myths elevated Eve as existing prior to Adam, and they spoke of the higher powers (or God) as deceiving Adam into believing that he was born first. These heretical stories also presented the serpent in a positive light as the one who brought true knowledge to Eve, who then enlightened Adam. The Gnostic mythology did not relegate Eve to the distant past, but gave her a continuing importance as the one who could communicate mystic knowledge and enlighten humanity. The believers in Ephesus were apparently turning

---

[305] Mowczko, *1 Timothy 2:12 in Context,* http://newlife.id.au/equality-and-gender-issues/1-timothy-212-in-context-3/. "Tertullian (160-220) identified the false teaching in the Ephesian church as an early, emerging form of Gnosticism. In his description of a developed Gnostic heresy, Tertullian used Paul's own expression of 'myths and endless genealogies', and he added, 'which the inspired apostle [Paul] by anticipation condemned, whilst the seeds of heresy were even then shooting forth.'

[306] Marg Mowczko: *"Adam and Eve in ancient Gnostic literature and 1 Timothy 2:13-14",* Marg Mowczko (3/9/2015), http://margmowczko.com/adam-and-eve-in-gnostic-literature/. More evidence for the existence of these first century syncretistic and pre/proto-Gnostic myths regarding Eve may be read in their original sources in this article.

[307] Ibid.

[308] Westfall, *Paul and Gender,* 73, 74.

away from the truth and believing this mythology (2 Tim 4:4). They were being duped by the foolish talk of false teachers (1 Tim 1:6) and old women, who led young widows to turn to Satan (1 Tim 4:7; 5:15). Paul's statements therefore, are an emphatic appeal to orthodoxy and the traditional biblical account."[309]

Thus, both Paul's assertion about Adam's prior creation and Eve's deception in the first sin may have been a refutation of the proto-Gnostic Eve heresy as well as a reminder intended to provoke humility among the church women who were assuming mastery[310] over men in teaching and leading in the church. Paul wanted to protect the women in the Ephesian church from being drawn into the local heresy that reversed the Genesis creation order and glorified a perverted characterization of Eve, but also wanted to protect them from the Eden-like temptation in which Eve desired an elevated position ("your eyes will be opened, and you will be like God, knowing good and evil," Gen. 3:5).

Further, no other Scripture even hints at any hierarchical significance based either on the order of creation or on Eve succumbing to temptation, who, unlike Adam, was due to being deceived. To assert that the order of the creation of Adam and Eve required that males exercise authority over females is logically problematic because animals were created before humans (Gen. 1). Genesis 1:26 asserts God's plan for humans to rule over all other creatures regardless of their prior creation. Superiority or ascendancy based on priority of creation would also be inconsistent with the absolute identity and equality of male and female so clearly portrayed in Genesis 1 and 2.

Third, the argument from verse 14 that women are by nature more vulnerable to deception and therefore should not hold authoritative teaching positions over men runs contrary to Paul's teaching in 2 Corinthians 11:2–4. In that passage, Paul's warning against deception had nothing to do with a more gullible gender, but rather expressed his concern that *both males and*

---

[309] Grenz, *Women in the Church,* Kindle loc 1565-1574.

[310] Westfall, *Paul and Gender,* 74. Based on the root meaning of αὐθέντης (*authentays*) as *to master,* Westfall asserts, "Without question, in the Greco-Roman culture, if the woman assumed the role of teaching and acting like a master over her husband, it would be considered abusive because it would have been humiliating."

females in Corinth might be led astray from devotion to Christ as Eve was deceived by the serpent.

Often overlooked in the story of Eve's deception is the fact that Adam "was with her" during the temptation (Gen. 3:6). Because Adam was present for the temptation, some have assumed that he was a silent observer. This assumption is the basis for the title of Larry Crabb's thought-provoking book, The Silence of Adam.[311] Some have suggested that Adam was complicit in Eve's sin because he failed to speak up and to exert his inherent responsibility for leadership to prevent her from falling for Satan's deception. However, there is absolutely nothing in Genesis 3 suggesting that a violation of gender roles contributed to Eve's deception or to their sin. Crabb's book is filled with helpful insights about relationships, but, while both Adam and Eve were quick to deflect blame, neither God nor Eve accused Adam of not providing better leadership, nor did Adam blame Eve for not seeking or following his direction rather than acting out of sinful independence. This in spite of both being in a blame-shifting mode.

With regard to the complementarian suggestion that women, being more naïve, should be excluded from a role requiring them to be able to discern Satan's falsehoods, Grenz queries: "Where do we read that the apostle dismisses women from such responsibility? Must we now read the apostolic admonitions that the Christian community discern truth, test the spirits and so forth as addressed solely to men, or at least as implying that men take the lead?"[312] The New Testament is not only replete with exhortations regarding exercising spiritual gifts without gender distinctions, the Old Testament also includes many portrayals of the involvement of both men and women in providing spiritual and moral instruction (see chapter 11). For example, Proverbs 1:8 is one of many proverbs emphasizing the role of a mother in teaching their children, "Listen, my son, to your father's instruction and do not forsake your mother's teaching."[313] Apparently, wise Solomon did not accept the idea that women's vulnerability to deception, exposed in the first temptation, made them unsuited to teaching God's truth to the most impressionable and least discerning students—children.

From a practical standpoint, think how throughout time, it has been

---

[311] Lawrence J. Crabb Jr., *The Silence of Adam* (Grand Rapids: Zondervan, 1995).

[312] Grenz, *Women in the Church*, Kindle Loc. 1609.

[313] See also Proverbs 6:20.

mothers who have played a primary role in teaching and warning their children to not be deceived by the wiles of sin and sinners. Arguably, many mothers take a considerably more active role than fathers. Paul reminded Timothy of the godly legacy he received from his mother's and grandmother's teaching of the Scriptures:

> I have been reminded of your sincere faith, which first lived in your grandmother Lois and in your mother Eunice and, I am persuaded, now lives in you also . . . But as for you, continue in what you have learned and have become convinced of, because you know those from whom you learned it, and how from infancy you have known the holy Scriptures, which are able to make you wise for salvation through faith in Christ Jesus. All Scripture is God-breathed and is useful for teaching, rebuking, correcting and training in righteousness, so that the man of God may be thoroughly equipped for every good work (2 Tim. 1:5; 3:14–16).

If in 1 Timothy 2:12 Paul instructed Timothy that women should not teach men, and if one contemporary application is that women should not teach in seminaries as some complementarians assert, doesn't it seem a little strange in either case that Paul would make such a strong statement in 2 Timothy about the role of Pastor Timothy's mother and grandmother in his theological training?

Additionally, it's important to remember that in this section of the passage, Paul is asserting the importance of women learning—a concept that was radically counter-cultural. The story of the first sin illustrates the importance of that. Eve's deception had terrible results. Adam's sin was deliberate. It was the kind of intentional sin the Scriptures often address with great seriousness.[314] But Eve's sin was less intentional than it was naïve. She was deceived. This understanding complements Paul's insistence that women learn (1 Tim. 2:12) and his illustration about the danger of not learning ("the woman . . . was deceived"). It suggests the importance of *liberating* women from the cultural gender restrictions, rather than favoring their continuation.

---

[314] For example, Numbers 15:27–31; Psalm 19:13; Hebrews 10:26; James 4:17.

It's as if he is saying, "Don't keep repeating this mistake of preventing women from full access to God's truth."

However, this counter-cultural liberation of women should never encourage women to be self-aggrandizing (1 Tim. 2:9) or domineering (1 Tim. 2:11), as was apparently the case in the Ephesian Artemis cult and perhaps as part of the growing problem of false teaching (1 Tim. 1:3–7, et al.). Was there a divisive argument between Adam and Eve over eating the forbidden fruit? Was Eve "pushy" with Adam about choosing what was forbidden? If so this might further explain Paul's insistence, in light of the stories of the creation and fall, that women should not be combative and divisive (*haysuxia*), or domineering (*authĕntĕō*) in their newly permitted role of teaching men. Rather, their learning must lead to peaceful unity (*haysuxia*) and "*full submission*" (πάσῃ ὑποταγῇ/*pasay upotagay*) to God's truth.

It is interesting that those who would use this passage to argue against women teaching men, nevertheless recruit and welcome them for teaching children and other women. If vulnerability to deception due to a feminine trait of gullibility prohibits women from teaching men, why on earth would they be encouraged to teach impressionable and yet untrained children and other supposedly gullible women (2 Tim. 3:14–17 with 1:5 and Titus 2:3–5)? That sounds like a recipe for colossal disaster—"the blind leading the blind" (Luke 6:39). Wouldn't it be better to have women teach men who, per complementarians, are less vulnerable? Wouldn't it be better to have men teach women and children? The fact that virtually no one argues for or practices this arrangement raises suspicion about what actually motivates (whether consciously or subconsciously) the perpetuation of limiting women's role in the church.

Thus, Paul's allusion to Eve's deception in 1 Timothy 2:14 is best understood in light of the multiple references in his letter to his concern about the prevalence of false teachers (1 Tim. 3:3–11; 4:1–5; 5:15) including female false teachers. Revelation 2:18ff specifically references this in a neighboring city and the influence of the Artemis cult noted in Acts 19 likely exacerbated the problem. Acts 13 recalls the efforts to hinder the spread of the Gospel in Pisidian Antioch by recruiting prominent Gentile women who had proselytized to Judaism: "But the Jews incited the God-fearing women of high standing and the leading men of the city. They stirred up persecution against Paul and Barnabas and expelled them from their region"

(Acts 13:50). To acknowledge that women have sometimes been vulnerable to being deceived by false teaching differs from assigning to them an innate and greater propensity based on gender. Rather, they, like men, must be afforded opportunities to learn. Incidentally, though supporting statistics may not be readily available, it seems undeniable that the vast majority of false religions and cults throughout history have been founded by males rather than females. Concerning 1 Timothy 2:14 Grenz writes:

> As Perriman explains, "Rather than claiming that men are less likely to be deceived, Paul chose references from Genesis to illustrate the disastrous consequences of a woman accepting and passing on false teaching." The women of Ephesus reminded Paul of the plight of the woman in Eden. Eve was deceived into believing certain erroneous statements, which she in turn passed on to Adam. In a similar manner the Ephesian women were susceptible to the deceit of the false teachers and to involvement in propagating their heretical beliefs.[315]

It is important to note that no other Scripture gives even the slightest hint that the temptation in Eden revealed something inherent to being a woman that necessitates that the feminine gender must always follow the leadership of men who do not have the same gender-based vulnerability. Although 2 Corinthians 11:3 mentions Eve's deception by the serpent's cunning, there is no assertion there, in 1 Timothy 2, or elsewhere that she was thereby more gullible by nature or more culpable than Adam. On the contrary, Romans 5:12–21 and 1 Corinthians15:21–22 clearly place responsibility for the fall on Adam.

Fourth, verse 15 says: "But women will be saved through childbearing— if they continue in faith, love and holiness with propriety." What is this salvation? Is it salvation from sin and the condemnation it brings? What "childbearing" is in view? Note that the definite article (τῆς/*tays*) is present in the Greek and therefore a literal rendering would be "the childbearing."

Paul cannot be making a soteriological assertion that women will be saved from sin and condemnation by bearing children as nearly all English

---

[315] Grenz, *Women in the Church,* Kindle Loc. 1617

translations unfortunately seem to suggest. This would not only be contrary to the clear soteriology of Scripture (we are saved by grace through faith in the finished work of Christ) but would also have devastating implications for childless women and for all males. Rather, in *"THE childbearing"* (τῆς τεκνογονίας/*tays teknogonias,* emphasis added), Paul referenced a very specific event, the most unique of all childbearings—the birth of Christ the Savior, in fulfillment of God's promise concerning Eve's *"offspring"* (Gen. 3:15). By His death and resurrection Jesus defeated Satan and liberated the broken creation from sin's curse, including the tragic curse of patriarchal oppression (Gen. 3:16).

Shockingly, the existence and significance of the definite article is not revealed by any mainstream English translation. The only version I found that somewhat acknowledges the definite article in the text of its translation is God's Word Translation: "However she [and all women] will be saved through the birth of the child, if they lead respectable lives in faith, love, and holiness." Better, the margin specifies, "Taken to refer to Jesus." In a *footnote*, the New Living Translation acknowledges the definite article in the second of two alternate readings: "or will be saved by accepting their role as mothers, or will be saved by the birth of the Child."[316] The Message seems to echo the Messianic hint in Genesis 3:15[317] in its rendering: "On the other hand, her childbearing brought about salvation, reversing Eve. But this salvation comes only to those who continue in faith, love, and holiness."

Is it possible that patriarchal bias once again affects virtually all the mainstream translations? They seem to affirm that the role of women is epitomized in bearing children[318] rather than revealing the exalted role of the first woman whose descendant's Offspring, Jesus, would save the world—"THE Childbearing of all child-bearings."

What are women saved from because of "<u>the</u> childbearing?" In the *context*, it would appear that it is not only salvation from sin and its condemnation, but more specifically, involves deliverance for believing women from sin's

---

[316] The capitalization of *"Child"* indicates that this alternative translation refers to Jesus.

[317] "And I will put enmity between you [the serpent] and the woman, and between your offspring and hers; he will crush your head, and you will strike his heel."

[318] Hopefully no one would minimize that motherhood is an exalted role, but, the typical complementarian translation of 1 Timothy 2:16 could feel painfully like the crass chauvinistic designation of the woman's place being *in the home, barefoot and pregnant.*

curse including the persistent gender wars and oppressive patriarchy that results from the fall. This interpretation of deliverance from male domination through Eve's Offspring not only fits the immediate context in which Paul had just mentioned Eve (verses 13, 14), but also the allusion to the Genesis passage in which sinful patriarchy was declared to be a consequence of the fall into sin: *"your husband will rule over you"* (Gen. 3:16). Salvation through the childbearing mirrors Paul's assertion about the new creation values Jesus inaugurated: "There is neither Jew nor Greek, slave nor free, male nor female, for you are all one in Christ Jesus" (Gal. 3:28).

In summary, interpreting the prohibition passages (1 Cor. 14 and 1 Tim. 2) in light of the focus and themes of the contexts and consistent with the corrected translations of key words in both, clearly refutes the traditional complementarian interpretation restricting women's roles in church. Paul's mandates are directed at protecting the values of <u>orderliness, appropriateness, and tranquility</u> in church gatherings (1 Cor. 14:26–33, 39 and 1 Tim. 2:8–9). Rightly understood, these passages place no gender-based restrictions on church ministry and leadership, but rather encourage women to learn and serve alongside men in *any and every* ministry capacity.

FOR DISCUSSION

(1) Describe a time when you were growing up when you knew someone who was a bully. How did you feel about it? If you have ever observed someone who was a church bully, talk about what they did and how you felt about it? Was anything done to stop the bully? What was it and was it effective? If nothing was done about the bullying, why do you think that was?

(2) Read 1 Timothy 2:12. Do you think Paul was talking about good authority or bad? Why? Why do you think Paul used a very unusual Greek word for "authority" that is not used anywhere else in the Bible?

(3) Read 1 Timothy 2:9. How do you believe Christian women should respond to this verse today?

(4) Imagine that an unbeliever hears that the Bible says, "A woman should learn in quietness and full submission" (1 Tim. 2:11). If

their response was that "the Bible is a misogynous book written by domineering men who wanted to oppress women," how would you answer them and explain the verse?

(5) How does the historical background about the female-dominated Artemis Cult in Ephesus and the proto-gnostic false teaching influence how 1 Timothy 2 should be understood?

(6) Explain what you believe Paul meant in 1 Timothy 2:15, "But women will be saved through childbearing—if they continue in faith, love and holiness with propriety." How would you answer someone who said that women receive salvation by bearing children?

(7) The theme of 1 Timothy 2 is "How to live in peace in the world and in the church." What do you believe God wants you to do this week to promote peace in your community and church?

11

Can You Believe What All
These Women Did?

Because it was God's plan for men to lead and women to submit, the Bible is full of examples of willful women who exercised authority over men in violation of God's plan and who were therefore rebuked for their rebellion against God's creation order for the genders. In this chapter, we will list the many times when women were called out for wrongfully assuming a position of leadership God never intended for them to have.

Oops! Wait a minute! There ARE NOT ANY examples in the Bible of a woman being rebuked for taking a position of leadership over men—**NOT ONE!** That's because it was NOT God's plan for men to lead and women to submit. That is a deeply entrenched myth that has permeated much of the church (and society) through the centuries. That error has frequently discouraged or restricted more than 50% of the church from even considering the possibility that God has gifted and called them to serve in ways that might have greatly affected the church and the world for God's kingdom. In reality, the Bible is replete with examples of women being *recognized and praised* for the leadership (at every level), teaching, and ministry roles they effectively carried out. They are honored, not rebuked, and this in cultures where patriarchy was pervasive and for the most part unassailed and unassailable.

If God's plan for women from the beginning of creation was that they are designed to be followers while men are designed to be leaders, and if women are therefore restricted from teaching and leadership positions over men, it would seem logical this arrangement would be confirmed throughout the

Scriptures. We would expect to find NO illustrations of women teaching or leading men unless any such reference came with a clear indication it violated God's intention and plan. Instead, what we find throughout the Scriptures is a plethora of positive illustrations of godly women teaching and leading men. The activities of these women are not treated as violations of God's order or as aberrations to His plan. On the contrary, what the women did is treated as if it were ordinary or normal, or, in some cases, as worthy of special honor. This is especially striking when we are reminded that the world of the Scriptures, both Old and New Testaments, was a very patriarchal world in which the norm was for male domination and the shocking exceptions were for female elevation.

It is time for another Reformation of the church. Although there have always been remnants within Jesus' church where women were encouraged to serve in any capacity, today there remains a huge percentage[319] where, although women minister in many essential roles without which the church would falter or fall (e.g. children's ministries), they are forbidden to serve in key leadership and teaching roles simply because of their gender. For too long churches have been held hostage by biased and incorrect understandings of a miniscule number of Bible verses that apparently few people in the pulpits or pews have had the interest, curiosity, or courage to investigate or challenge. If the church (or its leadership) is afraid to restudy the Holy Scriptures to be sure the "word of truth" is being "correctly handled" (1 Tim. 2:15), it has compromised its core values. We must repent of whatever motives prevent us from searching out what the Scriptures teach, whether pride, fear, laziness, apathy, pride, selfishness, arrogance, judgmentalism, resistance to change, idolatry, prejudice, chauvinism, or bigotry.

This chapter will address the questions: How does the Bible portray women regarding involvement in leadership, in communicating God's truth,

---

[319] Some of the largest denominations prohibit ordaining women along with numerous smaller groups and independent churches. While the number of women pastors is on the rise (three times as many as 25 years ago) only one out of eleven Protestant pastors is a woman. Christianity Today, 2/2017, "Study: Female Pastors are on the Rise," https://www.christianitytoday.com/women/2017/february/study-female-pastors-are-on-rise.html. Less than 40% of evangelical Christians are supportive of women pastors ("Study: 39% of Evangelicals Approve of Women Pastors," Christianheadlines.com, 3/14/27) but many of these belong to churches who do not agree with them and prohibit women from pastoring.

and in engaging in service for God? And, how does the Bible portray women in these roles in relationship to men?

It would not be difficult to demonstrate that although the Scriptures include many references to women in all the roles mentioned above, those references are often overlooked, ignored, minimized, dismissed, lied about, or misrepresented because of patriarchal bias. Carolyn Custis James suggests that the biblical stories of women and girls "are casualties to widespread cultural assumptions that men are leaders and women are born to follow."[320] Her insights are important to consider:

> We are cautioned not to get excited or to entertain big ideas for ourselves from the stories of women like Deborah, Esther, Priscilla, Lydia, Junia, and Phoebe, when their stories are in the Bible for our instruction and should fill our hearts and the hearts of our daughters with fierce passion and determination to give our all in service to Jesus.
>
> We aren't alerted to notice or called to aspire to the radical brand of bold and selfless leadership of Ruth the Moabitess or to follow the example of the hungry-to-learn Mary of Bethany and her courageous solo affirmation of Jesus' mission on the eve of his crucifixion.
>
> We completely miss how, for example, the young slave girl Hagar, barren Hannah, and the washed up childless widow Naomi are at least three female shapers of Judeo-Christian theology. Hagar teaches us the intimate side of the God 'who sees me.' Hannah's theology informs us of God's sovereign rule over everything from the womb to the throne. Naomi reassures us of God's stubborn relentless love (*hesed*) for us, what Sally Lloyd-Jones described as *'Never Stopping, Never Giving Up, Unbreaking, Always and Forever Love.'* The theology of all three women shows up in the writings

---

[320] James, Carolyn Custis, "Celebrate National Women's History Month with the Bold Women of the Bible" (3/3/ 2017): https://carolyncustisjames.com/2017/03/03/celebrate-national-womens-history-month-with-the-bold-women-of-the-bible/

of King David and is indispensable truth for believers in every generation.

It's worth mentioning that men lose out in this arrangement too, for not only do they also have much to learn from these strong women, ignoring them causes men to expect less from their sisters in Christ which, in turn, deprives them of strength, courage, and wisdom they need and that God means for them to gain from us. It is time we reclaimed these women's stories and reinstalled their portraits in their rightful place as Role Models for women and girls today. Without them, we will inevitably lower the bar for ourselves and our daughters when kingdom matters are every day at stake, when earth is emitting a distress signal, and when we cannot spare anyone in the monumental gospel ministry Jesus has entrusted to women and children?[321]

The women we will identify in this chapter who exerted strong and positive influence should not surprise us because the Old Testament gives no gender restrictions for any position of service, except the Levite Priesthood. Actually, there is no *stated* gender prohibition regarding the Levite Priesthood but the example is clear that only males filled that role. The Old Testament priests who served at the Tabernacle and Temple apparently were all male perhaps because God works in the world as it is, not as it ought to be. Therefore, the Scriptures sometimes temporarily accommodate pervasive cultural biases, such as patriarchy as was presented regarding the *concession passages* in chapter 5. It's also important to recognize that there was a very pragmatic reason for excluding women from serving as priests at the Tabernacle: "It would have been impractical to admit women on the regular roster of Temple ministry because women within the required age range of twenty-five to fifty were frequently 'unclean' due to their monthly period or childbirth."[322]

---

[321] Ibid.

[322] Marg Mowczko, "Old Testament Priests & New Testament Ministers," *Marg Mosczko* (blog), May 1, 2011, http://margmowczko.com/old-testament-priests-new-testament-ministers/

Further, the priests who ministered in the Tabernacle and Temple were *types* of Christ, our great High Priest. But, it is significant to note that at the same time, in Exodus 19:6, God declared the entire nation of Israel (without gender distinction) to be a "kingdom of priests" and in the New Testament, in Revelation 1:6, believers in the seven churches of Asia were declared by Jesus to be "a kingdom and priests" without gender distinction or limitation.

Mowczko argues cogently that the Old Covenant priestly gender limitation should not be applied to New Testament church leadership:

> The Old Testament Temple and the New Testament Church are in fact two very different organizations with different aims, methods and structures. Because of these differences, it is completely unreasonable to say that Christian women cannot be church leaders simply because the Old Testament priesthood was not open to them.

> Jesus brought in many changes with the New Covenant–new and better ways (Heb. 6:9; 7:19, 22; 8:6ff,). Priests were no longer needed as mediators between God and his people, because Jesus took on the roles as the ultimate Mediator (1 Tim. 2:5; Heb. 8:6) and the ultimate High Priest (Heb. 6:19-20; 7:23-28; 9:11ff).

> Under the Old Covenant, only the High Priest (a specially appointed, male Levite and a direct descendent of Aaron) could enter the Most Holy Place in the Temple, once a year, on the Day of Atonement.[4] Under the New Covenant, all believers (regardless of gender, ethnicity, social status, disease or disability, etc.), can enter the Most Holy Place, continually, by a "new and living way" through the blood of Jesus (Heb. 10:19-22). Wow!

> Furthermore, instead of a select few people, God has given all New Covenant men and women his Holy Spirit [Acts 2:17-18].[323]

---

[323] Ibid.

Under the Old Covenant qualifications for priesthood were *physical* (male descendants of Levi) whereas under the New Covenant, qualifications for ministry are *spiritual* and *moral*.

However, under the Old Covenant, women's participation in ministry was encouraged as illustrated by the Nazarite vow which involved taking "a special vow, a vow of separation to the Lord" and was open to "a man or a woman" (Numbers 6:2).

These Prophets Were Women

Although the prophets who wrote the Old Testament books were all males, there are extended passages within those books that were composed by female prophets such as Miriam (Ex. 15:21f), Deborah (Judg. 4:4; 5:1ff), and Huldah (2 Kings 22:14ff and 2 Chron. 34:22ff). Huldah became God's prophet to the king. One of Judah's most godly kings, Josiah, sought a message "of the LORD" to teach him how to respond to the newly rediscovered Book of the Law. Hilkiah the priest sought out the prophetess Huldah whose message is recorded in the Scriptures and was diligently followed by the King. Huldah was married but apparently there was no need for her to prophesy under the authority of her husband, Shallum.

It is striking to see how some prominent complementarians stretch the textual facts to the limit in their efforts to explain away the significance of the ministry of some of the Old and New Testaments' women. For example, the authors of Recovering Biblical Manhood and Womanhood (John Piper and Wayne Grudem) assert that Huldah's prophecy was done in a "private consultation" rather than in a public ministry (such as a male prophet would do).[324] They assert the same regarding New Testament prophetess, Anna (Luke 2:36-38).[325] A simple reading of the text about the prophetic role of those two ladies reveals how hard Piper and Grudem have to work to attempt to impose their biased insistence on these stories. Huldah's prophecy was delivered to the most powerful male in the nation, King Josiah, as well as to the high-ranking *delegation* he sent to procure her prophetic services: the high

---

[324] Cited by Marg Mowczko, "Hudah's Public Prophetic Ministry," *Marg Mowczko* (blog), February 19, 2018, http://margmowczko.com/huldah-prophetess/

[325] See more about Anna's public ministry of prophecy later in this chapter.

priest, the father of the future governor, the son of a prophet, the secretary of state, and the king's officer.[326] Any assertion that those six august males were the only audience is an argument from silence. Even so, would her ministry have been invalid if it had taken place in a different location with more people present? I thought the issue was teaching *men*—not where the teaching took place or how many were present. What is absolutely certain is that Huldah's ministry was not limited to women and children but was to a group of the most powerful men in the nation. Further, the prophetic messages of both Huldah and Anna are recorded in the Scriptures to teach generations of God's people, both males and females. Their prophetic ministries were anything but "private." Anna's ministry at the Temple was carried out in a public and perhaps crowded place which included both men and women.

Other female prophets were Nodiah (Neh. 6:14) and Isaiah's wife (Is. 8:3). Proverbs 31's famous description of the "wife of noble character" is one of the best-known chapters in Holy Scripture. It is the instruction of a woman taught to her royal son who passed on his mother's teaching to many generations of Jews and Christians: "The sayings of King Lemuel—an oracle his mother taught him" (Prov. 31:1). These inscripturated prophetic and teaching ministries by women were never restricted to audiences of children or females or in any other way. **These Holy Spirit-inspired female authors of holy Scripture have been teaching men authoritatively for thousands of years—every time men read these Bible passages or hear them taught.**

Deborah: Prophet, Judge, and Leader

It would be hard to imagine a more powerful Bible example of a woman teaching and having authority over men than Deborah. Judges 4:1–3 states (emphasis added): "Deborah, a prophetess, the wife of Lappidoth, was leading Israel at that time. She held court under the Palm of Deborah between Ramah and Bethel in the hill country of Ephraim, and the Israelites came to her to have their disputes decided." Deborah was a prophetess—she *preached* God's message to the men and women of Israel. She *led* the nation (men and women). She was a *judge* who held court and decided disputes for the Israelites, obviously exercising authority over both men and women. She

---

[326] 2 Kings 22:14ff and 2 Chronicles 34:22ff.

delivered God's message to General Barak about God's coming deliverance from their enemies, and on the Lord's behalf, commanded him to lead the army: "She sent for Barak son of Abinoam from Kedesh in Naphtali and said to him, 'The Lord, the God of Israel, commands you: 'Go, take with you ten thousand men of Naphtali and Zebulun and lead the way to Mount Tabor. I will lure Sisera, the commander of Jabin's army, with his chariots and his troops to the Kishon River and give him into your hands'" (Judg. 4:6, 7). God obviously placed her in a role of authority over a powerful man, the general over Israel's armies.

The inspired song by Deborah and Barak in Judges 5 indicates that they exercised leadership together over the princes, nobles, and the armies of Israel. Although she shared the credit with Barak (5:1), the text is clear that the overall strategy and orders (4:14) came from God *through her* to Barak and the nation. Some complementarians understandably have to try to find a way to represent something other than what the Scriptures unequivocally portray without embarrassment or apology. For example, some argue that Deborah was an exception contrary to the biblical rule of male leadership and that she had to overstep her normal place of female deference and submission to cover for Barak's cowardice. The complementarian assumption is argued based on Deborah's words to Barak in Judges 4:9: "'Very well,' Deborah said, 'I will go with you. But because of the way you are going about this, the honor will not be yours, for the Lord will hand Sisera over to a woman.'"

The attempt to take away from the significance of Deborah's leadership role is seen in the following suggestion: "The fight into which she ends up leading the people is a fight that should have been waged by Barak. When he is too afraid to go out and fight, she says she will go with him. But in consequence of, literally, hiding behind the skirts of Deborah, Barak will not gain honor from his victory."[327] Where, I ask, does *the text* indicate that Barak was "too afraid to go out and fight"? Wait a minute! Where does *the text* suggest that he was "literally" (?) "hiding behind the skirts of Deborah" (or even figuratively)? That language is slanderously demeaning to Barak and totally lacks support in the biblical record. It is a complementarian myth, apparently seen by them as a necessary attempt to misrepresent what the text clearly says so as to defend their biased position regarding gender roles.

---

[327] J. R. Daniel Kirk, *"Does Deborah Help?,"* Storied Theology (9/26/2011): http://www. jrdkirk.com/2011/09/26/does-deborah-help/

John Piper and Wayne Grudem are highly respected evangelical leaders and are two of the best known contemporary advocates of complementarian interpretation. By their complementarian perversion of the story they demonstrate their reluctance to recognize Deborah as demonstrating the validity of female leadership over men:

> "God has no antipathy toward revealing His will to women, nor does He pronounce them unreliable messengers. The differentiation of roles for men and women in ministry is rooted not in women's incompetence to receive or transmit truth, but in the primary responsibility of men in God's order to lead and teach. The instances of women who prophesied and led do not call this order into question. Rather, there are pointers in each case that the women followed their unusual paths in a way that endorsed and honored the usual leadership of men, or indicted their failures to lead . . . Deborah, a prophetess, judge, and mother in Israel, along with Jael, was a living indictment of the weakness of Barak and other men in Israel who should have been more courageous leaders."[328]

Really? Where does *the biblical text* give the slightest hint of an "indictment of the weakness of Barak and other men in Israel"? The absolute absence of any such statement in *the text* belies that complementarians seem intent on reading this passage through their bias-tinted glasses. Their minds are apparently locked shut to any possibility that the Scriptures could actually hold Deborah up as a model to godly women everywhere of God's plan and approval of women prophesying, leading, and even judging men.

In other words, complementarians utterly refuse to accept the possibility that the story demonstrates God's approval of a woman ministering to God's people as prophet, leader, and judge apart from any supposed failure or weakness of men who should have been leading instead. They have to explain it away as exceptional and contrary to God's "usual" order due to men's failure to lead. Further, they would assert, Deborah's remarkable leadership

---

[328] John Piper and Wayne Grudem, eds. *Recovering Biblical Manhood and Womanhood: A Response to Evangelical Feminism. Kindle edition,* location 1591.

and ministry are only acceptable because of Deborah's efforts to endorse and honor the more "usual" and legitimate male leader, Barak. They believe in a "differentiation of roles for men and women in order to lead and teach," hence cannot accept what seems to be a very straightforward and unequivocal biblical endorsement of a woman in a role of leading and teaching. It would be difficult to imagine a more obvious example of forcing one's gender bias onto the biblical text rather than allowing the text to speak for itself.

Deborah's prediction that Barak would not gain the honor of the victory because God would hand the opposing general Sisera "over to a woman" is not an indictment of any cowardice, weakness, or failure by Barak to assume the male role of authority. Rather it appears to be an acknowledgment that because of his request for her presence with him in battle, the honor for victory would be shared rather than sole credit going to him as the conquering general. It could also be a prediction of honor for Jael, another heroic woman, for her courageous and grisly dispatch of the enemy's leader with a tent peg hammered through his head. She, a woman, became God's instrument to kill the enemy's leader and thereby became the hero of the day for that assassination. Imagine if a female Navy Seal had pulled the trigger that killed Bin Laden. Even in our somewhat more favorable egalitarian environment, the *big news story* wouldn't have been about President Obama's great leadership. It would have been all about the *female seal* who killed Bin Laden. Can't you imagine the Hollywood movie that would follow?

Anyone who suggests that Barak was the appropriate leader who recruited Deborah due to his own cowardice, hasn't read the text carefully or honestly. After Deborah ordered him to lead the army, Barak pressured her to accompany him in battle (Judg. 4:8). She was already recognized as Israel's leader, judge, and prophet. She was Barak's superior, who, on God's behalf, commanded him to lead the military mission to the victory God promised. Deborah was not a leader BECAUSE the proper male leader was weak and inadequate or because he recruited her. She was already the nation's leader before Barak wisely asked her to help him in his military role. Though not a parallel circumstance, this would be like the President of the USA (think Deborah) ordering the top General of the US armed forces (think Barak) to launch an attack on an enemy. The president is the "commander in chief." Would it be cowardice if the general, recognizing the great respect the troops had for the president and how the president's presence would motivate and embolden every soldier, asked the president to join him in the command bunker to assist in directing the attack?

In any case, it is unnecessary and unwarranted to read into the story that the loss of honor Deborah predicted was due to Barak's cowardice or any lack of male leadership. It seems obvious that this traditional negative assessment of Barak is based on patriarchal bias imposed onto the text rather than on any actual exegetical evidence found within the text. I say that with full recognition (and shame) that for most of my life I read the passage through those same biased complementarian lenses. I taught that the only reason Israel had a female leader in this story was because no male would step up to his responsibility. I saw Deborah's leadership as a consequence of the nation's sin and the sin of those males who should have led (Barak and perhaps others). My patriarchal bias blinded me to what the text actually did and did not say. I was guilty of adding to the Scriptures[329] what was not there to protect my complementarian biased misinterpretation of God's Holy Scriptures.

There is zero biblical evidence that Barak's decision to ask Deborah to be with him was based on his *cowardice* to act as the legitimate male leader of the nation. He never was the leader of the nation. Deborah was! Rather, it may well have been a *brilliant and unselfish decision* based on his recognition of the army's respect for Deborah's already demonstrated leadership and influence. He was a great leader in his own right because he cared more about winning against Israel's enemies than about who got the credit, and because he did not allow gender-bias to prohibit his deference to Deborah's superior leadership. Barak recognized that the odds were stacked against his small, inexperienced, and greatly outnumbered army and understood that the presence of the nation's trusted and respected leader, Deborah, would inspire and embolden the troops and remind them of her prophetic promise that God would give them victory.

Gender bias is exposed when one considers what the reaction would doubtless be if the roles were reversed—if the story were about a Joan of Arc type female general who asked her male superior to ride beside her and to help her motivate the troops and lead them to victory. No one would say it exposed the woman's cowardice. Rather it would be hailed as a wise decision. The assumption that Barak's enlistment of Deborah's aid reveals his weakness

---

[329] Adding to the Scriptures is just as serious an offence as taking away from them, Revelation 22:18, 19.

and an appalling lack of proper male leadership in Israel is a perversion of the clear facts of the biblical story. Such a suggestion is not based on anything in the text, but springs from gender-biased patriarchal prejudice. Further, whatever Barak's rationale for desiring Deborah's presence beside him—even if it indicated a lapse in trust in God's promise—it takes nothing away from the leadership position Deborah was already competently filling prior to story of Israel's victory over Sisera. Nor does it diminish the indisputable affirmation of feminine leadership.

It should be noted that the purpose of Deborah's story is not to give us an *in your face* proof that it's okay for women to lead. While that could be argued from the story, the truth is perhaps even more powerful because the text doesn't need to say *"Notice this unusual incident of female leadership."* Rather, the validity of Deborah's leadership is just assumed. The text displays no need to defend or even to highlight it because it never was God's plan that only men should lead. She is just another of the Judges of Israel whose stories were told in this book.

The pervasive reality of patriarchy is not because of God's creation design. It is the horrific consequence of sin as predicted by Genesis 3:16. Patriarchy is ubiquitous not because God planned it so, but because that's what sinners do. Deborah is not a surprising exception to God's desired societal order. She illustrates the gender-equality that would be totally welcomed in an unfallen world, and what should be welcomed among those who pray, "let Your kingdom come and Your will be done on earth as it is in heaven" (Matt. 6:10).

In further support of Barak's good character and heroism, Judges 5:1 presents the glorious victory poem as the joint production of Deborah and Barak: "On that day Deborah and Barak son of Abinoam sang this song." Further, recognizing that Hebrews 11:32 lists Barak as one of the great heroes of faith with no mention of Deborah, it is difficult to accept the suggestion that Barak's request for Deborah's partnership in battle was anything but heroic. He is a hero of *faith*, not a coward or bad leader. He *believed* what God said through his prophet-leader Deborah (Judg. 4:6, 7) and he immediately requested that she actively participate with him rather than simply delegating the leadership of Israel's army to him. Hence, Barak was inducted into the Hebrews 11 faith hall of fame. If heaven (or the new earth) is a place for apologies, I suspect that there will be a long line of complementarians needing to ask Barak's forgiveness for their slander of his character and actions. I will be in that line. Barak was a godly hero, not an unspiritual coward or shameful wus.

In Hebrews 11:32, because of his faith, Barak is numbered with "Gideon, Samson, Jephthah, David, Samuel and the prophets." Far from being a weakling, he is memorialized for his heroic faith. His request for Deborah to stand beside him in leading the army was a recognition that in a day when spiritual compromise and rabid individualism ruled,[330] Deborah was the one person in the nation whom everyone knew spoke for God and stood for righteousness. Only she could unify a divided and spiritually bankrupt people. It was a daring, unselfish, counter-cultural, and godly move for Barak to give up his legitimate place of honor as conquering general riding alone at the head of Israel's victorious army and to invite Deborah, God's mouthpiece and ordained leader in Israel, to ride beside him.

Deborah did not lead because Barak was a coward and because God had to bend His patriarchal rules due to Barak's cowardly failure to lead. Her leadership had already been established before she received Barak's faith-filled request. Her established record of godly leadership is the reason he requested her partnership.

> "The prose and poem of Judges 4 and 5 . . . reveal that Deborah could not only prophecy, arouse, rule and fight, but also write . . . This song of praise, found in Judges 5, magnifies the Lord as being the One who enabled Israel's leaders to conquer their enemies. Out of the contest and conquest came the moral purification of the nation, and the inspiring genius of it was a woman daring and dynamic in the leadership of her nation. No character in the Old Testament stands out in bolder relief than Deborah—prophetess, ruler, warrior and poetess."[331]

Her leadership competence is further revealed in that after the military victory, she effectively ruled the otherwise recalcitrant nation and preserved

---

[330] "In those days Israel had no king; everyone did as he saw fit" (Judg. 21:25).

[331] *"All the women of the Bible: Deborah No. 2,"* Bible Gateway, https://www.biblegateway.com/resources/all-women-bible/Deborah-No-2

their peace and independence for forty years—an astonishing record in the time of the judges. She stands out among the heroes of Israel as one of the very few concerning whom not even a breath of criticism is recorded.

Deborah is such a powerful, biblical illustration of a female teacher and authoritative leader over God's people that the typical complementarian understanding that 1 Timothy 2:12 prohibits women from those roles is thereby *rendered strongly suspect and undermined.* If this understanding of the story of Deborah is correct, it seems impossible to view it as anything other than an exceedingly troublesome contradiction between two Scripture passages for those holding to the complementarian interpretation of 1 Timothy 2:12. On the other hand, the more accurate understanding of 1 Timothy 2 detailed earlier confirms the harmony and consistency of these two egalitarian-affirming passages.

Deborah joins a lengthy list of famous and effective women who governed nations. For example:

> Catherine the Great brought Russia out of feudalism. Joan of Arc united the dispirited troops of France, pulling along a frightened crown prince into battle and victory. In the sixteenth century, Queen Elizabeth I managed to end the bloodbath of religious persecution within England while keeping powerful enemies at bay. Her long reign allowed for a golden age of new ideas and exploration . . . The most populous democracy on earth, India, was led by Indira Gandhi for fourteen years. Golda Meir took charge in the crucial days following Israel's rebirth as a nation. Margaret Thatcher, along with Ronald Reagan, saw victory in the cold war."[332]

Female Leaders at the Very Top

While they don't necessarily have bearing on the subject of gender roles in the Scriptures, it is very interesting to note the Bible's references, without the slightest condemnation, to two female rulers of major Gentile kingdoms:

---

[332] Cunningham, Hamilton, and Rogers, *Why Not Women*, Kindle Loc 783.

the Queen of Sheba (1 Kings 10:1–3; 2 Chron. 9:1–12) and Candice, Queen of Ethiopia (Acts 8:27). With regard to the former, not only is the Queen of Sheba presented in a very positive light in the Old Testament account of her encounter with Solomon seeking to confirm and benefit from his wisdom, but also is given an exalted appraisal by Jesus for her exemplary spiritual passion (Matt. 12:42 and Luke 11:31). Jesus holds her up as a model to emulate and a standard against which others will be judged, NOT as a perversion of God's order for the genders upended by an inappropriate power grab or conceded because of the failure of men to step up to lead.

Women Teachers in the New Testament

More importantly for the church gender debate, the New Testament affirms women teaching men when it describes female prophets such as Anna (Luke 2:36ff) and Philip's four daughters (Acts 21:9). In neither case is there any indication that their prophetic ministry was limited to women and children. Regarding Anna Acts 2:38 indicates that "she gave thanks to God and spoke about the child to all who were looking forward to the redemption of Jerusalem." Would anyone actually argue that only women and children "were eagerly looking forward to the redemption of Jerusalem"? Obviously, her prophetic utterance in a very public setting (the Jerusalem Temple) included men.

Acts 2:17 (quoting Joel 2:28ff) asserts that "all flesh" including "daughters" and "women" would prophesy in the last days as a sign of the new age of the Spirit. We live in that age. Again, this female prophetic ministry was to be conducted without any gender restrictions as to their audiences. Similarly, Paul assumed women would prophesy in the Corinthian church (1 Cor. 11:5).

Included among the women who authored portions of the inspired Scriptures (thereby teaching every succeeding generation of male Scripture readers) would be Elizabeth and Mary (Luke 1). Others God used in special teaching roles were Mary who delivered an unforgettable prophetic object lesson (John 12:1–8) and the women who were the first witnesses and preachers of Jesus' resurrection (Matt. 28:1–18; Mark 16:1–10; Luke 24:1–10; John 20:1–18). From the time that Jesus was in Mary's womb (Elizabeth) to when He walked away from His empty tomb (Mary Magdalene), women were responsible for teaching their contemporaries and the church throughout history the theological significance and importance of those momentous events.

But Only Men Were Apostles . . . Or Were They?

Some complementarians find significance in the fact that Jesus called twelve men and no women to be His apostles. N.T. Wright weighs in on the subject:

> "Among the many things that need to be said about the gospels is that we gain nothing by ignoring the fact that Jesus chose twelve male apostles. There were no doubt all kinds of reasons for this within both the symbolic world in which he was operating and the practical and cultural world within which they would have to live and work. But every time this point is made—and in my experience, it is made quite frequently—we have to comment on how interesting it is that there comes a time in the story when the disciples all forsake Jesus and run away; and at that point, long before the rehabilitation of Peter and the others, it is the women who come first to the tomb, who are the first to see the risen Jesus, and are the first to be entrusted with the news that he has been raised from the dead. This is of incalculable significance. Mary Magdalene and the others are the apostles to the apostles. We should not be surprised that Paul calls a woman named Junia an apostle in Romans 16.7. If an apostle is a witness to the resurrection, there were women who deserved that title before any of the men."[333]

The initial twelve leaders of Jesus' new covenant community paralleled the twelve male patriarchs of God's old covenant community and hence were males. They were the foundation on which the new community was built (Eph. 2:20). More importantly, given the pervasive patriarchy of the

---

[333] Wright, *"Women's Service in the Church"*

first century, it should not be surprising that Jesus' first apostles needed to be males. To choose otherwise would almost certainly have been a great hindrance to the initial spread of the Gospel among both Jews and Gentiles. Like other temporary concessions to a culture that was oppressive, devaluing, and dismissive regarding women, starting with twelve male apostles was necessary and strategic. Even then, as the influence of the Gospel and Jesus' new humanity took hold and the church matured, female apostles were added.

Cunningham, Hamilton, and Rogers provide additional insight:

> Some have argued against women leaders in the church because Jesus called twelve men to be His disciples. They say that we should follow His example and appoint only male leaders in the church. If this is a valid argument, why narrow the qualification down to gender? Jesus also selected only Jews from one nation and one region—Galilee. Each of the ones He chose spoke Aramiac. Therefore, shouldn't we choose only leaders who are Aramiac-speaking Jews born in Galilee?"[334]

But if Jesus was inaugurating the kingdom values of the new creation, why didn't He place gender equality front and center by selecting some female apostles? Consider this:

> Jesus set a rather specific agenda for His three years of active ministry. He didn't confront all the other prejudices of His time either. He told His disciples that He had many other things to teach them, but they weren't ready yet [John 16:12]. He left the revolutionary step of taking the Gospel to the Gentiles first to Peter but primarily to Paul . . . Jesus did not confront slavery. He undercut its roots, but sadly it would take eighteen centuries before His followers were willing to see that.[335]

---

[334] Loren Cunningham, David Joel Hamilton, and Janice Rogers, *Why Not Women: A Fresh Look at Scripture on Women in Missions, Ministry, and Leadership* (Seattle: YWAM Publishing, 2000), Kindle, Loc 759, 767.

[335] Ibid., Loc 775.

Although none of Jesus' twelve apostles were female, the New Testament implied that women could be apostles. Ephesians 2:20 and 3:6 pair apostles and prophets together. As previously stated, women were prophets (Acts 2:17; 21:9; 1 Cor. 11:5). More specifically, Junia (Rom. 16:7) was a female apostle. While a few translations (NIV, NARSB) follow those Greek manuscripts that represent "Junias" as a male, other ancient manuscripts that designate "Junia" as a female are followed by equally respected translations (ESV, KJV, NRSV, NET). With regard to this translation dispute, N.T. Wright observes, "I note that there was a huge fuss in the translation and revision of the New International Version at the suggestion that Junia was a woman and not a single historical or exegetical argument was available to those who kept insisting, for obvious reasons, that she was Junias, a man."[336] Wright's unveiling of the apparently biased NIV translation process indicates that this might be yet another illustration of serious gender bias in one of the most popular and respected English Bible versions.

Scot McKnight is not at all flattering about why Junias should have been Junia and how he was finally changed to she:

> She was a woman whose name was changed to Junias because, so it was believed, the person was an apostle and an apostle can't be a woman. So some males changed the woman into a man and, presto, we got a man named Junias. The problem is that there is no evidence for a male name "Junias" in the 1st Century. The deed was done, and that's not our point: Junia remained Junias until, truth be told, the last quarter of the 20th Century when scholars realized the truth, admitted the mistaken history of interpretation, and acted on their convictions to restore the woman. Knocking off non-existent males is no moral problem, and raising a woman from the dead is a good thing. Junia is now inscribed in the best translations.[337]

---

[336] Wright, *Surprised by Scripture*, Kindle, 69.

[337] Scot McKnight, "Unveiling Paul's Women!" Jesus Creed (blog), 2/7/2018, http://www.patheos.com/blogs/jesuscreed/2018/02/07/unveiling-pauls-women/ #KYPJogUFWzWoCLR6.99

The emphasis of 1 Corinthians 12 is that ALL believers are given spiritual gifts (12:7, 11, 29ff) and are to exercise them in the church. 1 Corinthians 12:28 makes no gender distinction or restriction for those having the gifts of apostle, prophet, or teacher. Most Bible students view the apostolic office as the highest position in the church (under Christ), one which assumes authority over men and women, thus the evidence for female apostles is highly significant.

The Role of Women in Conjunction with Jesus' Ministry

Jesus' relationships and teaching were shocking in the first century due to His affirmation and elevation of women. Women played key roles in His itinerant ministry, death, resurrection, great commission, and church.

> The most striking thing about the role of women in the life and teaching of Jesus is the simple fact that they are there. Although the gospel texts contain no special sayings repudiating the view of the day about women, their uniform testimony to the presence of women among the followers of Jesus and to his serious teaching of them constitutes a break with tradition which has been described as being "without precedent in [then] contemporary Judaism" ... As Schreiner says, Jesus treated women with dignity and respect and he elevated them in a world where they were often mistreated." Hurley writes that Jesus did not perceive women "primarily in terms of their sex, age or marital status; he seems to have considered them in terms of their relation (or lack of one) to God."[338]

A group of women constantly traveled with Jesus and His disciples during His public ministry.

---

[338] *"Women in the Ministry of Jesus,"* Grace Communion International (2005), https://www.gci.org/church/ministry/women6b

Luke tells us that several women who had been healed helped support Jesus "out of their own means" (Luke 8:3). These included Joanna the wife of Cuza, the manager of Herod's household; Susanna; and many others. Although they were probably involved in meal preparation, Luke indicates a very significant role they played was to help to pay the bills . . . Although Christ worked with the cultural traditions of the first century, he ignored the limitations that had been placed on women by their culture. Women were free to follow him and to take part in his ministry to the world . . . Jesus welcomed women among his traveling coterie, allowing them to make the same radical commitment in following him that the Twelve did . . . That married women would be traveling with Jesus' group is striking indeed. Jesus expected men and women to mix freely.[339]

Luke 10:1–17 describes the time when Jesus sent seventy-two advance agents into every town where He was about to travel. Their ministry included kingdom proclamation and the healing of the sick. It must be gender bias behind the common assumption that these were all men, because nothing in the text requires that conclusion. Only two chapters earlier (Luke 8:3) it was mentioned that *"many"* women were among Jesus' traveling band of disciples. It seems safe to assume that they were included among the seventy-two.

A New Testament Yentl

Luke 10 also gives us the astonishing story about Martha and Mary. N.T. Wright observes:

Most of us grew up with the line that Martha was the active type and Mary the passive or contemplative type, and that Jesus is simply affirming the importance of both and even the priority of devotion to him. That devotion is undoubtedly part of the importance of the story, but far more obvious to

---

[339] Ibid.

any first century reader, and to many readers in Turkey, the Middle East and many other parts of the world to this day would be the fact that Mary was sitting at Jesus' feet *within the male part of the house* rather than being kept in the back rooms with the other women. This, I am pretty sure, is what really bothered Martha; no doubt she was cross at being left to do all the work, but the real problem behind that was that Mary had cut clean across one of the most basic social conventions. It is as though, in today's world, you were to invite me to stay in your house and, when it came to bedtime, I was to put up a camp bed in your bedroom. We have our own clear but unstated rules about whose space is which and so did they. And Mary has just flouted them. *And Jesus declares that she is right to do so.* She is "sitting at his feet"; a phrase which doesn't mean what it would mean today, the adoring student gazing up in admiration and love at the wonderful teacher. As is clear from the use of the phrase elsewhere in the NT (for instance, Paul with Gamaliel), to sit at the teacher's feet is a way of saying you are being a *student*, picking up the teacher's wisdom and learning; and in that very practical world you wouldn't do this just for the sake of informing your own mind and heart, but in order to be a teacher, a rabbi, yourself. Like much in the gospels, this story is left cryptic as far as we at least are concerned, but I doubt if any first-century reader would have missed the point.[340]

I remember a time when Gloria and I had attended a beautiful funeral at a Jewish synagogue and accompanied the family to their home afterward. In the midst of sharing memories, eating together, etc., the time was interrupted for a traditional Jewish liturgy related to the death. In our ignorance, Gloria and I thought nothing of standing together in the living room for the ceremony until a lady very discretely invited Gloria to the other room where all the ladies were gathered separate from the men. I was given a yarmulke to wear as I joined in the liturgy with the other men. The gender separation that day

---

[340] Wright, "Women's Service in the Church."

reminded us how shocking Jesus' inclusion of Mary with His male disciples must have been.

Barbara Streisand's lead role in the award-winning 1983 movie Yentl provides an excellent illustration of how offensive Mary's bold move must've been. Yentl is the story of "the odyssey of an Ashkenazi Jewish girl in Poland who decides to dress and live like a man so that she can receive an education in Talmudic Law after her father dies."[341] Mary's inserting herself into the men's club of rabbinical disciples who learned at Jesus' feet would have been at least as scandalous as Yentl's exposed subversive efforts—probably more so, yet Jesus defended and commended her: "only one thing is needed. Mary has chosen what is better, and it will not be taken away from her" (Luke 10:42).

An Unlikely Female Evangelist

Many Christians' familiarity with the well-known story of Jesus and the woman at the well probably mutes the shock factor of Jesus' strategic interaction with a woman. She was a five-times divorced woman, a currently immoral woman (in our culture she would doubtless have been labeled with some crude descriptors such as "slut" or "whore"), and in that culture, even more objectionable, she was a *Samaritan* woman. Jesus' appalling violation of cultural and Jewish norms was not lost on His disciples though they apparently sensed that they should keep their mouths shut and not question Him: "Just then His disciples returned and were surprised to find Him talking with a woman. But no one asked, 'What do you want?' or 'Why are you talking with her?'" (John 4:27). Note that the most troubling thing for the disciples regarding Jesus' interaction was not her ethnicity, as outrageous as that was, but rather was her gender. Jesus' identification with the oppressed, the outcasts, and the marginalized characterized His ministry, frequently with women.

Not only did Jesus engage this unlikely, soon-to-be-disciple in a deep theological interaction that included numerous remarkable doctrinal and eschatological revelations, He chose to give to her the clearest statement of His Messianic identity in John's Gospel: "The woman said, 'I know that Messiah

---

[341] *Yentl (film)*, Wikipedia, https://en.wikipedia.org/wiki/Yentl_(film)

(called Christ) is coming. When He comes, he will explain everything to us.' Then Jesus declared, 'I who speak to you am He'" (John 4:25, 26). She has been called Jesus' "first evangelist" because of her compelling witness and testimony that was key in teaching a number of local men about Jesus and in turning a significant number of people in her town to faith in Christ. Her sermon/testimony identified Jesus as the "Savior of the world" (John 4:42). No one had heretofore uttered that astonishing description of Jesus' identity and mission. Her role in leading a community to Christ and teaching them about Him is hard to reconcile with a belief that women are prohibited from teaching or exercising spiritual leadership over men. Jesus certainly acted like an egalitarian! Could this astonishing conversion of an entire community be replicated again and again today if women were unleashed for spiritual leadership? How often has this potential been stifled by complementarian bias?

Did Jesus violate God's order for the genders? Should He have found a Samaritan man instead so that His message could be delivered by a male? After all, the recipients certainly included men,[342] not just women and children. Of course not! Jesus knew exactly what He was doing. The meeting with the Samaritan woman was providentially directed and His decision to draw her into a deep theological discussion and equip her for an evangelistic mission was strategic on so many levels. It could not be more obvious that Jesus choose her because of who she was, not because a man wasn't available to preach His message to the Samaritan town.

Other New Testament Examples

It is even more startling that women were the first witnesses and proclaimers of Jesus' resurrection—the *first ambassadors of the inauguration of the new age* (Matt. 28:1–18; Mark 16:1–10; Luke 24:1–10; John 20:1–18). Some even suggest that Mary, as the first to believe in the resurrection, was the "first Christian" as well as the "first evangelist"[343]—spreading the ultimate Good News of Jesus' glorious resurrection. In that culture, women

---

[342] In John 4:28 "people" is ἀνθρώποις (*anthropois*) which means human beings, but sometimes designates men or husbands.

[343] A title some Bible teachers have also assigned to the woman at the well (John 4).

were often viewed as so inferior to men that they were not allowed to testify in court. Their testimony was considered unreliable. Yet Jesus chose to make them the first witnesses of post-creation history's most important event and those women's first audience was men—the about-to-be-founders and leaders of Jesus' church.

Jesus constantly violated gender norms in His ministry and practice with regard to women. His *first Gentile convert* was a woman who debated with Him and *won* (Matt. 15:21ff). Her concise teaching impressed Jesus' followers sufficiently to be remembered for inclusion in the Scriptures. Jesus allowed a woman to touch Him in public (Mark 5:25), another to kiss His feet (Luke 7:36ff), and yet another to anoint His head and feet and dry them with her hair (John 12:1ff). This chaste but shocking familiarity and startling intimate physical contact with women produced strong criticism of Jesus. The last-mentioned incident, Mary's anointing of Jesus' feet, was a defining moment in Judas' decision to betray Jesus. Jesus publicly humiliated him, one of the "Twelve," in favor of a woman (John 12:4ff; Mark 14:6–10).

Women played both lead and supporting roles in many of Jesus' parables. They held a prominent place in many of His "sermon illustrations."

1 Corinthians 7:32ff indicates that both genders could choose singleness over marriage in order to pursue *full time* ministry. This should not be surprising since a group of women made the same sacrifices as the twelve apostles in leaving everything to be discipled by and to minister to and with Jesus 24/7 during His itinerate mission (Luke 8:1–3).

Remember that all of the spiritual gifts to be used in the church including apostle, prophet, pastor, teacher, evangelist, administration, leadership, or governing (1 Cor. 12:28–31; 14:1, 26; Rom. 12:6–9; Eph. 4:11) were given to believers without any stated gender restriction or limitation. Stackhouse observes, "It is intriguing, however, and I think suggestive, that Paul's teaching about gifts and roles in the church is never sorted into gender-specific categories . . . I realize that Paul says that an elder is to be 'the husband of one wife' [1 Tim 3:2 NASB], but surely his point is faithful monogamy, and not the sex of the elder . . . Pressing this verse to mean that elders *must* be male would, by the same extreme logic, rule out single men as elders, including widowers who had been elders for years."[344]

---

[344] Stackhouse, *Partners In Christ*, 69.

However, there are those who claim that 1 Timothy 3:2 *requires* that pastors must be males, the husbands of one wife. If they insist on that literalistic understanding, then pastors cannot be single. They *must* be married (to one wife). Therefore, not only are single, widowed, or remarried men excluded, but also neither Jesus ("the Chief Shepherd," 1 Peter 5:4) nor Paul (an Apostle, a higher office than elder) could have met the qualification. Further, someone might legitimately ask, "Is that one wife *at a time?*" In that case, a pastor could have been through any number of divorces (including those for which he was the guilty party) and remarriages as long as he only had one wife at a time. Others might suggest that as long as a pastor continued to be married to one wife, he would not be disqualified for having girlfriends or mistresses on the side. He is, after all, still "the husband of one wife." These are of course ludicrous suggestions, but they expose the error of a flawed literalistic interpretation of "the husband of one wife" as eliminating "the wife of one husband" (a female) from pastoral service.

The fact is that Paul's leadership requirement is about CHARACTER not MARITAL STATUS or GENDER. A pastor must be "a one-woman man" (the literal translation of the Greek: μιᾶς γυναικὸς ἄνδρα), in other words, the kind of man who is sexually pure and, if married, faithful to his wife. He cannot be a flirt, a womanizer, a fornicator or adulterer. The same would be true of a lady pastor. This understanding of the phrase is confirmed by the comparative usage referring to a widow worthy of being put into the church budget (1 Tim. 5:9). She must be one who "has been faithful to her husband" (literally, "a one-man woman")—identically the same three Greek words only with the genders reversed (ἑνὸς ἀνδρὸς γυνή). The phrase does not mean that she is married. She is not. She is a widow. The issue in both phrases is not about gender or marital status but has to do with their *moral character*. They are a faithful person; pure in their relationships.

Additionally, 1 Timothy 3:11 could as well be understood as a reference to female deacons and elders rather than to "wives" which is a possibly legitimate translation, but less so than *"women"* (see additional discussion of this below). That would absolutely mean that women can be pastors. It is noteworthy that 1 Peter 5:13 and 2 John 1 may also refer to female elders/pastors.

Esteemed biblical scholar, Leon Morris, affirms agreement with John Stott's assessment of giftedness and the ordination of women:

> "If God endows women with spiritual gifts (which he does), and thereby calls them to exercise their gifts for the common good (which he does), the Church must recognize God's gifts and calling, must make appropriate spheres of service available to women, and should 'ordain' (that is commission and authorize) them to exercise their God-given ministry, at best in team situations. Our Christian doctrines of Creation and Redemption tell us that God wants his gifted people to be fulfilled, not frustrated, and his church to be enriched by their service."[345]

It is important to note that in numerous Pauline passages about teaching, there is absolutely no gender restriction, for example in 1 Corinthians 14:26, Colossians 3:16, and Hebrews 5:12 (if Paul was the author of Hebrews). When Paul commanded Timothy, "the things you have heard me say in the presence of many witnesses entrust to reliable men who will also be qualified to teach others" (2 Tim. 2:2), he used the gender inclusive Greek ἀνθρώποις (*anthrōpos*) which identifies a human being rather than ἀνήρ (*anēr*) which is an adult male. Rather than this passage providing *slam dunk* evidence for restricting teaching roles to males, Paul's word choice leaves the door wide open to both genders being "qualified to teach others."

Significantly, Paul's letters include at least eighteen references to women, a number of whom were clearly involved in church ministry and/ or leadership. For example, Romans 16, rather than being a boring recitation of the unfamiliar names of people Paul greeted in the Roman church whose stories are mostly inaccessible to us, gives a stunning snapshot of life in the first century church. It cannot be an accident that approximately one third of the names mentioned are of women whose roles in the church were diverse including apostle and deacon. Paul's obvious intent to honor these women in the church was a shocking departure from the cultural norms.

---

[345] Marg Mowczko, *"Leon Morris on 'Head' (kephale) in the New Testament,"* Marg Mowczko (1-/23/2013), http://newlife.id.au/equality-and-gender-issues/leon-morris-on-head-in-the-new-testament/

The low value of the female in the society was also reflected in the widespread practices of infanticide and abandonment of female babies. It was very common to raise only one daughter per family, which, together with maternal mortality, contributed to a shortage of women during the Roman Empire that created a population crisis. Therefore, when Paul gives honor and recognition to so many female members of the Roman church in Romans 16, it stands out as a significant deviation from the cultural practice and ideal.[346]

Women in Leadership over Men

Phoebe was a *deacon* (διάκονον/*diaconon*) and a great *leader* (προστάτις/ *prostatis*—literally: "one who stands in front/at the head of") in the church at Cenchrea (Rom. 16:1, 2).[347] Most translations call her *a great help, helper, or benefactor* rather than *a great leader*. It is difficult to not see this watered-down (deceptive?) translation as another indication of bias by the translators.

Though disputed, many Bible students believe that Paul specifically endorsed women as deacons or even as overseers in 1 Timothy 3:11 where the verse is better translated as, "In the same way women are to be worthy of respect." This translation is preferable to "their wives," which is the translation in versions such as the NIV, ESV, and KJV. A number of other versions do translate *gunaikas* as "women" (e.g. ASV, RSV, NASB, NRV, Young's Literal, New Century) rather than as "their wives." The word "their" is not in the original Greek. Some versions add "their" not as a translation but as an interpretation. The question could certainly be asked if the interpretive choice "their wives" reflects gender bias because it *forces* the reader who doesn't have access to the original Greek to assume the passage is talking about deacons' wives, thereby excluding any consideration of the possibility or probability that it may instead be talking about the qualifications of women for service as deacons and overseers (pastors/elders).

---

346 Westfall, *Paul and Gender,* 18, 19.

347 Elizabeth A. McCabe, *"A Reexamination of Phoebe:"* Society of Biblical Literature, https://www.sbl-site.org/publications/article.aspx?articleId=830

Further, that Paul in verse 11 is talking about *female* leaders rather than *wives* of male leaders, is supported by the primary meaning of *gunaikas* which most often refers to an adult woman as distinct from a man. While it is occasionally translated "wife," that is not its primary meaning. Further, comparing the identical Greek construction in verse 11 "likewise women" [γυναῖκας ὡσαύτως/*gunaikas hōsautōs*] and in verse 8 "likewise deacons" [Διακόνους ὡσαύτως/*Diaconas hōsautōs*] reveals that Paul could as easily be talking about women as overseers (bishops) as about women as deacons. If this alternative translation is correct, it is devastating for the complementarian view.

In Romans 16, women (Priscilla, Mary, Tryphena, Tryphosa, and Persis) were identified as "fellow workers," some of whom hosted (and perhaps led) churches in their homes (Rom. 16:5; Acts 12; 1 Cor. 16:19).

In the New Testament Priscilla was frequently named before her husband, Aquila (Rom. 16:3; 2 Tim. 4:19; Acts 18:18ff). This most probably indicated her preeminence over her husband as a teacher and leader. Acts 18:24–26 reveals Priscilla's role in teaching and mentoring a prominent male preacher, Apollos. Her role stands against those complementarians who insist that women should not teach in seminaries which train men, an office that they believe to be limited to males. Clearly Priscilla was not under the kind of restrictions complementarians assert from 1 Timothy 2:11–14.

Euodia and Syntyche, infamous for Paul's admonition to these apparently feuding females in the Philippian church (Phil. 4:2–3), are nevertheless referenced with honor as having "contended at my side in the cause of the gospel" and as being among Paul's "fellow workers." It would be very difficult to understand Paul's descriptors for these women as describing a secondary or less significant role in ministry. The two words portray partners working beside him, not subordinates working under or below him.

Paul's inclusion of Apphia as a recipient of his letter to Philemon leaves us wishing for more information: "Paul, a prisoner of Christ Jesus, and Timothy our brother, To Philemon our dear friend and fellow worker, to Apphia our sister, to Archippus our fellow soldier and to the church that meets in your home" (Philem. 1, 2). It seems probable that Apphia played a special role in the house church. The church is also specified as a recipient of the letter. Obviously, the letter was intended to be read aloud in a church gathering. The possible reasons for the culturally unusual reference to Apphia include that she was: (1) the wife of Philemon or Archippus, (2) the patron of the church perhaps as the owner of the house where it met, or (3) a minister of the church (much like Phoebe in Rom. 16). Mowczko argues persuasively for the possibility if not probability of Apphia's role as being one of official church leadership: "Rather than being the wife of Philemon, Apphia may have been a ministry partner. Philemon and Apphia (or was it Apphia and Archippus?) may have been missionaries, ministering in Colossae as Paul's emissaries.[348] Mowczko asserts that

> A few women involved in Pauline missions are mentioned in ministry partnerships with men, but many more are mentioned without any reference to a male relative: Phoebe, Euodia, Syntyche, Tryphaena and Tryphosa, Mary of Rome, Persis, Nympha, etc. It is not clear if these women were widows, single, or married. Nevertheless, they were active in ministry and prominent in their churches without, or despite, a husband. Apphia is likewise prominent and identified as an individual. She was certainly known well enough by Paul to be mentioned by him in his letter . . .

> Ross Kraemer suggests that Paul explicitly names Apphia because he sought her consent to his request concerning Philemon and Onesimus. That is, Paul "carbon-copied" Apphia into his letter to Philemon so that she would be aware of the situation Paul was writing about. However, the house church is also greeted in the letter. The letter would have been read aloud in a church gathering, and *everyone* would have been made aware of Paul's wishes concerning Onesimus.

> It seems that Paul's greeting to Apphia is some kind of respectful 'hat tip' to her. Just like Philemon and Archippus,

---

[348] Marg Mowczko, *"Apphia of Colossae; Philemon's Wife or another Phoebe,"* New Life: http://newlife.id.au/equality-and-gender-issues/apphia/

who are acknowledged alongside her, she was a minister in the church at Colossae, and quite possibly its patron.[349]

A New Testament Church with a Lady Pastor?

An often overlooked but another probable reference to a woman in church leadership is found in 2 John. John's second letter was addressed to "the chosen lady and her children" who, at the end of the short letter, was greeted by "the children of your chosen sister."[350] Identifying the unnamed lady (2 John 1), her sister (2 John 13), and both of their children, has not proven to be a simple task for interpreters. One suggests that the identity of this mystery woman is "baffling" and "impossible to settle."[351] Wescott asserts, "No interpretation can be accepted as satisfactory."[352] While John's paucity of details does make it challenging to make a 100% confident identification of the key players in 2 John, it seems obvious that gender bias has, for many interpreters, limited the *acceptable* options of possible identifications. What might seem to be an obvious possibility—that the letter is addressed to a female church pastor—is not even on most interpreters' radar screen of possible or tolerable options. This reminds me of someone who says that it is impossible to find their missing keys while refusing to hunt in the most obvious place they might have been lost.

Most Bible students argue that the reference was either to an individual female, metaphorically to the church at large, or to a particular congregation. Elwell and Yarbrough in their widely recognized introduction to the New Testament reference the "chosen sister" which, "some take to be a woman who

---

[349] Ibid.

[350] "The elder, To the chosen lady and her children, whom I love in the truth—and not I only, but also all who know the truth—because of the truth, which lives in us and will be with us forever ... The children of your chosen sister send their greetings" 2 John 1, 2, 13.

[351] Marvin R. Vincent, *Word Studies in the New Testament* (New York: Charles Scriber's Sons, 1887), Logos Bible Software, 2 John.

[352] Brooke Foss Wescott, *The Epistles of St John* (Grand Rapids: Wm. B. Eerdman's Publishing Company, 1966), 223.

allowed a church to meet in her house and others take to be a personification of a particular church."[353]

Those who prefer the interpretation that the "chosen lady" is a reference to the/a church often claim support in 1 Peter 5:13: "She who is in Babylon, chosen together with you, sends you her greetings, and so does my son Mark"—a passage that is commonly assumed to be an oblique reference to a church in a pagan environment.[354] Obviously not everyone agrees with that suggestion. Similarly, those who see the mystery lady of 2 John 1 as a personification of a church find a parallel reference to another church in the closing verse of 2 John (13), "The children of your chosen sister send their greetings."

In both references in 2 John the chosen ladies' children are understood to be the church members. In this lady-is-a-church view, the reference to some of her children walking in the truth is taken as a reference to the biblical obedience of the more consistent and mature church members. However, as will be pointed out below, rather than this supporting the lady personifying the church view, it complicates it. If the ladies are two churches and the children are two churches, the doubled reference seems redundant, awkward, and confusing. Some might attempt to offset this awkwardness by suggesting that the ladies represent the churches as a whole, while the children refer to the individual members. This doesn't seem to help very much.

On the other hand, if the first lady is a prominent lady in the church and/ or its *elder/leader* and her children are either her literal children or, more likely, church members, and if the "children of your chosen sister" represent the members of another female-led congregation, the passage makes a great deal of sense. It would be as if I wrote to a pastor friend and said, "Dear Pastor Thomas and church members . . . the members of Pastor Rodriquez' church send their greetings." John uses the same term "children" to refer to young believers in his earlier letter (1 John 2:12, 13) so it would be consistent with that usage to view these children as new believers in the church. As in most churches, "some" of the members were walking in the truth while others needed more encouragements to love each other (2 John 5, 6) and to be warned about the prevalence of deceivers (2 John 7–11).

---

[353] Walter A. Elwell and Robert W. Yarbrough, *Encountering the New Testament* (Grand Rapids, Baker Books, 1998), 369.

[354] "Babylon" is often suggested to be a veiled reference to Rome.

Why Does John Leave Us Guessing?

In either case—an actual woman or a congregation—why the anonymity or camouflaged references? In response, note that John doesn't name himself either, calling himself simply "the elder" in the opening verse. The most common suggestion for these anonymous references to "the elder . . . the chosen lady . . . her children" seems to be that it was to protect the parties from the threat of persecution. This is often asserted with regard to 1 Peter 5:13 ("she who is in Babylon"). However, the persecution argument for the lady-is-a-church view doesn't seem appropriate in Peter's letter in light of the fact that in the same verse (1 Pt. 5:13), Mark is *named* as also present in *"Babylon"* along with the chosen lady ("She who is in Babylon, chosen together with you, sends you her greetings, and so does my son Mark)." If Peter shied away from identifying the church (or it's female leader) in "Babylon" because he feared persecution might result, wouldn't he have been at least as likely to protect his "son Mark"? Further, Mark's name set alongside and parallel to the lady in Babylon make it more likely to be a reference either to a prominent lady in the church, most likely the pastor.

Others argue that perhaps John was averse to unnecessarily elevating individual church leaders (compare the need to correct celebrityism in 1 Corinthians 3—a problem that also seems endemic in contemporary Christian culture). This would be consistent with John's obvious decision to not identify himself by name in His Gospel[355] or in any of his three New Testament letters as well as the total absence of any named individuals in the first two letters. His references in 3 John to Gaius and Diotrephes are exceptional. Out of 28 New Testament chapters written by John, only this one chapter names any parties among his recipients. Some might argue that as there was no need for John to identify himself as "the elder" even as the female pastors in 2 John were so well known that there was no need to give their name.

Other interpreters who disagree with the lady-is-the-church interpretation assert that "the chosen lady" was either an unnamed lady in the church or that

---

[355] The anonymous fourth Gospel is called "The Gospel of John" because of the universal tradition that he was its author. The only probable reference to himself in the entire book is the rather oblique reference to the "disciple Jesus loved" in John 21:20.

"elect lady" should be translated as a proper name—Kyra,[356] lady Electa,[357] or Electa Kyra. This view had support within the first century of church history. If she was a real lady in the church, then it follows that "some" of her physical children or more probably some of her church members were following Jesus ("walking in the truth") and others were not. However, the suggestion that "chosen lady" (verse 1) should be translated as a proper name is undermined by the recognition that "chosen sister" (verse 13) would receive the same treatment. But, how likely is that both, being sisters, would have the same name, "Electa"? It is more likely that the two women are individuals, who, like Rufus in Romans 16:13, are described as "chosen" (the same Greek word).

Mowczko makes further helpful insights:

> Many have assumed that 'chosen lady' is used as a metonym, or metaphor, for a congregation, and does not refer to an actual person. This is despite the fact that no congregation is referred to as a 'lady' (Greek: *kuria*) in the New Testament or in later writings. On the other hand, many women are addressed, or referred to, as *kuria* in ancient papyrus letters and documents that still survive today. *Kuria* is a term that was often used for a high-status woman. The masculine form of the same word, *kurios*, is often translated into English as 'lord' or 'master,' indicating the status associated with this term.
>
> While *kuria* occurs only twice in the New Testament, both times in 2 John, the word occurs in other Jewish and early Christian literature. For example, it is used in direct address by Isaac to his mother Sarah in the *Testament of Abraham* (circa 100 AD), and by Perpetua's brother and father to their sister and daughter, respectively, in the account of Perpetua's martyrdom (202 or 203 AD). It is

---

[356] Robert Jamieson, A.R. Fausset, and David Brown, *Commentary Critical and Explanatory of the Whole Bible*, (1871), Public Domain, Logos Bible Software, in loc, 2 John.

[357] Clement of Alexandria believed Electa was the lady's name. Clement was an early church father who was born in 150 A.D. and died in 215 A.D.

used by Hermas (a freed slave) when addressing his female former owner, Rhoda, in the *Shepherd of Hermas* (circa 100 AD). Furthermore, Hermas frequently calls a woman who appears to him in visions as *kuria*. In the *Acts of Paul and Thecla* (circa 150 AD), Thecla is referred to as *kuria*, or 'mistress,' in relation to the maidservants. *Kuria* also occurs several times in the Septuagint, the Greek translation of the Old Testament in use during the early church period (Gen. 16:4, 8, 9; 1 Kings 17:17; 2 Kings 5:3; Psalm 123:2; Prov. 30:23; and Isa. 24:2).

It is a common word in pagan writings, too. In a manual of Stoic ethical advice called *The Enchiridion* (135 AD), the Greek philosopher Epictetus writes that the title *kuria* was used by men trying to flatter young women. Clearly, *kuria* is not a rare or obscure word.

Sarah, Perpetua, Rhoda, Thecla, and the 'ladies' mentioned in the Septuagint, were high status women; some were in charge of their own households. The lady greeted in 2 John is also, most likely, a high-status woman and a householder.[358]

What seems most probable is that John's letter was addressed to a prominent, office-holding woman with authority who was clearly held in high regard by the Apostle and by all the believers—*"whom I love in the truth—and not I only, but also all who know the truth"* (2 John 1). Wuest suggests: "The word 'lady' is *kuria* (κυρια). It is the feminine form of *kurios* (κυριος), which means 'lord, master.'"[359] The translation of *kuria* as "lady" masks the inherent reference to her position as mistress (NOT a reference to someone having an illicit affair but <u>the feminine form of *"lord/master"*</u>—the feminine *kuria* compared to the masculine *kurios*). It could well be translated "her

---

[358] Marg Mowczko, *"The Elder and the Lady: a Look at the Language of 2 John,"* blog: Marg Mowczko (7/16, 2017, http://margmowczko.com/elder-lady-language-2-john/.

[359] Wuest, *Wuest's word studies from the Greek New Testament: for the English reader* (Grand Rapids: Eerdmans), Logos Bible Software, in loc, 2 John.

lordship," or "her ladyship"—an appropriate rendering, but hardly acceptable for complementarian eyes.

What is both interesting and very troubling is that almost no traditional commentators mention even the *possibility* that the chosen lady could have been a pastor or leader in the church. While more recent writers are raising that possibility, I have yet to discover a traditional commentary that even acknowledges the possibility, much less giving it serious consideration. It would seem that the idea that the chosen lady could be a pastor or house church leader isn't even worth imagining as a possible interpretation. Could this be the result of pervasive patriarchal bias whether conscious or subconscious? There is *nothing* in the text that would prohibit this understanding. In fact, the most straightforward reading, "her chosen lordship," affirms it. Is this an illustration of self-reinforcing and self-perpetuating protection of patriarchy? There seems to be an unrecognized acceptance of circular reasoning—"This could not refer to a lady pastor because the Bible never mentions a lady pastor." Someone should vehemently object, "Wait a minute! What if this is a reference to a lady pastor? Then the Bible does mention a lady pastor."[360] If someone came to this passage totally free of gender bias (an impossible scenario) is it really such a stretch to think that they might come up with the idea that the "chosen lady" could refer to a church leader? Perhaps the reason so many interpreters have mentioned how difficult it is to interpret the meaning of "chosen lady"[361] is because patriarchal bias eliminates consideration of what might be the most obvious meaning—a female leader of the church.

Mowczko reasons forcefully against the lady-as-a-church interpretation and in favor of the chosen lady being a *leader* in the church:

> Furthermore, John addressed his second letter to 'the chosen lady' *and* to 'her children'. If the 'chosen lady' represents a church, who then are the children? If the 'chosen lady' is a congregation and the children are a congregation, then

---

[360] Remember that earlier in this chapter other possible references to a woman as pastor were made.

[361] Wescott, *"The Epistles of St. John:"* "On the whole it is best to recognize that the problem of the address is insoluble with our present knowledge. It is not unlikely that it contains some allusion, intelligible under the original circumstances, to which we have lost the key. 224.

John is addressing the same group twice. This simply doesn't make any sense. John used singular pronouns in the Greek when addressing the lady directly (in 2 John 1:4, 5 twice, 13 twice). For instance, in verse 5, John speaks directly to the woman and says, 'Now I ask you (sg) lady . . . ' This does not sound at all as though John were addressing a congregation. However, at other times in this letter, John used plural pronouns when referring to the lady and to her children'. The children were the church. The lady' is not a metaphor for a church; she was the church's leader."

For the first couple of hundred years following the day of Pentecost, most Christian churches were house churches. We have ample and, I believe, irrefutable evidence that some of these churches were hosted and led by women. In the New Testament, there are several women mentioned who were hosts and leaders of house church leaders. It seems that John's second letter was written to such a woman. The simplest and most straightforward explanation of who the 'Chosen Lady' in 2 John 1:1 & 5 was, is that she was a host and leader of Christian house church whom John addressed directly at times in his second letter. The most straightforward explanation of who her 'children' were, is that they are members of her household and congregation. It is very unlikely that the chosen lady was simply a mother. It is also unlikely that she symbolized a church. I believe that the chosen lady was a female house church leader.[362]

Probable references to women who hosted and led house churches include Priscilla along with her husband Aquila (Acts 18:26; Rom. 16:3–5, etc.), possibly *Chloe* (1 Cor. 1:11), *Nympha* (Col. 4:15), *Apphia* (with Philemon and Archippus) (Philem. 1:2).

Thus, it seems evident that unless someone reads 2 John 1, 2 through biased, patriarchal lens, a straightforward exegesis of the text would,

---

[362] Mowczko, *"Who was the chosen lady in 2 John?"* New Life (1/29/2011): http://newlife. id.au/equality-and-gender-issues/the-chosen-lady-in-2-john/

at minimum, allow for understanding the "chosen lady" as a leader of a house church and her "children" as its members, as a viable, if not strongly preferable, interpretation of the passage.

Jesus' Tacit Approval of Women Teachers in the Early Church

Jesus' letter to the church at Thyatira in Revelation 2 provides an indirect argument that women were accepted for teaching roles in the first century church and that this had God's approval. Jesus' letters to the seven churches of Asia in Revelation 2, 3 are a window on the early church revealing both its strengths and weaknesses. Jesus' condemnation of the false teaching by "Jezebel" at Thyatira is revealing both by what He says and even more, by what He does NOT say. Jezebel was probably not her actual name but was rather a characterization based on the horribly evil Old Testament Jezebel, queen of Israel whose idolatrous influence on her husband, King Ahab, and on the nation, was devastating (1 Kings 16-21; 2 Kings 9).

Jesus' message to the church at Thyatira was:

> Nevertheless, I have this against you: You tolerate that woman Jezebel, who calls herself a prophetess. By her teaching she misleads my servants into sexual immorality and the eating of food sacrificed to idols. I have given her time to repent of her immorality, but she is unwilling. So I will cast her on a bed of suffering, and I will make those who commit adultery with her suffer intensely, unless they repent of her ways. I will strike her children dead. Then all the churches will know that I am he who searches hearts and minds, and I will repay each of you according to your deeds (Rev. 2:20–23).

What is essential to note is that Jesus did not condemn the church for allowing a woman to be a prophetess or to teach. He condemned the church for allowing a woman to teach doctrinal error.[363] The problem was not THAT a woman taught. The problem was WHAT she taught. There is not a breath of criticism for having a woman teacher, but rather for tolerating false teaching. If it was wrong for a woman to teach in the church, it seems that the condemnation would have appropriately focused on that prior wrong-doing, which in Thyatira then opened the door to her erroneous doctrine. But that is not what Jesus criticized. It was the false doctrine of the self-proclaimed prophetess, not her gender. What Jesus did and did not condemn is a tacit approval of having women teachers in the church.

Summary of Biblical Roles for Women in Ministry

Thus, we have concluded that there are no gender-based restrictions for the office/role of teacher, pastor, elder, or bishop in the New Testament. Any gender restrictions must be argued from silence or implication. On the contrary, for those with eyes to see, there is overwhelming evidence suggesting that in the New Testament church, women exercised all the spiritual gifts including teaching, leading, governing, leading, and prophesying, and that they filled every role and office in the church including elder and deacon.

In summary, among other roles, the Scriptures indisputably identify women serving God's people (both men and women) as prophets, judges, leaders, teachers, and deacons, and almost certainly also as apostles and overseers (the same office as elders and pastors).

These observations are confirmed by Christian art from the first and second centuries which depicts women performing various ministerial functions including administering the Lord's Supper, teaching, baptizing, and leading in public prayers. Early church council records and tombstone epitaphs in Rome substantiate the presence of female bishops in the early church.

---

[363] There may also be a subtle implication that Jezebel was self-appointed to a teaching role (what 1 Tim. 2:12 disallowed) and that the church failed to remove her, in part because she commandeered the role, but more because of the false teaching she promulgated.

Just Imagine

What might happen if these scores of Bible stories and references to women leading and teaching God's people were celebrated in the church rather than neglected, minimized, or explained away? Tara Beth Leach remembers when, at sixteen years of age, she began reading her Bible cover to cover. "I can remember reading the stories of Deborah and Esther, and feeling emboldened to be a fearless female leader . . . When I arrived at John's Gospel and read about Mary being emboldened to proclaim the resurrection, my imagination was expanded. As a young woman reading that passage, I quickly shot up from my bed and began to pace around my room in excitement. I shouted. I prayed. I thanked God. And I began to see differently my role in God's kingdom."[364]

That exposes a significant problem. The gender-based ministry restrictions imposed on Jesus' church due to a faulty complementarian interpretation of the Bible have stifled the imagination of the church as to what could be. *We will not do what we cannot imagine*:

> Because women rarely teach, preach, and lead from up front, our imaginations will continue to be limited. When women don't teach, preach, and lead, we will continue to put them into the teal boxes of our churches: neat, quiet, and safe. Young girls sitting in the pews will never come out of their boxes, get their hands dirty, and boldly go where few have gone in their generation. Something happens to our imaginations when women preach: women in the pews come alive. When women teach, preach, and lead, women in the pews begin to open their confined imaginations and undo the narrative that their role exists in a perfectly fitted box . . . When women aren't on mission alongside of their brothers, the imagination of the bride of Christ is hindered—it can imagine only half of what it might be.

---

[364] Leach, *Emboldened: A Vision for Empowering Women in Ministry,* 113, 114.

The point is this: Women teaching, preaching, and leading today are not only important for the present church but also for the future church, for our sons and daughters. By encouraging our sons' and daughter's imagination now, we will see more men and women rise up together for the sake of the gospel. When women teach, lead, minister, evangelize, and preach, there is a ground swell, an uprising, Barriers are torn down, and the once-silenced mouths are opened. When women teach, led, minister, evangelize, and preach, the church's imagination is expanded and *made new.* Not only this, but we participate in something much bigger than ourselves. We stand in the middle of the grandest story ever told—that is, the story of God.

When women are seen leading, praying publicly, or doing things that they aren't often seen doing, other women are pushed to think critically about those tough passages. They are pushed to consider their own gifts. They are forced to ponder a false narrative they have embraced for far too long—that they are somehow less capable or less gifted than men in the kingdom of God.[365]

As we stand on the sidelines of Scripture watching the parade of amazing women who accomplished great things for God and made a difference in their nations, churches, and the world, let's allow our imaginations to be rekindled as to what is possible when God's vision for men and women serving side-by-side is embraced rather than rejected or stifled.

FOR DISCUSSION

(1) As you read chapter 11, were you surprised by how many women were involved in ministry and leadership throughout the Bible? Why or why not? How well do you think most churches do in teaching

---

[365] Ibid., 110–12.

about women in the Bible? What would you like to see happen in this regard?

(2) Describe the relationship between Deborah and Barak. Do you think God allowed Deborah to lead because Barak lacked the courage or faith to do so? What in the Bible supports or refutes that idea? Why do you think so many teachers and preachers advance the idea that Deborah had to step up because Barak was cowardly or unwilling?

(3) Name as many women as you can whom the Bible identifies as prophets, teachers, or church leaders? What does this suggest about God's plan for women in ministry?

(4) Why was the story about Mary and Martha so shocking? What does it teach us about God's plan for women?

(5) Describe what Jesus said and did regarding women during His three-year ministry. Why was this shocking in the first century culture? Based on what you see about Jesus' relationship to women in the Gospels, what do you think He would do about the gender roles issue in the church today?

(6) What are some specific things you could do to help your church to inspire and empower contemporary Miriams, Deborahs, Huldahs, Marys, Priscillas, Phoebes, and Junias? What do you see as the biggest hindrances to this happening?

(7) Spend time praying that the biblical pattern of women in positions of ministry, teaching, and leadership will be realized in Jesus' global church today.

12

Where Do We Go from Here?

If you have made it to this point I must express my deep thanks to you for joining me on this journey to discover what the Bible says about gender roles. Your perseverance is most likely an indication of your desire to please God and to discover what the Bible really says about this tremendously important subject. Thank you for considering my efforts to expose what I have come to believe the Bible actually teaches about gender roles in the church.

How Important Is the Outcome of This Debate?

God designed people to walk, run, and function on two legs. What happens if only one leg is present or functional? Although it is difficult and limits mobility, balance, and speed, it is possible to stand, pivot, hop, or jump on one leg. But the difference between operating on one leg compared to two is almost incalculable. Try bending your left leg up and tying it there so you can only use your right leg. Now attempt to walk or hurry across the room, or to bend over to pick something up, or to sit down or to get up from a chair using only one leg. Vacuum the rug. Carry a laundry basket down to the basement. Can you safely navigate going down the stairs? How about back up? Gather your garbage and take it out to your dumpster. Mow the lawn. Shovel the driveway. Hop out to your car and drive to the grocery store (imagine if it were a "stick shift"). Push a cart around the store and fill it with food. Carry the bags out to your car and put them in the trunk. After you carry the groceries into your house and put them away, attempt a few minutes of basketball in the driveway with your grandchildren, or perhaps take them bowling. How important is it to have two legs instead of just one?

What if men and women are like two "legs" God designed to mobilize the "Body of Christ," the church? What if the complementarian belief has in effect tied one "leg" up so the church hops along on only one? What would it mean for the effectiveness of the church to set the restricted leg free to mobilize both "legs"?

That's why I wrote this book!

In this final chapter, I hope to first briefly review, **where we have been**—to concisely cite the main points of this journey chapter by chapter—and then to give some practical answers to the question: **"Where do we go from here?"** We'll consider practical steps forward regardless of whether the reader agrees or disagrees with my conclusions about gender roles in the church.

Where We Have Been

This book tells the story of my personal journey—my lengthy, diligent, in-depth investigation into what the Bible actually says about gender roles. It describes what brought me to acknowledge that for over forty-five years of personal Bible study and of Bible-based preaching and teaching, I had *misunderstood and misrepresented* what the Bible actually teaches about gender roles in the church. To all whom I misled, **I apologize. I am sorry. Please forgive me!** As I type those words, I feel the heaviness of knowing I cannot undo what was lost or recreate what might have been if I had spent those years teaching and implementing the biblical truths that now seem so obvious. I know that God has forgiven me, but perhaps this book is for me somewhat of a redemptive process. Please don't let your journey be as slow as mine.

So where has this journey taken us?

The **opening chapter** described the years of intensifying study that ultimately led to my admission I had been wrong., and to my embracing what I now believe is the correct understanding of the Scriptures on this crucially important topic.

We were reminded that throughout the centuries of mostly wonderful church history, there were some terrible and shameful times when, with regard to very important issues, segments of the church or even most of the leadership of the church were horribly wrong. **Chapter 2** described two illustrations of very serious and consequential errors in church belief: (1) the time of unwavering adherence to a geocentric understanding of the universe and (2) the time when the horrific institution of slavery engulfed a huge part of the USA supported by large segments of the church and of pastors. Tragically, many who challenged those errors were criticized, slandered, ostracized, persecuted, or even martyred. Deep disagreement over slavery baptized the nation in ugly division and in the horrors of a bloody war which pitted brother against brother. Sadly, large parts of the church (mostly in the South) mirrored the same division as the nation and helped to inflame the dark passions which ignited the Civil War—a war that resulted in well over half a million deaths in the efforts to end the inhuman enslavement of millions of people made in God's image (more than 12% of the nation's population). We were reminded that "conviction" must be held accountable to a humble and teachable spirit. We must know our vulnerability to error and to deception whether by others by self.   We must never forget that the Bible has often, perhaps sincerely, been misused to perpetuate horrific evil, such as slavery. Those who do not learn from the past are destined to repeat it.

We learned in **chapter 3** that God created man and woman in His own image individually and distinct from gender. The account in Genesis 1 and 2 stressed again and again the identity, equality, oneness, mutuality, and partnership of male and female with no gender-based hierarchy in their relationship. Complementarians claim that God's intent and design for males to lead and females to follow are evidenced (1) by the order of creation, (2) by Eve's designated role as *"helper,"* and (3) by Adam's naming of Eve. These claims were shown to be completely unsubstantiated and a misrepresentation of the biblical text. The biblical creation account gives not a shred of support to the domination of men and the subjugation of women.

Chatper 4 revealed that rather than male authority being God's plan from the beginning, Genesis 3 clearly indicates that the rule of men over women is a tragic and evil consequence of sin's entrance into God's previously perfect world. Men ruling women was not God's intention but is Satan's corruption of the Creator's design. Male rulership is listed as one of a number of horrible results of sin, including painful childbirth; the cursed and thorn-infested ground; the necessity of sweaty, painful human toil; and death returning the body to dust. None of these express God's desire or plan but rather are the horrific legacy of human sin. We are no more called to make husbands rule over their wives than we are called on to make snakes crawl on their bellies, women to experience pain in childbirth, or weeds to take over our gardens. Other than making snakes crawl, humans make it their goal to eliminate all of these awful consequences of the Fall—except male rulership, the only aspect of sin's curse complementarians attempt to legitimize and perpetuate. No! Patriarchy is an *evil* to be eliminated from the church and society just as horticulturists strive to find ways to eliminate weeds from the farmer's field.

In **chapter 5** we discovered that two of the "concession passages" (Eph. 5:21–6:9 and Col. 3:18–4:1) address three parallel relationships: wives and husbands, children and fathers, slaves and masters. In the first century culture, each of these relationships was typically oppressive and unjust. In all three Paul calls on the oppressed and powerless parties to submit to the oppressing and power-possessing parties, who are then called on to treat the powerless with self-sacrificing love, kindness, and respect. None are instructed to take charge, be the leader, or tell the other to submit. Numerous factors detailed in this chapter reveal that the directives for the powerless parties to submit are *temporary concessions* for believers to make in order to preserve peace and unity and to promote rather than to hinder the advance of the Gospel. More significantly, at the beginning of the primary text (Eph. 5:21-6:9) is found not only a precedential command for total mutuality (e.g. every believer must submit to every other believer, Eph. 5:21), but also within the text are instructions to those in power to replace oppressive hierarchy with new creation values of the now-and-future kingdom of God in which all slaves are freed, and in which ethnic-, social-, and gender-based hierarchical distinctions are eliminated as signs of the coming Kingdom. All are one in Christ (Gal. 3:28).

Further it was shown in **chapter 6** that the two Bible passages (Eph. 5 and 1 Cor. 11) that use the word "head" to refer to the husband in relation to his own wife or to the man in relation to woman do not support an authority role for men. In those passages, "head" does not mean "having authority over," but rather it communicates "being the source of." This interpretation is not only confirmed by the contexts surrounding the two headship references, but also is illustrated by the meaning of "head" in many other contexts throughout the Scriptures.

Chapter 7 moved us to "ground zero" in the gender role debate, that is, the two (and only two) Bible passages that in any way might prohibit women from certain church roles, 1 Corinthians 14:33–35 and 1 Timothy 2:11–15. We learned that when we read these passages we are reading someone else's mail (they were addressed to the first century churches in Corinth and Ephesus) and that we must therefore understand the local history, culture, and circumstances and how these inform the interpretation of the relevant passages. We noted that however one interprets these prohibition passages, it must not contradict other clear passages such as 1 Corinthians 11:5 where Paul assumes that women will pray and prophecy in church gatherings. We also called attention to the misleading English translations of four key Greek words in 1 Corinthians 14:33–35 and 1Timothy 2:9–15, and briefly showed how those words, correctly translated, transform the gender roles debate in support of the egalitarian position.

Next **chapter 8** detailed numerous reasons the traditional complementarian interpretation of 1 Corinthians 14:33–35 is incorrect. In the larger pericope[366] in which those verses lie, Paul addresses three parallel situations causing *disruption* in the worship gatherings (untranslated tongues speakers, uninterruptable prophets, and perpetually talking women). The triple use of *sigaō* emphasizes the need to *defer* one's speaking to give opportunity for others to participate. The word *sigaō* does *not* communicate a prohibition from all speaking. In the third scenario Paul called on the Corinthian women to stop causing disorder by engaging in *non-stop talking* and by the *endless asking of questions*. The verses have nothing to do with holding a pastoral or other leadership role.

In **chapter 9** the correct meaning and translation of the three uses of *haysuxia* are one of two central issues in the challenge-laden second chapter of 1 Timothy—unquestionably the most important passage in the gender-roles conversation. Our study revealed that the word *haysuxia* does not communicate the idea of *silence* but of *serenity*—of displaying a *peaceable spirit and manner*. It is not about having a *quiet mouth*. This game-changing discovery is totally consistent with the theme of the chapter—*living peacefully without disruption, division, or conflict* (in the world, verses 1–7, and in the church, verses 8–15). This understanding of *haysuxia* is also consistent with

---

[366] A *pericope* is a section of a text (similar to a paragraph) that forms a unit of one coherent concept.

the need to address the dangerous threat of false teaching originating from the world-renowned, female-dominated Artemis cult, which was headquartered in Ephesus and dominated the city's financial stability, and also the threat from the unbiblical myths promoted by proto-gnosticism.

Although relevant material regarding the gender roles issue is found throughout the Scriptures, to some extent the arguments favoring complementarianism or egalitarianism swing on the disputed meaning of one word, *"authority" (authĕntĕō)*, found in 1 Timothy 2:12.[367] **Chapter 10** demonstrates that Paul does NOT prohibit women from exercising ordinary leadership/pastoral *authority* in the church, but rather that he prohibits women from unilaterally commandeering *aggressive authority* in order to *dominate* men. This bullying leadership is the opposite of what the entire chapter promoted: ***living peacefully without disruption, division, or conflict.*** An egalitarian understanding of this difficult chapter was shown to provide the most harmonious interpretations of several challenging assertions regarding the appearance of women, the order of the creation of Adam and Eve, deception and motivation in the first sin, and the meaning of salvation through childbearing.

In **chapter 11** we witnessed a long parade of illustrious Bible women who led, exercised authority and ruled over both men and women, taught God's people (including men), created Scripture content, and served God in nearly every conceivable capacity both among God's old covenant people, Israel, and His new covenant people, the church.

We saw that the way Jesus talked about, communicated with, empowered and treated women throughout His earthly ministry was shocking in His culture and is significant for the gender roles debate today.

What all these amazing women are recognized and honored for is impossible to reconcile with the gender-based restrictions placed on their contemporary sisters by the complementarian view. This is a powerful argument in favor of the egalitarian interpretation of Scripture—that is, that **the Bible places no gender-based ministry restrictions on women in the church.**

---

[367] "I do not permit a woman to teach or to have authority over a man."

Where Do We Go from Here?

The answer to that question depends on *where the reader is* regarding the gender roles issue. Therefore, let me respond to several scenarios. Before I do, let me assure my readers I will address the important question some are probably thinking about: **Should a person ever leave their church over the gender roles issue?** But, please don't skip ahead in the chapter without first considering what follows. Some of my readers may be saying,

I Haven't Made My Mind Up Yet

Despite having read this study, perhaps some are still undecided. They don't feel ready to commit either to the complementarian or egalitarian view as the correct interpretation and application of Scripture. If you are undecided I first recommend that you engage in serious, persistent prayer that God would give you wisdom[368] and that His Holy Spirit would teach you[369] as you continue to examine the Scriptures and other relevant resources on this issue. It might be helpful, as you review the earlier summary of the previous eleven chapters, to identify which gender-related biblical topics you feel unsettled about and then focus continued research on those. The footnotes in the relevant chapters will point the reader to helpful sources for further study. The bibliography at the end of this book also provides many additional resources. Here are some recommendations.[370]

The first is very accessible—four short, easy to watch and understand videos—while the second is a more substantial and exhaustive study.[371]

---

[368] "If any of you lacks wisdom, he should ask God, who gives generously to all without finding fault, and it will be given to him," James 1:5.

[369] "As for you, the anointing you received from him remains in you, and you do not need anyone to teach you. But as his anointing teaches you about all things and as that anointing is real, not counterfeit—just as it has taught you, remain in him," 1 John 2:27.

[370] Full disclosure: all of these recourses except the book presenting "Two Views" lean toward the egalitarian understanding of Scripture.

[371] My recommendations of resources are not blanket affirmations of agreement with everything within them.

- "Should Women Teach in Church?" is the title of four animated videos that creatively address the two most important gender role passages (1 Cor. 14 and 1 Tim. 2). These videos (4–9 minutes in length) are fun and easy to watch and are informative, thought-provoking, and Bible-centered. Don't underestimate the seriousness of these videos due to the medium (animation). They are a concise summary of key points in understanding these passages. *https://www.youtube.com/playlist?list=PLOMFMVk5oX41sBBX-U9kcfaB_trmKj3Ox*
- Cynthia Long Westfall's amazing volume, <u>Paul and Gender: Reclaiming the Apostle's Vision for Men and Women in Christ</u> (Baker Academic, Grand Rapids, 2016) is an exhaustive study of the relevant New Testament passages and how they relate to other Scriptures. It is packed with careful exegesis, scholarly research, relevant historical and cultural information, and also includes very helpful chapters on Creation, the Fall, and Eschatology as they relate to church gender roles issues.

These additional recommendations will be found helpful:

- Marg Mowczko writes an online blog that addresses gender role issues in the Bible. She is a diligent biblical scholar whose concise writings combine an understandable style with serious scholarship. Her blog, "Marg Mowczko: Exploring the biblical Theology of Christian Egalitarianism" is free by subscription. Her website, margmowczko.com, includes a treasure trove of past posts related to gender roles in the Bible.
- Another insightful blog (free subscription) is "The Junia Project" (juniaproject.com), which also has a huge cache of past postings on many biblical gender role topics.
- Two helpful books are <u>Women in the Church: A Biblical Theology of Women in Ministry</u>, Stanley J. Grenz, Intervarsity Press, Downers Grove, 1995;[372] and <u>Two Views on Women in Ministry</u>, ed. Stanley

---

[372] This book by Grenz helped to launch my several-year study because it was the first egalitarian presentation I read that was based on a high view of Scripture and careful exposition of the relevant texts. Since then my eyes have been opened to a flood of such resources that I was previously ignorant of.

N. Gundry and James R. Beck, Zondervan, Grand Rapids, 2005. This last resource includes chapters written by recognized biblical scholars who hold to the complementarian position and others who hold to the egalitarian position. It is a print version of a respectful debate.

- A specific resource (in addition to Westfall's outstanding work) regarding the meaning of *authenteo* in 1 Timothy 2:12 is by Jamin Hubner: "Translating αὐθεντέω *(authĕntĕō) in 1 Timothy 2:12*," Pricilla Papers, Vol. 129, No. 2 (Spring, 2015), http://www.academia.edu/24894103/Translating_αὐθεντέω_in_1_Timothy_2_12

- Of course, there is also the option of re-reading this book. Few people fully grasp or retain everything presented in a first reading.

Perhaps it would be productive to study the gender roles issue *in community with other believers*, such as in a small group or with a few friends who share your interest and have teachable attitudes. Remember the very beneficial process I described in my own journey when I was privileged to study this subject over many months in partnership with the elders and ministry team of the church I had served for over thirty years. The process and format we followed could be a model for others (see chap. 1), or, this book could be the guide and basis for a group study. The "For Discussion" section at the end of each chapter was included to facilitate group study.

Because the implications of this subject affect Jesus' church very significantly by potentially either excluding or including more than half of its members in leadership roles, to remain on the fence is not a good option. It is important to get this right—first because we need to correctly represent the Scriptures, and second because of how high the stakes are as we represent Jesus in a cynical culture. Regarding a different debatable and divisive topic which faced the first century church in Rome, Paul wrote: "Each one should be fully convinced in his own mind" (Rom. 14:5). Every follower of Jesus must be certain that they have opened their mind and heart to check their previously held position and/or to determine what their on-going position should be after a prayerful and sincere investigation into what the Bible actually teaches about gender roles.

Some reading this are not on the fence. Rather they might find themselves in the following uncomfortable circumstance:

I've Arrived at a Position, But It's Incompatible with That of My Spouse, Pastor, and/or Church

A difference of opinion that potentially leads to division in important relationships must be handled with great care, prayer, and attention to relevant Bible principles and examples. Maintaining unity in marriage,[373] family, and church is an extremely important value which must be strenuously guarded especially when there is disagreement.

In Romans 14, Paul gave the first century Roman believers *crucial principles* for dealing with debatable issues over which they could not agree. It's important to know that the disagreement over foods tainted by a connection to idols or over the "correct" day to hold as sacred were not topics which the Scriptures left up for grabs. Paul clearly took a position on both subjects elsewhere in his New Testament letters. But because not all were on the same page regarding their sincerely held beliefs on debatable issues, Paul insisted that they must protect the unity and harmony of the church. His commands in Romans 14 for the disagreeing Roman believers serve as powerful examples for us as we deal with a different divisive topic—that of gender roles in the church. Consider Paul's directives in Romans 14 as you contemplate your response to disagreement over gender roles in your personal relationships and your church.

When dealing with divisive issues in the church, Paul taught the following (I have taken the liberty to personalize and apply Paul's mandates and encouragements to the gender roles issue):

(1) You are to welcome and accept each other in Jesus' church without passing judgement on those who disagree with you about gender roles, 14:1, 10, 13

---

[373] This is certainly not an issue over which destroying a marriage is worthwhile. It is inconceivable that Jesus' command, "what God has joined together, let man not separate" (Matt. 19:6) would not apply to a lack of consensus on this theological topic. Strong marriages are those in which husbands and wives have learned to accept unresolved differences of opinion without constantly debating them or responding to each other with impatience, anger, manipulation, demands, threats, or rejection directed toward their dissenting spouse. Rather practicing mutual submission, love, respect, honor, and kindness are what the Scriptures require (Eph. 5:21–33; 1 Pt. 3:1–7).

(2) You must not look down on, despise, or condemn the people who differ with you regarding whether women are permitted to teach and lead in the church, 14:3, 10

(3) Remember that God accepts those who disagree with you about what women can or can't do in the church, 14:3

(4) Remember that God, not you, is the Master and Judge of those who disagree with you about the role of women in the church, 14:4, 10

(5) Remember that God can help those who disagree with you to stand even if you think they are wrong about gender roles, 14:4

(6) Understand that people who disagree with you about gender roles may *sincerely* believe that they are honoring and pleasing God by their position, 14:5-7

(7) Remember that the one who disagrees with you about male and female roles belongs to God and that Jesus died for them too, 14:8

(8) Don't forget that each of you must give account to God for your beliefs and practices regarding gender roles, not to each other, 14:12

(9) Decide to love those who disagree with you regarding God's plan for men and women, and determine to hold your differences in such a way that you do not hinder their spiritual life, cause them to stumble into sin, or unduly distress, injure, or harm them, 14:13–15, 20, 21

(10) Respect that some may honestly feel it would be wrong for them to adopt and practice your views about what women should or should not do in the church, 14:14

(11) Do not hold your good position about gender roles in such a manner that those who disagree might perceive it to be evil, 14:16

(12) Do not allow your stance on the roles of men and women to undermine higher values in God's kingdom such as righteousness, joy, and peace, 14:17

(13) Recognize that the manner in which you deal with your disagreement on a debatable issue such as gender roles determines whether you are truly serving God, 14:18

(14) Do not allow what you believe about women's roles in the church keep you from making every effort to maintain peace in the church and to help those who disagree to grow in maturity, 14:19

(15) When necessary to preserve unity and not cause harm to those who disagree with you, you may sometimes need to keep your gender-role convictions to yourself and not continue to debate them, 14:22

(16) Be diligent as you study the Scriptures to solidify what you believe about God's will for the roles of men and women, 14:5, 22.

Wow! Paul's use of an entire chapter to instruct this first century church on how to handle a theological disagreement sets a high bar for us to observe with regard to the gender roles debate: **know what you believe regarding debatable issues but do not destroy relationships or the unity of Jesus' church over them.**

Further, while disagreeing about gender roles, shouldn't we infuse our discussions with the fruit of the Spirit (Gal. 5:22, 23),[374] the "golden rule" (Matt. 7:12),[375] and the second greatest command (Matt. 22:39, 40)?[376] Can we justify throwing out these fundamental and essential ways of treating each other because of our differences regarding the role of women in the church?

Jesus said that it is by believers' love for each other, and by the preservation of unity in the church that all people will know that we are His disciples and may believe that God sent Jesus into the world (John 13:34, 35; 17:20–23). Disagreement over gender roles does not negate these things Jesus taught and prayed. We must remember that the world is watching not only what we do about gender roles in the church but also how we handle disagreement with each other over the issue. That can be a challenging tight rope to walk but we must try.

Think how similar some of these reminders are to Paul's call (e.g. in Eph. 5:21–6:9) to be willing to make difficult temporary concessions by submitting to others in order to preserve peace in the church and to promote the spread of the Gospel in the world. Even more relevant, recall that THE MOST IMPORTANT gender roles passage in the Bible, 1 Timothy 2, is all about *living peacefully in the world and in the church without disruption,*

---

[374] "But the fruit of the Spirit is love, joy, peace, patience, kindness, goodness, faithfulness, gentleness, self-control."

[375] "So in everything, do to others what you would have them do to you, for this sums up the Law and the Prophets."

[376] "Love your neighbor as yourself. All the Law and the Prophets hang on these two commandments."

division, or conflict. How tragically ironic it would be if someone promoted their complementarian OR egalitarian convictions in a way that damaged the *haysuxia* (peacefulness) which was the organizing theme of Paul's teaching on gender roles. Paul's instructions specifically forbade "anger and disputing" (1 Tim. 2:8) as well as imposing *domineering* or *bullying behavior (authĕntĕō)* on others (1 Tim. 2:11). Rather *submission* and *peaceableness* are required (1 Tim. 2:11, 12). To promote one's gender role convictions in such a way that *peace* is disrupted in the church would be the height of selfishness and hypocrisy, whether one is right or wrong on the issue. Okay then,

Should Someone Ever Leave Their Church Over the Gender Roles Issue?

Yes! Definitely! There, I got that out of the way. I believe that there are times that God may lead someone to leave a church over this issue. When and how they depart is crucial and will be discussed below.

But before we think about leaving, let's think about what the church is and should be. The church is the *family* of God (Gal. 6:10; Eph. 3:15; Heb. 2:11; 1 Pt. 4:17). Families are connected by birth or adoption. We who are in God's family are inseparably connected by both—*born again* by the Holy Spirit and *adopted* into God's family (1 Pt. 1:23; Eph. 1:5). Someone said, "You can choose your friends but you're stuck with your family." That doesn't sound very pleasant but if you think about it, it's good!

At the heart of being family is a *commitment* to love and loyalty regardless of disagreements and differences. My wife and I and our children don't bail out of our marriage or family because we don't agree about where to go out for supper, which political positions or people we should support, what color we should paint the family room, how and when someone should be baptized, what the Bible teaches about future events, whether a decision is great or awful, and a thousand other issues. Gloria and I are committed to each other *for better or for worse* even as we are committed to our children with every breath we have—even if we don't agree about every opinion, belief, or choice. We are family! To be sure, God permitted divorce in some circumstances because of the hardness of human hearts (Matt. 19:8), but while sometimes necessary and/or permitted, divorce was not His plan from the beginning.

Certainly, there may be times when hard-hearted believers bring unbearable stresses on personal or church relationships resulting in tragic but necessary separations or expulsions. But let's be clear that such is not how God desires it to be.

Unfortunately, many people in today's culture have **a consumer** relationship with their church rather than **a covenant** relationship. A covenant relationship is based on *commitment*. In such a relationship, though satisfaction and getting one's needs met is desirable, it is not essential. The covenant defines and preserves the relationship through harmony and discord. On the other hand, a consumer relationship is based on *personal satisfaction*—getting one's desires and needs met. The consumer is "loyal" to a relationship, business, or institution only as long as they are satisfied with it and are able to obtain the services and product they want at a cost they are willing to pay. If ever they feel that is no longer true of a business, they move on to a store down the road which will happily provide what they want. Imagine what would happen if people treated marriage as a consumer relationship rather than a covenantal one? Oh, wait! Many people do just that and leave in their wake broken promises, destroyed relationships, damaged children, and many other harms. Sadly, many "church hoppers" treat their *church* as a consumer relationship. Their theme song seems to be, *"This church is not my home, I'm just a passin' through. Another church looks better, so I'll try out their pew."*[377]

So how could we think lightly or casually about leaving our church family simply because we disagree over gender roles or some other debatable issue? That is absolutely not meant to minimize the importance of gender roles[378] but rather to confirm the high value of unity and love in Jesus' Bride, the church. Does this doctrinal issue rise to the level that one must leave the church they once felt God called them to? Consider how seldom someone choses or stays in a church because they are in perfect alignment on EVERY theological issue. That would be rare. Frankly, I don't even agree with all the doctrines

---

[377] For those unfamiliar with the old Southern gospel song, "This World Is Not My Home," this is a parody of *"This world is not my home, I'm just a passin' through. My treasures are laid up somewhere beyond the blue."*

[378] By this time my readers should be well aware that I believe that patriarchy in the church is evil, a masterstroke of Satan, a violation of Scripture, a great detriment to the church, and a blot on the church's testimony before a watching world.

and practices I myself embraced ten or fifteen years ago (totally apart from the gender roles issue). Hopefully that's because I'm still growing in my understanding and application of the Scriptures. I suggest that we normally choose a church family with which we agree on the *central doctrines* of our faith. But the likelihood is that in every church there are some doctrinal positions on debatable issues which we choose to tolerate and not fight about for the sake of love, unity, and testimony and because we value other things about the church.

Do you remember the old joke that has been adapted to many denominations? A Baptist pastor was shipwrecked alone on a deserted island. After thirty years by himself on the island, an off-course ship happened to notice smoke rising from the pastor's cooking fire on the beach. When they got to the island his rescuers were amazed to discover that he had built a small house and three different church buildings—all without any tools or building supplies. The puzzled ship captain asked. "Why are there three churches? You're the only person on this island." "That's easy," the castaway replied as he pointed to one of the buildings. "That one is where I go to church now and the other two are where I used to go." "But you're the only one here," the captain replied. "Why did you leave those two churches?" "That's easy," the castaway retorted, "I didn't agree with the pastor anymore."

If people left their church every time they didn't agree with something, they would run out of churches to move to . . . unless, like the castaway they kept starting their own new ones. Tragically that may be one of the motivations behind many church plants.

Stay with me, now! I will look at another side of this in a moment.

If someone leaves their church over gender roles, should they go to another church where they don't agree with some other doctrinal issue such as baptism, church government, prophecy, gifts of the Spirit, covenant or dispensational theology, music styles, involvement in politics, Calvinism or Arminianism, ministry to the poor, etc.? Does holding to complementarianism or egalitarianism take precedence over the many other doctrinal or ministry areas where disagreement may exist? Don't many Christian parents carefully explain to their children about aspects of the church with which they disagree? Isn't this seen as an opportunity to teach one's children how to disagree and still get along—a rather important life skill they will need in many relationships and circumstances, not just the church? Do you quit the football team because you don't agree with the coach 100%? Do you break off with some of your really good, long-term friends because you voted for different candidates in the last presidential election? Do you resign from your job because your boss has some different viewpoints or values than yours?

When someone contemplates leaving a church, they should carefully consider how their departure may affect the church. What ministry roles will be left vacant? What effect will the loss of their tithes and offerings have on the missionaries and staff the church supports and on ministry, building, and operational expenses? Will other members and the staff be discouraged? If the pastor has sacrificed for and served you faithfully, how will this separation affect him or her? What will leaving teach one's children about the church, relationships, and how to deal with conflict? If someone leaves because their beliefs about gender roles aren't affirmed by others, who will be left to influence growth and change in that area?

These considerations are not meant to be "deal breakers" in the consideration of leaving a church, but they certainly should be given serious thought and prayer. Remember that once we've become dissatisfied about something and have made a mental shift away from it, it's easy to look for other ways to rationalize and build a case for our contemplated action and to minimize any negative consequences. We become vulnerable to compiling a list of other imperfections or offenses to justify our departure. It becomes easy to forget the implications of what the church relationship is (or ought to be). We are family! God's family! We are in *covenantal* relationship with each other.

In other words, no one should lightly walk away from the church family of which they have been part. *Church hopping* has become a plague in the American church and does great harm to the kingdom of God. One church "grows" to the detriment or even the destruction of others.[379] Therefore, such a decision should be immersed in prayer and in careful weighing of the benefits and detriments. All that said, these considerations are absolutely not meant to suggest that leaving a church is never warranted or to induce unnecessary guilt for those who legitimately do.

So, let's return to that important question:

---

[379] The other side of the problem of church hopping is sheep stealing. An excellent study of this unhealthy, widespread practice is found in "Stealing Sheep: The Church's Hidden Problems of Transfer Growth" by William Chadwick (InterVarsity Press, 2001).

Should Someone Ever Leave Their Church over the Gender Roles Issue?

I believe that, in spite of all the factors just discussed, there are times when it is a valid decision for some people to leave a church over the gender roles issue. After all, the principles of Romans 14 cut both ways. When someone decides to leave a church over gender roles, it seems that whether or not I like or agree with that decision, I must love, accept, not look down on, judge, condemn, or harm that person. Isn't that what Romans 14 teaches? So, let's talk about *when and how* to leave.

How To Encourage a Change in Belief and Practice

Ideally, *prior to deciding to leave*, an individual should make every appropriate effort to influence positive change in the church leadership regarding the role of women in the church. How wonderful it would be if God could use an individual to influence a church to adopt a more biblical position and practice regarding gender roles. Thus, in my judgement, if a member has arrived at an egalitarian position but the church and its leadership operate in a complementarian mold, before finalizing a decision for departure, it would be worthwhile to first attempt to influence a better understanding of the Scriptures by the pastor/elders. Here are some suggestions for attempting to influence such a change:

(1) Engage in serious prayer that God would give you wisdom and proper motivation as you attempt to influence the leadership regarding gender roles. Pray for open hearts for the leaders and for a loving and wise spirit for yourself.

(2) After much prayer, when the Holy Spirit gives you release to do so, request a meeting with the pastor and/or elders to share your heart.

    a. If need be, ask for clarification regarding the church's position and exemplify listening with an open mind and heart.

    b. Describe your own journey to your current position on gender roles emphasizing what you believe the Scriptures teach.

c. Ask if the pastor and elders would consider looking at some resources regarding gender roles which you would recommend or supply—for example the ones suggested earlier in this chapter. Obviously, I would be thrilled if this book was recommended. I wrote it hoping to stimulate study and understanding about biblical teaching regarding gender roles.

d. Be sensitive to the fact that this is a very controversial topic and that the stakes are high if the church leadership changes its position.

(3) Carefully select the resources you will either provide or recommend. These could include books (discover if they prefer paper or digital copies such as Kindle or Nook), articles, CDs, digital copies, blogs, web sites, pod casts, etc. Be sensitive to their often over-busy and stress-filled schedules.[380] If they feel overloaded or overwhelmed, they may be tempted to procrastinate or disregard the study as an impossible task.

(4) Ask for permission to check back to inquire how their investigation is progressing, to discuss the things they studied (if they are willing), and to see if they have questions, need additional resources, are open to dialogue, or if they have arrived at any conclusions. If this opportunity opens up for further dialogue, be sure to display a humble and teachable spirit as you present your beliefs. Remember *haysuxia*.

(5) **Be patient!** Remember that I had a closed mind about gender roles for many decades. It took what I now recognize as a series of divinely orchestrated events to challenge me to investigate anew. Until then, I felt no need to seriously study this issue because I assumed the Bible clearly presented the complementarian viewpoint. Even once I embarked on a diligent investigation of the Scriptures regarding

---

[380] Many pastors consistently work fifty to eighty hours per week doing ministry. Between sermon preparation, pastoral care, discipling, meetings, and administrative work, a large percentage of pastors don't feel they have the luxury of engaging in a major study unrelated to the unrelenting sermon preparation required of them week after week. Many pastors prepare and preach three to five sermons and lessons every week—a huge time commitment.

gender roles, it took several years of study for me to become convinced of my new understanding.

(6) Vigorously reject the temptation to undermine the leaders or to sow seeds of distrust, dissention, or division in the church. Paul gave a very serious warning against harming the church in 1 Corinthians 3:17: "If anyone destroys God's temple, God will destroy him; for God's temple is sacred, and you [all] are that temple."

(7) Throughout this time, display a respectful, humble, loving, encouraging, and supportive spirit. Make yourself accountable to someone who will help you to maintain a proper attitude, to conduct yourself appropriately, and who will give wise counsel for you.

All that said, there may come a time when gentle efforts to produce change are rejected and truth must be spoken with grace and boldness. The time comes when injustice and oppression, however sincerely held by those imposing it, must be confronted as sin. To potentially disallow at least 50% of believers from any possibility of exercising their spiritual gifts and a calling God may have given them is a very serious matter. Sinful actions may be well-meaning, but they must be exposed for what they are. Ultimately, there should be calls for repentance and change—a challenge one must enact in a manner that is full of grace and truth.

Could this, even when done properly, still be divisive? Of course, it's divisive! But how divisive is the prohibition of more than half of the church population from even considering the possibility that God may have gifted and called them to serve in certain roles in the church? Of course, it's divisive! It is about perpetuating male power and privilege or tearing down walls of division, limitation, oppression, and injustice. Leaving a church appropriately may be a tacit way of confronting evil (no matter how sincere many of those who perpetuate it may be). Remember that many people, including Christians and pastors, sincerely defended the perpetuation of slavery. Thank God, some had the courage to stand against it, many even gave their lives to promote God-given equality and freedom.

I wonder if my journey might have started sooner had someone approached and confronted me in the manner just described? I don't know. I hope I would have responded with humility and a teachable spirit. The gentle encouragement by my daughter to read a book about gender roles was an important influence in the beginning of my journey.

Consider This: Is it a "Soft" Complementarian Church or a "Hard" One?

When someone is considering leaving a church because it believes that women, solely based on their gender, are excluded from certain leadership and ministry roles, it might be important to consider whether their complementarian position is what might be called "soft" or "hard;" "gentle" or "harsh."

A "soft" complementarian church values and respects women and affirms its gender-based restrictions in a gentle manner without a spirit of denigration or devaluation. Gender-limitations are not a frequently mentioned topic and when it is, efforts are made to emphasize all the roles which are available rather than those few that are not. With regard to marriage, mutual submission (Eph. 5:21) and the necessity of husbands practicing Christ-like, self-sacrificing love are emphasized to frame the instruction for submission by wives. Usually the gender limitations are taught as applying to marriage and church, but not to society in areas like business, politics, etc. There is an openness to considering expanded ways of inclusion for women in church ministry such as are suggested below.

A "hard" complementarian church, on the other hand, takes a more rigid and hardline stance about gender roles both in the church and in marriage. When taught, it may sometimes feel as if it is done in a harsh, rigid, and strident spirit. Women are spoken about or treated almost as second-class, and even when there is talk of "equality," the sense of being perceived as inferior remains. Typically, wives' submission to their husbands "as to the Lord . . . in everything" (Eph. 5:22, 24) is strongly emphasized along with the need for husbands to exert leadership.[381] At the same time, submitting "to one another," preferring others ahead of self, and self-sacrificing, lay-your-life-down kind of love get less attention. The teaching emphasis seems more on what women must *not* do in the church than on how they may freely minister. The gender-based roles of leader and submitter are seen as

---

[381] In Ephesians 5, husbands are never told to take charge, lead, or be the boss."

creation-based and inherent to what it means to be male and female. Further, women are believed to be more easily deceived and mislead and hence more vulnerable to temptation than men. Seldom is there any teachable spirit or openness to a reexamination of the biblical data on this topic. To even raise a question contrary to their patriarchal position would be to reject what God has clearly said and to compromise with the world. "God said it and that settles it!" is a common mantra. There is no openness to launching an effort to identify additional ways women might serve beyond their designated "place" in the kitchen, decorating committee, nursery, and in children's or ladies' ministries.

A person should be considerably more patient and cautious about leaving a "soft" complementarian church than a "hard" one. The possibility of contributing to positive growth and change regarding what the Bible teaches about gender-roles is much more likely in a "soft" complementarian church and, while there, the culture feels far less oppressive, devaluing, or even toxic than in a "hard" complementarian setting. When the complementarian position feels toxic, then leaving is considerably more important for consideration. There may be some situations which are so out of sync with the spirit of Jesus and the Scriptures that one is tempted to kick the dust off their feet as they leave (Matt. 10:14).

If Departure Is Inevitable, How Do You Leave?

If efforts to influence an investigation of and change regarding the gender roles issue are fruitless, some (not all) will conclude that separation from the church is inevitable.

Even in a "soft" complementarian church some may feel called to lovingly but firmly take a stand against the injustice and oppression of patriarchy much like many Christians have felt responsible to stand against slavery, racism, and injustice. Some may be convinced that to call attention to the importance of this issue requires radical action such as leaving a church which continues to exclude half of its members from any opportunity to serve in key leadership roles.

Others may sense the need to find a new church because they feel so strongly that their children, both daughters and sons, should worship and learn in an atmosphere where there are not stained-glass ceiling limitations; where based solely on their gender, all females are neither encouraged nor allowed to pursue investing their gifts and passions in church leadership either as a volunteer or a vocational pastor or in a preaching role.

A few may feel that God is specifically calling them (or their daughter) to serve in a ministry role which is not available in their current church, or they may desire to be in an environment where such a call would be affirmed and opportunities potentially arise. For them to follow God's calling they must be in a church which is open to such a role for a woman.

If a man who had the gifts and education for pastoral ministry and who felt called to serve as a pastor but had no opportunities or future prospects for such in the church he attended, would he be criticized if he left to attend a church where there was a realistic possibility of serving as a lay- or vocational-pastor? Wouldn't most people affirm that such a move was understandable, commendable, and necessary? What about a woman in the same situation who was in a church where there were not only no open doors for her gifts and call but rather only condemnation for even considering such? If she left that church for one where there was a realistic opportunity for her to serve with her gifts and calling, would she be affirmed in the same way as a man?

For some it is important for their daughters to grow up in an environment where all ministry options are possible and where their sons are taught to value women as their equals and as legitimate leaders in society and the church. The thought of one's children *never* seeing a woman preach in church or serve in leadership may be too difficult to contemplate.

Still others may determine a change is necessary because their distaste for and sense of injustice over the subjugation of women is too great for them to be able to continue to maintain a tolerant or positive attitude. Not wanting to stay and create division, they determine that maintaining a healthy attitude in what they view as a dysfunctional or even evil environment is not realistic if they remain in their church.

A dear friend falls into this category. They wrote to me:[382]

> Staying and just being peaceful and still would be a sin
> against the victims of injustice now and in the future ... I
> can no longer accept the gender roles debate being termed

---

[382] I obtained permission from my friend to share what they wrote.

'secondary theology' or an issue that isn't at the very center.[383] It's only a secondary issue to those in power. Only **they** have the luxury, and, well power, to make it so. The Civil Rights Movement is a great example of this. MLK's thoughts on being moderate and sedentary are very powerful and they directly translate to this discussion. The issue is so much more than just women being able to be elders. It's a question of the very nature of the God we serve, and a discussion about sin and the misuse of bearing the image of God both individually and systematically. Whether we immerse or sprinkle and how many times; regarding communion, does it become the actual body of Christ or is it just symbolic? ... those debates don't reflect on God's heart, but this one does.

If someone has become convinced that they must leave a church over the gender roles issue, I recommend that they prayerfully consider the recommendations that follow. These may be more realistic in a "soft" complementarian church than a "hard" one. In a "hard" complementarian church, confrontation and rebuke may be more appropriate—though always biblically-based and in love.

(1) First meet privately with the pastor and/or elders. Express gratitude for the ministry of the church and its leaders. Inform them that the departure is because of this theological issue, not due to disagreement over other issues, personal dissatisfaction with the pastor/leaders, or unresolved conflict with some members of the church.

(2) If possible, assure the leaders that you intend to speak well of them and that you will be careful to avoid behavior and communications intended to undermine the leaders or promote division in the church family.

(3) Ask the leaders how they would be most comfortable with you, when asked, briefly stating the reason for your departure with those who, because of relationship, should be informed. Prayerfully plan your statement so as to speak the truth with conviction but without

---

[383] If people were excluded from ministry and leadership in the church based on their race, would we consider that a "secondary issue"?

malice or intent to undermine, vilify, or divide. Stating the reason for departure appropriately not only is important for your integrity and witness, but also is important to avoid unnecessary suspicion or conjecture regarding why you left and to prevent people from wrongly filling in the gaps by assuming that there is some moral or other problem in your life **or** in the church or its leadership.

(4) Ask the leaders how they would like you to help to assure a smooth transition for any ministries you are currently involved in, including, if desired, being willing to help to recruit or train your successor(s).

(5) In many situations, it could be good to tell the leaders you intend to continue your tithes and offerings even after departing for some realistic period of time which you feel would be reasonable and helpful (e.g. two months). This gives the church time to attempt to increase giving or to adjust expenses without placing undue stress on the church budget. This assumes that you were a faithful and generous giver, as every follower of Christ should be—not all giving equal gifts, but all making equal sacrifices (1 Cor. 8:13–15).

(6) After departing, do not recruit or encourage others from your former church to follow you to your new church. Do not continue in your small group where your presence could be divisive and influence others to follow you to another church. Get involved in ministry and a small group in the new church where God leads you. Do not speak badly of the church you left and do not talk about it or its pastor(s) or other leaders in negative or disparaging terms. Remember Paul's words in Titus 3:2 (ESV), "speak evil of no one," and in Philippians 1:18, "But what does it matter? The important thing is that in every way, whether from false motives or true, Christ is preached. And because of this I rejoice. Yes, and I will continue to rejoice." When you must reveal the reason for your church change, do so in as positive a way as possible and without acrimony or denigration. If others choose to leave the church over this issue, you want to be confident that they feel that God truly led them and not that you tried to influence them.

All that said, regardless of whether someone stays or goes and regardless of whether one is committed to the complementarian or egalitarian position, nearly every church can and should become more welcoming and affirming to women and, with intentionality, could increase the participation of women in ministry. That is almost assuredly true of every church regardless of their position on gender roles. I would hope everyone who has read this book would want to help to see that happen.

How Churches Can Become More Affirming and Empowering to Women

Complementarian churches believe that *most* ministries are open to women. Egalitarian churches believe that *all* ministry positions are open to women. Therefore, it should be apparent that **all churches can work to open more doors for women and encourage them** to invest their time, experience, gifts, and wisdom to advance Jesus' church.

Complementarian Churches

Even a church that is complementarian could probably increase the visibility and number of women who minister in the many ways that are compatible with the church's beliefs. If, for example, a church believes that women should not be pastors or elders or have an official role of teaching men, there are scores of other ways they may minister and contribute greatly to the advance of Jesus' church. Appointing a task team to explore ways to strategically involve women in ministry consistent with the church's beliefs can lead to an intentional effort to welcome, recruit, and affirm women in every allowed ministry capacity.

For example, adding women to the elder board in an *ad hoc capacity* could bring their experience, gifts, ideas, and passion to the table without their having a vote or authority over men. If necessary, quickly adjust compensation levels for gender equity.[384] If a woman "director" has the same job description and responsibilities as a man titled "pastor," why would she

---

[384] This may also be a legal matter. Churches must act with integrity with regard to labor laws. Ignorance is not a valid excuse when a government agency knocks at the door. Besides, if you have read this, you can't plead ignorance any longer.

not be paid the same as he would? Even if the complementarian convictions prohibit her from being called "pastor" or "elder," why couldn't she participate in pastoral or elder meetings in an ad hoc or advisory capacity?

Think about a complementarian marriage. Just because the spouses believe that the man is the leader and the wife must submit doesn't mean that she isn't at the table as an active part of the decision-making process. Doesn't a wise and loving husband seek and consider his dearly loved wife's opinions and desires? Doesn't he sometimes (or frequently) defer to her, as Ephesians 5:21 requires ("submit to one another out of reverence for Christ")? Why would the same dynamics not be encouraged in a complementarian church as should be practiced in a complementarian marriage? Consider all the ways the "virtuous woman" of Proverbs 31 invested her skills for the good of her family and community. She was praised for far more than her domestic abilities. She was a successful entrepreneur. She was a wise teacher (31:26). If her husband was the chairman of the board, she was like the CEO and CFO of the "family business" (31:16, 24, 27, etc.). Her husband didn't feel threatened or undermined. He "praises her" (31:28). How would a church benefit if its women were similarly encouraged, unleashed, and empowered in its ministries?

Many complementarians would be comfortable with women preaching or team-teaching a Sunday sermon as long as they did so with the permission of and accountability to a male pastor. To do anything less than encouraging every allowable ministry involvement would be like tying a hand behind one's back and expecting to work as effectively as could be done with both hands. A one-handed church will never accomplish as much as a two-handed one and will never reach its full potential. Imagine what could happen if the "female hand" were set free to work in partnership with the "male hand!"

Transitioning Churches

What if a church has always followed the complementarian model but its leadership has now become convinced that the Scriptures support the egalitarian model—that is, there are no gender-based ministry restrictions? What should they do to implement the significant changes called for in this new understanding of God's plan for the church? What steps might they take in order to disciple the congregation through the relevant Scriptures and dramatically increase gender diversity in church leadership?[385] Consider these suggestions:

1. Acknowledge the errors of the past (wrong interpretation, teaching, and application of the Scriptures), express deep sorrow and repentance for the harms done, and ask for forgiveness. This could be expressed in a written statement to be posted on the church web site, Facebook page, and newsletter, and verbally communicated to the congregation on Sunday morning. This might call for some formal ceremony, when, for example, all the women and young women in the church are asked to stand while the leaders of the church sincerely communicate the confession and apology, ask for forgiveness, and share vision for change. This might be an ideal time to preach a special sermon or even better, to launch a multi-week sermon series on the topic to bring the congregation along in the change.[386] Some might prefer doing the study first and then making the public confession and commitment to a new direction.

2. Coinciding with this multi-week sermon series on gender roles could be a church-wide study of what the Bible teaches regarding gender roles. During this series, small groups could focus on the same themes as the sermons. Some churches might prefer to develop their own small group study guide based on their sermon series and suggest this book (or another) as a resource for those who wish to go deeper in the study. Or small groups could use this book and the "For Discussion" section provided at the end of each chapter to guide their small group interactions. It would be unwise to assume, after many years of complementarian teaching and practice, that everyone in the congregation will immediately adopt the new understanding. Therefore, asking the congregation to join the leadership on a three-month journey of Bible study regarding gender roles could unite the church in a new commitment to gender equality and to the

---

[385] In many churches, similar attention should be given to radically increasing ethnic diversity in church leadership. There are probably some similar dynamics, but that very important topic deserves its own extensive consideration.

[386] Consider this book as an outline and resource for a sermon series.

affirmation of women in every area of church ministry. Hopefully the emphasis in this chapter regarding the importance of maintaining peace and unity will be a help to minimize division even if there is disagreement.

3. As soon as the congregation would be supportive, create a diverse task team to formulate a strategic plan for gender diversity.[387] Having a female chairperson and a majority or at least an equal number of women on the team would be a powerful statement of the seriousness of the effort. It would be helpful if the pastor serves on the committee to show his support for their work. Included in the plan would be the recruitment of women to serve in leadership roles such as pastors,[388] elders, and ministry teams. This will obviously be different depending on the size of the church and its staff. The strategy should include goals, action steps, and a time-table, along with a statement about the anticipated benefits of this process. The strategy would be presented to the church leadership for input and/ or approval prior to adoption and implementation.

4. Cast a vision with the congregation in conjunction with the strategic plan for gender diversity. Church governance differs significantly from church to church. If appropriate, have the congregation vote to adopt and to implement the strategic plan.

5. Implement the strategic plan for gender diversity in the church.

Think of the benefits. Pete Gray, nicknamed "the one-armed wonder," was the first of only three one-armed baseball players who made it to the major leagues. Gray played minor league baseball for 10 years, batting 381 in his freshman season. One year he was voted the league's "most valuable player." As an outfielder, he caught the ball then transferred it from glove to hand with amazing speed. In 1945, he signed with the American league St. Louis Browns and played in 77 games. That season the Browns had a .600-win percentage when he played in the game and only .425 when he did not. His highlight was getting five hits and two RBIs in double-header sweep against the New York Yankees in legendary Yankee Stadium. Clearly Gray is an

---

[387] A similar plan to enhance ethnic diversity could be considered for another time.

[388] If the budget will not allow an additional staff person, consider starting with an unpaid woman pastor with a goal of moving her to a paid position when it is possible.

amazing exception to the limitations associated with playing with one arm. Gray's perseverance and ability are the stuff of legends. Very few players with only one arm could achieve even a fraction of his success. Perhaps Gray could be a metaphor for the church. What if many churches have for centuries been playing with one arm when they didn't have to? We should never diminish the accomplishments of all who have "played," but isn't it time for the church to play with two arms?

Already-Egalitarian Churches

Sadly, despite a growing number of Christians and churches which embrace an egalitarian understanding of the Scriptures, the number of women actually serving as pastors, associate pastors, elders, leaders, and preacher/teachers, while increasing, remains disproportionate compared to the percentage of women congregants. The number of female seminary students in the United States is on a steady rise providing a great recruiting ground for female pastors. In addition to senior pastor positions, hiring qualified women as associate pastors, children's pastors, youth pastors, music pastors, executive pastors, and business pastors—whether full- or part-time—would send a huge signal to young women and little girls about potential careers in Jesus' church. In a solo pastor church, there are many lay-person leadership and ministry roles that can be filled by qualified women including unpaid (perhaps part time) pastors.

As previously recommended, appointing a diverse task team to develop a strategic plan to implement gender diversity would be an excellent step. Affirmative action for increasing the number of women in pastoral ministry and on elder boards must be vigorously pursued.

Inviting qualified lay women and men to participate with the pastor in a preaching schedule or rotation could be implemented immediately and would have many benefits. Mentoring potential preachers, elders, and pastors of both genders is essential. Be intentional in determining who to ask to pray, sing, preach, give announcements, usher, greet, baptize, serve communion, and lead or serve on task teams and boards. Have both genders serve as visible *leaders* in ministries to children and teens to present models of partnership in ministry and to encourage the next generation of young men and women to affirm and to follow in the steps of Miriam, Deborah, Huldah, Anna, Elizabeth, Mary, Pricilla, Phoebe, Junia, and Apphia. In other words, normalize the involvement of women in every area of ministry. It's time to open the doors for women—not merely physical doors, but *ministry* doors—for those who for far too long have been forced to stand outside closed and locked doors.

Just Imagine

Imagine if a soldier who had lost a leg in Iraq woke up one morning with their missing leg supernaturally restored. Imagine how they would first tentatively put weight on it to see if it was really there and functional. Imagine them ecstatically leaping, jumping, walking, sprinting, doing jumping jacks, and engaging in all the things they used to do before losing a leg. Imagine the joyous celebration of those around them when they saw what they were now able to do.[389]

Imagine what might happen if a church that had grown used to one leadership "leg" suddenly had two—a masculine "leg" and a feminine "leg." Imagine what the church might accomplish that was previously impossible or, at best, difficult. Imagine the celebration of joy when the church began to function with both "legs."

Imagine if the man was no longer "alone" in church leadership as Adam was "alone"[390] in the original creation before God created Eve to be his partner. Imagine if men and women worked together to fulfill God's mission for the church even as Adam and Eve worked as equal partners to "fill," "subdue," and "rule" the earth and everything in it (Gen. 1:28).

Imagine the potential of opening the door to more than half of all church members to serve in ways in which the complementarian tradition has not allowed. Imagine the unleashed potential of leadership and teaching gifts that have been stifled, underdeveloped, or underutilized for decades or

---

[389] No one should minimize the worth of those who deal with handicaps or the amazing heroism of those who live with or who overcome physical or other kinds of limitations. To imagine a situation such as this paragraph visualizes should never be taken as diminishing the value and potential of people who face unique challenges.

[390] "The Lord God said, 'It is not good for the man to be alone. I will make a helper suitable for him'" (Gen. 2:18).

even for centuries. Imagine the infusion of feminine wisdom, intuition, and perspective that the church has largely been without in some of the most important planning and decision-making venues. Imagine experiencing the biblical insights and applications from a feminine viewpoint that have been almost entirely excluded from primary teaching settings. Imagine a new company of leaders and workers who have been marginalized for decades, suddenly being valued, elevated, engaged, employed, and followed. Imagine the potential of using two arms instead of one to build Jesus' church.

I remember a sermon I preached many years ago after which I received an unusually large number of positive responses. My earlier-than-usual preparation that week allowed me to go over the sermon ahead of time with Gloria. As she listened, Gloria made a number of excellent suggestions which I added here and there throughout my notes and then shared in my sermon on Sunday. Reflecting on the many compliments I received after the service regarding specific parts of the sermon that had touched or helped both men and women, I suddenly realized that virtually all of them referenced Gloria's additions to the message. It became apparent that my sermons are almost entirely masculine in the way they look at and apply Scripture to life, in the illustrations used, and in the perspective represented. When a single sermon included feminine ways of thinking, feeling, and teaching, the sermon's effect increased exponentially—with both women and men! I wish I could say that the lesson I should have learned from that sermon translated into my regular inclusion of Gloria and others both in preparing and delivering more gender-diverse sermons. Imagine the outcome if gifted women were regularly empowered to join the rotating teaching team and also invited to serve on a sermon-planning and research team to share personal and research insights and ideas that could be incorporated into a future sermon. They could be given the preaching calendar well ahead of time and then asked to email the pastor with the "cream" from their personal study and investigation of the texts.

It is important to recognize that when preaching and teaching roles are restricted to men, their messages are typically filled with vocabulary, illustrations, applications, interests, thought-patterns, values, and perspectives that reflect the experience, interests, and needs of men much more than women. While there is some overlap and gender stereotypes may be overemphasized, the fact is that male-produced and delivered sermons are heavily slanted toward the men in the congregation. Perhaps this is one reason why so many Christian women are appreciative of and responsive to some well-known, gifted female Bible teachers such as Beth Moore, Kay Arthur, and Priscilla Schirer. In those Bible studies, unlike the typical Sunday service, women are hearing God's truth from a teacher who much better understands and reflects how they think, feel, and perceive. She uses illustrations, vocabulary, and practical applications that resonate with them.

Of course, one could validly argue that God's truth is relevant to all ethnicities, ages, and genders and also that women can certainly benefit from male-styled teaching. But would it not then seem equally valid to argue that men would similarly benefit from female-styled teaching? After all, important portions of Scripture were written or spoken by women, for example: Exodus 15 (Miriam), Judges 5 (Deborah), 2 Kings 22 (Huldah), Proverbs 4 (Solomon's mother), Proverbs 31 (King Lemuel's mother), many portions of Song of Solomon (the Shulamite woman), and Luke 1 (Mary).

The benefits of gender diversity in leadership are confirmed in the business world. Studies have indicated that companies reporting the highest levels of racial and gender diversity brought in fifteen times more sales revenues than those with the lowest levels.[391] This is a stunning reminder of the value of having gender diversity in the highest levels of senior leadership. God made two kinds of people, male and female. When there was only one, God pronounced it "not good" (Gen. 2:18).

In a National Public Radio interview, advertising executive and consultant Cindy Gallop suggests what companies miss out on when they don't bring women into leadership includes:

    a.   They miss out on "radically innovative and different perspective" because "diversity drives innovation," and

    b.   They miss out on a huge amount of money that could be made when women who are the primary purchases of everything and who are much more connected than men, "share everything in ways men don't" because they are naturally "chatterers, gossips, and advocates." When their needs and wants are met, they spread the word. This has tremendous impact because they are and are connected to one half of the population.

---

[391] Johnson, Joshua, A1 (a daily radio program on National Public Radio, 1/18/2017.

Responding to the question "Why does diversity bring about innovation?" Gallop responded: When you bring a diverse set of people together to wrestle a problem to the ground you will get: a faster solution, and a more creative one that typically meets the customer or clients' needs.[392]

Imagine these same benefits experienced in the church as a result of the inclusion of women in the leadership.

Could it be that the Creator's penetrating observation, "It is not good for the man to be alone" (Gen. 2:18), could appropriately be applied to leading, learning, teaching, and responding to God's Word and worship? Is it possible that the Creator's plan for male-female partnership and co-dependency was intended to extend far beyond the creation mandate, marriage, and parenting so as to permeate and enrich all other areas of life, including unrestricted participation in church ministry at every level?

Remember God's first mission for Adam and Eve was assigned to them in partnership: "So God created man in his own image, in the image of God he created him; male and female he created them. God blessed them and said to them, 'Be fruitful and increase in number; fill the earth and subdue it. Rule over the fish of the sea and the birds of the air and over every living creature that moves on the ground'" (Gen. 1:27, 28).

Even so, God's mission for His church was delivered to all His followers in partnership regardless of gender. Tara Beth Leach reminds us that

The early church was obsessed with the mission of God in Christ. They were mad about living and sharing the mission. Every conversation, every story, and every miracle was connected to mission . . . It's about the mission. We live in a changing world. Many say that the church is in decline; some say we need CPR. When I think of CPR, I don't care if it's a man or a woman doing it! We simply need to join God in his grand rescue operation, and we need all hands on deck. We need both men and women with dirt under their finger nails. We need men and women on the road to proclamation. A mission is at hand; it's time to get on with

---

[392] Ibid.

it. When women are held back from using their gifts simply because of their gender, the people of God will continue to be hampered and not live into the fullness of the mission we have been invited into. Friends, there is a mission before us, and we must get our act together. This then, is not merely a *justice* issue; rather, it's a *mission* issue."

It's about *mission*. And as long as women are held back in the church, I believe the church will continue to miss out on the fullness of mission we have been invited to participate in.[393]

In Conclusion

As I reach the end of this story of my personal journey to discern what the Bible teaches about gender roles, it is my conclusion that the overwhelming evidence of Scripture powerfully supports the egalitarian position which asserts that <u>there should be no gender-based restrictions for ministry or leadership in Jesus' church</u>. The passages used to support a complementarian view excluding women from certain ministry roles and functions have been shown to be erroneously translated and/or inaccurately interpreted.

On the contrary, even the primary passages typically used to support gender-role discrimination, when rightly translated and interpreted, <u>assume that women will teach and exercise authority over men</u>, but define what attitudes and spirit are inappropriate for women while in those roles.

Please Forgive Me. I Was Wrong!

Based on this cumulative and compelling evidence, I believe that I need once again to apologize and ask forgiveness for my incorrectly teaching gender restrictions in the church for most of my pastoral ministry until not long before my retirement in September of 2016. Although I did so sincerely, believing I was correctly representing the teaching of the Bible, I am now convinced that I was wrong—very wrong! Thankfully, this has never been a significant emphasis of my teaching, but nevertheless it was erroneous and

---

[393] Leach, *Emboldened: A Vision for Empowering Women in Ministry,* 109, 99.

detrimental and doesn't diminish my error and its damage to others and to Jesus' church. My greater sin was supporting and implementing unbiblical gender role restrictions in the churches where I was the pastor without seriously questioning what I had been taught and without doing my own serious investigation of whether it accurately reflected what the Scriptures actually taught.

My sin was in ignorance but that does not erase my guilt. It was wrong that in the three churches I pastored over nearly fifty years I did not allow or encourage women to fully invest their gifts and passions for the glory of God and the advancement of His mission. I grieve that my teaching on gender roles in the church was not only biblically incorrect, but also restrictive, offensive, and potentially oppressive to women as well as to many people inside and outside the church. The fact that my former complementarian position was sincerely held, graciously received, and the fact that I believed it to be an accurate portrayal of biblical truth doesn't erase that it was wrong and that it has done harm to individuals and to those churches. The effectiveness and witness of those churches were undoubtedly negatively affected. I am deeply sorry and ask for forgiveness.

I hope that my late-in-life discovery of the biblical teaching on gender roles can be an example of the need to others, young and old, to keep studying and growing till death or Jesus' return. I can hardly wait to see what other understandings of Scripture I now have that need to be adjusted or changed. Whether or not I discover that I have been wrong in my interpretation related to other topics, I want to be certain that I do not misrepresent the Scriptures! By God's grace I never want to stop growing. Actually, I believe that all of God's children will, in the new heaven and earth, be launched on a new adventure of learning for all eternity during which their learning curve will be unhindered by the limitations imposed by depravity and all of its perversions in our ability to think and learn without bias. Just imagine!

It is my sincere prayer that this study will help to open the door of ministry to godly and qualified women to serve in leadership and preaching roles which will affect lives, churches, and communities in exciting new ways to advance the Kingdom of God. I pray that I and those who have joined me in this journey will be passionately committed to always growing in our knowledge and practice of the Scriptures, in love for God and neighbor, and in engagement in the Good News mission of Jesus to redeem and restore His sin-ruined creation to its original perfection to the glory of God!

On August 28, 1963, during the epic Civil Rights Movement, from the steps of the Lincoln Memorial in Washington D.C., Dr. Martin Luther King Jr. delivered a speech for the ages often characterized by four words he passionately repeated again and again, *"I have a dream."* His speech was permeated with striking quotations from the Old Testament prophets.

I don't want to minimize or diminish in any way Dr. King's iconic and nation-changing speech which cast a vision for a racially bias- and prejudice-free United States of America. Neither do I wish to imply that the gender restrictions wrongly imposed on women, evil as they have been, are equal to slavery and to subsequent generations of systemic racial bias, injustice, and oppression which Dr. King tirelessly opposed. But I would like to call attention to parallels of inequality, injustice, and oppression in the segregation of women from leadership in the church. I would like to borrow and adapt some of Dr. King's words to highlight the long-overdue emancipation of women in the church. The following is taken from near the end of Dr. King's vision and clarion call with my gender-specific modifications:

- *"I have a dream that one day Jesus' church will rise up and live out the true meaning of the words: 'We hold these truths to be self-evident, that all men and women are created equal.'*
- *"I have a dream that one day in all the churches of America, the daughters of formerly oppressed women will be able to sit down together with former complementarian patriarchs at the table of church governance.*
- *"I have a dream that my three grown sons will one day worship in churches where their sister would not be judged or limited by the identity of her gender but by the goodness of her character and calling. I have a dream today.*
- *"I have a dream that one day in every denomination, previously oppressed girls will be able to join hands in equality and partnership with enlightened male pastors and liberated female pastors. I have a dream today.*
- *"I have a dream that one day every valley shall be exalted, every hill and mountain shall be made low, the rough places will be made plain,*

and the crooked places will be made straight, and the glory of the Lord shall be revealed, and all flesh, both men and women, shall see and proclaim it together."

Turning from the words of Dr. King's speech to the words of the ninth century BCE prophet Joel, I call attention to another liberating vision the Holy Spirit inspired in Joel 2:28, 29: "And afterward, I will pour out my Spirit on **all people**. Your sons **and daughters** will prophesy, your old men will dream dreams, your young men will see visions. Even on my servants, both men and **women**, I will pour out my Spirit in those days."

On the Day of Pentecost, immediately following the death, resurrection, and ascension of Jesus, the Spirit-filled Apostle Peter, quoting Joel, heralded the inauguration of the already/not yet New Creation, coincidental with the birth/beginning of Jesus' new people of God, the church: "This is what was spoken by the prophet Joel: 'In the last days, God says, I will pour out my Spirit on **all people**. Your sons and **daughters** will prophesy, your young men will see visions, your old men will dream dreams. Even on my servants, both men and **women**, I will pour out my Spirit in those days, and they will prophesy'" (Acts 2:17, 18).

I invite you to join me in prayer:

> **Our Father Who fills the heavens, let Your Name be hallowed. Let Your Kingdom come and Your will be done on earth as it is in heaven. Help us to believe and to practice that vision today as a beautiful "sign" of Your now-and-future Kingdom on the earth in which "there is neither Jew nor Greek, slave nor free, male and female. For we are all one in Christ Jesus."[394] May the showers of Pentecost swell into a flood of women and men proclaiming the Gospel. In the emancipating Name of Jesus we ask these things. Amen!"**

---

[394] Galatians 3:28.

FOR DISCUSSION

(1) How do you feel about the comparison of an individual functioning with only one leg to the church functioning with only one "leg" in leadership roles, that is, the masculine "leg"?

(2) After reviewing the chapter summaries, tell how a particular chapter was helpful to you. If there is another chapter about which you still have a lot of questions, describe what is unclear to you. Have your group share their insights regarding the questions you identified.

(3) Review Paul's sixteen principles for dealing with divisive and debatable issues (Rom. 14). Which of these sixteen identifies behavior or attitudes you need to work on regarding the gender roles debate? What do you intend to do?

(4) How would you explain to someone what it means to be complementarian or egalitarian? Which is the position you hold to? Briefly share with your group why you believe the Bible supports that view.

(5) If someone told you they were thinking about leaving their church over the gender roles issue, what counsel would you give them?

(6) What are a few ways your church could increase the involvement and visibility of women in the church ministry? What can you do to try to make those a reality?

(7) Spend time praying that God will give unity to His churches as they diligently seek to know and do His will regarding gender roles in the church. Pray that God's Spirit will fill and empower you as you encourage and participate in this process to the glory of Jesus.

Select Bibliography

This bibliography does not list every source cited in the book. The source information of those is provided in the footnotes. The following identifies select books, English Bible versions, and a few major blogs which are cited throughout.

BOOKS

Arndt, William F., and Gingrich, Wilbur, eds. *A Greek-English Lexicon of the New Testament and Other Early Christian Literature*. Chicago: The University of Chicago Press, 1957.

Beck, James R. ed. *Two Views on Women in Ministry*. Grand Rapids: Zondervan, 2009.

Brown, Francis, Driver, S.R., and Briggs, Charles A., eds. *The Enhanced Brown-Driver-Briggs Hebrew and English Lexicon*. Peabody: Hendrickson Publishers, 1996.

Crabb, Lawrence J. Jr. *The Silence of Adam*. Grand Rapids: Zondervan, 1995.

Cunningham, Loren and Hamilton, David Joel, and Rogers, Janice. *Why Not Women: A Fresh Look at Scripture on Women in Missions, Ministry, and Leadership*. Seattle: YWAM Publishing, 2000.

Dickson, John. *Hearing Her Voice*. Grand Rapids: Zondervan, 2014.

Elwell, Walter A., and Yarbrough, Robert W. *Encountering the New Testament.* Grand Rapids: Baker, 1998.

Erickson, Millard J. *Introducing Christian Doctrine.* Grand Rapids: Baker, 2001.

Evans, Rachel Held. *Searching for Sunday.* Nashville: Thomas Nelson, 2015.

Gombis, Timothy G. *Paul: A Guide for the Perplexed.* New York: T&T Clark, 2010.

Grenz, Stanley. *Women in the Church: A Biblical Theology of Women in Ministry.* Downers Grove, IL: Intervarsity Press, 1995.

Gundry, Stanley, and Beck, James R., eds. *Two Views on Women in Ministry.* Grand Rapids: Zondervan, 2005.

Jamieson, Robert, Fausset, Jamieson, and Brown, David, *Commentary Critical and Explanatory of the Whole Bible.* Robert Jamieson, Edinburough: Oliphants Ltd, Edingurgh, 1871.

Kostenberger, Andreas J., and Schreiner, Thomas R., eds. *Women in the Church: An Interpretation & Application of 1 Timothy 2:9–15.* 3rd ed. Wheaton: Crossway, 2016.

Leach, Tara Beth. *Emboldened: A Vision for Empowering Women in Ministry.* Downers Grove, IL: InterVarsity Press, 2017.

Lee-Barnewall, Michelle. *Neither Complementarian nor Egalitarian: A Kingdom Corrective to the Evangelical Gender Debate.* Grand Rapids: Baker Academic, 2016.

Louw, Johannes P., and Nida, Eugene, eds. *The Greek-English Lexicon.* Philadelphia: American Bible Society, 1988.

Myers, A. C. *The Eerdmans Bible Dictionary*. Grand Rapids: Eerdmans, 1987.

Payne, Philip B. *One in Christ: An Exegetical and Theological Study of Paul's Letters*. Grand Rapids: Zondervan, 2009.

Piper, John, and Grudem, Wayne, eds. *Recovering Biblical Manhood and Womanhood: A Response to Evangelical Feminism*. Wheaton: Crossway, 2006.

Poulton, Paul. *Genesis for Ordinary People*. Eugene, OR: Resource Publications, 2014.

Stackhouse, John G. *Partners in Christ: A Conservative Case for Egalitarianism*. Downers Grove, IL: Intervarsity Press, 2015.

Swanson, J. *Dictionary of Biblical Languages with Semantic Domains: Greek (New Testament)*. Oak Harbor: Logos Research Systems, Inc., 1997.

Vincent, Marvin R. *Word Studies in the New Testament*. Peabody: Hendrickson Publishers, 1886.

Walvoord, J. F., and Zuck, R. B., eds. *The Bible Knowledge Commentary: An Exposition of the Scriptures*. Wheaton: Victor Books, 1985.

Wescott, Brooke Foss. *The Epistles of St John*. Grand Rapids: Eerdmans, 1966.

Westfall, Cynthia Long. *Paul and Gender: Reclaiming the Apostle's Vision for Men and Women in Christ*. Grand Rapids: Baker Academic, 2016.

Wright, N.T. *Surprised by Scripture*. San Francisco: Harper One, 2014.

Wuest, K. S. *Wuest's Word Studies from the Greek New Testament: For the English Reader*. Grand Rapids: Eerdmans, 1997.

Young, Robert. *Analytical Concordance to the Bible*. Grand Rapids: Eerdmans, 1994.

ONLINE BLOGS

Custis, James, Carolyn, carolyncustusjames.com
"The Junia Project." Junia.com

McKnight, Scott. Patheos.com/blogs/:Jesus Creed/

Mowczko, Marg. *Exploring the Biblical Theology of Biblical Egalitarianism.* margmowczko.com

ENGLISH BIBLE VERSIONS

English Standard Version, Wheaton: Crossway, 2008.

King James Version, 1611.

The Message, (Eugene Peterson). Colorado Springs: Navpress Publishing Group, 2002.

The New American Standard Bible, Grand Rapids: Zondervan Publishing House, 2006.

New International Version, Zondervan Publishing House, Grand Rapids: Zondervan, 1984.

New King James Version, Nashville: Thomas Nelson Publishers, 1975.

New Living Translation, Carol Stream: Tyndale House Publishers, 1996,

New Revised Standard Version, Philadelphia, American Bible Society, 1997.

The New World Translation, Pittsburg: Watchtower Bible and Tract Society, 1961.